THE

GRENVILLE PAPERS.

VOL. I.

THE

GRENVILLE PAPERS:

BEING

THE CORRESPONDENCE

OF

RICHARD GRENVILLE EARL TEMPLE, K.G.,

AND

THE RIGHT HON: GEORGE GRENVILLE,

THEIR FRIENDS AND CONTEMPORARIES.

———

EDITED, WITH NOTES,

By WILLIAM JAMES SMITH

———

VOL. I.

AMS PRESS
NEW YORK

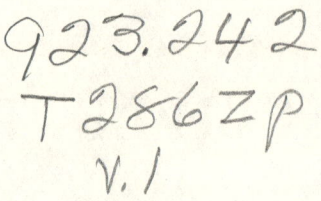

Reprinted from the edition of 1852, London
First AMS EDITION published 1970
Manufactured in the United States of America

International Standard Book Number:
  complete set: 0-404-06150-8
  volume 1: 0-404-06151-6

Library of Congress Catalog Card Number: 72-119154

AMS PRESS, INC.
New York, N. Y. 10003

PREFACE.

The correspondence of the several members of the Grenville family and their contemporaries contained in these volumes, extends over a period of more than thirty years, commencing in 1742; but the most interesting and important part of it is that which comprises the seven concluding years of the reign of George the Second, and the first ten years of that of George the Third.

It consists principally of letters to and from Richard Grenville, Earl Temple, and his next brother, the Right Honourable George Grenville, the two eldest surviving sons of Richard Grenville, Esq., of Wotton, by his marriage with Hester Temple, sister and coheir of Sir Richard Temple, Viscount Cobham of Stowe, to whose peerage she succeeded by special remainder, at his death in September, 1749. A few weeks afterwards she was advanced to the title of Countess Temple, and died in October, 1752.

Richard Grenville, the eldest son, was born September 26, 1711, and, having been educated at Eton, was sent at the age of eighteen, under the care of a private tutor, a M. de Lizy, to travel in Switzerland, Italy, and France. He remained upon the Continent more than four years, and soon after his return to England, at the

General Election in 1734, he was chosen, through the influence of his uncle Lord Cobham, to represent the Borough of Buckingham, and in subsequent Parliaments he sat as one of the Knights of the Shire for the county of Buckingham. He succeeded to the Earldom of Temple upon the death of his mother in October, 1752, and inherited the large estates of Stowe and Wotton.

In the year 1736 he obtained a very considerable accession of fortune by his marriage with Anna Chamber, one of the daughters and coheirs of Thomas Chamber, Esq., of Hanworth, by Lady Mary, daughter of Charles, second Earl of Berkeley. Miss Chamber, having lost her parents at an early age, was brought up under the guardianship of her aunt the well-known Lady Betty Germaine, with whom she constantly resided until her marriage.

Lord Temple became First Lord of the Admiralty in the Administration formed by Mr. Pitt in November, 1756, and in the following June he was made Lord Privy Seal. In December 1758 he was constituted Lord-Lieutenant and Custos Rotulorum of the county of Bucks, and in February, 1760, he was made a Knight of the Garter.

During the greater part of Mr. Pitt's glorious Administration, Lord Temple certainly took a very active, though, perhaps, not very ostensible part in the affairs of Government. Since Mr. Pitt's marriage with Lady Hester Grenville, Lord Temple had become his most intimate and affectionate friend, and was very confidentially trusted by him, to a great extent, during the long and frequent illnesses which entirely prevented his own personal attention to the arduous duties of his office as Secretary of State. Upon these occasions much responsibility was deputed to Lord Temple, and it has been said by a contemporary writer, apparently with considerable probability of truth, " with respect to Lord Temple, that as the war and his management of it was the chief occasion of Mr. Pitt's being so much distinguished, so his intimate connection with that gentleman was the principal cause why this peer became so conspicuous and celebrated."

At the accession of King George the Third, he continued to be Lord Privy Seal until Mr. Pitt went out of office in October, 1761, upon the question of war with Spain, when he resigned at the same time; and from that period commenced the unhappy estrangement from his brother, George Grenville, who remained in his office as Treasurer of the Navy, and adhered to the policy and influence of Lord Bute, which were soon after more openly avowed by the latter being appointed Secretary of State, upon the dismissal of Lord Holdernesse, and subsequently first Lord of the Treasury upon the removal of the Duke of Newcastle.

Lord Temple now became one of the most active and zealous leaders of opposition to the Administration of Lord Bute, and, in consequence of his open encouragement and patronage of the celebrated John Wilkes, he was dismissed from his office of Lord Lieutenant of the county of Bucks, in May, 1763.

He continued in opposition to the Administration subsequently formed by Mr. Grenville, until May 1765, when he became reconciled to his brother George, and ever afterwards remained upon the most affectionate terms with him.

Although Lord Temple was several times called upon by the King to assist in forming a Ministry, yet he never again accepted office in any subsequent Administration. He had a serious difference of opinion with his friend, Mr. Pitt, upon the formation of that Government in 1766, in which the latter assigned to himself the office of Lord Privy Seal, and became Earl of Chatham. Their enmity was now as remarkable as their former friendship had been sincere, and they continued in the most bitter personal and political animosity, until their final reconciliation in the autumn of 1768; and from that period they again acted together with equal zeal in opposition, and were agreed in all political questions, excepting only that which regarded the taxation of America, in which Lord Temple invariably supported the policy of George Grenville, and the Stamp Act.

I shall hereafter take occasion to speak more at large of the character and political career of Lord Temple. During the latter years of his life, he, in great measure, retired from politics, and devoted himself to the improvement and embellishment of his favourite residence at Stowe, where may still be seen the remains of his architectural taste, and talent for landscape gardening.

He seems to have most sincerely and constantly deplored the loss of Lady Temple, who died in April, 1777. After her death he sought consolation in the society of his nephews and nieces, more particularly of George Grenville the younger, who eventually succeeded to his title and estates, and who had recently married the daughter and heiress of Earl Nugent, of Gosfield Hall, in Essex. Sir Nathaniel Wraxall, in describing a visit to that place, in 1776, mentions among the guests, who attracted most attention,—

"The late Lord Temple, then far advanced in life, and very infirm. In his person he was tall and large, though not inclined to corpulency. A disorder, the seat of which lay in his ribs, bending him almost double, compelled him in walking to make use of a sort of crutch[1], but his mind seemed exempt from any decay. His conversation was animated, brilliant, and full of entertainment. Notwithstanding the nickname of 'Lord Gawky,' which he had obtained in the satirical or party productions of those times, and which we may presume was not given him without good reason, he had nevertheless the air and appearance of a man of high condition, when he appeared with the insignia and decorations of the Garter, seated at table."

Lord Temple's death was occasioned by his having been thrown from a pony carriage in the Park Ridings at Stowe. His skull was fractured by the fall. He became insensible, and so continued, without any signs

[1] "Lord Temple's cane," or crutch, was the subject of the following lines in a handwriting which I have not been able to identify, but they are dated

"*Nuneham, August 13th.*

"Hail, sacred staff! tho' some may think I err,
To Clement's crozier thee I must prefer:
More hallowed office! for 't is thine to guide
The man, to virtue and to wit allied:
When you support him o'er the rugged plain,
Britannia's truest friend you then sustain:
Shouldst thou (avert it Heaven!) betray thy trust,
Honour would fall, and Freedom kiss the dust."

I found these lines accompanied by an outline sketch of Lord Temple's portrait, a whole length, with his *cane*, as he appeared in the House of Lords in 1778. It was drawn by Lady Mary Grenville, afterwards Marchioness of Buckingham. It corroborates Wraxall's description of him, and it is no doubt an accurate, though somewhat caricature portrait. A label from his mouth is inscribed, "*I am come to express my highest indignation and contempt*," &c., &c., and the expression of his countenance is in accordance with the sentiments he is uttering.

of returning consciousness, until he died a few days afterwards, on the 11th of September, 1779.

The Right Honourable GEORGE GRENVILLE was born October 14th, 1712. After being educated at Eton, and Christ Church, Oxford, he entered upon the study of the Law, and was called to the Bar; but at the desire of his uncle, Lord Cobham, he relinquished that pursuit, and devoted himself to politics. He represented the borough of Buckingham in successive Parliaments, from 1741 until his death in 1770. In December, 1744, he was made a Lord of the Admiralty, and of the Treasury in June, 1747. He was Treasurer of the Navy in 1754, and continued in that office, with some intervals, until May, 1762; when, having separated himself from Lord Temple and Mr. Pitt, and become attached to Lord Bute, he was made Secretary of State. In October following he left that office to be First Lord of the Admiralty; and subsequently, upon the resignation of Lord Bute in April, 1763, he was appointed First Lord of the Treasury and Chancellor of the Exchequer.

After his dismission in July, 1765, he never again accepted any appointment in the Government.

It is unnecessary in this place to discuss the political events in which Mr. Grenville was concerned. They will be found related in his own DIARY, which forms an important feature in these PAPERS; and it will, I believe, be found to throw new light upon several transactions, particularly some relating to party changes, which have hitherto been but very imperfectly understood, and be considered a very acceptable addition to the history of that part of George the Third's reign to which its contents refer. In this Diary he relates his daily conversations with the King at the time that he filled the office of first Minister; and their discussions show the anxious personal interest which George the Third so early evinced in all the most minute affairs of his Government, and the confidence he reposed in the Administration of Mr. Grenville.

The principal measure with which Mr. Grenville's name has become associated in history is that of the American Stamp Act. It has been said, and I believe with truth, that he was not the author of that measure; but that he adopted it, and ever defended it with the utmost zeal and ability, cannot be denied. The measure was patriotic, and well-intentioned on the part of Mr. Grenville, but the result was unfortunate. It was not, however, until the result became known that it met with so much of party condemnation, for it is notorious that the Stamp Act originally passed both Houses of Parliament with very little discussion and less opposition.

One of the latest acts of Mr. Grenville's political life was the Bill for Regulating the Proceedings of the House of Commons on Controverted Elections, which he introduced in March, 1770. It has been described by Mr. Hatsell; a most competent authority, as " one of the noblest works for the honour of the House of Commons, and the security of the Constitution, that ever was devised by any minister or statesman."

Mr. Grenville's parliamentary abilities, and his extensive knowledge of the forms and privileges of the House, were frequently mentioned by his contemporaries, and it was at one time his ambition to be Speaker of the House of Commons. Mr. Pitt said of him, so early as 1754, that he was " universally able in the whole business of the House, and, after Mr. Murray and Mr. Fox,

certainly one of the very best Parliament men in the
House;" and I may add the testimony of Horace
Walpole, that "Mr. Grenville was confessedly the
ablest man of business in the House of Commons, and,
though not popular, of great authority there, from his
spirit, knowledge, and gravity of character."

The character of George Grenville, as a statesman, has
been drawn by the master-hand of Edmund Burke, and
though the passage has been often quoted, it should not,
therefore, be omitted here. It occurs in his celebrated
Speech on American Taxation, in April, 1774.

"Here began to dawn the first glimmerings of this new colony
system. It appeared more distinctly afterwards, when it devolved
upon a person to whom, on other accounts, this country owes very
great obligations. I do believe that he had a very serious desire
to benefit the public. But with no small study of the detail, he
did not seem to have his view, at least equally, carried to the total
circuit of our affairs. He generally considered his objects in
lights that were rather too detached.

"Whether the business of an American revenue was imposed
upon him altogether; whether it was entirely the result of his own
speculation; or, what is more probable, that his own ideas rather
coincided with the instructions he had received, certain it is, that,
with the best intentions in the world, he first brought this fatal
scheme into form, and established it by Act of Parliament. No
man can believe that at this time of day I mean to lean on the
venerable memory of a great man, whose loss we deplore in common. Our little party differences have been long ago composed,
and I have acted more with him, and certainly with more pleasure
with him, than ever I acted against him.

"Undoubtedly Mr. Grenville was a first-rate figure in this
country. With a masculine understanding, and a stout and
resolute heart, he had an application undissipated and unwearied. He took public business not as a duty he was to
fulfil, but as a pleasure he was to enjoy, and he seemed to have
no delight out of this House, except in such things as some way
related to the business that was to be done within it. If he was

ambitious, I will say this for him, his ambition was of a noble and generous strain. It was to raise himself, not by the low pimping politics of a court, but to win his way to power through the laborious gradations of public service, and to secure himself a well-earned rank in Parliament, by a thorough knowledge of its constitution, and a perfect practice in all its business.

If such a man fell into errors, it must be from defects not intrinsical; they must be rather sought in the particular habits of his life; which, though they do not alter the groundwork of character, yet tinge it with their own hue. He was bred in a profession. He was bred to the law, which is, in my opinion, one of the first and noblest of human sciences; a science which does more to quicken and invigorate the understanding, than all the other kinds of learning put together; but it is not apt, except in persons very happily born, to open and to liberalize the mind exactly in the same proportion. Passing from that study, he did not go very largely into the world, but plunged into business, I mean into the business of office, and the limited and fixed methods and forms established there. Much knowledge is to be had undoubtedly in that line, and there is no knowledge which is not valuable. But it may be truly said, that men too much conversant in office are rarely minds of remarkable enlargement. Their habits of office are apt to give them a turn to think the substance of business not to be much more important than the forms in which it is conducted. These forms are adapted to ordinary occasions, and, therefore, persons who are nurtured in office do admirably well as long as things go on in their common order; but when the high roads are broken up, and the waters out,—when a new and troubled scene is opened and the file affords no precedent,—then it is that a greater knowledge of mankind, and a far more extensive comprehension of things is requisite than ever office gave, or than office can ever give. Mr. Grenville thought better of the wisdom and power of human legislation than, in truth, it deserves. He conceived, and many conceived along with him, that the flourishing trade of this country was greatly owing to law and institution, and not quite so much to liberty; for but too many are apt to believe regulation to be commerce, and taxes to be revenue. Among regulations, that which stood first in reputation was his idol. I mean the Act of Navigation. He has often professed it to be so. The policy of that Act is, I readily admit, in many respects well understood.

But I do say, that if the Act be suffered to run the full length of its principle, and is not changed, and modified according to the change of times, and the fluctuation of circumstances, it must do great mischief, and frequently even defeat its own purpose."

The Solicitor General, Wedderburn (afterwards Lord Chancellor, and Earl of Rosslyn), spoke, in reply to Burke, upon this occasion; the following extract, in which he alludes to Mr. Grenville, is taken from a manuscript copy of his speech, corrected by himself, and sent to Lord Temple. I believe the speech has not been printed.

" I had no intention, when I came into the House, of addressing you upon the general question of this day, a subject on which my sentiments have too often troubled the House; but some things have fallen from the honourable gentleman who spoke last that compel me to entreat their indulgence, for under the impressions his reflections have made upon my mind I protest I should know no rest nor peace, had I omitted any opportunity of expressing my dissent to such doctrines and to such representations.

" The honourable gentleman has gone into a long detail of past measures, and a very large censure of characters that are now no more. He has spoken, respectfully indeed, of a late very eminent person, of whom I am unable to speak without emotion; but he has neither done him that justice with which the latest posterity will treat his memory, nor has he spoken of him as the general voice of a grateful people would, even in this moment, express itself of his person, his conduct, his acts.

" I blame not those who, in considering the present state of affairs in America, choose to review the measures of the last ten years. To expose past errors is a part of political wisdom; but if that review is turned from the measures themselves, to the conduct and characters of the persons engaged in them, prejudice and passion will corrupt the judgment as to the past, and such a review mislead us the more as to the future measures.

" I feel no such bias, and am not conscious of a wish to disparage the motives or the conduct of any man who has ever taken an active part in an American question. For those with whom

I have most differed on that subject I entertain the highest personal consideration ; but 1 confess I feel the warmest zeal to vindicate (as far as my poor abilities can) the motives and the conduct
of that great Minister who first planned the measures with regard
to America, to which, unjustly, so much mischief has been imputed.

" The House has been told that the honourable gentleman
(whose loss has at some time been deplored on every side of the
House) was unfortunately so framed that, with good intentions,
he had not sufficient liberality of mind for the direction of public
affairs. Two circumstances in his education are said to have contracted his mind, for otherwise I suppose he was not so *unhappily
born*, but that he might have possessed as extensive a mind as
other men, who, it seems, are *born* for Government. The first was,
that he happened to be bred to a profession, which, in the early
part of his life, had engaged him in the most assiduous study of
the laws and constitution of his country. From this illiberal course
of study he had acquired some unfortunate habits and prejudices,
unknown to those who are happily ignorant under what form of
Government they live.

" A second unfortunate circumstance was, that my much lamented friend, when he had finished this course of study, did not
go into the world, but plunged into the business of office. Going
into the world is a term too large for my narrow comprehension ;
if it means that he neither played nor dressed, nor was a member
of any of the fashionable clubs, I believe it may be true; but his
birth and his talents introduced him to an early intimacy with
the first men of his age, and in the best, though not, perhaps,
the most fashionable company (if fashion is confined to the follies
of young men), his life and habits continued to be undissipated,
and he had not, even then, emancipated his mind from a daily
application to the various parts of public business. He passed by
regular gradations from one office to another. Whatever related to
the Marine of this country he had learnt during his attendance at
the Admiralty. The Finances he had studied, under a very able
master, at the Treasury. The Foreign Department was for a time
entrusted to him. The proper business of this House was for
several years his particular study.

" In almost every various office of the State he had acquired
a practical knowledge, improved by theory, and from the general
course of his observation and researches he had adopted principles

and habits, which the firm temper of his mind would not stoop to abandon or unlearn, in complaisance to the opinions of any man. Such, Sir, were the disqualifications under which Mr. Grenville was called forth to the first situation in Administration, at a time when ancient prejudices were still respected, and before it was understood that parts were spoilt by application, that ignorance was preferable to knowledge, and that any lively man of imagination and fancy, without practice in office, and without experience, might start up at once a self-taught Minister, and undertake the management of a great country in difficult times.

"I have attempted, Sir, to state to you what Mr. Grenville was, and how qualified for the office he undertook, not with the partiality of a friend who reverences his memory, but from the very circumstances imputed as a disadvantage to him. I shall now state what I understood to be the system he adopted, and the ideas he pursued with regard to America, when he formed the plan of the Stamp Act; but permit me first to view the situation in which he was called upon to act."

Mr. Wedderburn proceeds with a long exposition of Mr. Grenville's system of Finance, and concludes by asserting that his

"intention only was to do justice to the memory of the honourable gentleman who proposed the Stamp Act, to vindicate his motives, and to place his character in a just point of view."

The following is an extract from the "*Extra Official State Papers*," published by Mr. Knox, who was intimately acquainted with Mr. Grenville, and who was for some time Under Secretary of State to Lord Hillsborough :—

"Mr. Grenville, under a manner rather austere and forbidding, covered a heart as feeling and tender as any man ever possessed. He liked office, as well for its emoluments as its power; but in his attention to himself he never failed to pay regard to the situations and circumstances of his friends, though to neither would he warp the public interest or service in the smallest degree : rigid in his opinions of public justice and integrity, and firm to inflexibility in the construction of his mind, he reprobated every suggestion of the political expediency of overlooking frauds or evasions in the payment or collection of the revenue, or of waste or extravagance in its expenditure. But, although he would not bend any measure out of the strict line of rectitude to gain popularity, he was far from being indifferent to the good or ill opinion of the public; and that tediousness and repetition which his speeches in Parliament, and his transactions with men of business, were charged with, were occasioned by the earnestness of his desire to satisfy and convince those he addressed, of the purity of his motives, and the propriety of his conduct; and while there remained a single reason in his own mind that he thought would serve those purposes, he could not be content to rest upon those he had already adduced, however convinced and satisfied his hearers appeared to be with them.

" Inheriting but a small patrimonial fortune, he had early accustomed himself to a strict appropriation of his income, and an exact economy in its expenditure, as the only sure ground on which to build a reputation for public and private integrity, and to support a dignified independency; and it was the unvaried practice of his life in all situations, as he has often told me, to live upon his own private fortune, and save the emoluments of whatever office he possessed; on which account, he added ; ' the being in or out makes no difference in my establishment or manner of life. Everything goes on at home in the same way. The only difference is, that my children's fortunes would be increased by my being in, beyond what they would be if I remained out; and that is being as little dependant upon office, as any man who was not born to a great estate can possibly be.' "

An anonymous writer in December, 1765, thus sums up the character of Mr. Grenville :—

" Calm, deliberate, economical, and attentive ; steadfast to business, early and late ; attached to no dissipations or trifling amusements ; always master of himself, and never seen, either at White's with the gamesters, or at Newmarket with the jockies. Regular and exact in his family, and discharging, in the most exemplary manner, every social and religious duty. What is a labour and a fatigue to other men was his greatest pleasure : and those who knew him best in the management of affairs acknowledge that his discernment, capacity, and application were quick, enlarged, and indefatigable.   No minister was ever more easy of access, or gave a more patient or attentive hearing to such as applied to him ; and though he entered upon the management of affairs at the most critical conjuncture, with many and great prejudices on certain accounts against him, yet his steady, upright, and able conduct had conciliated the minds of men to him ; and nothing, perhaps, could give the wiser and more rational part of mankind better hopes, and better expectations, than to see a man of these distinguished abilities, of this unwearied attention, and of this unblemished integrity, again serving his country, in one of the highest and most important offices of State."

While the inflexible integrity of Mr. Grenville's conduct secured to him the esteem and affection of his political contemporaries, so honourably evinced by these public testimonies of the consideration in which he was held as a statesman, it should also be mentioned that, in his private life, and in his domestic relations as a husband, a father, and a friend, the family traditions of Mr. Grenville's character approach the highest point of excellence.

Mr. Grenville married in 1749, Elizabeth, daughter of Sir William Wyndham, and sister to the Earl of Egremont and Lord Thomond.   She died in December, 1769, and Mr. Grenville survived her only until the 13th of November following.

By this marriage Mr. Grenville had a numerous family.   Of his three distinguished sons, the eldest, George, having succeeded his uncle in the Earldom of Temple, was afterwards created Marquess of Buckingham, and was the grandfather of the present Duke of Buckingham and Chandos.   The second son, the late Right Honourable Thomas Grenville, who died recently at a very advanced age, had filled several high offices in the

State, and bequeathed to his country one of the most splendid libraries ever formed by a private gentleman. The youngest son, William Wyndham, afterwards Lord Grenville, who died in 1834, will be known to posterity as one of the most eminent statesmen in the latter years of the reign of George the Third.

By the marriages of his four daughters, Mr. Grenville's descendants are now most numerous, and are connected with all the highest and most distinguished families of rank in the kingdom.

The Right Honourable JAMES GRENVILLE, second brother to Lord Temple, came into Parliament for Old Sarum, in 1741, and afterwards sat for Bridport and Buckingham. He held at various times the offices of Lord of Trade and Plantations, Deputy Paymaster of the Forces, and Cofferer of the Household. He died in 1783. The eldest son of James Grenville was created Lord Glastonbury; but he never married, and that title became extinct upon his death in 1826.

The Right Honourable HENRY GRENVILLE, third brother of Lord Temple, was Governor of Barbadoes from 1746 to 1756, and afterwards sat in Parliament for Bishops Castle and Thirsk. In 1761 he was sent Ambassador to Constantinople; and on his return from thence, in 1765, he was appointed a Commissioner of Customs. He died in 1784.

THOMAS GRENVILLE, the youngest brother of Lord Temple, was a Captain in the Navy, and a very distinguished officer. He sat in Parliament for a short time as Member for the Borough of Bridport. He was killed in the action off Cape Finisterre in May, 1747, while in command of H.M.S. *Defiance.*

LADY HESTER GRENVILLE, the only sister of Lord Temple, was married, in 1754, to William Pitt, afterwards Earl of Chatham, by whom she was the mother of the late Right Honourable William Pitt.

Lady Chatham survived her husband many years, and died in 1803.

It remains only to mention that Lord Temple's papers have always been preserved at Stowe. They are much less numerous than might have been expected, and doubtless many of the letters were destroyed by himself, in accordance with the opinions which are so well described in the following extract, from his pamphlet on the *Seizure of Papers,* printed in 1763:—

"Papers relate to the affairs of business and property; the advantages, title, and security of which depend upon them; but that is not all. Every man who has papers, has his secret and confidential correspondences; his private studies, researches, and pursuits, whether of profit, entertainment, or improvement. His *papers* contain all these. The merchant has his secrets of trade; the philosopher his discoveries in science. Every accurate man has the impenetrable secret of his circumstances; the state of his affairs. Many have their WILLS, *Settlements,* and dispositions of their estates, sealed up in silence, not to be broke, but with their own heart-strings. These are to be found among their *papers.* A man's riches may be there in things known to none but himself; and his poverty may from thence *only* appear, the unseasonable discovery of which may involve him in irreparable ruin. *Papers* are the depositories of our fortune; the trustees of our credit, character, and reputation; the secretaries of our pleasures. They are our closest confidants; the most intimate companions of our

bosom ; and, next to the recesses of our own breasts, they are the
most hidden repository we can have. Our honour and fame, our
estates, our amusements, our enjoyments, our friendships, *are*, and
even our vices *may be* there: things that men trust none with, but
themselves ; things upon which the peace and quiet of families,
the love and union of relations, the preservation and value of
friends depend. Secrets that may cost a man his life ; secrets (of
which there are many) that though they can neither affect life nor
liberty, yet some men would rather die, than have discovered ; the
revealing of which may render life insupportable, may dissolve
every tie of nature, loosen every bond of society, and put an utter
end to the comfort of existence.

"It is for these reasons that wise men not only keep their
papers with the greatest care, but at convenient seasons purge their
repositories, and destroy those that ought not to be preserved,
after the immediate purposes of them are answered. They have
above all, a special care into whose hands their secret papers
shall come after they are dead ; a precaution that every man owes,
not only to himself, but to his family and friends, perhaps to his
country."

All that remained of Mr. Grenville's Papers were
eventually deposited at Stowe. A considerable portion
of them had been brought from Wotton by his son, the
Marquess of Buckingham, and were arranged in port-
folios with those of Lord Temple.

The late Duke of Buckingham and Chandos, a few
years after his father's death, brought more of the
Grenville Papers from Wotton House to Stowe ; and
I discovered the remainder about seventeen years ago
in one of the bedrooms at Buckingham House, Pall
Mall, in a very large chest, of which the contents were
unknown, and which had evidently remained unopened
and untouched since it was brought from Mr. Grenville's
residence in Bolton Street, soon after his death. The
whole of these several collections of papers were re-
arranged by the late Duke of Buckingham and myself;

b 2

and it was his Grace's amusement, at intervals for several years, to make the selections, which are printed
in these volumes. The Duke did not intend that the
publication of them should take place until after the
death of his uncle, the late Right Honourable Thomas
Grenville. The latter, however, survived the Duke
more than seven years; and from various causes the
publication has been delayed, until the papers were
recently placed in my hands to prepare for the press,
by the present Duke of Buckingham and Chandos,
with a desire that I should carry into execution what
I knew to have been his father's wishes upon the
subject.

Mr. Grenville was most methodical and careful in the
preservation of his papers: the whole of them were folded
and endorsed, chiefly by himself, and placed in alpha-
betical and chronological order, and it would appear
that he never destroyed any letter he received, however
trivial its import. The applications from all classes of
persons for places in the Customs and Excise alone,
during Mr. Grenville's tenure of office, were almost in-
credibly numerous. It was his habit to keep the draughts
of his own letters; many of them in his own hand,
some in that of Mrs. Grenville or his children, and
more in that of his secretary, Mr. Charles Lloyd.
There is little doubt but that many valuable documents
were lost among the large mass of papers destroyed by
the fire which consumed Wotton House and its contents
in October, 1820.

With respect to the letters addressed to Mr. Grenville
by the AUTHOR of JUNIUS, which will be printed in
the concluding volumes of this correspondence, it will
be sufficient to say for the present, that there is not a

particle of truth in all the absurd tales which have been invented, as to their preservation or discovery. In the proper place I shall have an opportunity of explaining that there was no mystery attached to them, beyond the anonymous nature of the author's communication.

WILLIAM JAMES SMITH.

Conservative Club, St. James's Street,
December, 1851.

CONTENTS

OF

THE FIRST VOLUME.

1743.

1754.

1761.

Page

CORRIGENDA.

VOL. I.

Page 34, note [3], *for* p. 1 *read* p. 11.

  ,, 49, line 15, *for* February 3 *read* February 13.

  ,, 55, line 1, *for* [2] *read* [1].

  ,, 78, note [1], *for* Society of Antiquarians *read* Society of Antiquaries.

  ,, 96, line 2, *for* 1750 *read* 1751. Frederick, Prince of Wales, died on the 20th of March, 1750–51.

  ,, 126, line 11, *for* mortality *read* morality.

  ,, 157, note [3], *for* Lady Francis *read* Lady Frances.

  ,, 193, line 10, *for* Carysfoot *read* Carysfort.

  ,, 236, the last note, *for* [1] *read* [2].

  ,, 238, last line, *for* [1] *read* [2].

  ,, 402, The Earl of Lincoln to Earl Temple. October 9, 1761. This letter has been accidentally misplaced; it should have been inserted according to its date, on page 394.

  ,, 406, line 10, *for* white as the snow on salmon, *read* white as the snow on Salmon.

  ,, 421, note [2], *for* Russian *read* Prussian.

  ,, 470, note [1], *for* Carrington *read* Carington.

CORRIGENDA.

VOL. I.

Page 325, line 4, *for* Marlborough, *read* Marburg, a small fortified place in Hesse.

Page 383, line 16. The Lord Grantham alluded to was an old Dutchman, named Henry de Nassau, who was created Earl of Grantham in 1698. He was for a long time Chamberlain, and a kind of *Polonius* to Queen Caroline. He died in 1754.

Page 425, line 16, *for* former, *read* latter.

Pages 480–481. Of the three letters dated October 10, the *first* is misplaced: it should have been the *last*.

VOL. II.

Page 114, line 12 and line 15. There is probably some error in the figures, but they are correctly copied.

Page 155, line 26. Mr. Walkub means Mr. Henry Wauchope, M.P. for Bute.

Page 170, line 6, *agreeing* is the right word; it is often used in the sense of *agreeing on*.

Page 246, line 13, and page 497, line 31. The person alluded to in both instances was the Rev. John Home.

GRENVILLE PAPERS.

VISCOUNT CORNBURY[1] TO MR. GEORGE GRENVILLE[2].

Cornbury[3], August 3, 1742.

How uncertain are appearances! When first I saw your handwriting this morning, it gave me great delight. I imagined it would inform me that I should see you soon, and that I should see you here, which were two things I particularly wished for; and, besides, I longed to know what was become of you, for I did not know where to find you out and ask you these questions.

[1] Henry Hyde, Viscount Cornbury, eldest son of Henry, fourth Earl of Clarendon. He died in May, 1753, a few months before his father. Bolingbroke's *Letters on the Study and Use of History* were addressed to this young Lord, whose sister, Catherine, Duchess of Queensberry, was the well-known patroness of Gay. Lord Cornbury is mentioned by Walpole as the author of a few pamphlets, some tragedies, and a comedy; to the latter Walpole contributed a preface, printed at Strawberry Hill, in which Lord Cornbury is described as possessing "one of the best hearts that ever warmed a human breast;" and Lady Mary Wortley Montague, in expressing her sorrow for his untimely death, says, "He had certainly a very good heart: I have often thought it a great pity it was not under the direction of a better head. . . . . . His desire of fixing his name to a certain quantity of wall, is one instance, among thousands, of the passion men have for perpetuating their memory."

[2] At this time M.P. for the Borough of Buckingham.

[3] Cornbury Park, in Oxfordshire; formerly the residence of the Lord Chancellor Clarendon, now the property of Lord Churchill.

Instead of this, you will give me leave to say that I found your letter as disagreeable as a letter from you could be, for it acquaints me that you are passed by me without health, after having been at Cheltenham to seek it. It mortifies me, too, another way, by marking out to me a way in which I might have been useful to you, when I am not able to undertake it. I have had sickness enough myself to feel the obligation I have to you for thinking of me for a companion when you are not well; and, besides the real satisfaction I should have in being useful to you, and the pleasure I should find in your company, I am in your debt, you know, upon that very account, so that you cannot, I hope, doubt that I would most readily embrace your offer to accompany you to the south of France[1], if it were in my power; but the little good I found from my last travels made me exclude that remedy from my schemes of health, even when I wanted it (which, I thank God, with tolerable care, is not now the case, even after my long imprisonment); and, considering myself as fixed and settled at home (not to be useless or idle there), I embarked myself in several businesses, which, little as they are with respect to anybody but myself and my own family, as I have squared all my affairs accordingly, could not be left without much inconvenience and dis-

---

[1] Mr. Grenville had been for some years in a weak state of health, and was now about to undertake a tour in France for the amendment of it. In a letter from Mr. George Lyttelton to Pope, dated December, 1739, he says, "George Grenville is in a fair way of recovery; the waters (of Bath) agree with him, and he mends in all respects. Cheyne says he is a giant, a son of Anak, made like Gilbert, the late Lord Bishop of Sarum, and may therefore, if he pleases, live for ever: his present sickness being nothing but a fillip which Providence gave him for his good, to make him temperate, and put him under the care of Dr. Cheyne."—*Phillimore's Life of Lord Lyttelton*, vol. i. p. 127.

order to them. Some part of that business I should have been rejoiced to have shown you here, some improvements in this park, some useful and agreeable repairs to this house, which I could not, with any ease to myself, leave unsettled and unpaid, and go out of England, besides other matters that keep me in it.

In short, I have bought a team of oxen and cannot come, I have built a house and cannot come, I have every excuse but that of having married a wife; and who knows but even that may happen to me in my present disposition to be fixed in this country, and settled at home. I am, indeed, as happy at this home now as a man can be who has neither parents, nor children, nor mistress, nor wife.

Friends I have had here, and need not, I hope, tell you that no friend I have could make me happier than yourself. Some cold weather we have had since I came here, but we now bask in the sunbeams which gild our prospects, and which are so very pretty that they do not want gilding, if it were not so much the fashion.

I cannot quite understand why Lady Suffolk [1], Mr. Berkeley, and yourself took so much pains to avoid making an humble servant happy, as you must have done in this expedition, when you dined at one inn within five miles of me, and were to lie at another ten miles off from me. I will venture to say that we could

---

[1] Henrietta Hobart, widow of Charles Howard, ninth Earl of Suffolk, at this time the wife of the Hon. George Berkeley, youngest son of the second Earl of Berkeley. Lady Suffolk had been Mistress of the Robes to Queen Caroline, and a well-known favourite at the Court of George the Second. Her character, drawn by Swift and Walpole, together with a biographical account, will be found prefixed to the edition of her Letters published, under the editorial care of the Rt. Hon. John Wilson Croker, in 1824.

have taken as much care of a sick man here, as at any other inn upon the road, and may be have amused those that were well, as tolerably. One thing, however, I have learnt from this, that I should be in no pain for you if you do go abroad, as to any straggling parties, for it will be a strange thing if a man should not know how to avoid his enemies, who showed so much skill in avoiding his friend.

But if I have gained this satisfaction upon your account, I have the mortification at the same time to be no longer able to do myself the credit in this country of mentioning Lady Suffolk and Mr. Berkeley as my friends; for, after what has happened, I should not be believed.

I wish I could name to you, as you desire, some person whom you could like to travel with. If you persist in your scheme of staying three months only, I could wish Mr. Pitt[1] would go with you for both your sakes, though not for mine, since, if he stays in England, I have some hopes of seeing him this summer.

You know what vast benefit Lord Chesterfield[2] received by such a jaunt, short as it was; and I should think his court could not be unreasonable enough not to be glad he should take the means of confirming his health, which another session, after such a one as the last, might chance to shock.

But give me leave to say to you, that if your own health makes it necessary for you to leave England, you cannot be in the right to think of returning to a winter and a parliament.

[1] William Pitt, afterwards Earl of Chatham, at this time M.P. for Old Sarum.

[2] Philip Dormer Stanhope succeeded to the earldom of Chesterfield on the death of his father in 1726. He died in 1773.

I do not know that any party is worth killing oneself for, and I think I do know that a party is what, whether one will or no, one must finally act for. I say the more upon this, because, if I know you, your zeal is not according to knowledge, with regard to your own constitution. I could therefore wish, that you might stay with more ease of mind, that you could, if possible, make your party with some acquaintance, with whom you knew you could agree everywhere but in the House, if you can guess yet with whom you shall, or shall not, agree there. Don't be indolent in settling this party for yourself. I think you have made me long to hear that you are out of England, as much as I used to long to feel myself out of it; but still I think my lot now is cast, and my mind is fixed to this country, and except when I think of you (if you leave it) I shall not even wish myself out of it.

In this land where I grew, I shall flourish or wither, as my own nature and culture, and the disposition of the land, and the influence of the heavens, will decide. Every thought of mine is now confined to serve this country while I live, and manure it when I die. Both, you'll say, in a very little proportion, but yet according to my ability, and in discharge of the debt I owe to it. Indeed there is some more satisfaction in thinking of this country and living in it, than there has been. God grant that the interior prospect may be as happy as the exterior view is likely to be honourable. It is not canting to make that a prayer even in a letter, for to compass that great end, our prayers, perhaps, as much as our actions, must operate, since, to effect that, the *minds* of men (which are in the hands of Providence) must cooperate more than they seem disposed to do at present.

I cannot end this long tedious letter without again talking to you about your health. I wish you would ask whoever you trust whether *made* asses' milk would not be a good thing for you to take now. It is made of snails and aringo roots, and other ingredients very strengthening, and healing, and cooling. I inclose to you the receipt[1] for it, because I have known great good done by it, to persons who have had your complaints, but do not take it without advice, for I know, too, that it may be improper.

You will think, from talking like a politician, I am, on the sudden, talking like an old woman. If you should, I shall not be the first politician you and I have heard talk so. However, that I may not talk as long as an old woman, let me release you, after I have first assured you (if I need assure you) that I am ever, &c., &c.   CORNBURY.

Let me hear from you sometimes, and especially if you go out of England. Since your health is out of order, I shall long the more to hear from you.

'T is like reading newspapers in time of war. My stay here is uncertain, but I believe I shall go away the middle of next week for ten days or a fortnight, part of which time I shall be at Woburn with Mr. Murray[2]; and after that, stay here till September, when I expect my father here. I mention this, because any friend of mine who was not acquainted with him, might like as well to take some other time to see me here. I believe

---

[1] The receipt has not been preserved.

[2] The Hon. William Murray, younger son of Lord Viscount Stormont, afterwards Lord Chief Justice, and Earl of Mansfield. He was at this time in Parliament for Boroughbridge.

he will stay till some time in October, and part of the time he stays here I shall, I believe, ramble into Worcestershire, &c.

Pray make my compliments to Mr. Pope[1] when you see him.

VISCOUNT CORNBURY TO MR. GEORGE GRENVILLE.

London, August 16, O.S., 1742.

I HAVE but this moment received yours, my dear Mr. Grenville; and this is post-day, and I am in company, and engaged in company the rest of the day; my letter must therefore be short, though I had more to say than I have at present.

I am here for a few days only upon business, and then return by Woburn to Cornbury, which I hope you will see another year, and like as much as I do.

I wish I could have come sooner, to have seen you before you went. I have had, however, the pleasure to learn from Mr. Pitt how much you were mended, and have no doubt the south of France will quite re-establish your health.

Pray let me hear from you sometimes when it is quite easy to you to write; I hope you know it can only be pleasant to me upon those terms. Make, I beg you, my best compliments at Argeville[2]. Make Lady Bolingbroke[3] think well of me, if you can. I am afraid she

---

[1] Pope has complimented Lord Cornbury in the following lines:—
> " Would you be blest? despise low joys, low gains;
> Disdain whatever Cornbury disdains;
> Be virtuous, and be happy for your pains !"

[2] Lord Bolingbroke's seat in France, near Fontainebleau.

[3] Clara de Marsilly, niece of Madame de Maintenon, widow of the Marquis de Villette, and second wife of Henry St. John, Viscount Bolingbroke. She died in 1750.

does not just now believe I love and honour her as much as you know I do. Nobody can love and honour you more than yours, &c.   **C.**

Pray make my compliments to Sir John and to Lady Lambert, if she is returned [1].

MR. WILLIAM PITT TO MR. GEORGE GRENVILLE.

Clifden [2], Sept. 1, 1742.

MY DEAR GRENVILLE,—I cannot tell you the pleasure I received at Marble Hill [3] yesterday in reading Mr. Berenger's [4] letter from Paris. We talked of you by the hour. I will not tell you all we said of you, but one of our tendernesses and what we all agreed in was, that we wished not to see you these six or seven months at least. Till I knew how you bore your journey, I own I had a thousand fears for you; I have now but one left, which is, that the sudden change in your health may make you neglect the care of yourself. I hope you have consulted the physician at Argeville, and have resolved to guide yourself by his directions as to the air you will go to live in. Our people here are certainly no judges of that matter. I have just been told by Mr.

[1] This letter is addressed to Mr. George Grenville, "*chez Mons. le Chevalier Lambert, Banquier, à Paris.*"

[2] Clifden, in Buckinghamshire, then the residence of Frederick, Prince of Wales. Mr. Pitt had been for some time attached to the household of His Royal Highness.

[3] Marble Hill, Twickenham, was built by King George the Second, as a residence for the Countess of Suffolk. Henry, Earl of Pembroke, was the architect; and the gardens were laid out after a design by Pope.

[4] Lord Cobham's nephew; a son of his youngest sister, Penelope Berenger.

Schutz, that his son received little or no benefit at Aix, but mended instantly at Lisbon : I don't mention this to you to recommend Lisbon, but as an instance that the air of Aix is not the properest for your complaint. I have seen none of your family since we parted. I shall leave this place in a week and go and rejoice with your friends at Wotton[1], Stowe[2], and Hagley[3], upon the great amendment you have already found. Murray is to meet me at Hagley, who talks of you as I do, or as you do of him. I beg you will not write to me, but if Mr. Berenger will have the goodness to give me a line, let him direct to me under cover to Mr. Ritzau in Pall Mall.

Adieu, my dear George, and remember perpetually how many of us you will oblige by taking care of yourself.—Ever yours most affectionately, W. PITT.

VISCOUNT CORNBURY TO MR. GEORGE GRENVILLE.

Cornbury, Oct. 14, 1742.

IT was with great pleasure, dear Sir, that I received your letter from Le Teil. At first sight the length of it made me very happy, even before I had read it, since it not only showed me how many of your thoughts you allowed to me, but seemed to promise that your health was extremely mended, since I flattered myself you knew too well the regard I have for you to imagine that you could please me by hurting yourself in the least. But when I had read it, I could not but regret the fatigue my letter must have given you after your journey, and

---

[1] Mr. Grenville's seat in Buckinghamshire.
[2] Lord Cobham's seat.
[3] The residence of Mr. George Lyttelton, in Worcestershire.

wished you had had company or amusement to have
shortened it. We have known together what a bad inn
in France can be, but I know nothing is so bad as being
alone in such a place; so that I flattered myself that the
indifferent account you give of your health proceeded
rather from fatigue and disgust (of both which, by
your own account, you must have had a great share
since you left Argeville), and that rest and amusement
in a good air, with the help of some time, too, will
reconcile you better to the scheme you have submitted
to. And, indeed, I am the more in haste to answer
your letter, because I would use whatever little interest
you allow me to have with you, to dissuade you from
those thoughts of returning this winter, to which the
disagreeableness of your situation might naturally enough
have led you. But I beg you will consider that your
journey was not a party of pleasure, but a prescription,
and that the operations of climates can only be effectual
from time, so that to give up a method to which your
physicians have advised you, because you do not immediately find the benefit you expected (and which has been
occasioned by your own fatigue, perhaps, or some accidental ill weather, or being weary of the place you are
in): this would not, give me leave to say, be doing
justice to yourself, or, what I know you consider more,
not doing justice to your friends, who have a right to
your giving them the satisfaction of taking all reasonable ways to re-establish your health. You know very
well how necessary time is in this sort of remedy, and
therefore I hope you will think no more of returning this
winter to England.

What may be the business of next winter few persons, I believe, if any one, can tell; but if there should

be none of any consequence, your presence will not be necessary; and if there should, you know very well how unfit the fatigue of such another attendance would be for you, till your health is re-established, and how far it is from being your duty to throw yourself away. What the fogs and rains and winds of an English winter are you know full well, and what the fatigue of the journey will be you have lately experienced, to which you must add all the difference of the approach of winter. Put, therefore, from your thoughts, as far as you can, believe me, all the cares of this scene, till you have fitted yourself to bustle in it, and that you may do that, give yourself up to the strictest attention to your health for this winter. By your own account (allowing for the fatigue of travelling) I rather hope, notwithstanding what you say, that your health is mended, since your cough has left you, and that you find no alteration for the worse, notwithstanding the fatigue of your journey.

I am glad Mrs. Pitt[1] will pass her time so pleasantly. Mrs. Cleland, by this time, is at Argeville, and will not a little continue to mend even that society. Mr. Murray has given me, this recess, a great deal of his time, and consequently made mine, as you will easily believe, very delightful. He gave me above a fortnight here, and most of the rest of his time we rambled together. Mr. Pitt has not yet been here, but I expect him in a few days. Mr. Murray was not gone from hence when I received your letter. I need not tell you how much he

---

[1] Probably Mrs. Anne Pitt, the eldest sister of William Pitt, Earl of Chatham. Mr. Croker says, " She was remarkable in society, even to old age, for a great decision of character and sprightliness of conversation." She died in 1780.—*Notes to Suffolk Correspondence.*

is your friend, and I can assure you he joins heartily with me in hoping we shall not see you this winter.

I shall long to hear that you are fixed at Aix, or in any place as proper, and that your friend is returned to you. I interest myself in his health, not only as it is of, consequence to yours, but I really wish him well for wishing you so.   CORNBURY.

<hr>

MR. PITT TO MR. GEORGE GRENVILLE.

London, October 21, 1742.

DEAR GRENVILLE,—If Mr. Berenger[1] be still with you, I beg you will tell him I have not words to thank him for the pleasure his letter gave me. I don't trouble him with a letter, because I think it more probable he has left you, and that I shall have an occasion of acknowledging the favour when I see him in England, before my letter could follow him back from Aix, should he set out from that place. What shall I say to you, my dear George, of England? I should not tell you how much every friend you have here (which is every acquaintance you have here) interests himself for your perfect recovery. I say I think I should not tell you so, knowing, as I do, the warmth of your gratitude, for fear you should fancy yourself obliged to come home to thank them for their concern for you. I can venture to assure you, in the names of them all, that they will not charge you with the least insensibility to their inquietudes for you, if you should defer making your acknowledgments in person to them till May, or April at soonest. To speak seriously to you, my dear George,

---

[1] Moses Berenger, Esq., who married Penelope, youngest sister of Lord Cobham.

of a subject I think as serious as anything in the world, let us prevail upon you to give till next spring to the establishment of your constitution; and be assured while you are doing so, you are conferring the highest obligation upon your friends, and upon none of them more than myself.

I am sorry Mr. Berenger is forced to leave you, because of all men living you most want a friend to put you in mind of attending to the care of yourself: you can have no idea how much care you ought to take of yourself, unless you could hear how mankind talk of you, and how earnestly they wish to see your health perfectly restored and confirmed. I saw Mrs. Grenville[1], your mother, very well yesterday. The rest of your house I have not seen for this month, but have the pleasure of hearing they are all well. I shall set out for Stowe to-morrow, and not return till the Parliament meets, which it will do the sixteenth of November. When writing is not troublesome to you, give me the pleasure of hearing of you: I live in Cork Street, Burlington Buildings.

Adieu, my dear George, and be assured no one can be with a more perfect esteem than myself, most faithfully and affectionately yours.   W. PITT.

MR. GEORGE LYTTELTON[2] TO MR. GEORGE GRENVILLE.

Wickham, October 24 (1742).

DEAR GEORGE,—Nothing ever gave me more joy than the last accounts we have received from France of your

---

[1] Hester Temple, second sister of Lord Cobham, and widow of Richard Grenville, of Wotton.

[2] George Lyttelton, eldest son of Sir Thomas Lyttelton, of Hagley,

being so near a perfect recovery; but let me beg you, my dear George, not to trust too much to it, or think of leaving that air from which you have received so much benefit, to come in winter into that of Westminster Hall and the House of Commons, which for your case is certainly the worst in the world. When I ask this of you, I give you the most disinterested proof of my love, for in one of those places I shall want you extremely, and would risk anything but your safety for the advantage of your assistance there; not that if you were present, you or I either could do any good, but that in the painful race I am to run, it would be a great satisfaction and support to me to have you by my side. I know you will wish yourself there, but don't let that wish nor the zeal of your heart for a lost cause make you forget, that if by returning too soon you relapse into your illness, all the assistance and pleasure you can give to your friends—all the advantage and honour you can propose to yourself—will be entirely defeated. True wisdom, you know, is proportioning means to ends, and whatever ends you have in view, the first great means to them must be good health; acquire that, my dear

by Christian, daughter of Sir Richard Temple, of Stowe. He was at this time M.P. for Oakhampton. He succeeded to the Baronetcy at the death of his father, in 1751, and was created Baron Lyttelton in 1757. Lord Hervey, in his *Memoirs of the Reign of George II.*, thus describes Mr. Lyttelton :—" In his figure, extremely tall and thin : his face was so ugly, his person so ill made, and his carriage so awkward, that every feature was a blemish, every limb an incumbrance, and every motion a disgrace; but as disagreeable as his figure was, his voice was still more so, and his address more disagreeable than either. He had a great flow of words that were always uttered in a lulling monotony, and the little meaning they had to boast of was generally borrowed from the commonplace maxims and sentiments of moralists, philosophers, patriots, and poets, crudely imbibed, half digested, ill put together, and confusedly refunded."

George, and reserve yourself for better times. I would say a great deal to you upon the state of public affairs, and the scene that is opening to us at the meeting of Parliament, if I had any means of conveying my letter to you, except the post; but I have often experienced that to send one abroad with such things in it is a sure way to make it miscarry, and I had rather you should hear from me than that my letter should stay at the Post Office.

I will, therefore, only tell you what no Ministry, either old or new, can have any concern in, that Mrs. Lyttelton[1] goes happily on with her breeding, that I am very well, and your friends at Hagley much as they used to be.

Mrs. Fortescue[2] is in town, very busy in furnishing my house for her daughter and me; in the meanwhile we are at Wickham in great tranquillity. West[3] has the gout, which he is very glad of, as it will probably be the best cure for a feverish disorder he has been indisposed with some time. Kitty and he join with my wife in sincere congratulations upon your amendment, and

[1] Lucy, daughter of Hugh Fortescue, Esq., of Filleigh, Devonshire. She was married to Mr. Lyttelton, in June, 1742, and, dying in January, 1747, was the subject of the well-known Monody.

[2] Mrs. Fortescue was the daughter of Matthew, Lord Aylmer, and second wife of Hugh Fortescue, of Filleigh. She died in 1767, at the age of 80.

[3] Gilbert West, son of Dr. West, who published an edition of Pindar. His mother was a sister of Lord Cobham, and he was, consequently, first cousin to Mr. Lyttelton. He was the author of Observations on the Resurrection, a version of Pindar, and some other poetical works. Mr. Pitt procured for him the Treasurership of Chelsea Hospital. He resided at Wickham, in Kent, where he was often visited by Lyttelton and Pitt. It was at Wickham that Lyttelton is said to have received that conviction under which he composed his Observations on the Conversion of St. Paul. West died in March, 1756, from a stroke of paralysis, which brought to the grave, says Dr. Johnson, " one of the few poets to whom the grave might be without its terrors."

wishes for your recovery. How ardently I wish it no
words can tell you; every day I live convinces me more
of the value of such men as you, and makes you more
dear to your most affectionate,   G. LYTTELTON.

MR. WILLIAM MURRAY TO MR. GEORGE GRENVILLE.

Lincoln's Inn, 3rd Nov., 1742.

DEAR GEORGE,—I have long had a strong impulse to
write to you; you are much in my heart, and often in
my thoughts. I am very impatient for your recovery,
and rejoice in the favourable accounts I hear. I rambled about as usual during the leisure time I had, and
amongst other places I was at, I spent three days most
agreeably at Hagley, with our friends Lyttelton and Pitt,
where you may believe you was not forgot. You guessed
right, too, that I should probably be at Cornbury, for
your letter to my Lord, which makes very obliging
mention of me, found me there. I can send you no
news of your friends; to tell you they are extremely
anxious about you is none. Pope is at Bath, perched
upon his hill, making epigrams, and stifling them in
their birth, and Lord H——y [1] (would you believe it?) is

---

[1] John, Lord Hervey, eldest surviving son of the first Earl of Bristol
of that name, by his second wife, daughter of Sir Thomas Felton
and Lady Elizabeth Howard, daughter and heiress of the third Earl of
Suffolk. Lord Hervey's most entertaining *Memoirs of the Reign of
George the Second* have been recently published from the original
manuscript, with Notes and a Biography from the pen of the Right
Hon. John Wilson Croker. Lord Hervey died in August, 1743. The
libels mentioned above probably refer to a political ballad said to have
been written by Lord Hervey. A copy of it was sent by Horace Walpole to Sir Horace Mann, October 16, 1742.—See *Walpole Correspondence, collected edition*, vol. i. p. 235.

writing libels upon the King and his Ministers. It does not become him to be so employed. Mrs. Smith [1] has left all the Bradford estate to my Lord Bath [2], upon the death of Mr. Newport without issue, who is a lunatic to a degree of idiotcy, and never can recover. They say, when it all comes in, for part now belongs to this Earl of Bradford, who is, and has been a lunatic for many years, it will be near 12,000*l.* a year; but perhaps this is magnified. I have been concerned in a cause about it, and therefore I know 't is reckoned a very great estate. She has left Small, the surgeon, her personal estate, which is said to be worth 50,000*l.*, and she has given George Wilson, whom you know, 1000*l.*, which I am very glad of.

You know as much of foreign news as we do; we are told affairs in Germany go very well, and as to domestic, they wait the meeting of the Parliament.

I have a friend and near relation at A——on, a lady whose acquaintance you would be pleased with, and who would show a great regard to any one I have so great a friendship for as I have for you. Let me know if your route is like to lie that way, and I will send you a letter to her. No man more ardently wishes to see you return soon to us in strength and health than your most affectionate, &c., W. MURRAY.

---

[1] Mrs. Smyth, of Chelsea, who had been mistress to the late Lord Bradford, and by whom she had a son, who changed his name by Act of Parliament from Smyth to Newport. Lord Bradford left her a considerable estate, which she disposed of at her death as above mentioned.

[2] William Pulteney, recently created Earl of Bath.

MR. RICHARD GRENVILLE[1] TO MR. GEORGE GRENVILLE.

November 22, 1742.

DEAR GEORGE,—I will begin a long letter to you by thanking you for the great instance of your kindness which you have so lately given me, by consenting to submit the government of yourself, at this critical conjuncture, entirely to me; if I refuse to take it, there are people enough here who will be glad of it, I assure you, the moment they see you enter St. Stephen's Chapel. However, that I may still retain my credit with you, I will begin by telling you that I have this morning consulted Dr. Hulse about you, who, upon hearing your letter read, consents to your coming home whenever you please. By him and your own account all your friends here are governed. I long to see you, and could I but flatter myself I should see you well, I should have nothing left to wish. You are to take up your quarters when you come either at my house or Lord Cobham's[2]. Berenger is not yet come, and has already drawn for near 500*l*.

Mr. Dodington[3] has writ a very fine and civil letter to Lord Cobham, owning his marriage, and acquainting him that, though it is of a long date, yet he has no

---

[1] Richard Grenville, afterwards Earl Temple. He was at this time Member for the county of Buckingham.

[2] Sir Richard Temple, Viscount Cobham, of Stowe.

[3] George Bubb Dodington, afterwards Lord Melcombe. He was at this time M.P. for Bridgewater. He married a Mrs. Beghan. Horace Walpole says, " Mr. Dodington has at last owned his match with his old mistress: I suppose he wants a new one."—See *Walpole Correspondence*, vol. i. p. 245. Lord Hervey, also, in his *Memoirs of the Reign of George II.*, pp. 431-34, has given an amusing account of the character of Dodington.

children. Poor old Carter, of Buckingham[1], is dead, and there has been the devil to pay there about the choice of a burgess: Mr. Read has struck for the government of the Corporation, but I think we shall defeat him entirely; however, it will cost me a journey thither.

The latter part of your letter is very political, and so great an alteration do three months make that you appear as unknowing in them as any French marquis of them all. Your hero is not the hero he was when you left him. Lord Cobham and Lord Gower[2] have refused going to the cabinet, and we have had very warm work in the House of Commons the first day upon the Address. Pitt[3] spoke like ten thousand angels; your humble servant was so inflamed at their indecency that he could not contain, but talked a good while with his usual modesty. Jemmy[4], too, was all on fire, but could not get a place. We divided 150 against 259. We reckon ourselves, however, 200; and it is inconceivable how colloguing and flattering all the ministers are to all of us, notwithstanding our impertinence. We understand it, indeed, but had rather they should behave so to us than we to them. Who but young Bathurst[5] to answer me, in the most ridiculous, indecent, stupid

[1] One of the burgesses of Buckingham, and, consequently, one of the thirteen electors for the borough.

[2] John Leveson Gower succeeded his father as second Baron Gower, in Sept., 1709. He was made Lord Privy Seal in 1742, and in 1746 created Viscount Trentham and Earl Gower. He died Dec. 25, 1754.

[3] Mr. Pitt's speech upon this occasion was not reported; neither was that of Mr. Grenville, nor the reply by Mr. Bathurst.

[4] James Grenville, younger brother to Richard and George Grenville; at this time in Parliament for Oakhampton.

[5] Henry Bathurst, second son of Allen, Lord Bathurst. He was now M.P. for Cirencester. Having joined the Leicester House party, he was made Solicitor General to the Prince of Wales in 1745. After the death of Frederick he went over to the Court party, and in 1754

speech that ever was made. It was melancholy, but entertaining enough, to see them skulk in with their tails betwixt their legs, like so many spaniels, to the tune of above 40. Our friends are not yet come. Your brother Denton [1], as a great independent country gentleman, thinks it beneath him to attend. We shall have a glorious day [2] about the 16,000. We shall then see also who are Hanoverians, and who Englishmen.

Adieu, my dear George; be not in too great a hurry to see us, but according as you find yourself, and the different airs you pass through. Believe and be assured we all love you most cordially.

CAPTAIN THOMAS GRENVILLE [3] TO MR. GEORGE GRENVILLE.

Romney, off Cape St. Vincent, February 28, 1742-3.

DEAR BROTHER,—I believe you will not grudge the trouble of reading this letter, since it is to tell you the

was made a Judge of the Court of Common Pleas. He was advanced to the dignity of Lord Chancellor, and to the Peerage by the title of Baron Apsley, in 1771. By the death of his father in 1775 he succeeded to the earldom of Bathurst; and, having reached his 86th year, he died in 1794. Lord Campbell, in his most amusing work, the *Lives of the Lord Chancellors of England*, says that "perhaps the most memorable act in the life of Lord Chancellor Bathurst is, that he built Apsley House, now the residence of the illustrious Duke of Wellington, where once stood the *Hercules' Pillars*, the inn frequented by Squire Western."

[1] George Denton, Esq., of Hillesden, M.P. for the borough of Buckingham.

[2] The debate took place on the 10th of December, on the motion of Sir William Yonge, to grant 265,190*l.*, for defraying the charge of 16,000 Hanoverian troops. Pitt and the Grenvilles denounced the question, and moved that the troops should be dismissed. Pitt was opposed on this occasion by his great Parliamentary rival Murray (now become Solicitor General), in one of his best speeches. Sir William Yonge's motion was carried by a majority of 251 to 181.

[3] Thomas Grenville, the youngest of the Grenville brothers. He

good news of my having taken a very rich prize [1] from the West Indies, which I have carried to Gibraltar, and am now out again in quest of another; but as we may meet with some difficulties in the condemning her, and as she cannot be proceeded against (being a register ship) in any other court but the High Court of Admiralty of England, I will give you a very circumstantial account of my taking her, and of my proceedings since, that you may lay the case before some civilian, and have his opinion upon it. I believe you know Dr. Lee, and I think he is the properest man to apply to in this case.

On the 18th of February, in the morning, we discovered a large ship, which we chased all day, but having little wind we came up with her very slow; however, I continued the chase all night, and in the morning we saw her again about eleven o'clock; being pretty near in with C. St. Maries, we both fell in among some Portuguese fishing-boats, one of which I saw put aboard of the chase, and he immediately stood right in for the land, at which time, there being but little wind, several Portuguese fishing-boats went ahead and towed him. Upon seeing this, I called to the boats about me, desiring them to tow me, and promising them rewards, which they accordingly did. About one, being pretty near within gun-shot of him, and he having French colours out, and I my English, I fired some shot at him to bring him to, but all to no purpose. About three he run

was a captain in the Royal Navy, and at this time was the representative in Parliament for the borough of Bridport.

[1] Horace Walpole says, " I am not partial to the family, but it is but justice to mention, that when he (Captain Grenville) took a great prize some time ago, after a thousand actions of generosity to his officers and crew, he cleared sixteen thousand pounds, of which he gave his sister ten."—*Walpole Correspondence*, vol. ii. p. 189.

ashore upon a little island of sand, which lies off Faro in Portugal, and within about half an hour I came to an anchor, at about a cable's length and a half distant from him. As I stood in near him he had struck his colours, so that I immediately sent Mr. Bowdler, my first lieutenant, with orders to fetch the captain of her aboard to me with all his papers.

When he came he informed me that he was a Frenchman from Vera Cruz in the Spanish West Indies, bound to Cadiz; that he was loaded with cochineal, indigo, balsams, and chests of silver; and that the reason of his going ashore in hopes to escape us was, because the patron of the first Portuguese fishing-boat that was aboard him, had assured him that there was a war declared between the English and French, and that the ship in sight (meaning my ship) was an English man-of-war, which sailed extremely well, and which he could avoid by no other means.

Upon this information I immediately gave orders for getting her off, which we effected in about an hour's time, to my great joy, and on the 24th I arrived with her at Gibraltar.

Now, the remarks I have to make upon this are these: —in the first place it is to be observed, that upon the island of sand where this ship run ashore there were no forts, no guns, nay, not even any inhabitants; that his running ashore upon it was occasioned by the false information of these Portuguese fishing-boats, who gave it him in the view of having the chests of silver, &c., put into their boats to carry ashore, and which they partly succeeded in, since twenty-two chests of silver were saved in their boats by a Spanish captain or supercargo, who had the charge of all the cargo, and some other Spaniards. And, moreover, that if the King of Portugal should ever reclaim this ship, under pretence of breach of neutrality (which, however, is never understood to be such where there are no forts nor guns), he may very justly be answered, that in the beginning of the war a very rich English ship, whose name I have forgot, but one White was master of her, was taken off the same island by a Spanish privateer, and though often reclaimed by the King of Portugal, the claim was never admitted by the King of Spain, and the ship never restored, which is a certain fact. The King of Portugal may also be told, that we ought rather to complain of the breach of neutrality of the side of him and his subjects, seeing the Portuguese fishing-boats not only gave him, the Frenchman, a false information to our prejudice, but also assisted him in towing his ship ashore, and saved part of his cargo for him besides.

Thus much for the taking her; now for my proceedings since. Upon my arrival at Gibraltar, I found that a clause in the Act of Parliament for giving prizes to the captors, prevents the Deputy Judge of the Admiralty there from taking any cognizance of this prize, since she comes from Vera Cruz, whence the Flota ships come, and her cargo is registered. I have, therefore, caused the depositions of the chief officers, &c., of the prize, to be taken before the Deputy Judge of the Admiralty there (which are very full, and quite sufficient to condemn her), and they will be brought home by Mr. Samuel Savage, my purser, whom I have likewise chosen my agent, jointly with one Mr. Wombwell, a merchant at Gibraltar. Now, if these depositions are found sufficient to condemn her, well and good; but for fear they should not, I have wrote to Mr. Matthews to desire discretionary orders to proceed home with the prize myself, in case her coming home should be insisted upon in the High Court of Admiralty of Great Britain.

Now the two points I want to be resolved by civilians are these: whether they think the manner of taking her any sort of breach of the neutrality of the King of Portugal, and whether they think the High Court of Admiralty will insist upon the ship's being brought to England; and for God's sake, if it is possible, let me have their answer while I am at Lisbon, where I shall be from about the 8th of March till about the 23rd. Mr. Ezekiel Hall, merchant in London, is Wombwell's partner at Gibraltar, so that if you will let him know that Wombwell is my agent, he may be useful to you. The value of the ship's cargo is computed at about 120,000*l.* or 130,000*l.* sterling, of which, if we condemn her, I shall share about 30,000*l.* or 40,000*l.* Make all our family and friends partakers of the pleasure this news will give you, for I write this while an English ship is lying to, waiting for it, and I have time to write to nobody else.

THOMAS GRENVILLE.

Note, that in all the sworn depositions it is affirmed that the Portuguese patron of the fishing-boat assured them that there was war between the English and French, and that that was the reason of their running ashore.

MR. GEORGE GRENVILLE TO CAPT. THOMAS GRENVILLE.

Stowe, June 10, 1744.

HETTY[1] showed me your letter, which she received last post, and that determined me to be beforehand with

---

[1] Hester Grenville, afterwards married to William Pitt, Earl of Chatham.

you, and to thank you par avance for the letter you promise me. We received intelligence from Mrs. Catherine
that the Paultons[1] party are to follow us to Amesbury[2],
but at the same time she told me I despaired of seeing
you there, even if I had broken my faith with my Lord
Cobham for another day or two.

This consideration made us turn a deaf ear to the
voice of the charmer, though indeed she charmed very
wisely. At our arrival here we found my Lord and
Lady[3] and Madlle. Harriett[4] engaged in the pleasures of
three-handed cribbage, and were vain enough to flatter
ourselves that we were extremely welcome, though we
broke in upon the solitude of the place, and turned
those agreeable tête-à-têtes which must happen amongst
three people only, into parties quarrées. Hetty got here

---

[1] Paultons, in the New Forest, the residence at this time of James
Grenville. It subsequently belonged to Mr. Hans Stanley.

[2] The seat of the Duke and Duchess of Queensberry.

[3] Anne Halsey, Lady Cobham: she survived her husband and died
in 1760.

[4] Miss Harriett Speed, sister of Colonel Speed; a very intimate
friend and relation of Lord and Lady Cobham. After Lord Cobham's
death, Miss Speed still continued to reside with Lady Cobham, who
retired to a property belonging to her father, the old Manor House at
Stoke Pogis, formerly the residence of Sir Christopher Hatton and Sir
Edward Coke, and the well-known locality of Gray's Poem called *The
Long Story*, which originated in circumstances attendant upon a visit
paid by Miss Speed, accompanied by Lady Schaub (widow of Sir Luke
Schaub), to the residence of the Poet in the village of Stoke, in order,
by Lady Cobham's request, to invite Gray to the Manor House, as the
ladies were desirous of being acquainted with him. The absence of
Gray upon the occasion of this visit gave rise to the humorous incidents described in the poem. In a letter to Wharton in 1761, Gray
mentions—" My old friend Miss Speed has done what the world calls
a very foolish thing: she has married the Baron de la Perrière, son
to the Sardinian Minister, the Count de Viry. He is about twenty-
eight years old (ten years younger than herself), but looks nearer
forty."

about a week after us, and the day before yesterday we were surprised with the laughing and laughter-promoting Jemmy [1]; and now the scene begins to thicken here, since the Lord of Ashendon and his fair lady come to-morrow, and Lady Blandford [2] and Miss Wyndham [3] have agreed to lay aside their hoops next Tuesday morning, and by the assistance of post-chaises intend to be at Stowe before the evening. For my own part, I have been engaged ever since I came here in endeavouring to carry our new Turnpike Act into execution, but have met with almost as many difficulties, and as much opposition to the mending of our ways in the country, as to the reforming our manners in town; however, I don't think the one quite so desperate as the other, but hope that with the assistance of a dry summer it may succeed: whereas our political affairs seem as if they would not be much bettered by this summer's campaign. Menin, you know, is taken, and Ypres is supposed to be so by this time. Ostend, Aeth, Mons, and Tournay come next, which, I suppose, will be glory enough for the British arms for this year. 'Tis said that the Dutch and English have solicited Prince Charles of Lorraine to command our army in Flanders, but that he declines it because he is already at the head of an army of twice the number, consisting of troops more aguerried and somewhat more obedient to him than per-

---

[1] James Grenville.

[2] A Dutch lady named D'Jong. She was now the widow of Sir William Wyndham, having been his second wife, and by whom he left no issue. The first husband of this lady was William, Marquess of Blandford.

[3] Miss Wyndham, daughter of Sir William Wyndham, by his first wife, Lady Katherine Seymour, daughter of Charles, Duke of Somerset. She was afterwards married to Mr. George Grenville.

haps he may expect to find the English, Dutch, and
Hanoverians. 'T is still a most problematical question
whether the King will go, or no, and every letter brings
different accounts.

Pope [1] is dead at last, or at least all that is mortal
of him. He has left 200*l.* to Gilly West [2] after the
death of Mrs. Blount [3], to whom he has given 2000*l.* for
her life, and then it goes to her sister. His papers he
has left to be published at the discretion of Lord Bolingbroke; and, when published, they are to be the property
of Mr. Warburton [4], to whom, and Mr. Spence [5], of Oxford, he has given his library.

I am very glad to hear that you are likely to lose
Jemmy Berenger, as the change is likely to be so much
to his advantage. I heartily wish it may, because I
believe he very well deserves it should. I am desired
to inquire after another cousin of ours, which is Captain
West [6]. A sister of his, who is married to Mr. Dayrell,

---

[1] Pope died on the 30th of May, 1744. Speaking of Pope's will,
Lady Mary Wortley Montague says, "On the whole it appears to me
more reasonable, and less vain, than I expected from him."

[2] Gilbert West, see *ante*, page 15, *note.*

[3] Mrs. Martha Blount, the well-known friend of Pope; described
in the will as the youngest daughter of Mrs. Martha Blount, of Wel-
beck Street, Cavendish Square.

[4] Afterwards Bishop of Gloucester.

[5] The Rev. Joseph Spence became known to Pope from being the
author of an *Essay on Pope's Odyssey, &c.*, in 1727, "with the
criticism in which," says Dr. Johnson, "Pope was so little offended,
that he sought the acquaintance of the writer, who lived with him
from that time in great familiarity, attended him in his last hours, and
compiled memorials of his conversations. The regard of Pope recommended him to the great and powerful, and he obtained very valuable
preferments in the church." Spence was accidentally drowned in his
garden at Byfleet, in Surrey, in 1768.

[6] A son of Dr. West, by Maria, eldest sister of Lord Cobham; he was
afterwards an Admiral, and was with Byng at Minorca.

of this neighbourhood, complains that they have not heard of him a great while, and that Mrs. West neglects to send them the accounts she receives. Whenever, therefore, you write to Hetty, you will do a kind thing in telling her what you hear of him.

I find that the taking of the *Northumberland*[1] is thought a great loss by everybody, but we are quite ignorant of the particulars of the capture, the circumstances of which are very differently related. I see by your letter to Hetty that you are ready to sail. I don't know how to wish you to continue in the disagreeable place where you now are, but I hope when you do sail that it will not be very far, and consequently that we may meet before winter, and pass it together. At all events, let me know what is to become of you as soon as you can, and love me always as well as I do, which is the best wish I can make for my own honour and happiness. Adieu, my dear Tom.

I shall leave this place in a week at furthest, and therefore beg that you will direct your letters for me at my mother's, in Clifford Street, where I will give you notice of all my motions. Hetty does not write to you by this post because I told her I would. Everybody here talks of you, and loves you, and she not the least.

---

[1] On the 4th of June, the *Northumberland*, a new ship of 70 guns and 480 men, commanded by Captain Watson, cruising in the Channel, fell in with three French men-of-war. The *Northumberland* sustained a very unequal conflict for three hours with amazing activity and resolution, till unfortunately Captain Watson was mortally wounded : she then struck her colours by order of the master, who was therefore afterwards sentenced by a court martial to spend the remainder of his life in the Marshalsea prison. The French carried the *Northumberland* in great triumph into Brest, where Captain Watson died.—*Campbell's Lives of the Admirals*, 1812, vol. iv. p. 487.

MR. GEORGE GRENVILLE TO CAPT. THOMAS GRENVILLE.

Stowe, October 22, 1744.

DEAR TOMMY,—Though we had but little hopes of poor Jemmy Berenger's[1] safety, from what we read in the newspapers, yet the certainty of his ill fortune, which we received last night by the account sent by you to Harry[2], could not help affecting us all extremely. Poor lad! His ill genius continued constant, and persecuted him to the last. He has never left your ship but to his ruin.

The first time he missed an opportunity, in some degree, of making his fortune, and the last, of saving his life. May this victim (and indeed it is a great one, considering the habitudes we had with him, and how well he deserved) atone at least for your safety. A blow so near one cannot but make one tremble for what is nearer; and yet methinks this sort of accident is not usual; and when I talk this language my love and low spirits speak rather than my judgment. My mother, I hear, bears this loss very indifferently. This was an aggravation that I was much afraid of, and for that reason Hetty and I agreed, before we received your account, that it would be very proper for her to go up to London, and be with her. Accordingly, she set out the day before yesterday, and is with her before now; so that she has just missed your letter to her, which came last night, together with that from Harry, and which I imagine contains the same unfortunate story:

[1] He was on board the *Victory*, of 110 guns, Admiral Sir John Balchen's ship, which, with 900 men, was lost off the island of Alderney.

[2] Henry Grenville, fourth son of Richard Grenville, Esq., of Wotton, by Hester Temple.

be that as it will, I have taken care of it, and will send it to her by to-morrow's post. I expect to hear from her the day after to-morrow: if my mother is very bad, I will go up to town directly; if not, I shall stay here ten days longer, and make a visit to Mr. Waller[1], and to Marble Hill, in my way to London, where I shall be about the 7th or 8th of next month. This was my purpose upon a supposition that you would pass this winter in London, and that you would not be able to get there before that time; but I see by your letter to Harry that there is a talk of your going to the Mediterranean. I hope 't is without foundation, and need not say how great a disappointment it would be to me; since, though I could not comply with the letter of your last kind request to me, the reasons of which I will tell you more fully when I see you, yet I reckoned with the greatest joy upon fulfilling the spirit of it. If this report of sending a new fleet into the Mediterranean should be true, and that your ship is to be one of it, I imagine you will at least be permitted to go to town for some little time to settle your prize affairs; in which case I beg you will send me word immediately when it will be, and I will certainly meet you there, and put off my visits to another time. Everything wears a melancholy face. The miserable situation of the public you see in every newspaper, and it seems to me very difficult to tell exactly the means of redressing it; and even those which are the likeliest methods, we are not the masters to make use of: however, we shall try by this winter whether the experience of the past may not add some weight to the reasons so often urged, and whether the public calamity, in which all are involved alike, may not in-

---

[1] At Hall Barn, near Beaconsfield.

duce some little consideration in those whom interest alone can persuade. As to our private vexations, you are fully apprized of them, so that I can say nothing new to you on that head, but must wait for the event to decide upon them. News, you may imagine, whilst I am here, I know but little of, but what I do I will tell you. There is yet no account of Coni[1] being taken, notwithstanding that the King of Sardinia, 't is agreed, was repulsed in his attempt to raise the siege: so that the fate of Italy, which seems in some measure to depend upon the success of that siege, is still uncertain. A battle is every day expected in Bohemia, which, if the Queen of Hungary loses, will put an end to her hopes in Germany, as the taking of Coni will to the King of Sardinia in Italy, though the success on either or both of these places will not be decisive in their favour. We have received an account from our armies in Flanders, that a great fracas has lately happened between the English and Hanovers, who till that time had agreed very well; the dissensions having prevailed chiefly between the English and the Dutch, each nation accusing the other as the author of the dishonour of this campaign. This, with the contempt which the French have expressed for us, makes the scene complete in Flanders. I am told that Mr. Rowley's fleet is in great distress; this, perhaps, may be the reason of the talk of reinforcing him. As to domestic news, you will have seen in the newspapers that the Duchess of Marlborough and Lady Granville[2] are both dead the same day. The latter has

---

[1] Siege of Coni. See *Gentleman's Magazine*, 1744, p. 567.

[2] "Yesterday morning," writes Horace Walpole on the 19th of October, 1744, " carried off those two old beldams, Sarah of Marlborough, and the Countess Granville." Lady Grace Granville, youngest daughter of John Granville, Earl of Bath, and wife of George, first Lord Car-

left a great estate to her son Lord Carteret; the will of the former is not yet opened, the executors not being all in town. The contents of it excite the curiosity of all the world, particularly of the inhabitants of this place, because she had declared in her lifetime that she had left a provision for Mr. Pitt[1]. He is still at Bath, and (as Jemmy, who called upon him there in his way from Butleigh, says) in a very bad way, having never been able to get rid of the gout in his bowels ever since it first seized him before you left London, in the spring. The Bath waters have done him no good. This is a grievous misfortune to him, since, if it does not affect his life, it may perhaps disable him, and make a cripple of him for ever; though, for my own part, I cannot help thinking that his youth and ease are most likely to get the better of it in a great degree. I wish this good news may contribute to it. Mr. Waller[2] has had as great a misfortune, by a humour falling upon his ears, which, added to his former complaint, has made him so entirely deaf, that he has by times been utterly unable to converse with his family except in writing.

I suppose you know Dr. Ayscough's[3] good fortune in being appointed preceptor to Prince George, with a salary of 500*l.* a year. This, with his other circum-

---

teret, after whose death she was herself created Viscountess Carteret and Countess Granville: she was succeeded by her only surviving son, John Lord Carteret, who became Earl Granville.

[1] She bequeathed to Pitt a legacy of 10,000*l.*

[2] Edmund Waller, M.P. for Wycombe, at this time a leading member of the opposition. He was appointed Cofferer of the Household, in December following.

[3] Dr. Ayscough married, in November, 1745, Anne, sister of Mr. George Lyttelton, to whom he had been tutor. He had been also Clerk of the Closet to Frederick Prince of Wales, and was subsequently Dean of Bristol.

stances put together, will make matrimony sit easy upon him. Everybody here is well. GEORGE GRENVILLE.

MR. RICHARD GRENVILLE TO MR. GEORGE GRENVILLE.

January 8, 1744–5.

YOUR will, like that of most arbitrary princes, is not much to your subjects' palates, but must be obeyed, and your will only, upon this subject, would be obeyed.

I intend to set out the day before the Marlow Election, and shall be in town the same night. As to the call, I take it for granted it is next to impossible it should take place; but I think it is quite impossible I should be taken into custody, if the House should be called over, when you stand up and in a moving manner acquaint the House that I have for ten years together been a most exact attender, that I have had a great deal of private business to settle, and that you will pawn your word to the House that I shall certainly be in town on the 16th.

Let me know as soon as you can, or at least before I come up, whether you think things are, or are like to be, in such a situation as to prevent my return here, that I may resolve upon taking up or leaving my family behind. Sir Edward is very happy with Lord Cobham's answer, and is much devoted to us in particular, I believe, notwithstanding his eagerness the other day. It is a pleasure to us here to read what is going forward in town by way of news, though, for one, I protest I feel myself no more concerned in it, than when I read of the exploits of our very good friend and neighbour Kouli Kan.

Give yourself no trouble about the parish officers, only

take care of the naval ones, and provide a most excellent station for poor Tom[1], that if the public be not
benefited by your administration, your family at least
may, which is so far at least doing good, and is about as
much as is expected from any placeman's hands. We
have danced four nights together *successfully*, as Lord
B——[2] would say, and to-night I shall have my swill,
being engaged with the most potently vigorous dancer of
these parts, Mrs. P—tt[3]. Tell Lord Barrington[4] since
he won't come down to us, we must go up to him, and
since he will not be a Lord of Trade, he may, I dare
say, soon be a lord of whatever he pleases. Poor Hillsborough[5] I have a fellow-feeling for. I have sent to
Buckingham for fear you should not have writ, as I desired you would. Adieu, dear George, and don't kill

[1] Captain Thomas Grenville.

[2] Probably Charles, the sixth Lord Baltimore, at this time M.P.
for Surrey, and a Lord of the Admiralty. He died in 1751. Horace
Walpole ascribes to him a similar *Malaprop* mode of expression:
" It will be a new æra, or, as my Lord Baltimore calls it, a new
area in English History," &c.; and upon another occasion he mentions
him as " the best and honestest man in the world, with a good deal of
jumbled knowledge."—*Walpole Correspondence*, vol. ii. pp. 174 and 308.

[3] Probably Mrs. Anne Pitt, see *ante*, p. 1, *note*.

[4] William Wildman, second Viscount Barrington, son of John, the
first Lord, by Anne, daughter and co-heiress of Sir William Daines
of Bristol. He was at this time Member for Berwick. He filled
many offices of the State, having been at different times a Lord of
the Admiralty, Master of the Great Wardrobe, Secretary at War, Chancellor of the Exchequer, and Treasurer of the Navy. He died in
1793.

[5] Wills Hill, Viscount Hillsborough, M.P. for the borough of Warwick. In 1751 he was advanced to the Earldom of Hillsborough in
Ireland, and subsequently made Baron Harwich, and Earl of Hillsborough in the Peerage of Great Britain; and Marquess of Down-
shire in that of Ireland. In 1763 he was appointed a Commissioner
of Trade and Plantations; Joint Postmaster-General in December,
1766; and Secretary of State for the Colonies in 1768. He died in
1793.

yourself with attendance.   How does Pitt do?   Let him
know I enquired of you after him, for I am not yet
resolved to forget entirely all my old friends.

MR. GEORGE GRENVILLE TO CAPT. THOMAS GRENVILLE.

Admiralty Office, May 13, 1745.

I RECEIVED your letter, my dear Captain, and though
I am sorry that I cannot at all times congratulate you
on the accomplishment of whatever you wish, yet give
me leave to tell you that, as rich as you are, you want
money more than you do honour; and therefore I wish
you joy most sincerely of your 3000*l.*, and hope your
next cruize will bring you a great addition to both the
one and the other.   How the d——l came the swift-
sailing *Falkland* to miss of her ship, and the *Augusta*
to come up with hers so soon?   I am afraid their
beauty and perfections are a little journalier.   I showed
that part of your letter which related to the cleaning
at Kinsale to the Board, and we immediately wrote to
the Navy Board to take all possible care to put everything at that yard into order immediately for the cleaning
of ships.

The orders to Captain Hamilton are to clean all ships
of his squadron at Kinsale; but if, after this notice has
been given to the Navy Board, you still find the same
difficulties in cleaning there, write to the Board, and we
will endeavour to have you clean at Plymouth, though
the former is what we should wish if it is feasible.
There are no thoughts, I believe, of changing your
station, or putting you under any other command than
that of Captain Hamilton, unless you desire it, which

by all I can find is very far from your intentions, so
that you are likely to stay where you are a good while.
The House of Commons has, as you will hear, made
a strict and severe inquiry into the engagement near
Toulon, and has ordered Admiral Matthews, Admiral
Lestock, and six captains, Burrish, Norris, Ambrose,
Williams, Frogmore, and Dilke, and the lieutenants of
the *Dorsetshire*, to be tried at Court Martial for their
behaviour [1]. Captain Norris was half tried in the Mediterranean, pursuant to an order of the last Admiralty,
and the minutes of the trial were transmitted to us
during the time of the House of Commons' inquiry;
by which it appeared that, after having tried him for
eight days, when the facts came out very strong, the
Court Martial declared that, he being out of the King's
service, they could not try him. This was thought extraordinary, as they had examined all the witnesses
Captain Norris could produce; and the minutes being
laid before the House, the whole proceeding was so very
bad that the House unanimously voted them to be arbitrary, partial, and illegal; in consequence of which Mr.
Rowley must be recalled; so that in this session the
three admirals and half the Mediterranean fleet have
been censured in some measure. There was a division
to excuse Mr. Matthews from being ordered to be tried;
but it was carried that he should be tried, by a majority
of 258 against 73. Mr. Pelham [2] was of the minority,

---

[1] The result of the court martial was, that Admiral Matthews was
declared incapable of again serving in the navy; Lestock was acquitted; and some of the captains were visited with different degrees
of disgrace.—*Coxe's Pelham Administration*, vol. i. p. 222. *Parl. Hist.*
vol. xiii. pp. 1201-17.

[2] The Right Honourable Henry Pelham, first Commissioner of the
Treasury. He came into Parliament for the borough of Seaford in

and your humble servant of the majority, which has not usually been the case with either of us; and I am afraid the zeal we have shown to bring delinquents to justice, and to endeavour by that means to restore the discipline and spirit of the Navy, has not made us very popular with part of the fleet; but if that is so, tant pis for them, and so much the more necessary is an inquiry if the Board of Admiralty is scarce strong enough to dare to undertake it; for my part I will, as long as I have a seat here, which I think it is now settled I am to have till the next sessions; if not, I shall at least leave it with more pleasure than I took it.

Since I began this letter many material things have happened. We have been beat in Flanders, and Tournay will certainly be taken. I send you enclosed the account of this unfortunate action[1], as given in the Gazette, to which I refer you for all the particulars of that fatal day; only I will add, that it is universally agreed that the Duke behaved with the greatest spirit and intrepidity; so, in general, did all our troops. The Dutch horse behaved scandalously; their foot but indifferently; the Hanovers very well.

The loss of the battle is imputed to the ill-behaviour of the Dutch in the left wing, who did not venture to attack the foot they were ordered to on that side, and to Brigadier General Ingoldsby, who several times refused to attack that on the right hand, though commanded several times by the Duke and Marshal Konigsegg, and by a Hanover major-general, who attacked it in his sight

1718, and afterwards represented the county of Sussex until his death in 1754. He had been Paymaster of the Forces, and Secretary at War, before his appointment to the Treasury in 1743.

[1] The battle of Fontenoy, in which William, Duke of Cumberland, suffered a defeat.

with two Hanover battalions, which were cut to pieces, whilst Ingoldsby looked on with four choice English battalions; for which neglect, or, not to mince the word, poltronnerie, he is to be tried as soon as he recovers his wounds. Many of the Dutch are likewise ordered to be tried for their behaviour that day. The Dutch have sent reinforcements, and so have we, by drafts from the English Guards here, and by three entire regiments from hence. The Government have likewise ordered 1500 men to be drafted from Ireland in about three weeks, and have insisted on our getting a convoy for them. This obliges us to change your situation, and that of Mr. Keppel, for a little while; and as you are foul you will cruize at Portsmouth, and then return to your former station. I little thought of your turning a convoy; but as the embarkation is to be from Cork, and in such a hurry, we can find no other ships to perform that service; besides which, upon the whole, I cannot say I am very sorry, as you will be cleaned sooner and better at Portsmouth than at Kinsale, and 't is only one trip to Ostend; besides, I am interested in it, for perhaps I may some way or other have a chance of seeing you, and settling many things which it is impossible to write about. I want to tell you what our situation is; to know what you wish yours should be.

There are no news here; but people hang their heads about this battle. Many stories are told with regard to it. We have not heard one word with regard to Mr. Martyn or the French fleet since the account you gave us of the latter, which you are much commended for giving.

We heard from Mr. Martyn a day or two before, who had received an account of them from a victualler ship, which they took and sent back to France; and upon this intelligence he sent us word that he had called a Council of War, and resolved to follow them, but does not say how far. Since which time we have heard nothing from them; and thence we conclude that he is not in the Soundings, because we imagine some ship or other by this time must have seen or spoke with him. We have had many reports from Ireland of their having taken and destroyed the whole French fleet; but none more authentic than a hearsay from a Portuguese ship, said to have put into Cork, which this moment appears to be only hearsay; for we have heard by an express from Mr. Martyn this moment, that he put into P. Egmont Sound with all his squadron without success, not having been able to get up with the French squadron, who were upwards of 80 leagues ahead of him, in the way to Cape Breton. God send us good news somewhere or other, or else send us a peace. Adieu, my dear Tommy, let me hear of you often, which, next to seeing you, is the greatest pleasure you can give me. We are all well. Mr. and Mrs. Grenville have been gone to Wotton this week, together with Hetty.   G. G.

MR. GEORGE GRENVILLE TO MR. RICHARD GRENVILLE.

Admiralty Office, Oct. 3, 1745.

DEAR BROTHER,—I came here last night from Stowe, and intend this afternoon or to-morrow morning to go and look after our lawyers.

Nothing new from the North since your last accounts, but the city is giving great marks of their zeal and loyalty, having offered any sum of money that the King wants towards suppressing this rising. The run upon the Bank[1] still continues, though in a less degree. Orders are given to bring over the 6000 Hessians hither. Last night we had an account, which may be depended upon, that the King of Prussia has broken his armistice, if it is true he ever entered into one, and has fallen upon Prince Charles, whom he has beat all to pieces a second time. They talk of above 4000 Austrians killed upon the spot[2]. Our sea news still continues good, and our continent news bad. The French have raised the siege of Aeth, and it is said, upon this diminution of our forces in Flanders, they are marching directly to attack the remainder of our army there.

We have an account from New England, that two more French East India ships, and the third South Sea ship, which was reckoned as rich as either of the other two, have put into Cape Breton, and are all three in our possession.

The *Tigress* Privateer has taken a ship bound from Brest to Calais, and so to the South Sea, which is valued at above 150,000*l*.

I found those I went to in so d——d a humour that it was impossible for me to execute your commands as to examining the papers. Nobody met me at our turnpike meeting except our Buckingham Trustees, so that I thought it not prudent to overturn the act of a full meeting in so thin a one. Adieu.

GEORGE GRENVILLE.

[1] An immediate rush was made upon the Bank of England, which, it is said, only escaped bankruptcy by paying in sixpences to gain time. —*Lord Mahon's History of the 'Forty-five*, p. 89.

[2] The battle of Soor, in Bohemia, in which the Austrians were defeated by the King of Prussia. The conquerors lost 2600 killed and wounded, and among the former Prince Albert of Brunswick.

I opened my letter again to tell you a piece of news which I have just heard, and which rejoices me most exceedingly. John Stuart, whom we all know, is not killed or wounded, but is a prisoner safe and sound in Edinburgh, but another Captain John Stuart is killed, which occasioned the mistake.

MR. GEORGE GRENVILLE TO MR. RICHARD GRENVILLE.

Admiralty Office, Oct. 5, 1745.

DEAR BROTHER,—Nothing very extraordinary has happened in the political world since my last letter. The Queen of Hungary ordered her troops to attack the Prussians, so that she has brought this defeat upon herself.

The last accounts from the North[1] say that the Highlanders have begun plundering part of the country between Edinburgh and Berwick, particularly a house of Lord Somerville's. This manner of proceeding may be an unfortunate one with respect to those upon whom it falls, but cannot be more so to them than to the party that suffers it, whose hopes I think it must entirely destroy if carried to any length.

It is now said again that the Castle of Edinburgh is in great want of provisions; that the Governor of the Castle ordered the inhabitants of the city to supply him, and threatened, in case of refusal, to burn the town, and beat it down about their ears.

They obeyed for two or three days, but then the Highlanders threatened them with the same fate, and

[1] See a very interesting account of the state of Scotland at this period in Lord Mahon's *History of the 'Forty-five*, pp. 60–62.

with military execution, if they continued it any longer, upon which they desisted immediately, and the magistrates have applied to the King, stating their miserable situation, and beseeching him to give orders to the Governor not to execute his threats. The answer to the application I don't know, but I imagine 't is a favourable one. Two letters have been found, the one in Dorsetshire wrapped up in a handkerchief, the other near Canterbury in the inside of a large mohair button, both of them talking of a designed landing in the West, and of assistance to that landing by some Roman Catholic gentlemen; but both of them being found at the same time makes people suspect their authenticity, and think it not likely that two such letters should be lost by accident. We have no accounts of any preparations for an embarkation in any of the ports of France, which I own surprises me a good deal; but the Ferrol fleet is not yet sailed, which, perhaps, may be destined this way, though 't is said that they are designed for the Havannah; but I think it extraordinary if our mortal enemies should make no use of the present opportunity of distressing us; if they do not, it looks to me as if they were distressed themselves.

.   .   .   .

GEORGE GRENVILLE.

MR. GEORGE GRENVILLE TO CAPT. THOMAS GRENVILLE.

Admiralty Office, Oct. 10, 1745.

MY DEAR TOM,—I would not have let so much time pass without giving you some account of this part of the world, if I had thought it possible that my letters could

reach you; but you have been so quick in your motions
of late, that all attempts of that sort would be fruitless,
and I am obliged even now to catch you flying, for you
will receive orders with this to proceed with what other
ships can put to sea from Corunna, and we are afraid
some other attempt may be made upon the fourteen rich
East India ships who are now in the defenceless bay of
Galway on the back of Ireland. Two ships are already
gone to convoy them home, and two more are to be sent
by Admiral Martyn. What a deplorable condition have
we been in since my last letter to you! but I hope to
God we are now in a way to get out of it. I will not
repeat to you all the particulars of this unfortunate
transaction, which you will have seen in the printed
papers almost as fully as I can give them to you. Many
mutual complaints and accusations are generally the
consequences of all public misfortunes, and so they are
of this, but where the blame really is, I will not pretend to decide. Sir John Cope, who is so much concerned in it, is recalled from Berwick in order to have
his conduct examined by a Court Martial. The French
are gone, or going, into winter quarters, after having
taken and razed Aeth. Our troops are at last all ordered home to defend England. Marshal Wade is set
out for Doncaster to form his army, which is to consist
of three battalions of those who came lately from
Flanders, two Irish regiments landed the other day at
Chester, six Dutch battalions, and one other Dutch
battalion at Berwick, besides about 500 of the remains
of Sir John Cope's army, and eight battalions of our
own troops ordered from Williamstadt to Newcastle
directly, with three regiments of horse, and two of dragoons, so that he will have a body of 15,000 or 16,000

men, which, I hope, will be sufficient to put an end to this affair. We have just heard that the Castle of Edinburgh[1] has fired, and killed 40 or 50 of the Highlanders, and made a sally, and introduced a large quantity of provisions in the Castle, and that the rebels have thereupon taken the resolution of marching southward. These are all our politics at present, for no other will bear the talking of whilst we are in this distress. Lord Cobham came to town this very day. The Lord of Wotton comes next Monday, and with him Mademoiselle Hetty. Everybody that you are concerned for are well. I wish that Mr. Martyn's fleet were ordered farther from the coast to the southward, for I own I am very much afraid for them this season. Adieu, my dear Tom, I have a thousand things to say to you, but have not time, for the express stays for my letter. Love me as I love you, and I desire no better, except that you should come home safe and sound, and rich, but above all safe, as for *sound* and *rich*, that as fortune shall order.   George Grenville.

MR. GEORGE GRENVILLE TO CAPT. THOMAS GRENVILLE.

Admiralty, October 15, 1745.

My Dear Tom,—I was very sorry to hear of the bad condition in which your Commodore and the greatest part of Mr. Martyn's fleet returned to Plymouth, not only from the mischief already done, but from the apprehensions I am under of what may happen to them upon these winter cruizes in so dangerous a station as just off the Lizard, which I do assure you has given

[1] See Lord Mahon's *History of the 'Forty-five*, p. 62.

me many an uneasy hour, and would have done so even
if you had not been amongst them : judge then, my dear
Tom, what my anxiety would be with that addition.
Thank God, his next cruize is ordered *well to the westward*, and consequently in a more honourable, more
advantageous, and a less fatiguing, less dangerous station. You will know long before this can reach you
that you are to make part of his squadron for this
cruize. This cursed rebellion has overthrown all our
schemes, but when that vanishes, as I hope it will soon,
I flatter myself our projects will revive with redoubled
strength, " if," as Milton says, " the blind fury of party
does not interfere with her abhorred shears," and slit
our thin-spun political life, of the duration of which no
man can pretend to form a guess. Mr. Legge tells me
he has writ to you this post, and inclosed I send you a
letter from Miss Hester, so that I take it for granted
that you are thoroughly informed of our Admiralty
transactions, and of the lives and histories of the family
of the Grenvilles. News from the North have been very
scarce of late, which I am afraid does not look as if the
rebels were about to disperse, as it has been reported,
since in that case the ways would be open, and we
should have tidings of what was doing there every hour.

The last accounts from that part of the world says,
that they have about 9000 men, that they have above
400 horse, and were to set out from Edinburgh on
their march southward as this day, but whether by
Carlisle or Berwick is uncertain. A French privateer,
with officers, arms, and money, is got to Montrose, and
we are afraid that others steal by us to the ports on the
east coast of Scotland, in spite of all our cruizing ships
and sloops. I don't hear of any embarkation of a num-

ber of men, unless the four Spanish men-of-war which
the Spanish frigate taken lately by the Privateer gives
an account of, were destined to land men and money in
Ireland.   'T is generally reported that there is some
person of distinction on board of that frigate, who is in
a common sailor's dress, and is amongst the other prisoners unknown.   Report has already made this person
of distinction the Pretender's second son, but I have not
seen anything authentic that can induce me to think
this extraordinary story well founded; and therefore I
believe it has no other grounds, but that the eldest brother came to Scotland in such a vessel.   So much for
news.   I wish, my dear Tom, that I was as confident of
your succeeding in everything to the utmost of my desires, as I am that you will do your duty and deserve it;
nor is this the language of my affection and partiality,
though I am equally happy in having both for you, and
receiving both from you.   Adieu: the Parliament meets
on Thursday, and everything is in a hurry.   Write to
me ten lines before you go to sea, if you have time,
and if I can, you shall hear from me again next post.
God bless you.   George Grenville.

Have you received a letter of mine sent to Admiral
Martyn six weeks or two months ago?

MR. GEORGE GRENVILLE TO CAPT. THOMAS GRENVILLE.

Admiralty Office, December 28, 1745.

Dear Tom,—I wrote two letters for you at Portsmouth, and one to you at Deal, which, however, contained nothing important, and therefore you will have

no loss of them. I did not expect that I should still be to write to you, because by this time I hoped to have seen you here ; but such is the uncertainty of our affairs at present, that we can reckon upon nothing ; however, I still flatter myself that you won't continue where you are long, though 't is possible your stay there may not be shorter than mine at the Admiralty, but that I leave to fortune, which has many more considerable events to decide: in the mean time, whilst I am here, the pleasantest thing I can do is to believe that my being here may, in some way or other, contribute to your ease or satisfaction. I received your last letter at Wotton, where I made an excursion for three days with the Duke and Duchess of Queensberry [1], and Mr. Pitt. Hetty [2] was gone from thence to make a visit to her friend Lady Litchfield [3], so that I saw nothing of her, but heard of her twice that she was very well. Jemmy [4] was there, and Harry [5] with his love Peggy [6] went down yesterday. We left them on Thursday, and my first care was to comply with your request of making Mr. Netherton a purser, in short I found one out for him, and we signed the warrant for him to be purser of the *Lys* yesterday, so that you have nothing to do but to send him up to

[1] Charles Douglas, third Duke of Queensberry, and his wife, Catherine Hyde, daughter of Henry, Earl of Clarendon and Rochester. The Duchess died in 1777, and the Duke in the year following. They are particularly remembered for their affectionate friendship to Gay.

[2] Hester Grenville, afterwards Lady Chatham.

[3] Diana, daughter of Sir Thomas Frankland, and wife of George Henry Lee, third Earl of Litchfield.

[4] James Grenville.

[5] Henry Grenville.

[6] Miss Margaret Banks, a sister of John Hodgkinson Banks, Esq. She was a celebrated beauty, and was married in October, 1757, to Mr. Henry Grenville.

the office to take it out as soon as he pleases. Do you know that this can't give you half so much pleasure as it has given to me?

Admiral Vernon[1] has complained so often, and desired so often to be recalled, that whilst I was at Wotton the Board took him at his word, and sent him an order for that purpose; indeed, his behaviour has been in some respects a most extraordinary one.

I agree with you as to the French invasion, which I cannot believe is any longer intended to be carried immediately into execution now the rebels are got northward, but if we spoil all our line-of-battle ships, by keeping what formed the Western Squadron in the Downs all the winter, instead of cleaning them, and putting

---

[1] Admiral Vernon, so well known by his boasting temper, his success and his miscarriages, was a man of undoubted talent, but ill qualified by his character to govern those under him, or to obey those above him. Vernon was raised to the rank of Admiral of the White in April, 1745. He was immediately appointed to the command of the Fleet for the defence of the Channel and north coast, and in that situation his vigilance has been greatly commended. The Board of Admiralty, however, having found fault with some of his dispositions of the force, he complained bitterly, and, after an angry correspondence, desired leave to strike his flag. The Admiralty, finding it useless to give orders which were always cavilled at, complied with this request. Hereupon the Admiral, who seems to have thought the public would support him against the Government, published two pamphlets, in which he revealed the orders he had received, and published, without leave, his official correspondence. The Admiralty visited this offence in the most severe manner. Admiral Vernon was called upon to attend the Board. When he appeared, the Duke of Bedford asked him if he was the publisher of the two pamphlets. He declined to answer the question. The Duke of Bedford then informed him, that the Board, after such a refusal, could not but consider him as the publisher. He stated his surprise that he should have been asked such a question, and withdrew. The next day, the Duke of Bedford saw the King, and signified to the Board the King's pleasure that Vice-Admiral Vernon should be struck out of the list of flag-officers.—*Lord John Russell's Introduction to the Bedford Correspondence*, vol. i. pp. xlvi., xlvii.

them in order for the spring, 't is possible a more feasible and more sensible project for an embarkation may be supported by the Brest Squadron in March or April next. This seems to me to be the case, but I am no seaman, and therefore leave the consideration of it to those that are.

The Duke is besieging Carlisle, where 300 or 400 of the rebels are left in garrison [1], the rest are got into Scotland, and 't is thought will soon join their other body at, or near, Stirling.

Adieu, my dear Tom; many people ask after you, because many people love you, but nobody better than your most affectionate, GEORGE GRENVILLE.

COL. RICHARD LYTTELTON [2] TO CAPT. THOMAS GRENVILLE.

Cleveland Court, February 3, 1745-6.

MY DEAR TOM,—I know not where this letter may find you, or if you will get it at all, but write to thank you for your kind congratulations. I long to see you in town, where I hope you will live with the Duchess without jealousy; and though you are divorced as my wife, I will receive you as a mistress, and she on any terms you please.

[1] It was supposed by Prince Charles that these men and their officers were left at their own request, " yet," says Lord Mahon, " the result was most fatal to them, and the determination to leave them most unwise."—*History of the 'Forty-five*, p. 95.

[2] Colonel Richard Lyttelton, fifth son of Sir Thomas Lyttelton, and afterwards a Knight of the Bath. He had recently married the Lady Rachel Russell, the sister of John, Duke of Bedford, and widow of Scrope Egerton, Duke of Bridgewater. He was appointed Commander-in-Chief of the island of Minorca, and was subsequently Governor of Guernsey. He died in 1770.

The Cabinet and other our Governors, who had laid
down, have retaken their parchments, so that my lords
of Granville[1], Bath[2], Winchilsea[3], Carlisle[4], Bathurst[5],
Sandys[6], &c., stand a fair chance of being in opposition,
unrespected the rest of their lives, as the present
ministry will in all probability be much confirmed and·
strengthened by this weak effort of those infant Atlases,
Bath and Granville, whose backs must have been broken
by the burthen, had they had strength to lift it fairly
on their shoulders[7].

Commodore Smith set out this morning for Scot-

[1] John Carteret, Earl Granville.

[2] William Pulteney, Earl of Bath.

[3] Daniel Finch, seventh Earl of Winchilsea, and third Earl of Not-
tingham, succeeded his father in those titles in January, 1730, having
previously represented the county of Rutland in several Parliaments.
He was at this time, and subsequently for a short period, First Lord
of the Admiralty. He died in August, 1769, in his 81st year.

[4] Henry, fourth Earl of Carlisle, K.G., succeeded his father in May,
1738. Before his accession to the Peerage he had represented in
Parliament the borough of Morpeth. He died September 4, 1758.

[5] Allen, first Lord Bathurst. He died in 1775, at the age of 91.

[6] Samuel, first Baron Sandys of Ombersley. He was Chancellor
of the Exchequer in 1741, and was made a peer in 1743. He had
previously sat in Parliament for Worcester. He died in 1770.

[7] It was at this juncture, and in consequence of the intrigues of
Lord Granville and Lord Bath, and the King's absolute refusal to make
Pitt Secretary at War, that the Duke of Newcastle, Mr. Pelham, and
the whole of the Cabinet and Chief Officers of State, sent in their
resignations, and the King endeavoured to form an Administration with
Lord Bath at the head of the Treasury; Lord Granville, Secretary of
State; Lord Winchilsea, First Lord of the Admiralty; Lord Carlisle,
Lord Privy Seal, &c. Lord Granville, it is said, had actually kissed
hands upon his appointment, but in less than forty-eight hours the
new Ministers found there was not the slightest chance of making a
successful stand against so powerful an opposition. The King was
therefore obliged to send to Mr. Pelham, and desire him and his
colleagues to return to their employments. Mr. Pitt was made Vice-
Treasurer of Ireland, and soon after appointed to the lucrative office
of Paymaster of the Forces, and at last, by the force of his genius

land to take the command of Byng's squadron. Only think of him going post to Edinburgh.

Adieu, my dear Tom, may all honours and success attend you, and believe me, most faithfully, yours.

R. LYTTELTON.

MR. PITT TO MR. GEORGE GRENVILLE.

Lincombe, August 25, 1746.

MY DEAR GRENVILLE,—As Jemmy[1] informs me you designed to give me the pleasure of hearing from you soon, I write this to notify my intention to leave this place in two or three days, by which means your letter would not find me before I shall embrace you in town. I propose to take our Wotton friends in my way, and if I can, Barrington.

I have a request to you, which I desire you will allow me to take for granted, by not hearing a refusal, for which there cannot be time while I stay here. My request is, that Mr. Hoare[2] may copy a gentleman's picture, which he lately drew, and which he will touch at London or elsewhere, as occasion offers. I hope to find you looking just as you did when he and I had you under consideration. I will defer all further discourse till we meet. W. PITT.

and talents, acquired in the highest degree the favour and confidence of his sovereign.

[1] James Grenville.

[2] Williame Hoare, a fashionable portrait-painter, for many years resident at Bath, where he was much employed by the visitors. He painted a portrait of Mr. Pitt, which was formerly at Stowe. He was one of the original members of the Royal Academy, and a constant exhibitor there until his death in 1792. His son, Prince Hoare, was afterwards the Foreign Secretary to the Royal Academy.

MR. PITT TO MR. GEORGE GRENVILLE.

Bath, October 29, 1746.

MY DEAR GRENVILLE,—I join most heartily with you in your grief for the loss of a man of more worth and honour than most he has left behind him. Poor Lady Suffolk bears this terrible stroke[1] with all the composure that strength of mind can give. This turn of mind may, perhaps, be better for her health in the beginnings of her affliction; but, I believe, there is less resource from time for her, than if she gave way to more violent marks of it. In the midst of your concern for the dead, let me assure you that I am most sincerely touched with your kind attention to the living; your friendship will ever be deemed by me among the first of public honours and private comforts. In the gloomy scene which I fear is opening in public affairs for this disgraced country, there is nothing to rest upon but the pleasure of esteeming and sharing the esteem of those who deserve to have lived in better days. I had postponed my leaving this place till towards the meeting of Parliament, before I received the favour of yours. I am better considerably, but not so much as I appear, having still some of the same impressions upon the old part. I desire you will embrace for me the Wotton Grenvilles: the Lincoln's Inn Fields Grenville will have a letter from me before this reaches you. Believe me most unalterably and affectionately yours.   W. PITT.

[1] The death of her husband the Honourable George Berkeley.

ADMIRAL ANSON[1] TO MR. GEORGE GRENVILLE.

Plymouth, November 4, 1746.

DEAR SIR,—My not finding your brother[2] here has given me a great deal of uneasiness, but cannot conceive any accident has happened to him, for D'Anville's ships were in no condition to attack him, if they happened to meet with him, and he must have got to the eastward of the ships that fell in with the Barbadoes convoy; his being short of water, and the finding the winds contrary, must have obliged him to put into Ireland, and the easterly winds have kept the packet from getting to England, which must be the reason we have not heard of him. I find you have destined him for the Canarys, with Captain Montague; nobody can wish them more success than I do; but I differ in opinion with you, for, by the scheme the enemy pursues, they will not put it in the power of two or four ships to part them, for their convoys are strong, and no French or Spanish trade permitted to sail unprotected; but I know what you intend him will be more agreeable to him than any other station, and therefore resign my right and title to him, though you cannot esteem him more than

Your obliged and faithful humble Servant,

G. ANSON.

[1] Admiral George Anson was appointed to the command of an expedition and voyage round the world. He sailed from England in September, 1740 and anchored at Spithead on his return in June, 1744. In December following he was made Lord of the Admiralty and came into Parliament for the borough of Heydon, In the spring of 1747, he was sent to cruize off the coast of France, and falling in with the enemy's fleet off Cape Finisterre, after a gallant action he entirely disabled them. In June, 1747, Anson was raised to the Peerage by the title of Baron Anson, and was subsequently First Lord of the Admiralty. He died in June, 1762.

[2] Captain Thomas Grenville, at this time in command of the *Defiance*.

THE DUKE OF BEDFORD[1] TO MR. GEORGE GRENVILLE.

Bath, November 11, 1746.

DEAR SIR,—I have long intended to have returned you thanks for your letter[2] of the 24th of last month, and at the same time have given you my opinion in relation to what you mention in it about the undertaking early next Spring—our intended expedition against Canada. But I really have had occasion to write so many letters, and have had so much business, that I have put it off from day to day in the hopes of finding a leisure time. I hope by this time all your fears for Accadie are vanished, as I cannot think it possible, by the accounts we have had, that Duc d'Anville can have made any impression there. As by the ill success of that squadron, I think our original scheme is as entire as ever, I enclose to you my thoughts on that head in the copy of a letter[3] I wrote by last night's post to Mr. Stone, in answer to one I had just received from him by order of the Duke of Newcastle, desiring me to transmit to him my opinion about the destination of the troops now in Ireland, under the command of General St. Clair. I hope this will have its effect in keeping the troops this winter in Ireland, and that all proper measures will be immediately concerted for setting the expedition forward very early next Spring[4].

BEDFORD.

[1] John, fourth Duke of Bedford, at this time First Lord of the Admiralty.

[2] The letter here referred to is printed in the *Bedford Correspondence*, vol. i. p. 155.

[3] It is printed in the *Bedford Correspondence*, vol. i. p. 182.

[4] " The favourite plan of the Duke of Bedford was to send an expedition to North America, and conquer Canada. In conformity with his

THE DUKE OF BEDFORD TO MR. GEORGE GRENVILLE[1].

Bath, November 24, 1746.

DEAR SIR,—I agree with you in all your reasonings in your letter of the 19th instant with regard to the neeessity of determining immediately whether the expedition designed against Canada shall proceed early in the Spring, in order to be beforehand with the enemy, as well in recovering what possibly we may have lost this year (I mean Annapolis Royal) as in attacking them in their own settlements on the River of St. Lawrence. I am likewise sensible that in case it shall be determined to go on with this expedition, that it is absolutely necessary to dispatch a sloop forthwith with orders to the several Governors on the Continent to assure, in His Majesty's name, their respective Assemblies, that a considerable force both of troops and ships shall be sent from hence to North America, as soon as the season of the year will permit, in order to attempt the reduction of Canada, and at the same time to require the several Governments to furnish their quotas for this expedition.

But the day before yesterday I received a letter from the Duke of Newcastle, with an account that (notwithstanding all the arguments I had made against it in my letter to him of the 10th instant, and of which I enclosed you a copy) it was determined unanimously in

request, preparations were made on a sufficient scale for the purpose. Had he been allowed to order the sailing of the expedition which was prepared, it is most probable the conquest of Canada, would not have been reserved for the Seven Years' War. But the indecision or timidity of the Duke of Newcastle delayed, and finally broke up, the expedition." —*Lord John Russell's Introduction to the Bedford Correspondence*, vol. i. p. xlviii.

[1] Part of this letter is printed in the *Bedford Correspondence*, vol. i. p. 196.

the Cabinet Council, to order the troops late under the command of Lieutenant-General St. Clair, and now in Ireland, to return immediately to England. I must own this has thoroughly convinced me that the intended expedition is entirely laid aside, as I cannot possibly conceive that a determination could be taken to remove these troops, harassed as they were, at such a season of the year as this, without there was an absolute necessity for so doing, in order for the defence of this country against a French invasion. If that is the case, and troops cannot at present be spared from Scotland for that purpose, I must own I see no probability of their being spared early enough next Spring to permit these troops to go on this expedition with any prospect of success; and besides, these troops by their continual embarkations would be so harassed, that they would hardly be fit for this service, which I think particularly requires troops to be complete, and in good health, as there is no possibility of recruiting them in North America.

With regard to the Navy Debt, I think that nothing can stand in competition with it, as I fear that, if a considerable sum of money is not granted this year towards the lessening of it, His Majesty's Naval Service must entirely stand still, or, which is worse, be overturned. I doubt not but that Mr. Pelham, upon this being stated to him, will be very ready to do what lies in his power to supply the necessities of the Navy, and enable us to keep our credit till the next sessions of Parliament. If it can be done in no other way, I fear it will be necessary to raise another half million more than was first intended, as I cannot think it possible that, during a French and Spanish war, the public can be induced to suffer the Navy to be neglected. I do not write to Mr.

Pelham on this subject, for the same reason you have till now deferred speaking to him about it, I mean the adding supernumerary distresses to those he must now necessarily labour under. But as I think it is absolutely necessary that something should be done immediately in this affair, and as I think it will be both better done by you by word of mouth, and with less trouble to Mr. Pelham, than it could be done by me in a letter to him, I would beg the favour of you to mention it to him, both as from me and yourself, and by his answer we shall be able to judge what it is possible (considering the present exigencies of the public) may be granted to us.

I fear that if Admiral Davers is recalled from Jamaica it will be out of our power to confer that command on Commodore Smith, as I believe Admiral Mayne had the greatest encouragement given him to expect it, both by Lord Sandwich and Mr. Anson, and with mine, and I thought the joint consent of the whole Board. Though I do not personally know Commodore Smith, no one can have a greater regard for him than I have, upon account of the universal good character he bears, both as a seaman and an officer, and I am very sensible that the command he now has is far from being grateful or profitable to him, and farther that he has acquitted himself in it to the satisfaction of H.R.H. the Duke. But, at the same time, I cannot forget the much harder duty Admiral Mayne has undergone as President of the Court Martial at Deptford, and I think that after the mortification he has been obliged to go through in his submission to the Lord Chief Justice (which the Court Martial ignorantly, though innocently, drew upon themselves), it would be unjust in us not to do what

lay in our power to countenance him, and through him
the whole Court Martial. I hope the Board will be
willing to defer determining who shall succeed Mr.
Davers in the command, till Mr. Anson's return, who
will be able to inform them what has passed between
him and Admiral Mayne upon that subject.

BEDFORD.

MR. GEORGE GRENVILLE TO CAPT. THOMAS GRENVILLE.

Admiralty Office, April 2, 1747.

MY DEAR TOM,—You will be surprised and sorry, but
not either one or the other half so much as I am, when
I tell you that your ship and the *Bristol* are both
ordered under the command of V. A. Anson, as long
as from the information he has of the strength of the
enemy he judges it necessary[1]. Mr. Anson and Mr.
Warren set out from Portsmouth the next day after you
left London; and this regulation was settled whilst we
were at dinner, for the next day, at the Board, I found
the order prepared for signing. As I knew nothing of
it, I refused peremptorily to sign it, and bid Corbett
write to Mr. Anson to know what he intended to do

---

[1] Lord John Russell alludes to this circumstance in his *Introduction
to the Bedford Correspondence*, vol. i. p. xlix. " An instance of the
Duke of Bedford's confidence in Lord Anson, appears in a letter written
by the Duchess to the Admiral when his flag was flying at Plymouth.
Two of the Lords of the Admiralty, Lord Sandwich and Mr. Grenville,
had brothers in the command of ships. Mr. Grenville, wishing to
obtain for these officers a separate command, contrived that an order
for Admiral Anson not to keep their ships above seven days with him
should be prepared for signature. But the Duke indignantly refused
to sign the order, and the ships were placed unconditionally under
Anson."

with you: this stopped the order that day, but yesterday the importance of it was pressed in the strongest manner, and that Mr. A. would have but few ships out with him; and what would be the consequence if the Brest fleet should be superior, and beat us, &c., &c., &c. To all this I replied, that the same language of *ifs* and *ands* had been used to me two years together, and that I was quite sick of it a third time; that the Admiralty had all promised me this cruize, with repeated vows and oaths; that I had already been used very ill upon this occasion, and that I would never consent upon any terms to release that promise; but, if they thought it proper and honourable, they must break it. Lord Vere[1] sent me word that he would answer with his life that Mr. Anson would not keep you above a week with him; and how could that injure you, as his orders are then to permit you to go in execution of our former orders. These arguments did not prevail upon me to change my resolution or to sign those orders; but the Board are so much afraid, or so little anxious about keeping their word so solemnly given, that they have signed the order and gratified Mr. Anson in his request. I have not been at the Board to day, nor don't much care if I never go again, so much am I vexed at their behaviour to me, which I think I have not deserved, and will not forget, though I hope, after the bustle this has occasioned, that you will not be detained long.

I have received a letter from Vice-Admiral Steuart,

---

[1] Lord Vere Beauclerc, third son of the first Duke of St. Alban's; at this time a Lord of the Admiralty, and M.P. for Plymouth. In 1750 he was made Lord Vere of Hanworth. He married Mary, eldest daughter and co-heir of Thomas Chamber, Esq., of Hanworth. Lady Betty Germaine was her aunt. Swift called her " Lady Betty's saucy niece."

in which he states the irregularity of my request for
giving you the *Berwick's* and *Woolwich's* men in preference, which he says would be deemed a glaring instance
of partiality, and inconsistent with his duty; that your
ship has but fifteen sick, whose room he will supply,
and seven short of complement, and bears twenty-five
supernumeraries; that Captain Boscawen has not a man
given him, but that he will try and send you away contented.

I shall write an answer to this next post. Let me
hear from you, and what your Admiral says upon this
bustle, which I dare say he has heard all the particulars
of, though not a word from me. Write to me directly;
and so adieu, my dear Tom.   GEORGE GRENVILLE.

ADMIRAL ANSON TO MR. GEORGE GRENVILLE.

Portsmouth, April 3, 1747.

DEAR SIR,—The reason of my not mentioning the
Defiance and *Bristol's* going out of the Channel with
me, to you before I left the town, was, that I did not
think of it myself till the moment I left the town; they
shall be detained from putting the Board's orders in
execution as short a time as possible; if there should
be any service, I know they would both of them be
glad to be in it. As Captain Pritchard of the *Devonshire* has got the gout to that violent degree as not to
be able to go to sea, I intend to give Captain West an
order to command her, Mr. Warren having consented
to take him upon my recommendation, and I think he
cannot serve in a properer or more honourable way.

I desire you will not be among the number of my friends that neglect to write to me now and then when absent; you know letters sent to Plymouth will find their way to me, and you cannot do a greater pleasure to, dear Sir, &c., &c.   G. ANSON.

ORDERS BY GEORGE ANSON, Vice-Admiral of the Blue Squadron of His Majesty's Fleet, Commander-in-Chief, &c., to CAPTAIN THOMAS GRENVILLE, Commander of His Majesty's Ship the *Defiance*.

April 7, 1747.

IN case of separation by any unavoidable accident before the fleet goes out of the Channel, with the wind hard westerly, and you should not have got to the westward of Torbay, Portland Road is the place of rendezvous; if to the westward of Torbay, and you cannot get up to Plymouth, Torbay is the rendezvous; and if to the westward of Plymouth, then Plymouth is the place of rendezvous. Dated at Spithead, the 7th of April, 1747, on board the *Prince George*.   G. ANSON.

By command of the Admiral, PHP. STEPHENS.

MR. ANDREW GUTHRIE[1] TO MR. GEORGE GRENVILLE.

Defiance, at Spithead, 16th May, 1747.

SIR,—As I believe it to be my duty, I, most unwillingly, beg leave to acquaint you with the nature of the fatal accident which happened to your brother, Captain Grenville[2], on the third of May. We were engaged

---

[1] Surgeon to Captain Grenville's ship, the *Defiance*.

[2] The lamented death of Captain Grenville is mentioned in Anson's letter to the Duke of Bedford, as First Lord of the Admiralty, describ-

near two hours before he was wounded, by a large
splinter from the ship's side, on the quarter deck, which
shattered the bone of his left thigh in several pieces
near two-thirds of its length, and tore all the muscles
about it in the most miserable manner. He was immediately brought down to me; I examined the wound,
and, to my great concern, plainly saw that it was a most
desperate case, but the only possible means that could
be used then to save his life was to amputate it above
the wounded part, which he agreed to, and I immediately took it off. He bore it with a surprising constancy and firmness of mind, never making the least
complaint. He was afterwards moved into my cabin,
where I constantly attended him; he lived near five
hours, sensible most of the time, but very faint with the
great loss of blood and excessive pain, until a little
before he died, which happened without any struggle,
sleeping as it were insensible into death.

As it was my greatest ambition to please him when
living, I thought it no less my duty to take the utmost
care I could of his body, that it might be carried home.
The next day I opened his body, embowelled and filled
it with proper things to preserve it, then wrapped it in

ing his celebrated action off Cape Finisterre. Of Captain Grenville,
he says, " he was by much the cleverest officer I ever saw." George
Lyttelton, writing to Thomson on the 21st of May, says, " I wish you
joy of Anson's success: an action that does him great honour, and of
great benefit to his country, but the joy of it is palled to our family by
the loss of poor Captain Grenville, one of the most promising young
men in the Navy, and who, had he lived, would have been an honour
not to his family only, but to his country. I never saw in any man
a finer mixture of spirit, temper, and judgment. He fought and died
with the gallantry of Sir Philip Sidney." A column was erected to
his memory, by his uncle Lord Cobham, in the gardens at Stowe, on
which are inscribed some beautiful lines by Lyttelton.

a cerecloth, and put it into a coffin lined with lead. As I have endeavoured to do everything for the best, I hope to have your approbation, which will make the great loss I have sustained by his death the easier.

If you thought proper I should be glad to have leave to come along with his body, and take care of it until it is safely delivered, as it is the last thing I can do to show my regard and gratitude to him, and hope you will be pleased to obtain me their Lordships' leave to be absent from the ship for some time, for that purpose. Hoping you will excuse this trouble, I am, with the greatest respect, &c., &c. ANDR. GUTHRIE.

COLONEL SPEED [1] TO MR. RICHARD GRENVILLE.

Camp at Zanoven, June 29, 1747.

MY DEAR MR. GRENVILLE,—Till within these five days we have been very inactive, but upon intelligence of the enemy's making a motion towards Maestricht, our army marched from Liere to this place; but the enemy we hear are now returned to Louvain, where the King of France is; we expected an engagement before now, and it is the opinion of many it cannot be long before we have one, from our situation; we have a very large country to defend, which covers Holland from

[1] Colonel Samuel Speed, the writer of this letter, was the fellow soldier and very intimate friend and relation of Lord Cobham. When he added in the postscript that *he expected the whole army to be engaged in an hour's time*, he little expected that in such a brief space he should have received his death wound from two bullets through the head; yet so it happened. There was formerly a very good portrait of Colonel Speed, at Stowe, which represented him as a very handsome man, apparently about forty years of age.

Bergen-op-Zoom to Maestricht; there are about twelve
thousand men in Zealand, and a large detachment at
Hogstraten, near Breda: the enemy on their side make
as large detachments, so that ten or twelve thousand
men may encounter each other, but when a decisive
action may happen is very uncertain; our out parties
have small skirmishes happen almost every day: the
losses on either side are too inconsiderable to mention
—thirty men is the greatest number that has been lost
at a time this campaign: some members of Parliament
have asked leave to go to attend their elections, but
I do not hear H.R.H. has consented for them to go.
Our situation at present is a very critical one, and does
no doubt afford great matter for conversation in England.   God knows what the event may be, I hope favourable, but you shall hear from me the first motion we
make.

I should, my dear friend, have written to you on the
melancholy news I had heard, could I have given you
the least consolation which I wanted myself: your
family have my constant good wishes and prayers; the
latter you will laugh at me for when in spirits, but that
you know I am used to, and hope to see those days
again.   When you see Dick Berenger, pray tell him I
take it unkind he did not answer my letter, which I
earnestly desired he would.   When you are most at
leisure I beg you will write me a line to let me know
how you all are, for the accounts I have hitherto had
afford very little satisfaction.   I desire my compliments
to Mrs. Grenville[1] and Miss Banks, and though it is

---

[1] Anna Chamber, daughter and co-heir of Thomas Chamber, Esq.,
of Hanworth, now married to Richard Grenville, afterwards Earl
Temple.

my misfortune to be a useless friend, you have not in the world a more sincere one. SAM. SPEED.

The camp takes its name from the head-quarters, which often happens to be a small village, but the army lays near Hasselt, about six leagues from Maestricht.

I had not an opportunity to send this as dated: we are now before the enemy, and expect the whole army will engage in an hour's time. Yours till death,

S. SPEED.

Sunday, June (July) 1, N.S.

MR. PITT TO MR. RICHARD GRENVILLE.

London, June 30, 1747.

MY DEAR GRENVILLE,—I am this moment arrived from Sussex [1], victorious as yourself, after being opposed by Mr. Gage and the Earl of Middlesex [2]. It is certain my own success does not give me a more sincere pleasure than yours does. I find no account from Jemmy [3] which I hoped by this time: not that his last leaves any

[1] Pitt was at this time Paymaster of the Forces. He had just gained his election for Seaford, one of the Cinque Ports, for which borough Mr. William Hall Gage had been previously the member.

[2] Lord Middlesex, eldest son of the Duke of Dorset, and Master of the Horse to the Prince of Wales, was elected for Old Sarum. Horace Walpole says of this Lord, that "his figure, which was handsome, had all the reserve of his family, and all the dignity of his ancestors. His passion was the direction of operas, in which he had not only wasted immense sums, but had stood lawsuits in Westminster Hall, with some of those poor devils for their salaries. The Duke of Dorset had often paid his debts, but never could work upon his affections, and he had at last carried his disobedience so far, in complaisance to, and in imitation of, the Prince, as to oppose his father in his own boroughs."—*Memoirs of George II.*, vol. i. p. 97.

[3] James Grenville was elected member for Bridport.

room to fear for him, but I shall be glad to hear it was well over. Jack Pitt[1] is likewise silent as to his state ; his last account was very sanguine, but general. I confess I am not without apprehension for him and Hodgkinson[2]. Elections in general go better than the most warm expectation could promise. Doneraile[3], at Winchilsea, offered thousands without making the least impression. Would to God our victories were not confined to our own little world! A full detail of the late action[4] I have not yet seen ; the clearest and best makes it evident that the British and Electoral troops did all that can be expected from men overpowered by numbers, the whole weight being upon them. The Duke has done himself great honour by the efforts he made in person during the action ; but most of all, in my opinion, by the very orderly and able retreat of his own wing, and the facility he afterwards gave to the right wing of Austrians to make theirs. Ligonier[5]

[1] John Pitt, one of the Commissioners of the Board of Trade, and son of George Pitt, of Strathfieldsaye. He was elected for Wareham.

[2] R. Banks Hodgkinson was elected for the borough of Wareham in 1751, upon the resignation of Mr. John Pitt, who was chosen for the town of Dorchester.

[3] Arthur St. Leger, Viscount Doneraile, Comptroller of the Household to the Prince of Wales, had been previously member for Winchilsea : he was unsuccessful on this occasion, but he was elected for Old Sarum.

[4] The battle of Lauffeldt, in which William, Duke of Cumberland was defeated, and, Walpole says, " was very near taken, having through his short sight mistaken a body of French for his own people. He behaved as bravely as usual : but his prowess is so well established, that it grows time for him to exert other qualities of a general."—*Letter to Sir Horace Mann. Walpole Correspondence*, vol ii. p. 198.

[5] Sir John Ligonier, a general officer of the highest military reputation. He had been created a Knight Banneret on the field of Dettingen in 1742. He became Earl of Ligonier in the Peerage of Great Britain in 1766, and died in 1770, at the age of 91.

and, I believe, Conway[1] prisoners; Lord Albemarle[2]
and Bland slightly wounded: Commodore Fox's falling
in with St. Domingue Fleet is a little cordial, and comes
most critically for the elections.

When do you think of being at Wotton? Let me
know, for I am at present upon the parish. Lady
Charlotte refers me, till her return in August, for a
final answer about my Lodge. Since we parted I have
seen somebody at dinner at Bedford House. I am as
much puzzled as ever, and as great a changeling. I
am Mrs. Grenville's and Miss Hebe's most devoted
Servant, and ever yours.

LORD BARRINGTON TO MR. GEORGE GRENVILLE.

September 5th, 1747.

DEAR GEORGE,—It falls to my lot always to convey
bad news to you: what you said the other day about

---

[1] Colonel Henry Seymour Conway, second son of Francis, Lord
Conway. He had been Aide-de-camp to the Duke of Cumberland at
Culloden. Horace Walpole, in a letter to Mr. Montague on the subject
of the battle of Lauffeldt, says, " Harry Conway, whom nature always
designed for a hero of a romance, and who is *deplacé* in ordinary life,
did wonders, but was overpowered and flung down, when one French
hussar held him by the hair, while another was going to stab him: at
that instant an English serjeant with a soldier came up, and killed
the latter, but was instantly killed himself: the soldier attacked the
other, and Mr. Conway escaped, but was afterwards taken prisoner,
and is since released on parole."—*Walpole Correspondence*, vol. ii.
p. 197.

[2] William Anne Keppel, second Earl of Albemarle, K.G. He distinguished himself at the battles of Dettingen and Fontenoy. He
commanded the right wing at the battle of Culloden, and on the departure of the Duke of Cumberland he was left Commander-in-Chief of
all the King's forces in Scotland. He was appointed Ambassador to
the Court of France, and died suddenly at Paris, December 22, 1754.

poor Speed was prophetic. He was shot through the head with two bullets while he was encouraging the picketts and loading his musquet. I thought it right to send Lord Cobham early notice of this, that poor Harriett[1] may hear it in the least shocking manner, and I have wrote to him by this post accordingly. The French are battering Pucelle and Cohorn in breach, but they cannot make any great progresses yet.

Fox[2] is worse, and I think in danger. If anything happens, as I must go to-morrow to Beckett, I trust my affairs in your hands. Say anything about me or for me that you think proper, and give me your advice what to say and do for myself. In these things being early is everything. I will add nothing more to you, who can and will do more for me than for yourself, for in what concerns your friends your laziness will not operate, nor your modesty prevent your doing what should be done. Yours most affectionately. B.

MR. GEORGE LYTTELTON TO MR. GEORGE GRENVILLE.

Hagley, September 21, 1747.

DEAR GEORGE,—I would not give up the hopes you have flattered me with, of seeing you here, 'till I heard of your being returned to town, but as they are now quite disappointed, I must adjourn them 'till another year.

In the mean time Mr. Pitt and I have been contriving

---

[1] Miss Speed, sister to Colonel Speed.

[2] Henry Fox, afterwards Lord Holland. He was at this time Secretary at War, and it is evident that Lord Barrington was willing to succeed him in that office, as in fact he did a few years afterwards.

some considerable new improvements to make you the more inexcusable if you do not visit us then; though, indeed, I think if there were no other reason to bring you to us, but the desire we all have of your company, that alone would leave you without an excuse, if you don't let us share you with Wotton and Stowe. Thomson[1] is just come to us, and as he is very unwilling to leave this place soon, I wish, that instead of returning to town on the 7th of next month, as I intended to do, I could be allowed to stay 'till the 14th. If Mr. Campbell be in town, as he told me he should, and you are there too, there will, I imagine, be no difficulty in it, even though Legge[2] should be out of the way, as perhaps he will desire to be if it should prove a good season for cock-shooting. Be so kind as to let me know how this will be by the first return of the post, and with my best compliments to Mr. Pelham, ask his leave for me to prolong my holidays[3] 'till that time, unless he has other commands for me; I mean in case there be a Board without me, for if there be not I will certainly be there by the 7th.

[1] Thomson was a frequent guest at Hagley. Lord Lyttelton procured him a pension of 100*l.* a year, and when he subsequently took office under Mr. Pelham's administration, he appointed Thomson Surveyor-General of the Leeward Islands, from which he derived about 300*l.* a year. He displayed his gratitude to his benefactor by some lines in the *Castle of Indolence* (canto i. st. 65, 66), descriptive of Lyttelton's character. He died August 27, 1748.

[2] Henry Bilson Legge, also a Lord of the Treasury. He was a younger son of the first Earl of Dartmouth, and successively represented in Parliament the boroughs of East Looe and Orford, and the county of Southampton, and filled the several offices of Secretary of the Treasury, a Lord of the Admiralty and of the Treasury, and Chancellor of the Exchequer. He married Mary, Baroness Stawel, and died in August, 1764. His widow remarried in October, 1768, to Wills, Earl of Hillsborough.

[3] Lyttelton was at this time a Lord of the Treasury.

Poor Sam Speed! I most heartily condole with you on his brave unfortunate death. What a havock of virtue has this cursed war made, and how cruelly have we in particular suffered by it! I pray God we may not have great public as well as private reasons to wish it had ended a year ago.

Adieu, my dear George; all here are much yours, and none more affectionately than your most faithful

G. LYTTELTON.

MR. OSWALD[1] TO MR. GEORGE GRENVILLE.

November 5, 1747.

DEAR GEORGE,—Since writing my last I have been seized with a fever, which raged for some days with a great deal of violence, but is now quite over and I recover tolerably well. Nor would this have prevented my attending my friends on the first day of the session, but the situation of my wife, which I mentioned in my last, puts it out of my power at least sooner than after Christmas.

I heartily wish affairs abroad were to go on as much to your wish, as those in the Senate in all probability will, where I am confident the Admiralty will not want any concurrence they desire to whatever project they think necessary for the public service. Nor shall my expectations, I assure you, be extremely sanguine, even with all these advantages. While the game is played in Flanders, a sort of fatality seems to attend whoever

---

[1] James Oswald, at this time M.P. for Fife. He was made a Lord of Trade in 1751, and subsequently a Lord of the Treasury, and one of the Vice-Treasurers of Ireland.

holds the cards. I was in hopes when the game came to be played in Holland, the tables might turn, but Bergen-op-Zoom has almost totally finished those hopes. The Dutch liberty is now certainly over, but has its extinction produced discipline and an army? Has anything yet appeared since the change which points that way? Perhaps it may be necessary to settle the family affairs of the Stadtholder, before the Councils of that unhappy people admit of a proper firmness. But is this a time for so much prudence, and such distant views of future security? Does the temper and spirit of those in management there seem to be changed? Will not the same spirit of prudence so unaccountable now that danger is at their very gates, produce the same pusillanimity both in council and action as it has done hitherto, when perhaps prudence and caution with their effects were much more reasonable? These are doubts and fears perhaps unreasonable in themselves, augmented by distance and ignorance of the true situation, but they are what makes the prospect extremely dismal to me.

What I wrote you in my last with regard to the Highlands is I fancy false, as I then suspected it; but the temper, spirit, and insolence of our Jacobites is certainly such as I wrote you, though I really think them as impotent as they are ridiculous. Archy Stewart's[1] trial ended on Saturday. The taking of the evidence lasted from Monday till then, during all which time the jury sat inclosed, except one interval of about ten hours, which was absolutely necessary, and indulged

---

[1] The trial of Archibald Stewart, Provost of Edinburgh, and M.P. for that city, upon a charge of complicity with the rebels. He was acquitted.

by the judges. I did not attend the trial myself in any part of it, though I read the informations of the counsel, which is a sort of summary of the pleadings in law reduced to writing; but from what I can hear from the lawyers, and indeed in general, both the points of law and the proof have turned out more palpably in Stewart's favour. This makes me curious to see the evidence, which I could wish were printed. Meantime, if one was to pronounce from appearances, I could wish there had been no trial at all, at least no second trial, which seems to indicate so thorough a persuasion of his guilt on the part of the prosecutors, as made a step taken, which, if law, is certainly hard, if they were persuaded of his guilt on improper evidence. It is weak if these prosecutions were carried on so violently, so determinedly, without such persuasion of guilt, and only for the purpose of distressing an individual. It is cruel, if persuaded of guilt from proper evidence, which ought, but did not convict him before a partial jury. How fatal is the case that no justice can be had for the C——n in Scotland: but all will be screened; the length of this whole affair, so long an imprisonment in the Tower, so long so solemn a trial will lead to reflections, and some one or other of these reflections must be made. You will make me happy in my retirement if you are so good as to write me. I should wish to know something of what happens above, and perhaps at so great a distance it may be no breach of secrecy to acquaint me of some things even before they do happen.

What is your scheme of money? If I knew, perhaps I might ask to subscribe. Could I obtain a subscription? As I could not flatter myself that my being either at London or absent from it, could be either useful or detrimental to the public. What makes me most uneasy is the inability I shall be in of serving some few of my friends, for whom, had I been present, I should probably have asked favours. May I hope to obtain them when absent? I will ask or not as you write me it is proper. In the jumble of ecclesiastical affairs perhaps I might have served my brother. I once mentioned him to Lord Chesterfield for some dignity in the Church, as he has two small livings, but am afraid his channel is not the right one: could you advise or assist me? Recommend me to all your friends, and believe me ever, &c.　　　　　　　　　　　　JAMES OSWALD.

MR. PITT TO MR. GEORGE GRENVILLE.

April 26, 1748.

DEAR GRENVILLE,—I have just time to tell you all I have learned of the preliminaries[1] on my arrival in town this morning, after an absence of two days. They are signed by France, England, and the Republic of Holland: the outlines I understand to be much the same as the Marshal of Saxe's overture, except that Guastalla is added to Parma and Placentia for Don Philip. I most heartily rejoice with you on this happy event; happy, I call it, because absolutely necessary to our very being.

Sir William Yonge[2] tells me he left you very well,

---

[1] Of the peace signed at Aix-la-Chapelle. The Definitive General Treaty between all the belligerents was signed on the 18th of October following.

[2] Sir William Yonge, M.P. for Honiton, and one of the Vice-Treasurers of Ireland. He had been a Commissioner of the Admiralty and of the Treasury, and Secretary at War. He died August, 1755. The

and I most sincerely hope he tells me truth. I could more easily pardon any of the fictions in which he sometimes deals than one on this occasion.   W. PITT.

MR. PELHAM TO MR. GEORGE GRENVILLE.

April 30, 1748.

DEAR SIR,—I had the favour of your letter yesterday, and am much obliged to you for your kind congratulations on the late happy event of signing the preliminaries. I look upon it as almost a miraculous deliverance for this country and the Republic, considering the great and successful army of France, and the weak and unfortunate one of the Allies. It must be owned we have fought it to the stumps, and that being the case with ourselves as well as our Allies, we are certainly well off. The terms are much the same as were talked of last year; the Duchy of Guastalla is added to Parma and Placentia as an establishment for Don Philip: the whole to revert to the present possessors, in case

character of Sir William Yonge is thus drawn by Lord Hervey: "Without having done anything that I know of, remarkably profligate, anything out of the common track of a ductile courtier, and a parliamentary tool, his name was proverbially used to express everything pitiful, corrupt and contemptible. It is true he was a great liar, but rather a mean than a vicious one. He had been always constant to the same party: he was good-natured and good-humoured: never offensive in company: nobody's friend, nobody's enemy. He had no wit in private conversation; but was remarkably quick in taking hints to harangue upon in Parliament: he had a knack of words there, that was surprising, considering how little use they were to him anywhere else. He had a great command of what is called Parliamentary language, and a talent of talking eloquently without a meaning, and expatiating agreeably upon nothing, beyond any man, I believe, that ever had the gift of speech."—*Lord Hervey's Memoirs of the Reign of George the Second*, vol. i. p. 48.

the King of Naples comes to be King of Spain, or Don Philip should die without issue male. A restitution of conquests on both sides, excepting what is allotted for the Spanish Infant as above; and the cessions made by the Empress Queen to the King of Prussia by the Treaty of Dresden, and to the King of Sardinia by that of Worms: both which are confirmed. The Republic of Genoa and the Duke of Modena are to have their own again. Cessation of arms in the Low Countries immediately, and elsewhere in six weeks. The Queen of Hungary's minister has protested, and the King of Sardinia has not yet signed; but I make no doubt both will come in to the General Treaty, because they can do nothing else. I have now told you all the principal articles in this Treaty; but as they are not published, I think you had better not mention these particulars as having them from authority. We do not see the use in laying the preliminaries before Parliament; I hope the next sessions will meet early, and that we shall then be enabled to show the work complete. You are very good in offering to come to town; but as the waters agree with you, I hope you will not think of stirring from Bath sooner than you first designed. We have a Board complete at the Treasury, and I look upon the sessions as over, our last Money Bill having passed the House of Commons last Friday. I am sorry to tell you that His Majesty has determined his journey for Hanover as soon as the House is up. It is always best when he is amongst us; but as Peace is near at hand, I don't think his absence of equal ill consequence as it would have been, had not the preliminaries been signed. This great and unexpected news meets with general approbation.

Your uncle[1] seems unaffectedly well satisfied. There are those who look down, but that is rather a symptom of the wisdom of the measure than of the integrity and good faith of those dejected gentlemen.

I am, dear Sir, &c., &c.   H. Pelham.

LADY DOROTHY HOBART[2] TO MR. GEORGE GRENVILLE.

May 12, 1748.

I am so well convinced that I have a pleasure in writing to you, that it would be unnecessary to ask myself any questions upon that subject. I feel obliged to you for giving me so good an account of yourself and your sister, and therefore I think I cannot tell you so too soon.

I believe my aunt Suffolk[3] would be pretty well if her good nature did not make her so sensible to other people's distresses, however I hope she will find herself better when she is quietly settled at Marble Hill; the day of our departure is not absolutely fixed, but I imagine it will be about Monday or Tuesday. They say the House will be up on Friday, that His Majesty may go on Saturday[4]. We have had as yet no summer, but I supped at Ranelagh last night, and hope to go to Vauxhall this evening.

So far was wrote yesterday. Lady S. says she is quite ashamed and angry with herself for not having wrote to

---

[1] Lord Cobham.

[2] Daughter of John Hobart, first Earl of Buckinghamshire, married, in 1752, to Sir Charles Hotham. She died in 1798.

[3] Henrietta, Countess of Suffolk.

[4] The King prorogued the Parliament, and set out immediately for Hanover.

you, but the headache must be her excuse. Poor Lady Mary [1], finding it was necessary for her to see Lord C., determined to put a conclusion to this affair by returning home, and in pursuance of this resolution she is to go home this evening : she is certainly in the right, but I own I tremble for the event. The good account you give of yourself makes me impatient to see you. I have a strange propensity to think you in the right, and as a proof of it, follow your example, and without further ceremony bid you adieu.

The King has ordered his equipages to-morrow at 4 o'clock in the afternoon. Lord Herbert [2] is made Earl of Powis, Lord Kerry an Earl of Ireland, and Sir —— King [3] Lord Kingsborough.

[1] Lady Mary Campbell, youngest daughter of John, Duke of Argyll : she married, in 1747, to Edward Viscount Coke, eldest son of Thomas, Earl of Leicester, who died in 1753, during the life-time of his father. Lady Mary separated from her husband about this time : she remained a widow, and survived until 1811. In one of Walpole's letters to Sir Horace Mann in January, 1748, he says :—" Lord Coke has demolished himself very fast ; I mean his character : you know he was married but last spring : he is always drunk, has lost immense sums at play, and seldom goes home to his wife till eight in the morning. The world is vehement on her side ; and not only her family, but his own, give him up ;" and a few months later writing to Conway, he mentions Lord Coke, and that " Lady Mary has made him a declaration in form, that she hates him, that she always did, and that she always will. This seems to have been a very unnecessary notification."—*Walpole Correspondence*, vol. ii. pp. 208-224.

[2] Henry Arthur Herbert, grandson of Richard, second Lord Herbert, of Cherbury, so created in 1743, and was afterwards advanced to the Earldom of Powis, having married Barbara, niece of William Herbert, third and last Marquess of Powis. Lord Powis died in 1749.

[3] Sir Robert King, created Earl of Kingsborough, in Ireland. He died in 1755, when the Peerage became extinct, but he was succeeded in the Baronetcy by his brother, who was successively created Baron Kingston in 1764, Viscount Kingsborough in 1766, and lastly, Earl of Kingston in 1768.

THE REV. CHARLES LYTTELTON [1] TO MR. RICHARD GRENVILLE.

Aldersbrooke, in Essex, January 5, 1748–9.

I WAS favoured with my dear Mr. Grenville's letter sent me hither from town by the last post. Had I not been in waiting at Court when Billy [2] went to Wotton, I should certainly have accompanied him thither, but I was detained by my Chaplain's duty 'till the end of last week, and on Monday was glad to come over hither for a little country air. This place is but six miles from town, so my chariot and pair easily conveys me, but as I am grown of late so bad a horseman, I find it a difficult matter to take longer journies, else I want not a very warm inclination to spend some days with my Wotton friends.

As it is a year since I had your evidences and muniments under consideration, the paper you sent me wants some explanation; if you will take the trouble to bring the parchment books, &c., to town, I shall then soon refresh my memory with the state of your pedigree, and the difficulties which occurred to me at the time I endeavoured to draw it up.

I think we shall easily reconcile Moreri, and the Not-

---

[1] Third son of Sir Thomas Lyttelton of Hagley, by Christian Temple, sister to Lord Cobham. He was at this time Chaplain to King George the Second; he was rector of Alvechurch in Worcestershire; Dean of Exeter in 1748; and in 1762 he was made Bishop of Carlisle. He was for some time President of the Society of Antiquarians. He died unmarried in 1768.

[2] William Henry Lyttelton, sixth son of Sir Thomas. He was appointed Governor of South Carolina in 1755, and subsequently Governor of Jamaica. He was made an Irish Peer by the title of Baron Westcote in 1766, and succeeded to the family estates by the death of his nephew, Thomas, the second Lord Lyttelton, in 1779, when that Peerage became extinct: it was recreated in his favour in 1794. He died in 1808.

ley Register, with regard to the marriages of Isabella Gifford and Isabella Mareschall, by looking into Dugdale's accounts of the families of Fitzhamon, Clare, Gifford, and Valence, and particularly Sir Robert Atkyns's pedigree of Fitzhamon, in his History of Gloucestershire. I am not sure whether I assigned the right arms to Joan de Arsic, wife of Sir Eustace de Grenville, and daughter of —— Arsic, Baron of Cogges. I have lately met with his true bearing, and therefore you will please to add it to your pedigree, in case it be not there already (viz.): Or, a chief indented Sable.

I return to town on Saturday, and hope to receive any further commands you have for me, or that I shall soon have the pleasure of seeing you in Pall Mall. Your most affectionate, &c., &c.   C. LYTTELTON.

MR. PELHAM TO MR. GEORGE GRENVILLE.

Woburn Abbey, Monday Night.
(September 11, 1749.)

DEAR SIR,—I was extremely concerned to hear of Lord Cobham's indisposition, but by your letter I flatter myself that there are great hopes of his recovery. Undoubtedly at his time of life these attacks are dangerous, but I have myself known recoveries after many shocks of this kind. We will endeavour to do our business as well as we can without you, and if anything is necessary to be signed, whilst two remain in London, we can easily send a messenger down to you with the warrants for your signature. I hope Lord Cobham will be so well recovered by the next week that we may have the pleasure of seeing you then in town; but if not, I beg you will not put yourself to any inconvenience, or make yourself uneasy about it. I go to London to-morrow, and shall see Mr. Lyttelton the next day, with whom I will settle everything, as events shall happen. When you have a proper opportunity, which I hope will be soon, I beg you will make my compliments, and believe me, &c., &c.   H. PELHAM.

THE HON.[1] GEORGE GRENVILLE TO THE HON. RICHARD GRENVILLE-TEMPLE.

Upper Brook Street, September 24, 1749.

DEAR BROTHER,—I have taken care of all the letters entrusted to me, and inclosed I send you Mr. Fisher's answer to that which you wrote to him.

I took the first opportunity to speak to my mother upon the subject of your intended application[2], which in general she approves of; but as far as it relates to herself, she says she should be sorry anybody should think her desirous of any step of this kind in any other light than as the properest means of transferring it to her children. I showed the copy of your letter to my brother Jemmy and to Mr. Pitt, both of whom think it very properly turned, but as the latter is very strongly

---

[1] Sir Richard Temple, Lord Viscount Cobham, died on the 13th instant, and his sister, Mrs. Grenville of Wotton, having succeeded, by special remainder, to the title of Viscountess Cobham, her sons were, consequently, entitled to the prefix of "Honourable." For the sake of brevity, this title having been once acknowledged, will, for the future, be omitted. The eldest son of Viscountess Cobham adopted the additional surname of Temple.

[2] That their mother shold be created a Countess, with remainder to her issue male.

of opinion that it ought to be asked without any previous intimation of it, or feeling the ground beforehand,
I have deferred doing more in it till I have further
directions, which I was the more inclined to wait for,
as Mr. Pitt told me that he and my brother Jemmy
are to be with you to-morrow, and you will then have
an opportunity of talking over the whole very fully with
them, for which purpose I have given to Mr. Pitt the
copy of your letter, and desired him to deliver this to
you, and if you will send me the result of your opinions
I will execute them directly. My wife desires her best
and kindest compliments to you and to my sister, with
which I join, and am, &c., &c. GEORGE GRENVILLE.

MR. GRENVILLE-TEMPLE TO MR. GEORGE GRENVILLE.

Thursday, September 28, 1749.

DEAR BROTHER,—I had the pleasure of meeting with
so strong an approbation of the step intended, and in so
many different lights, that I did not hesitate a moment
in sending you the letter which I was forced to trust to
hands a little uncertain, the post being gone out; if you
received it, as I hope, last night, I imagine I may hear
some sort of answer by to-morrow's post, but if the
letter has miscarried I send you the inclosed, desiring
you to seal it, and deliver it as soon as may be.

With regard to the titles, BUCKINGHAM I cannot
depart from on any account, if it can be had, but I do
not find my affairs in a state to part with 700l. or 800l.
more for the difference of writing TEMPLE as a title,
instead of it as a name. I think it is next to impossible
that what I ask should be refused; but as nothing is

quite impossible in the political world, I can only say, I am very indifferent about the event as to my own mind, in every light but that of being refused so errand a trifle.

My love to your spouse [1], and so adieu! Pitt is in raptures at Stowe.

Pray send me the inclosed back if you have delivered the other,

----

MR. GEORGE GRENVILLE TO MR. GRENVILLE-TEMPLE.

Upper Brook Street, September 28, 1749.

I RECEIVED your letter last night, dear Brother, and in consequence of it, carried the letter inclosed in it to the Duke of Newcastle [2]. I obeyed your directions, and gave him your letter with very little introduction. As soon as he had read it he expressed to me his desire of doing anything to oblige you, in general terms, but very strongly. I stated to him very shortly the nature of the request [3], and added some expressions to show that I thought it of no great importance. After this, many things passed between us which it is too long to enter into the particular detail of till I see you, but the conclusion was, that he desired me to assure you that he would use his *utmost* endeavours that it may succeed according to your desire, that he would represent it to the King in a day or two, and seemed not to doubt

----

[1] Mr. Grenville had been recently married to Miss Elizabeth Wyndham, the daughter of Sir William Wyndham, and granddaughter of Charles, Duke of Somerset.

[2] Thomas Holles-Pelham, Duke of Newcastle, at this time Secretary of State.

[3] As before stated, for a promotion in the peerage, in favour of Viscountess Cobham, their mother.

of its being complied with; he asked me if he should write to you to-night, or whether I would tell you how earnest he would be in what might contribute to please us, and that he would defer writing to you himself till he could give you the King's answer, which he hoped to do in two or three days. I left this to his choice, and he desired me to make you his excuses to-night, and say that he would write to you very soon.

Upon the whole, I look upon your application as complied with, as far as His Grace can promise. He talked as if he was to ask the King for the title of Earl Cobham, which obliged me to say that the words referring to Lord Cobham in your letter did not intend that, for I thought you was inclined to BUCKINGHAM; he immediately objected that it was already bestowed, which I denied, but said I would leave that to be settled hereafter, if the rest was granted, but that no title should be mentioned.

He then asked me whether you designed to include in this all that are in the former limitation, that is to say, Mr. L———[1], &c. I said that I apprehended your letter did not apply for that, and I could say nothing to it. This is the sum total of our conversation, which was ended with many and the strongest assurances of friendship and regard to us, by which I conclude that you will not meet with much difficulty in the thing, but perhaps you may in the name; however, I would not enter into that, as it seemed premature till the other was settled. Adieu. GEORGE GRENVILLE.

---

[1] Mr. George Lyttelton, who was in remainder through his mother, Christian Temple, to the titles enjoyed by Lord Cobham on failure of issue male of the elder sister, Hester Temple, now Viscountess Cobham.

MR. GRENVILLE-TEMPLE TO MR. GEORGE GRENVILLE.

Stowe, Saturday, September 30, 1749.

MY DEAR GEORGE,—I cannot tell you how much pleased every one is here with the manner of His Grace's proceeding, and how much good we promise to our little society from this event, which the more it has been sifted has appeared the more proper and expedient in every light. We all take it for granted the thing is done. I only write this to apprize you more particularly about BUCKINGHAM, which is probably the only difficulty remaining. If you are spoke to upon it, I think it will be proper to mention the instance of Devonshire and Exeter, supposing always, that if the Heralds' Office was to be examined, there are a great many more of the same examples; next, to show the extreme propriety of my having it, on account of the real service it may do me in the borough[1], and my having the best estate in the county. Was it not for the real service it will do me, I know no difference whatever betwixt one form of letters and another, and I am sure if I had had BUCKINGHAM, and Lord Hobart[2] had applied for BUCKINGHAMSHIRE, I should not have cared one tittle: however, when this has been insisted upon and explained as far as is prudent and necessary, we will not kick down an excellent pail of milk by a wrong-headed obstinacy, but desire the title of Countess TEMPLE. If I have the King's consent by to-morrow's post, I shall be in town on Tuesday in

[1] Of Buckingham.

[2] John, Lord Hobart, had been recently created Earl of Buckinghamshire.

order tv wait upon the Duke of Newcastle on Wednesday, and pay my duty to the King on Thursday. I take it for granted it is to be done forthwith, which gives the greatest grace to it.

It will be proper to fix something exactly about Hetty[1], as it will be necessary to know what to call her, and I should think the Heralds' Office would be the proper place to send to even if she determines to go to Court; but I only mention this, leaving it to her to do as she will, and so adieu! with all our compliments to Mrs. Grenville.

I wish you would employ anybody to search for precedents in the Heralds' Office as soon as you hear of the King's consent to the Earldom. I will write to Lyttelton about the limitations, which I think in no light with the expense, but, above all not to fret the King, who dislikes them, especially as Lyttelton has thoughts of applying himself, some time or other, for a Peerage[2].

THE DUKE OF NEWCASTLE TO MR. GRENVILLE-TEMPLE.

Claremont, September 30, 1749.

DEAR SIR,—I had the honour of your letter by Mr. Grenville, and though I very sincerely condole with you upon the death of poor Lord Cobham, I cannot but take a very sensible part in the situation you are in, so agreeable to your friends and servants, and so material and

----

[1] When her mother was created a countess, her daughter would, of course become, by courtesy, Lady Hester Grenville.

[2] Lyttelton succeeded his father in the baronetcy in 1751, and was made a peer by the title of Baron Lyttelton, in November, 1756. Horace Walpole says of him, that "'his great ambition was to go to Heaven in a coronet."

useful to the King and your country. I shall endeavour to deserve the continuance of that friendship with which you honour me, and I am very ready in this and in all other instances to do my part in the manner and at the time you desire it.

The request you make to the King of conferring a further title upon your mother, to be limited afterwards to you and your brothers, is undoubtedly a very natural and reasonable one, and I hope and believe will meet with no difficulty. The only thing I shall submit to you, and that I shall leave entirely to your own determination, relates singly to the point of time[1], whether it might not be as well to defer it 'till winter or some time after the meeting of Parliament, as to propose it just now, so soon after Lord Cobham's death and before you have had an opportunity of appearing at Court.

I mention this purely for your own consideration, and am ready to do in it just as you wish. I am the more inclined to mention it, as the King has lately had a good deal of solicitation about Peerages, &c., which in three weeks or a month may be a little forgot. I beg you would not misunderstand me; your answer to this letter shall determine me to do my best towards obtaining what you propose, in the manner and at the time you shall desire it. I hope to have the pleasure of seeing you when you come to town, and will wait upon you as soon as I know you are in London. The Duchess of

---

[1] The application for the earldom was first made to the Duke of Newcastle on the 28th instant; and, considering that Lord Cobham had died only on the 13th instant, it is not surprising that the Duke should suggest the propriety of deferring it until a more convenient season. Dodington has recorded, however, in his Diary, under the date of October 15th, the following—" At Leicester House. The Grenvilles presented for the title of Temple."

Newcastle[1] and I join in our compliments to Mrs. Grenville-Temple.

I am, dear Sir, very sincerely,
Your most affectionate humble Servant,
HOLLES NEWCASTLE.

MR. GRENVILLE-TEMPLE TO THE DUKE OF NEWCASTLE.

Stowe, October 1, 1749.

MY LORD,—Nothing can be more obliging than the kind manner in which your Grace is pleased to answer the letter I took the liberty to trouble you with, and the readiness you are so good as to express, in laying before His Majesty a request which you do me the great honour not to think unfit. As to the time, since your Grace seems to make some doubt upon that, I confess I could wish that your Grace had taken me out of the difficulty of deciding that, by determining the thing yourself, because possibly some reasons for delay may occur to your Grace of which I cannot be so proper a judge; but since you have had the extreme goodness to leave me to chuse at what time I should wish an application might be made to the King in my favour, upon a matter which I have presumed to recommend to your Grace's protection, I own every reason which I conceived in my poor judgment to be strong ones, that led me so soon to ask this favour, would determine me yet more strongly to wish to receive this great mark of His Majesty's condescension and goodness, and of your Grace's countenance and friendship, as early as may be,

[1] The Duchess of Newcastle was Lady Harriett, daughter of Francis, Earl of Godolphin, and granddaughter of John, Duke of Marlborough.

and without drawing into the delays which sometimes happen upon these occasions. Your Grace sees that I have, in obedience to your commands, taken upon me to chuse in a matter which I should most willingly have submitted to your Grace, if your letter had given me to understand that you yourself had laid any very great stress upon any objections that may arise in point of time. I trust that you will easily feel for me that the grace and pleasure of these things depend so much upon their being carried into execution before they become the subject of discussion and conversation, that you will forgive me for desiring to repeat my first request to you as to time, as well as to the substance of the favour I have presumed to ask. Mrs. Grenville-Temple desires me to assure Lady Duchess of her most humble respects, and your Grace may be very certain that I shall pay mine to you the very moment I can come to town ; being, with the greatest gratitude and respect, &c., &c.

Richard Grenville-Temple.

MR. GRENVILLE-TEMPLE TO MR. GEORGE GRENVILLE.

October 3, 1749.

Dear Brother,—By this post I have time to send you a copy of my last letter to the Duke of Newcastle, which will inform you more precisely of our present state: I likewise send you his. I believe somebody [1] is offended; but when I recollect Legge and Campbell [2] on your account, and Mason [3] on my own, I think there

---

[1] Mr. Pelham is, no doubt, here referred to. He probably thought that the application should have been first made to him.

[2] Legge and Campbell were both in office at this time.

[3] Probably Mason, the poet, for whom he had desired some preferment.

can be no real complaint that I have thought fit to apply where I have always met with most favour. As to BUCKINGHAM, if you find that nail will not drive, let us resort to TEMPLE immediately, as TEMPLE will appear most decent to the world, and justify the more strongly this early application; besides, if the disposition of obstructing remains, this will be a handle for a longer delay, and BUCKINGHAM may hereafter be a pretence for a further step. In my last letter, I rather desired you would defer your journey hither, but as you will be the best judge whether this matter will be settled so soon as to require me to be in town Tuesday or Wednesday in the next week, you will take your own measures accordingly, remembering that Monday remains the day fixed for the ancient and loyal, unless I change it upon this account, and the quarter sessions I had forgot.

I think it not in the least likely that I should be in town before Tuesday or Wednesday, and if this meets with further delays, I shall be very cavalier indeed about it, though I shall not think I have the least reason to complain of the Duke of Newcastle; on the contrary, every reason to be satisfied.

MR. GEORGE GRENVILLE TO MR. GRENVILLE-TEMPLE.

Upper Brook Street, October 3, 1749.

DEAR BROTHER,—Mr. Lloyd delivered to me your letter of Saturday, and I received yesterday that which you put into the post at Aylesbury: as mine came safe I hope the Duke of Newcastle has received that which you wrote to him at the same time, and if so, he may speak to the King in consequence of it to-day.

I have been this morning with Mr. Pelham, in order to remove any difficulties that might arise from his not having been informed of it sooner. I found him but just arrived from Greenwich, and extremely engaged, so that I had but very little time to speak to him. I told him that you had directed me to communicate to him the request that you had desired the Duke of New-castle to lay before the King, and that you flattered yourself with having his assistance in obtaining that mark of the King's favour. He seemed not to know what it was, but when I had told it him, asked me why you should wish it so soon, as no Government would long refuse it to you. I repeated to him the reasons you mention in your letter to the Duke of Newcastle, and he concluded with saying, to be sure, he wished you success in everything you desired. It was so late before I could see him, that I could not hope to see the Duke of Newcastle to-day if I had gone to him. I propose waiting upon His Grace to-morrow morning, and if he tells me that he has spoken, and that the King has con-sented to it, I will delay my journey, as I take it for granted he will have informed you of it by to-night's post; but if nothing has been done in it, I will keep my purpose, and you may depend upon seeing me on Thursday morning, for I should be very sorry to put off my journey unnecessarily, as everything is fixed for it, and it will be very difficult for me to make it the week after. Before I received your letter I had sent to Mr. Mason, and promised to bring him down with me. If you do not receive the account of its being done by to-night's post, you cannot hear of it before Friday or Sunday evening, and the utmost of my stay cannot ex-ceed Monday, because there are none of the Treasury

but Mr. Pelham and myself in town; it would, therefore, be only shortening my stay a day or two, if you
should set out as soon as you hear it is done, and we
might come to town together. I am in a great hurry,
so adieu, my dear Brother. GEORGE GRENVILLE.

Norbonne Berkeley[1] is better, and I believe will
recover.

VISCOUNT COBHAM[2] TO MR. GRENVILLE.

Stowe, November 26, 1749.

DEAR BROTHER,—Having left no orders for my votes
to be sent to me, I know not the least in the world how
Master Speaker and his boys go on, nor should I be at
all inquisitive about it, were it not that I have so many
friends on one side of the school for whom I interest
myself, and therefore would not willingly be absent on
any day when the two armies are likely to engage at
all in earnest; if they, those patriot placemen of opposition, continue as contemptible as they were when I
left them in town, as I wish them, and as I think they
will be at least all this session, perhaps I might be at
liberty to indulge myself in a thousand schemes which I
have here, some tending to pleasure, others to profit.

---

[1] Norbonne Berkeley, M.P. for Gloucestershire. He was the son
of John Berkeley, Esq., by Viscountess Hereford. He claimed, and
established his right to the Barony of Botetourt, in 1764, and was
subsequently appointed Governor of Virginia, when Sir Jeffery Amherst was displaced from that office, in 1768. He died in 1776. The
Barony of Botetourt is now merged in the Dukedom of Beaufort.

[2] Upon his mother being created Countess Temple, Richard Grenville
assumed the courtesy title of Viscount Cobham, and Mr. George
Grenville will, in future, be styled Mr. Grenville.

If there is a man of candour and veracity in the world,
all the honest-hearted women of London, of which
there is such plenty, all, all cry out, and always have
cried out, why it is good Mr. George Grenville: why
then, if it is good Mr. George Grenville, perhaps he
will tell me very ingenuously, and as nakedly as his
modesty will permit him, when, from the general opinion
and appearance of things, such business is likely to
come on, as an honest independent courtier may not be
ashamed to come to town for, such for example as the
reduction of the interest, or any plan of government to
which any reasonable, or considerable, or troublesome
opposition, is likely to be made. I do not mean to
expect that you should be a sorcerer, and dive a hundred fathom deep into the heart and plans of our great
cousin, the man mountain, but I mean that you should
tell me what I think I was at all times able to tell a
Denton or a Lowndes, which is when they would be
wanted, and how long in all probability. I did swear by
the French play, that play which has been so much
sworn at, that I would be in town ready to get my teeth
knocked down my throat by Monday next; and in performance of that solemn oath, I am ready to set out,
unless I can be absolved by Pope P—— thoroughly,
entirely, and without repining. Shall I, in that case,
if I obtain not absolution, come with bag and baggage?
—that, that's the question. Must I, that is should I, for
what I should I must, stay in town one week, two weeks
or three, and eris mihi Magnus Apollo[1], greater than
Pitt, or Jemmy, to whom I scorn to write upon this

[1] " If Mr. Horne answers this letter handsomely, and in point, he
shall be my great Apollo."

              Junius—Private Note (No. 37) to Woodfall.

occasion, that Pitt, who has an Enfield of his own
within an hour of town, and never feels for the unfloated
bowling-greens of others, who has determined with his
deputy to withdraw all advice and correspondence from
me upon that head. I say I scorn to ask of them
what I am to do; but do you, to whose sage counsel
I have referred the linen and the chariot, tell me what
in fitness, decency, and decorum, I am to do : upon your
veto I give up all thoughts of delay, but with your
consent I shall indulge myself as long as I may in this
world, ready to change it for a better like a good
Christian when I must, and not 'till then.

A thousand thanks to the Earl of Buckinghamshire
for the letter [1], which will save me ten guineas, as well
as prevent my setting a bad example, and so, with compliments to my sister, I am, &c., &c.   Cobham.

MR. PITT TO MR. GRENVILLE.

Pay Office, January 20, 1749-50.

Dear Grenville,—It is with much concern that I
hear the waters do not continue to agree with Mrs.
Grenville as they promised to do at first. I have almost
experience enough of the Bath waters to be a physician
with regard to them, and as such, I advise Mrs. Grenville to discontinue them a little, and try them again
in small quantities, and with some corrective adapted to
her case, before she entirely gives up the use of them.
I have done what I advise, many times, and with great
benefit.

I should not take it ill if you was to call in some other

---

[1] A hint about the peerage fees.

of the faculty, and I will add, that notwithstanding all the opinion I have of Duncan [1], there are certainly at Bath men more knowing in all the various effects of those waters, and the several ways of qualifying them, according to the inconvenience they occasion, than he can possibly be. I hope you and Mrs. Grenville will pardon this officiousness, and perhaps take my advice. News, I have none to tell you; when we meet, we shall have, no doubt, matter to quid nunc upon. The Mutiny Bill at present employs all our time, and all our rhetoric on all sides. We fought the Oath of Secrecy yesterday: the requisition to disclose is now placed in the Courts of Justice. The next point will be the revision, and Tuesday the day for it. I hope you both find Bath not void of amusements, and that virtù contributes its part towards it. Whenever you return, I believe you will find us idle enough, all prospect of great attacks being over. Adieu, dear Grenville, and believe me, very affectionately yours,

W. PITT.

MR. PITT TO MR. GRENVILLE.

Pay Office, January 25, 1749–50.

LATE as it is, and tired as I am with the Mutiny Bill, which we have just finished in the Committee, I can't forbear taking this post to return a thousand thanks for the honour and pleasure of a joint letter I received from Bath. To begin, the first, as in duty bound, with the lady, my patient, I will own that, however vain I might be of my skill in physic, I did not expect to be feed so

---

[1] An eminent physician. He was created a baronet in August, 1764. Sir William Duncan married Lady Mary Tufton, eldest daughter of Sackville, Earl of Thanet. He died in September, 1774.

infinitely higher than the most eminent of the profession, by the honour of some lines from Mrs. Grenville's own fair hands. The fee, indeed, would have risen in its value if these lines had given a better account of her health; but though they are short in that respect, yet, they speak such good spirits that I will hope perfect recovery can't be far off. I wish extremely I could, in obedience to her commands, send any receipt for the immediate attainment of it; I should be not a little glad if I could but help her to any one for high dice, and the poultry-yard in consequence of it; but till I can teach blind chance to see and discern those she ought to favour, (which, though an excellent physician, I am not oculist good enough to do,) I can promise no kind of assistance.

I now come to my dear Mr. Grenville, but will not detain him with much discourse. What you heard about the Mutiny Bill is in fact this. The exception to the Oath of Secrecy is now declared to be, the case of a requisition of any Court of Justice to give evidence relating to a sentence of a Court Martial. The Attorney moved it; the Solicitor spoke for it; my Lord Cobham declared for it, and in a manner that did him credit. It was opposed (properly speaking) by none, but disrelished by many; more of this when we meet.

I will be sure to take care of you Monday next. The post is going, so adieu! It is impossible to be more sensible than I am of the manner in which you and Mrs. Grenville are so good to accept my most sincere wishes for your health and happiness.   W. Pitt.

GEORGE, PRINCE OF WALES [1], TO VISCOUNT COBHAM.

Leicester House, April 26, 1750.

MY LORD,—I am obliged to you for your affectionate expressions of concern for my misfortune in losing the best of fathers.

Your attachment to me gives me great pleasure; and I am, with great regard,   GEORGE P.

MR. JAMES GRENVILLE TO VISCOUNT COBHAM.

Paultons, July 13, 1752.

IT was not fraternal fondness nor any such low motive that excited my epistolary ardour in writing to you from London, but since the purest actions of my life are fated to undergo the worst interpretations that friend or enemy can put upon them, I shall submit to my hard fortune, and persist in being what my new acquaintance Martinelli calls himself—a malheureux honnête homme. I wish it was in my power to give you satisfaction, in making an ample description of the circumstances which attended the late fire at Lincoln's Inn [2]. As Virgil, Tasso, Dante, and Ovid in his conflagration of the world, had succeeded with so much general applause in those animated descriptions of fire, I chose to leave untouched a part of poetry in which I despaired of beating my rivals, and I shall still continue in the

---

[1] Afterwards King George the Third. Frederick, Prince of Wales, died on the 20th of March.

[2] Numbers 10 and 11, in Lincoln's Inn New Square. The fire happened on the 27th of June, and broke out in the chambers of Mr. Wilbraham, about one in the morning.

same modest diffidence of my own force: unless you insist upon my taking down the lyre and giving you a specimen of my genius.

I must indeed confess that I ought to have been more exact in what relates to your deeds. Not a syllable of any other paper belonging to you was affected by those flames than what perished in the counterpart of your marriage settlement.

Perhaps it would have been better fortune to you if they too had suffered, as the destruction of deeds by such fires always serves to make good the titles of those estates, which the subsistence of them frequently invalidates. There was an Act of Parliament for making good the deeds that perished in the Temple fire. There will be one next sessions for those which were destroyed in this. If I was too inaccurate in the circumstances of a calamity which affected you, perhaps you have been as little accurate in one that may affect me. You talk of leaving Stowe and going into Northamptonshire, but not one word about the time when, which, nevertheless, is a circumstance which it much imports me to know; and I do humbly implore your goodness to let me be fully apprized of that circumstance, forthwith the whirl of my motions being to depend much thereupon.

I suppose you know with what danger and difficulty Mr. Yorke[1] escaped from the fire.   J. G.

---

[1] Mr. Charles Yorke, second son of the Lord Chancellor Hardwicke, was the principal sufferer in this calamity. He not only very narrowly escaped with his life, but the whole of his library of books, manuscripts, and papers, were entirely destroyed, including the valuable state papers of his great uncle, Lord Somers, which having recently come into possession of the Hardwicke family, had been deposited in Mr. Yorke's chambers. Lord Hardwicke has given an animated description of the

MRS. FORTESCUE [1] TO MR. GRENVILLE.

Ebrington, October 18, 1752.

SIR,—I should have acknowledged the receipt of your letter sooner had not the purport of it [2] for some time absolutely incapacitated me from setting about anything.

I had indeed lived with my dear Lady Temple for a long series of time in an uninterrupted course of friendship, a happiness few enjoy, as there are but very few that are fashioned with those lasting materials that are requisite to constitute a true friend : she was possessed of every quality that could possibly make her a most valuable treasure to her friends, but this is a subject I cannot long dwell on, tears fall so fast that I can see no light. I condole with you all, and shall as long as I live love you all, and consequently interest myself in whatever relates to the children of my dear Lady Temple, whose virtues I shall not take upon me to enumerate to you, but give me leave to indulge in the mention of what among other beauties of the mind I have often admired in her, viz., that she had joined to a most masculine understanding all the compassionate, tender, gentle softness of her own sex, without any of those trifling opiniâtreties about peccadillos which are so frequently seen amongst the generality of our sex ; but I ought to consider who I am writing to, and that in dwelling on the value of what we have lost, I may make wounds still green bleed afresh: I will therefore only

fire, in a letter to the Duke of Newcastle, which is printed in *Harris's Life of Lord Hardwicke*, vol. ii. p. 466. Among the title deeds lost were all those belonging to Lord Leigh's estate.

[1] See *ante*, page 15, *note*.

[2] The announcement of the death of his mother, the Countess Temple, which happened on the 7th of October.

thank you for your goodness in preventing my abrupt hearing of the melancholy news of my dear friend's death, for this I shall always acknowledge as a great mark of your good nature and feeling disposition.

I heartily wish you and your amiable lady a long course of health and happiness, and am,

Sir, &c., &c.

Lu. Fortescue.

My kind compliments wait on Lady Esther, and Lord and Lady Temple.

MR. PITT TO MR. GRENVILLE.

Bath, November 16, 1752.

Dear Sir,—I wish extremely that it had been in my power to be the bearer myself of a thousand very sincere thanks for your obliging invitation to Wotton, but I find my health, though very much mended, stands in need of as long a course of these waters as I can take, before necessary business of office will call me to town; which leaves me no time for the pleasure of waiting on you, at Wotton the dry, whose paths of pleasantness I should be happy to tread. Don't imagine that I intend, by the epithet dry, to be flippant upon the cleanness of your walks; having experienced the merits of the soil in the autumnal season oftentimes, to my great satisfaction: but à propos of clay, J. Pitt[1], that great master, (together with his journeyman Hoare[2],) lives in clay up to the elbows; and I think with great success: the

---

[1] See *ante*, page 66, *note*.

[2] A sculptor at Bath, brother of Hoare the painter. He was now employed upon a marble monument to the memory of Captain Thomas Grenville.

H 2

model of the figure is almost done, and promises to be a very good one. The monumental part of the design, I find, upon examination, not to be so contracted in depth, as to make any saving in solid marble ; on the contrary, there will be more contents of marble. This we have gone over very minutely ; though this at first hearing must appear a little extraordinary, it will soon be explained by one consideration, which is this : the two feet reduced of the depth, are saved in that part which would have been let into the wall : by this means the profile of the monument, projecting forward from the line of the church wall will be full as deep as it would have been in the other design ; and no light being left between the columns and the back of the edifice, the profile comes to take up more marble, by being made solid.

Perhaps I am about as clear as the Doctor in Mo-lière, tout cela fait, que votre fille est muette : but when it is properly explained to you, you will be satisfied as we are, that the thing is so. The sum of our calculations therefore is that the trophies being restored according to your desire, the other savings in the work may stand against the increased quantity of marble ; and that the extraordinary consumption of time taken up in modelling, and dancing after my friend Jack, being brought into consideration, Mr. Hoare's proposal of no abatement is not unreasonable. I thought I owed it to Hoare, to say this after having expressed another opinion in a former letter to you.

I beg my humblest compliments to Lady Hester and Mrs. Grenville.   W. PITT.

MR. PITT TO EARL TEMPLE.

Monday, March 19, 1753.

MY DEAR LORD,—I remain under so great uneasiness with regard to the part you shall determine to take upon the Duke of Bedford's question [1], that I cannot help presuming on your friendship and infinite goodness to me, so far as to trouble you upon it. If you should entertain any thought of supporting or going with the question, give me leave, my dear Lord, to implore you to lay it aside, as I am deeply persuaded that nothing could be so fatal to me and to all our views, so nothing imaginable could give me a concern equal to seeing your Lordship take such a step. I need a thousand pardons for this liberty, and I trust your kind and affectionate friendship has them to bestow upon the man who loves you with the most warm and tender friendship.

W. PITT.

If you will call in this evening, the satisfaction to my mind will be infinite.

---

[1] The question alluded to was the motion intended to be made on the following Thursday, in the House of Lords, by the Duke of Bedford, to have all the papers laid before the House relative to the charge of Jacobitism, made by Lord Ravensworth on the authority of a lawyer named Fawcett, against the Bishop of Gloucester, Stone, sub-preceptor to the Prince of Wales, and Murray the Solicitor General. Mr. Pitt's intreaties show the part which Lord Temple was inclined to take upon this question, and they appear to have had sufficient weight to have prevented his giving any support to the Duke of Bedford's motion, either by speaking or voting. In fact, only four lords accompanied the Duke below the bar, consequently there was no division, and the motion was negatived.

MR. POTTER [1] TO MR. GRENVILLE.

Friday Night, January 11, 1754.

DEAR SIR,—I took the liberty of leaving my name at Lord Temple's door this morning, and depend upon your favour to inform him that my principal business in town was to desire his assistance towards the nomination of Mr. Wilkes [2] as High Sheriff of Bucks. You have been so good as to give me leave to rest that business in your hands. Lady Packington's [3] steward goes down to Aylesbury on Monday, and has received orders to engage her tenants in my interest *singly*, the name of Wilkes being too well remembered at Worcester to be entitled to any favour from the Tories of that county.

While I am writing, I receive an account that Lord Temple has a tenant at Ashendon named Bates, a Quaker preacher. There is in Aylesbury but one

---

[1] Thomas, second son of John Potter, Archbishop of Canterbury. He was a barrister-at-law of the Inner Temple, and Recorder of Bath. He came into Parliament at the general election in 1747, for St. Germans, and at that time he was Secretary to the Princess of Wales. Horace Walpole, writing to Sir Horace Mann, in November of that year, mentions him as a young man of great promise—" The world is already matching him against Mr. Pitt." His subsequent career, however, did not correspond with these anticipations. He was M.P. for Aylesbury in 1754, and afterwards sat for Oakhampton. He held the offices of Joint Vice-Treasurer of Ireland, and Paymaster of the Forces. He inherited a very large property from his father, amounting, it was said, to at least 70,000*l.* He died at his seat called Ridgmont, in Bedfordshire, June 17, 1759.

[2] John Wilkes, so often to be mentioned hereafter in these volumes, was probably indebted to Potter for his introduction to Earl Temple, with whom he subsequently became so intimately acquainted.

[3] The manor of Aylesbury, and considerable property there, formerly belonged to the Pakington family of Westwood, in Worcestershire, from whom it was purchased by George, Marquess of Buckingham.

Quaker, named Edmunds; I have reason to think he is well inclined to me, but Bates, I am told, can make him warmer in his zeal. If there is the shadow of a reason against Lord Temple's laying his commands upon Bates, I beg he would not undertake it. If there is no reason against it, Lord Temple has already been so good, that when I show him how it is in his power, I know I need not ask him to serve me.

I set out to-morrow morning for Bath. Should any incidents arise which would make my attendance in London proper, I presume to depend on your friendship for a hint. I am, with the greatest truth,

Your faithful and obliged Friend and Servant,
THOS. POTTER.

MR. PITT TO MR. GRENVILLE.

Bath, January 29, 1754.

DEAR GRENVILLE,—You would have been troubled with a letter from me, in consequence of my commission to Mr. Hoare, if I had not hoped to have made my report to you in person long ago; but gout, and much proper pain in both feet, has prevented, and lameness still prevents, my return to town.

I conclude you have already received a petition from Mr. Hoare, praying farther time; indeed it is a very necessary request, however unjustifiable the cause of the necessity may be. I found, when I came here, the architectural part of your brother's monument a good deal advanced; but the principal thing, the figure, not only not begun, but the second model, which he had designed to work from, by no means without great objections to it. His brother, the painter, who interests himself much for the excellence of the thing, has made several designs of a figure, and particularly one which seems to me to have great merit. It is simple, graceful, and in the manner of the ancients, though the drapery be modern, and, above all, it has a happy expression in the attitude. This is to be the model for the statue; but your patience is like to be thoroughly tried, for a twelvemonth or more will be the least time necessary to allow the sculptor, with any hopes of the statue coming out not quite unworthy the noble subject. I need not say how much I long to be amongst you. I am sorry to see, every post, in the papers, that there are so many public reasons to make me impatient till I see my friends, besides the many private ones that always make me wish myself in Upper Brook Street.

W. PITT.

MR. POTTER TO MR. GRENVILLE.

Bath, February 8, 1754.

DEAR SIR,—Mr. Pitt tells me that there is an opportunity to congratulate you. I am fond of all such opportunities, and therefore it is no wonder if I embrace the present. I wish, indeed, it were less complicated in its nature, and the removal of anxiety had less share in the occasion of rejoicing, but since occasions of condolence will happen, may they ever end in congratulations. Your two boys have been dangerously ill, and are perfectly recovered. I know how much you and Mrs. Grenville have suffered while they were ill, not to feel with you upon the re-establishment of their health.

I am interested in all that concerns you; and when I say you, I take the liberty to consider Mrs. Grenville in the good old sense, as bone of her husband's bone. May those bones long continue united, and may all that springs from them be an increase of your mutual happiness.

Receive the old-fashioned wishes of an old-fashioned heart. Mr. Pitt has had a smart fit of the gout: this, I doubt not, he has told you: but perhaps he has not informed you that he is the picture of health. I hope he is not a hypocrite. You will expect to hear something of myself, but as I can give you no accounts that will please you, I will only say that I propose being in town in about ten days, with an intention to return hither as soon as the elections are over.

THOS. POTTER.

MR. PITT TO MR. GRENVILLE.

Bath, March 6, 1754.

DEAR GRENVILLE,—The post of this day has brought a much worse account of Mr. Pelham than your letter which had given me much uneasiness. I am infinitely concerned at the state of his health. I hope, however, there is room to think that he may be safe from any present danger, as he began to mend. I am myself still suffering much pain, under the third attack of the gout in both feet. I am indeed much out of order, and worn down with pain and confinement: this gout which I trusted to relieve me has almost subdued me: I am the horse in the fable, non equitem dorso, non frænum depulit ore. I must, however, endeavour to look forward

to ease and health in reversion, and support myself as
I can.   Mr. Pelham's illness fills me with infinite concern.   I hope this will find Mrs. Grenville perfectly well
of her cold.   I desire my humblest compliments to her,
my very affectionate remembrance to Lord Temple: I
don't trouble him with the repetition of my pains and
miseries.   I am, &c., &c.   W. Pitt.

MR. PITT TO SIR GEORGE LYTTELTON AND THE GRENVILLE
BROTHERS.

March 7, 1754.

My dearest Friends,—The shock of Mr. Pelham's
death has affected me so powerfully, as not to leave me
in a proper condition to write.   I am sensibly touched
with his loss, as of a man, upon the whole, of a most
amiable composition: his loss as a minister is utterly
irreparable, in such circumstances as constitute the present dangerous conjuncture for this country, both at home
and abroad.   But as I am unable to write long, as well
as that generals, in the present exigency, are unavailing,
and can, at best, unburden an oppressed mind, I will
contract my thoughts to the consideration of the distressful state of things, looking forward for the resources
that may be left for this country, instead of wandering
into regrets, which a full heart is apt to do.

I will offer to the consideration of my friends but
two things: the object to be wished for, the public;
and the means; which the object itself seems to suggest; for the pursuit of it, my own object for the public,
is, to support the King in quiet as long as he may have
to live; and to strengthen the hands of the Princess of

Wales, as much as may be, in order to maintain her power in the Government, in case of the misfortune of the King's demise. The means, as I said, suggest themselves : an union of all those in action who are really already united in their wishes as to the object : this might easily be effected, but it is my opinion, it will certainly not be done.

As to the nomination of a Chancellor of the Exchequer, Mr. Fox [1] in point of party, seniority in the Corps, and I think ability for Treasury and House of Commons business, stands, upon the whole, first of any.

Doctor Lee [2] if his health permits is Papabilis, and in some views very desirable. Te Quinte Catule, my dear George Grenville, would be my nomination.

A fourth idea I will mention, which if practicable, and worth the person's while, might have great strength and efficiency for Government in it, and be perfectly adapted to the main future contingent object, could it be tempered so as to reconcile the Whigs to it : I mean to secularise, if I may use the expression, the Solicitor General [3], and make him Chancellor of the Exchequer. I

---

[1] Henry Fox, afterwards Lord Holland. He was at this time Secretary at War.

[2] Dr. Lee was Treasurer of the Household to the Princess of Wales. He was afterwards Dean of the Arches, and a Judge of the Prerogative Court. He died in December, 1758. Horace Walpole mentions Lee at this time, as " an unexceptionable man, sensible, of good character, the ostensible favourite of the Princess, and obnoxious to no set of men : for though he changed ridiculously quick on the Prince's death, yet as everybody changed with him, it offended nobody ; and what is a better reason for promoting him now, it would offend nobody to turn him out again."

[3] It is now well known that the operation proposed by Mr. Pitt would have been by no means agreeable to the subject of it, for of all men who had arrived at a certain eminence in the law, Murray at least was one who had resolved to rise by his profession alone. He loved

call this an idea only; but I think it not visionary, were
it accompanied by proper temperaments.   I write these
thoughts for Lord Temple, his brothers' and Sir George

his profession, and had pursued it with more than the usual ardour
and success of his persevering countrymen.   Lord Campbell says, that
" from a high feeling that his destiny called him to reform the juris-
prudence of his country, he sincerely and ardently desired to be placed
on the Bench, and the special object of his ambition was, to be Chief
Justice of England, with a peerage. . . . . All impartial ob-
servers declare that he invariably refused to go out of his profession for
any promotion."—*Lord Campbell's Lives of the Chief Justices*, vol. ii.
p. 380.   Only two years later, with what determination did Murray,
when Attorney General, resist the splendid offers of the Duke of
Newcastle, who, to suit the purposes of the moment, and to retain his
services in the House of Commons, tempted him with almost unlimited
terms: the Duchy of Lancaster for life ; tellerships and reversions;
a pension of six thousand a year, &c: but Murray was not to be bought:
he meant to rise by his profession: he was Attorney General, and he
would succeed to the vacant Chief Justiceship.   If he were not to be
Chief Justice, he would not remain Attorney, and he would not accept
the former without the peerage in addition.   Lord Chancellor Hardwicke, who did not desire the rivalship of Murray in the House of
Peers, encouraged the hesitation of the Duke of Newcastle; but Murray
was determined, and the result is well known.   How little likely is it,
therefore, that even when only Solicitor General he should have consented to Mr. Pitt's idea of *secularization.*   It is interesting to specu-
late upon Mr. Pitt's motives for this proposition.   It would not have
removed Murray from the House of Commons, and therefore he would
still have remained a rival orator.   Did Mr. Pitt shadow forth a
peerage and the Treasury for himself, or was it to prevent the ascendancy
of Fox?   The Duke of Newcastle might remain Secretary of State:
Fox, Murray, Dr. Lee, or George Grenville, might be Chancellor of the
Exchequer, but who was to be First Lord of the Treasury?   It is evident from the correspondence between Pitt, the Duke of Newcastle,
and Lord Hardwicke, that the former was bitterly disappointed at the
ministerial arrangements which were subsequently made, and in which
he was not included, nor even consulted.   He remained only Paymaster
of the Forces.   The cause assigned in reply to his complaints was, the
continued disinclination of the King to admit Pitt to any office which
should require his personal communication with the sovereign; but
that in some measure to soothe his disappointment, several of his
friends, such as Mr. George Grenville, Sir George Lyttelton, Mr.
Legge, &c., had been promoted to offices in the Administration.

Lyttelton's consideration only, or rather as a communication of my first thoughts, upon an emergency that has too much importance and delicacy, as well as danger in it, to whoever delivers their opinion freely, to be imparted any farther.

I am utterly unable to travel, nor can guess when I shall be able : this situation is most unfortunate. I am overpowered with gout, rather than relieved, but expect to be better for it. My dear friends over-rate infinitely the importance of my health, were it established : something I might weigh in such a scale as the present, but you, who have health to act, cannot fail to weigh much, if united in views.

I will join you the first moment I am able, for letters cannot exchange one's thoughts upon matters so complicated, extensive, and delicate.

I don't a little wonder I have had no express from another quarter.

I repeat again, that what I have said are the breakings of first thoughts, to be confined to you four; and the looseness, and want of form in them, to be, I trust, excused in consideration of the state of mind and body of

Your ever most affectionate,

W. PITT.

As nothing is so delicate and dangerous, as every word uttered upon the present *unexplained* state of things, I mean *unexplained*, as to the King's inclinations towards Mr. Fox, and his real desire to have his own act of Regency as it is called, maintained in the hands of the Princess; too much caution, reserve, and silence cannot be observed towards any who come to fish or sound your dispositions, without authority to make direct propositions. If eyes are really turned towards any connection of men, as a resource against dangers apprehended, that set of men cannot, though willing, answer the expectation without countenance, and additional consideration and weight added to them, by marks of Royal favour, one of the connection put into the Cabinet, and called to a real participation of councils and business. How our little connection has stood at all, under all depression and discountenance, or has an existence in the eyes of the public, I don't understand: that it should continue to do so, without an attribution of some new strength and consideration, arising from a real share in Government, I have difficulty to believe.

I am, however, resolved to listen to no suggestions of certain feelings, however founded, but to go as straight as my poor judgment will direct me, to the sole object of public good.

I don't think quitting of offices at all advisable, for public or private accounts: but as to answering any further purposes in the House of Commons, that must depend on the King's will and pleasure to enable us so to do.

MR. PITT TO EARL TEMPLE.

(March 7, 1754.)

My dear Lord,—I return my answer to Jemmy's and Sir George's dispatch directed to you, and accompany it with this line to give you my apprehensions of Sir George's want of discretion and address, in such soundings as will be, and have been, made upon him, with regard to the disposition of his friends.

I beg your Lordship will be so good to convene your brothers and Sir George, and communicate my letter to them, which is addressed to you jointly. It is a most untoward circumstance that I cannot set out immediately to join you. I am extremely crippled and worn down with pain, which still continues. I make what efforts I can, and am carried out to breathe a little air. I write this hardly legible scrawl in my chaise.

Let me recommend to my dear Lord to preach prudence and reserve to our friend Sir George, and if he can, to inspire him with his own.

I heard some time since that the Princess inquired after my health : an honour which I received with much pleasure, as not void, perhaps, of some meaning.

I have writ more to-day than my weak state, under such a shock as the news of to-day, will well permit.

Believe me, my dearest Lord,
Ever most affectionately yours,
W. PITT.

Fox will be Chancellor of the Exchequer, notwithstanding any reluctancy to yield to it in the Ministers : George Grenville may be offered Secretary at War ; I am sure he ought to be so. I advise his acceptance. The Chancellor is the only resource; his wisdom, temper, and authority, joined to the Duke of Newcastle's ability as Secretary of State, are the dependance for Government. The Duke of Newcastle alone is feeble · this, not to Sir George.

MR. PITT TO EARL TEMPLE.

Bath, March 11, 1754.

MY DEAREST LORD,—I hope you will not disapprove
my answer to Lord Chancellor [1]. I include in you your
brothers, for your Lordship's name is Legion. You
will see the answer contains my whole poor plan; the
essence of which is to talk modestly, to declare attachment to the *King's* government, and the future plan
under the Princess, neither to intend nor intimate the
quitting the service, to give no terrors by talking big,
to make no declarations of thinking ourselves free by
Mr. Pelham's death, to look out and fish in troubled
waters, and perhaps help trouble them in order to fish
the better: but to profess and to resolve bonâ fide to
act like public men in a dangerous conjuncture for our
country, and support Government when they will please
to settle it; to let them see we shall do this from *principles of public good,* not as *the bubbles* of a few fair
words, without effects (all this civilly), and to be collected by them, not expressed by us; to leave them
under the impressions of their own fears and resent-
ments, the only friends we shall ever have at Court,
but to say not a syllable which can scatter terrors or
imply menaces. Their fears will increase by what we
avoid saying concerning persons (though what I think
of Fox, &c., is much fixed), and by *saying very expli-
citly,* as I have (but civilly), that we have our eyes open

---

[1] Mr. Pitt refers to a letter addressed by him to Sir George Lyttelton, with the intention that it should be shown to the Lord Chancellor:
it was accompanied by a private letter to Sir George: both are dated
Bath, March 10, and are very curious specimens of Pitt policy. They
are printed in *Phillimore's Memoirs and Correspondence of Lord Lyttelton,* pp. 449–453.

to our situation at Court, and the foul play we have had offered us in the Closet: to wait the working of all these things in offices, the best we can have, but in offices.

My judgment tells me, my dear Lord, that this simple plan steadily pursued will once again, before it be long, give some weight to a connection, long depressed, and yet still not annihilated. Mr. Fox's[1] having called at my door early the morning Mr. Pelham died is, I suppose, no secret, and a lucky incident, in my opinion. I have a post letter from the Duke of Newcastle[2], a very obliging one. I heartily pity him, he suffers a great deal for his loss.

Give me leave to recommend to your Lordship a little gathering of friends about you at dinners, without ostentation. Stanley[3], who will be in Parliament: some attention to Sir Richard Lyttelton[4] I should think proper; a dinner to the Yorkes[5] very seasonable; and, before

[1] Mr. Pelham died about *six o'clock* on the morning of Wednesday, the 6th instant. The activity of Fox upon this occasion is remarkable. He was at Mr. Pitt's door *early:* in the Diary of Bubb Dodington, we are told that he was at Lord Hartington's *before eight o'clock* in the morning; and a letter from Lord Hardwicke to Mr. Pitt, in the *Chatham Correspondence*, mentions " a certain person " (meaning Fox) " who, *within a few hours* after Mr. Pelham's death, had made strong advances to the Duke of Newcastle and myself."

[2] This letter is not to be found in the *Chatham Correspondence*.

[3] Mr. Hans Stanley, of Paultons, in the New Forest. He was a grandson of Sir Hans Sloane, and M.P. for the borough of Southampton. He was subsequently a Lord of the Admiralty, and employed on several diplomatic missions to Paris, &c. He died in 1780.

[4] He had recently been made a Knight of the Bath. He was M.P. for Brackley.

[5] There were at this time four sons of the Lord Chancellor in Parliament, viz., Philip (afterwards Lord Royston, on his father's being made Earl of Hardwicke), M.P. for Cambridgeshire; Charles Yorke, Member for Reigate; Joseph Yorke, for East Grinstead; and John Yorke, for Higham Ferrers.

things are settled, any of the Princess of Wales's Court. John Pitt[1] not to be forgot: I know the Duke of B——[2] nibbles at him: in short liez commerce with as many members of Parliament, who may be open to our purposes, as your Lordship can. Pardon, my dear Lord, all this freedom, but the conjuncture is made to awaken men, and there is room for action. I have no doubt George Grenville's turn must come. Fox is odious, and will have difficulty to stand in a future time. I mend a little. I cannot express my impatience to be with you.

W. PITT.

MR. PITT TO MR. GRENVILLE.

Bath, March 14, 1754.

MY DEAR GRENVILLE,—The favour of your letter of the 12th instant was very intelligible and very acceptable. The kind and affectionate manner in which you wish me amongst you, adds to the impatience I already had of being there to a degree almost intolerable. I am making all the efforts possible to prepare me for the journey. I am carried down stairs, and packed up like a bale of goods in my chaise, to inure me to motion. I begin to bear it upon smooth ground without much uneasiness; my appetite returns, my pains subside, and my nights are tolerable: if no relapse comes, I hope a week will go a good way towards enabling me to crawl, if not to walk. As soon as I am capable of that degree of self-motion, I will set out.

You cannot, my dear Grenville, in any situation ever so critical, need my assistance. My warmest wishes,

---

[1] John Pitt was now M.P. for Dorchester.
[2] The Duke of Bedford.

absent or present, you will always have; but I have much need of seeing the faces of my friends again, after a long absence, and tedious scene of pain and confinement. My most affectionate remembrances to the brothers, and most humble compliments to Mrs. Grenville. W. PITT.

SIR GEORGE LYTTELTON TO MR. GRENVILLE.

Hill Street, Monday Evening, 18th March, 1754.

MY DEAR GRENVILLE,—I wish you would let me know your opinion, whether I shall send an express to Mr. Pitt to morrow or not. I think that things are now as much settled as they are likely to be 'till the dissolution of the Parliament, and he will be impatient to know some particulars. If he is coming to town the express will meet him on the road. I have had no answer from him to my last letter; have you? In case you think I should send an express, be so good to tell your brother Jemmy to send the man to me to-morrow morning about half an hour after ten; and as you have seen Fox's letter, I wish you would write yourself an account of it, which may be sent with mine. If you choose that the express should go early in the morning, send him to me to-night, any time before 12 o'clock.

MR. PITT TO EARL TEMPLE.

Bath, March 24, 1754.

MY DEAR LORD,—Not being able to write much to-day, I beg your brother George will excuse my writing separately, and receive my thanks for his letter in this to your Lordship. I hope my letter[1] to the Duke of Newcastle will meet with the fraternal approbation. It is strong, but not hostile, and will, I believe, operate some effect. I am still more strongly fixed in my judgment from the state of things as it opens, and will open every day, that the place of importance is employment, in the present unsettled conjuncture. It may not to us be the place of dignity, but sure I am it is that of the former. I see, as your Lordship does, the treatment we have had: I feel it as deeply, but I believe, not so warmly. I don't 'suffer my feelings to warp the only plan I can form that has any tendency or meaning; for making ourselves felt, by disturbing Government, I think would prove hurtful to the public, not reputable to ourselves, and beneficial in the end, only to others. All Achilles as you are, Impiger, Iracundus, &c., what would avail us to sail back a few myrmidons to Thessaly! Go over to the Trojans, to be revenged, we none of us can bear the thought of. What then remains? The conduct of the much-enduring man, who by temper, patience, and persevering prudence, became adversis rerum immersabilis undis. I am so tired I cannot hold my head down to write any longer. A fine Secretary of State I should make. Ten thousand compliments to the ladies, and warm effusions of heart, breathed, not expressed, to yourself, my dearest Lord.   W. PITT.

---

[1] This letter is not to be found in the *Chatham Correspondence*, nor is there any copy of it among the *Grenville Papers*. The deficiency, however, has been supplied by the author of an article on the Life of Lord Chatham, in the *Quarterly Review*, No. CXXXI. p. 216, where extracts from the letter in question are given from the *Hardwicke MSS.* Mr. Pitt had enclosed it to Sir George Lyttelton, open, for his own perusal, and to be shown to the Grenvilles, before it was sealed and sent to the Duke of Newcastle.

I hope to be able to set out in a week. I am much mended in my general health, but not half a man yet; were I a legion of men they would be all yours. Be so good not to leave my letters in your pockets, but lock them up or burn them, and caution Sir George to do the same.

MR. PITT TO MR. GRENVILLE.

Bath, March 24, 1754.

DEAR GRENVILLE,—I hope you was so good to excuse my not thanking you for your very kind letter in one addressed to yourself, by my packet of yesterday. I cannot refuse myself the pleasure of supplying that omission to-day, though it be only to write a letter worthy of a profound politician of these dark times, that is, to say nothing. When the day will dawn (for to my poor eyes it is not even twilight at present), I cannot guess : when it comes, may it show us a view men will see with pleasure, and not wish to change! I am deep in a world that is very entertaining; or rather, the demolitions of the metaphysical world, which that intellectual Sampson of Battersea [1] has pulled down about our ears, but with this difference, that here the Hero is the Philistine, and the poor saints are crushed.

I have gone through the Essay on Human Know-

---

[1] Lord Bolingbroke. Mr. Pitt alludes to a collected edition of his works, which happened to be published on the morning of Mr. Pelham's death, the 6th instant, and which gave rise to the well-known Ode, by Garrick, in which are the following often-quoted lines :—

> " The same sad morn, to Church and State
> (So for our sins 't was fixed by fate)
> A double shock was given :
> Black as the regions of the North,
> St. John's fell genius issued forth,
> And Pelham's fled to Heaven ! "

ledge, and will confess that fine as it is, and irresistible
as the vogue for writings of that kind may be, I cannot
think it the greatest performance that ever was, as I had
been made to expect. Old matter new dressed, and
often tawdrily enough; trite observations emphatically
imposed for most sagacious discoveries, and much falla-
cious reasoning, or else want of that clearness of conception and luminous discernment to which the author
so particularly pretends. I could almost wish him alive
again, that he might have the pleasure of reading that
stupid fellow (as he calls him) Warburton's[1] answer,
and that we might have the entertainment of reading his
Lordship's reply. I endeavour, you see, to keep my
mind as far as I can, abstracted from what you gentlemen at London are pleased to call the great world,
and which we philosophers at Bath call the little; and
instead of such trifles as the government of millions,
fate of kingdoms, and system of Europe, to hold our
minds fixed on the contemplation of nature's system,
and intellectual and moral worlds. But I will descend
so far from my sublime occupations as to hope that a
part of your little world, namely a certain family in
Brook Street, is in perfect health. I desire my most
humble compliments to Mrs. Grenville, and am, my
dear Grenville's   Most affectionate,

W. PITT.

MR. PITT TO MR. GRENVILLE.

Bath, April 6, 1754.

DEAR GRENVILLE,—I can write but a few words,
having a bandage on my arm, after being blooded for a

---

[1] William Warburton, afterwards Bishop of Gloucester.

feverish cold. You know so thoroughly my heart about public matters, that not even one word is necessary on that subject; nor is it, I hope, more necessary to tell you that the Treasurer of the Navy gives me great pleasure, especially if the office be allowed to claim its right of succession, in virtue of the precedent lately made [1]. A better right it will have (whether it will be allowed or not), the ability of the possessor of it to serve his country in a higher sphere; for, some time or other, weight in Parliament will be considered as an ingredient, at least, among the qualifications of a man for the first offices of business. You can't read what is written: my hand can hold out no longer; but it shall to assure Mrs. Grenville, and the House of Grenville, of my humblest compliments. W. PITT.

MR. PITT TO EARL TEMPLE.

Bath, April 8, 1754.

MY DEAR LORD,—I cannot, without some little difficulty, return you my warmest thanks for your kind letter, having been blooded on account of a feverish cold and sore throat. I was much out of condition to answer the great packets with which I was honoured; nor was I the better for the efforts of mind I was forced to make·

I am better this morning, and hope to surmount this slight attack in two or three days.

Per varios casûs et tot discrimina rerum, I cannot

---

[1] The precedent of Mr. Legge's removal from the office of Treasurer of the Navy to which Mr. Grenville had succeeded, and Mr. Legge being made Chancellor of the Exchequer.

say, tendimus.ad Latium. Where my sole wishes tend
ultimately is to retreat[1]; but when or how? In the
mean time, I see with great pleasure the Treasurer of
the Navy and the Cofferer[2]. George Grenville's turn
must come for greater things; there I lay the stress;
for my own poor self, I sincerely wish His Majesty's
affairs in Parliament all success in the hands to which
they are committed. I esteem and love Legge[3]: Sir
Thomas Robinson[4] is a very worthy gentleman. This
is all I think of public matters; very concise, but all I
can possibly utter, if I were put to the rack.

My picture[5] will before now have come to your
Lordship's hands, or rather I shall have had the honour
to present myself before you in my very person; not only
from the great likeness of the portrait, but, moreover,
that I have no right to pretend to any other existence
than that of a man, en peinture. My arm will not
allow me to write more.   W. PITT.

I hope you will, by Sir George's means, learn the

---

[1] The same desponding wish is mentioned by Mr. Pitt in his letters
to the Duke of Newcastle and Lord Hardwicke. He seems to have
been occasionally much depressed in spirits by the continued pain and
sickness which had so long afflicted him; but as his health improved,
the energy and activity of his mind returned, and we hear no more of
that ignoble retreat, by which the destinies of England might have
been changed in the events of the " Seven Years' War."

[2] George Grenville was now appointed Treasurer of the Navy, and
Sir George Lyttelton became Cofferer of the Household.

[3] Henry Bilson Legge. He was now Chancellor of the Exchequer.

[4] Sir Thomas Robinson had just succeeded the Duke of Newcastle
as Secretary of State. He had been previously employed in some
diplomatic missions:—a Commissioner of Trade and Plantations;
Master of the Great Wardrobe, &c. He was made Lord Grantham
in 1761, and died in 1770.

[5] The portrait of Mr. Pitt, painted by William Hoare of Bath.
This picture was formerly in the collection at Stowe.

sum of my answers[1] to the great honour done me by express.

MR. PITT TO EARL TEMPLE.

Bath, May 3, 1754.

MY DEAR LORD,—Though I did not hear the departure of my most obliging visitors this morning, I have done nothing but feel it this whole day. Accept this scrawl from a lame hand, addressed to you both, and be assured it conveys, in the few words I can write, the warmest sense of your goodness in coming so far to visit the sick. Sick I retract, for lame is all I can in conscience call myself; and that right to the dear retreat I am so enamoured of, I think is leaving me every day. In a word, I think the cheering countenances and sweet converse I have enjoyed for two days, will go a great way, both literally and figuratively, to set me upon my legs again.

I have reconsidered Mr. Hoare's labours of yesterday, and I find it the very best thing he has yet done, in point of likeness. He thinks so himself, and will finish it con amore, as the painters say. For the present, farewell, my dear Lord Temple, and dear Grenville, and may you both have as much pleasure in London as I have had for eight-and-forty hours at Bath.

W. PITT.

---

[1] Probably referring to the Duke of Newcastle's letter to Mr. Pitt, of the 2nd instant, and the letters of the 5th and 6th instant, from Mr. Pitt, to the Duke of Newcastle and Lord Hardwicke; see *Chatham Correspondence*, vol. i. pp. 95–103.

MR. PITT TO EARL TEMPLE.

Bath, May 23, 1754.

My DEAR LORD,—I am still the same indolent inactive thing your Lordship saw me; insomuch that I can hear unmoved of Parliaments assembling, and Speakers chusing, and all other great earthly things.

I live the vernal day on verdant hills or sequestered valleys, where, to be poetical, for me, Health gushes from a thousand springs, and I enjoy the return of Her, and the absence of that thing called Ambition, with no small philosophic delight: in a word, I envy not the favorites of Heaven, the few, *the very few*, quos æquus amavit Jupiter, the dust of Kensington Causey[1], or the verdure of Lincoln's Inn Fields[2].

I propose to be in London about the 7th or 8th of June, when I must not hope to find your Lordship there.

I shall dispatch my necessary business as fast as I can, and pursue you to Stowe, where the charms, so seldom found, of true taste, and the more rare joys and comforts of true friendship, have fixed their happy residence. There it is that I most impatiently long to enjoy you and your works. I lay myself at the feet of Lady Temple and Miss Banks, and am, my dear Lord Temple's truly devoted,　　　　　　　WM. PITT.

My affectionate remembrances to the Brotherhood.

---

[1] George the Second constantly kept his court at Kensington Palace.
[2] The Duke of Newcastle's town residence was in Lincoln's Inn Fields, at that time a more fashionable quarter of the town than it is now considered.

LADY HESTER GRENVILLE[1] TO EARL TEMPLE.

(October, 1754.)

THE most expressive manner I can find of offering the thanks I would pay to you, my dearest Brother, for what has so lately passed with you on my subject, is to beg you would measure them by the degree of gratitude due to the happiness you have bestowed upon me by the most affectionate conduct in a circumstance so important to my happiness. The receiving the approbation of a brother whom I admire as much as I love, is a heartfelt joy that will not admit of description, though your declared friendship for Mr. Pitt, and his own superior merit secured me from any apprehensions, but such as arose from what prudential views might suggest to you; but you remembered them only to add to your kindness by not urging them to our unhappiness.

Every way I have millions of thanks to offer you for your love to him, to me, and for those expressions of affection and regard which give me a double joy, as they will recommend me further to your friend, to whom I wish to be recommended by every endearing circumstance, feeling that pride and pleasure in his partiality for me which his infinite worth not only justifies, but renders right.

You will easily imagine, my dear Brother, how great my happiness is, that in taking new engagements, I am, if possible, more closely united to my own family, which I have ever, and must ever, love and honour so highly.

I feel my obligation so great *to Lady Temple upon

---

[1] It will at once be seen that this and the following letter refer to the intended marriage of Mr. Pitt and Lady Hester Grenville.

this occasion, that I must give her the trouble by a letter.

I should have preferred coming to Stowe to have repeated more fully what my heart dictates towards you and Lady Temple, but I hear you are immediately to have company, which, for many reasons that you can supply, I should chuse to avoid, and therefore hope, till I am at liberty to see you, you will accept my present acknowledgments and assurances of being, my dear Brother, most faithfully,

Your affectionate and obliged Sister,
HESTER GRENVILLE.

MR. PITT TO EARL TEMPLE.

(October, 1754.)

My DEAREST LORD,—I cannot suffer a day to pass without expressing a few of the thousand things I feel from your kindest, most amiable of letters to Lady Hester Grenville. You sent me from Stowe the most blessed of men, and every hour I live only brings me new and touching instances of the unceasing goodness and most affectionate and endearing partiality towards me, of the kind, noble, and generous fraternity to which it is my glory and happiness to be raised. Don't imagine, my dearest Lord, that these are the exaggerations of a heart thinking and talking of the brother of her that for ever fills it. I can say nothing to you that my heart has not always given you before this last transcendant and tender mark of your friendship and highest confidence. Your letter is the kindest that ever glowed from the best pen speaking the best heart. I should say

a million of things about the charm of style and manner
of it, if I was not too much filled and touched with the
endearing matter of it. If it did not look like an expression more of a lover than a friend, I should say,
I love, to the very pen that wrote it. What do I read
in it, from the first line to the last, not only the same
warmth of affection, but the same amiable delicacy of
manner that I read in every word, and smallest instance
of behaviour while I was at Stowe, and which even the
best and kindest friends cannot put into their actions
unless their minds are truly Grenville. How generous and
how delicate it is in you to state me in the too flattering
lights of your own partiality to the eyes of Lady Hester,
and to help to furnish her with a kind of justification of,
I fear, infinitely too great a sacrifice of her establishment. I see I have run into a long letter, intending
only a note. I must yet add one word to Lady Temple,
but let that one word imply acknowledgments and gra-
titudes without number. You cannot read, for I cannot
write, as Lady Hester does me the honour to wait for
me. Ever, ever your most affectionate, obliged, and
happy friend. My best compliments to Miss Banks,
and many thanks.

EARL TEMPLE TO MR. WILKES.

Stowe, October 12, 1754.

RETURNED from the expensive delights of Berwick [1],
and all the sweets of Edinburgh, I hope this will find

[1] According to his biographer Almon, the " delights " of a Berwick
election cost Wilkes between 3000*l.* and 4000*l.*, and he was besides

you in good health, spirits as usual, and with an excellent cause. It is very gracious and kind in the pious
Æneas, after his conversion, after the Love feast, to
keep up that of friendship with one, who has so slender
a claim to be admitted to the table of the Saints[1]; but
I am sorry to hear you are exalted to so high a story of
faith and godliness, because great may be the fall thereof,
and this Scotch taste of architecture is so contrary to the
fashionable style of building in this country, that I fear
it will never prevail, and that you will return to your
humbler roof of mortality and every social virtue, with
as much ardour, as if you had never deviated into the
higher regions of cherubim and seraphim, or the conversion of Wilkes, compared with that of St. Paul;
however, if I should live to see you in the bosom of
our father Sir George[2], I shall only now and then drink
to the pious memory of the delightful moments I have
passed in your wicked company, and begin to attach

unsuccessful in his opposition to the Delaval interest. Fox, writing to
Lord Hartington on the subject of this election, says, " Mr. Wilkes, a
friend it seems of Pitt's, petitioned against the younger Delaval, chose
at Berwick, on account of bribery only. The younger Delaval made a
speech on his being thus attacked, full of wit, humour, and buffoonery,
which kept the House in a continued roar of laughter. Mr Pitt
came down from the gallery and took it up in his highest tone of
dignity. He was astonished when he heard what had been the occasion of their mirth. Was the dignity of the House of Commons on
so sure foundations, that they might venture themselves to shake it?
Had it not, on the contrary, by gradations, been diminishing for years,
till now we were brought to the very brink of the precipice, where, if
ever, a stand must be made?"—*Memoirs by Lord Waldegrave*, Appendix, p. 147.

[1] Lord Temple here probably alludes to the well-known club at
Medmenham Abbey, of which fraternity Wilkes, Potter, Sir Francis
Dashwood, and Lord Sandwich were distinguished members.

[2] An ironical allusion to Sir George Lyttelton, and his *Essay on
the Conversion of St. Paul.*

myself to all the interested pursuits of this world, as the sure road to a better.

It is impossible for me to ask, and as impossible not to wish to see you here, before that great day of Judgment which will decide of the fate of Berwick and of you; however in all events, I fancy I may depend upon meeting you in town soon after the birth-day, which is the date of all good courtiers, or a little before the meeting of Parliament, which is the æra of every honest independent country gentleman, and there will be some happy minute in some lucky hour betwixt them both, which will probably afford me the pleasure of seeing again the kind host of Aylesbury, to whom I am, and ever must be, in the nature of things,

My dear Sir,

A most affectionate and

Obedient humble Servant,

TEMPLE.

Lady Temple, Miss Banks, and I, desire to assure Mrs. Wilkes, Mrs. Mead [1], and your good uncle of our best respects. The good man Jemmy just this instant steps in to bid me tell you how much he is yours.

MR. PITT TO MR. GRENVILLE.

Sunday, October 27, 1754.

MY DEAR GRENVILLE,—You will not have wondered that the letters I have addressed to Wotton or Stowe, since I left you, have not been any of them superscribed to you.

----

[1] Mrs. Mead was the mother of Mrs. Wilkes.

Lady Hester has left you, and not only Wotton is, as it always must be, most agreeable to remember, but you will both, I know, pardon me for saying, you and Mrs. Grenville are now the first persons in your own house. How many, and how truly affectionate, are the thanks I owe to the goodness and friendship of these two persons. The trouble you have taken, and particularly your kind attention to expedite the most interesting work of Mr. Nuthall[1], is a most obliging instance of it. He writes me word that you will have the draughts Wednesday next. If so, I flatter myself the writings may be engrossed by about the 4th or 5th. If I am so happy as to find no objections arise to the completing my felicity from the dear object of it, when I see her, might I not hope that the 6th or 7th of November might be the day from which I shall date all the real honour and happiness of poor life? You will, I am sure, allow every degree of impatience in me to be reason itself; but not to urge *my reason*, your own will suggest to you the approaching opening of Parliament, and variety of other calls upon my time and necessary attentions, as real and very pressing motives to accelerate what I confess I should press with equal impatience were they all out of the question.

I trust Lord Temple will have an ear for arguments of such weight; besides that his Lordship will have just days enough to look round a scene that must be viewed often before it is at all understood. I will write to Stowe as soon as I have seen her who is to decide

---

[1] Mr. Thomas Nuthall, a confidential solicitor, employed by Mr. Pitt to prepare his marriage settlements. He was appointed Solicitor to the Treasury in 1765, and died very suddenly in 1775, from fright and excitement, caused by his being attacked by a highwayman on Hounslow Heath. See *Chatham Correspondence*, vol. ii. p. 166.

almost, if possible, of my wishes.   In the mean time, I recommend to your kindness to dispose his, which I know are both of them disposed to my hand, to make your most grateful and affectionately devoted friend happy, as soon as may be, without precipitating Lady Hester's intentions.   Must I not count every moment till the world sees me the most honoured and blessed of men !   .   .   .   .   .

MR. PITT TO EARL TEMPLE.

Salt Hill, Friday Night, November 1, 1754.

I AM, thank Heaven ! so far in my way towards London ; that is, my dearest Lord, within hours, but far from a few, of seeing again every perfection of human nature in Argyll Buildings.   You perhaps begin to suspect a summons to you to leave Stowe, which you so kindly allowed to be served upon you, is coming. Not so ; Lady Hester has granted to my most ardent and respectful supplications, the 15th, a day, however late for my tender impatience, infinitely good in her not to think too early.   This leaves my dear Lord master of his motions, as to the journey of happiness to his most loving friend, which he was so kind to offer at any warning ; but though I will not teaze you in one character, shall I persecute in another ?   Reason of State says, Lord Temple can hardly be in town too early : his eyes will be ever the best, and sure the more wanted, as some eyes he too often trusts to can go but to one loved object.   What your brother Harry's letter will have intimated about Hagley merits attention.

I understood Thursday, at the Bath, from William

Lyttelton[1], who has wishes and prospects of going to America, that the most obliging, and I hope agreeable offer, will be made to your Lordship, in case his seat vacates. This is one reason of State, and I think not weak, for your presence among your friends. Many others, rather seen in the mass than in detail, must occur.

I had conversation this day, at Reading, with Lord Fane[2]. I foresee an event growing out of that petition. His Lordship I have known from boy's age, and his worth and honour inferior to none. His language is very manly: to your humble servant very obliging, upon my public situation. So much for politics. How shall I thank you for the kindest and most agreeable letter that ever flowed even from your own pen? not by my pen, but with my life; by telling you that life is happy, and that the inestimable present you have given me could alone have made it so. I should not say too much if I added, that this life, happy as it is, is at your call. Never were words so fine and touching as those which I now repeat. Why must I blot this happy paper with the miserable name of Queensberry. I have writ to the poor Duke[3], to inquire of their health,

---

[1] He was soon after appointed Governor of South Carolina.

[2] Charles, second Viscount Fane in the Peerage of Ireland. He was now Member for Reading. He had been employed in several diplomatic missions at Florence, Turin, and Constantinople. He died in 1782.

[3] Mr. Pitt here alludes to a dreadful calamity which had befallen the Duke and Duchess of Queensberry, by the death of their son, Lord Drumlanrig, who was killed by the accidental discharge of his own pistol, in their coach, while they were on a journey to London, accompanied by his newly-married wife, Lady Elizabeth, a daughter of the Earl of Hopetoun, and she died of consumption a little more than a year afterwards.

which I dread to hear. Dear Lady Temple has more
room in my thoughts than in my paper. All happiness
to Miss Banks. Adieu.

MR. PITT TO MR. GRENVILLE.

Saturday, November 2, 1754.

I WRITE to my dear Grenville from a place where it is
impossible I should give much time to anything but one.
I never can thank you as I feel for your kind letter
which this day brought me, and Mrs. Grenville for the
infinitely obliging prolongation of that concluding letter.
How shall I say what I ought for the additional trouble
I am now perhaps giving you in the person of Mr. Nuthall? I conceive there may have been some want of
sufficient explanation of my wishes with regard to the
estates in reversion. Give me leave to state in a few
words how I understand it. Having reasons, of a sort
I am sure you and Lady Hester will approve, against
tying all those contingent estates, I proposed that by
an after settlement in the most proper manner to be
judged of by you, the Sunderland estate should be settled in the strictest manner, but those estates that come
under the Duchess of Marlborough's will should be left
at my disposal. My reasons are these : that I thought
myself bound by every tie to take care of Mr. Spencer's
debts in case I succeeded to his estate, which I could
only do by a power over these lands from the Duchess.
I also wished, in case of such a large fortune, to have
elbow-room for a town house of some expense, perhaps
one near town, and particularly to be in a condition to
purchase Old Sarum. But in case I should succeed to

K 2

the estates of the Duchess of Marlborough only, I meant, and I mean, that they in like manner should be strictly entailed. If you should recollect any of these reasons to have been mentioned, or should now not think them improper, I conceive the draughts may be easily altered to this plan. I write in a way not to state business very clearly, but I trust your goodness will supply what I ought to have better explained.

A thousand pardons for all the loads I venture to lay upon your friendship. As we shall have the pleasure of seeing you in town Thursday, I will take no more of your time now, than to repeat how much I feel I abuse that goodness and infinite kindness I must ever most gratefully and affectionately love. Yours most unalterably,

W. PITT.

The 15th Lady Hester has had the goodness to grant. How late a day for me, and yet how early for her!

MR. FOX TO MR. GRENVILLE.

Holland House, Saturday night, November 16, 1754.

DEAR SIR,—We are to meet to-morrow night on Oxfordshire [1]. I will wait on you previously for half an

[1] The Oxfordshire Election petition was now the cause of great party animosities. The Sheriff returned all the four candidates, and they all petitioned, complaining of undue election and double return. After a very long debate on the 18th of November, and on many subsequent days, it was eventually decided that Lord Parker and Sir Edward Turner were the sitting members, and that Lord Wenman and Sir James Dashwood had not been duly elected. The sum of money spent on this occasion was enormous. Walpole writes to Sir Horace Mann, " A knowing lawyer said to-day, that with purchasing tenures, votes, and carrying on the election and petition, five-and-fifty thousand pounds will not pay the whole expense."

hour wherever you will appoint, or at eleven on Monday morning. If the former, send a note to me to be left at White's; if the latter, or any other time, it will be time enough to appoint it when we meet at Lord Maccles-field's [1]. If we meet now determined not to agree, I flatter myself we shall however disagree so as that it may be the last time. If you say this is unavoidable, I will disagree with you even in that, and in everything relating to this election at Hindon, and I hope never in anything else. I am, most sincerely yours,

H. Fox.

THE COUNTESS TEMPLE TO EARL TEMPLE.

Saturday (December 28, 1754.)

To keep up a custom, I must write to you, though I have not much to say; there is one piece of news, which is much to the King's honour, and shows a great deal of good nature: when he heard of my Lord Albe-marle's [2] death, he immediately gave my lady a pension

---

[1] George, second Earl of Macclesfield: he died 1764.

[2] See *ante*, page 67, *note*. Lord Albemarle was taken ill after supper and died in a few hours, at Paris, where he was the British Ambassador. He married Lady Anne Lennox, sister of Charles, second Duke of Richmond. She died in 1789. He was succeeded by his son George, Lord Viscount Bury, Lord of the Bedchamber to William, Duke of Cumberland. Horace Walpole, mentioning his death to Sir Horace Mann, says, "Everybody is so sorry for him!—without being so; yet as sorry as he would have been for anybody, or as he deserved. Can one really regret a man who, with the most meritorious wife and sons in the world, and with near 15,000*l*. a year from the Government, leaves not a shilling to his family, lawful or illegitimate (and both *very* numerous), but dies immensely in debt, though, when he married, he had 90,000*l*. in the funds, and my Lady Albemarle brought him 25,000*l*. more, all which is dissipated to 14,000*l*."—See *Walpole Correspondence*, vol. iii. p. 97, where Lord

of twelve hundred pounds a year. She was very much
shocked when Lord Bury told her the news; but as
soon as he came into the room, bid him not speak a
word, for she knew what he was come about; she was
sure his father was dead, for she had seen him the night
before, and it never failed. When this came to be explained, it was only a dream: she thought she saw
him dressed in white; the same thing happened before
the Duke of Richmond's death, and often has happened
before the death of any of her family. Methinks I see
you laugh!   I am, your most affectionate,

A. TEMPLE.

EARL TEMPLE TO MR. GRENVILLE.

Thursday night (May 8, 1755.)

DEAR BROTHER,—That wise, virtuous, and able statesman Sir G. L.[1] told Mrs. Grenville, it seems, at parting,
that it would be necessary for you to look in upon this
delightful town about once a week. I little thought
that I should ever adopt one tittle of his sentiments,
and yet I cannot help saying that I wish you would try
it this once, and see how you like it. Oblige me so far
and come as soon as you can; in the firm confidence of
which I remain, &c.   T.

The Brest squadron is in the Bay of Biscay, consisting
of twenty-five ships of the line, as I hear. Boscawen
there, too, with at least half that number. The Lord
preserve us! Many affectionate compliments. I have

Dover, in a note, refers to the *Mémoires de Marmontel*, for an interesting account of this magnificent spendthrift: and see also *Walpole's
Memoirs of George the Second*, vol. i. p. 82.

[1] Sir George Lyttelton.

deferred to the last moment giving you the trouble of this piece of advice relating to your own expedition.

EARL TEMPLE TO MR. GRENVILLE.

May 29, 1755.

DEAR BROTHER,—The accident which has happened to Lady Betty Germain[1] of setting herself on fire in two places, which I suppose you have heard of, has amongst other ill consequences obliged me to put off my journey to Stowe till Saturday or Sunday se'nnight. I am the more mortified at this, as I have not heard that Mrs. Conway[2] and Miss Stapleton[3] have left you, I saw

[1] Daughter of Charles, second Earl of Berkeley, and widow of Sir John Germaine, who left her a very large fortune, including the estate of Drayton, in Northamptonshire, which at her death she bequeathed to Lord George Sackville. When her father was Lord Lieutenant of Ireland, Swift was his chaplain, and Lady Betty was consequently much in the Dean's society, and she remained his friend and frequent correspondent for many years after. She is often mentioned in his letters and poems. Lady Betty's elder sister had married Mr. Chamber, of Hanworth—they had two daughters, who, having lost their parents early, were brought up entirely under the guardianship of Lady Betty; the eldest became the wife of Lord Vere Beauclerc, afterwards Baron Vere of Hanworth; and the youngest the wife of Richard Grenville, now Earl Temple. Lady Betty died at her house in St James's Square, in December, 1769. Nothing is now known of the accident mentioned in Lord Temple's letter.

[2] Second daughter of Sir John Conway, of Bodrhyddan, by Penelope Grenville, daughter of Mr. Richard Grenville, of Wotton. She was, therefore, aunt to Lord Temple.

[3] Second daughter of James Russell-Stapleton, Esq., by Penelope, eldest daughter of Sir John Conway. Miss Stapleton died unmarried, in 1815. Her youngest sister married Sir Robert Salusbury-Cotton, Bart., and had a son and heir, the present Lord Viscount Combermere, G.C.B.

some little glimpse of hope that I might possibly have the pleasure of their company at Stowe.

Lady Betty gets better daily, and we now stay only as she seems much to wish it, and we arè sure would most willingly have done the same for us, in the same situation. The French politics of bringing home six ships of the line and three frigates, can be reconciled to no sense whatever, but the unintelligible one of English politics. It is very lucky for us, that the same epidemical distemper of incapacity should spread itself so wide as to produce fortunate and salutary effects for this country. I cannot by letter add anything to what we talked over, when we last met.

In statû quo, a little better or a little worse, is the whole gradation of political speculation at this time, and I am in statû quo.　　　　　TEMPLE.

MR. JAMES GRENVILLE TO MR. GRENVILLE.

July 15, 1755.

DEAR BROTHER,—This day arrived an express from Admiral Boscawen. It is said to bring an account that part of the French squadron fell in with part of ours about the 18th or 20th of last month, in a fog off Cape Race, the southernmost point of Newfoundland.

Two 60-gun ships of theirs taken, the one armé en flûte, with eight companies of grenadiers on board, the other en guerre; the first struck immediately. The other was attacked home by Captain Howe[1], and made

---

[1] Afterwards Admiral and first Earl Howe. He succeeded his brother, the third Viscount Howe, who was killed in a skirmish, at Ticonderago, in 1758.

resistance, 'till Boscawen's ship coming up she too struck. They say a third struck, but got off in the fog.

My intelligence is uncertain which fired the first broadside. The fog continuing, he took a run towards Louisburg, in hopes of finding more, and, looking into that harbour, could see only four of them got in. Among those, he thinks he saw the second in command. Where the others are at present, no account is yet come. There is a report that fifteen French sail of the line have been seen in the Channel.

Signals were made yesterday to the whole fleet at Spithead, to prepare for immediate sailing.

J. GRENVILLE.

MR. POTTER TO MR. GRENVILLE.

(Near the end of September, 1755) [1].

DEAR SIR,—It is too important not to run some little hazard of this letter's miscarrying, in order to give you a hint of what has lately passed since you left London. I went thither last Friday, and heard from your brother the substance of what had passed in the conversations at Powis House [2]. He told me too the report of those con-

---

[1] This letter is not dated, but Mr. Potter says it was written when he was hastening on the road to Bath, to see Mr. Pitt. In the *Chatham Correspondence* will be found a letter from Mr. Pitt to his nephew, dated from Bath, Sept. 25th, 1755, in which he alludes to his *recent* arrival at that place, and of his intention to return to London *in about a week;* from this, and other internal evidence, I have fixed the date of Mr. Potter's letter to Mr. Grenville as above mentioned.

[2] Mr. Pitt had lately held several conferences at Powis House, with the Lord Chancellor Hardwicke, and also with Mr. Charles Yorke, and the Duke of Newcastle, the particulars of which are related in *Harris's Life of Lord Hardwicke,* vol. iii. pp. 27-34.

versations made by the D—— was, that Mr. P. was so much *personally incensed* against him as to be induced *on no terms whatever* to undertake the two measures [1].

This was received with great indifference, and it was said that the defection of six or seven men could not create any disturbance to a measure so popular.

That this measure was not only right but *popular*, that the people of England loved *Hanover*, that these measures were necessary for its defence, and the acclamations of all mankind on his arrival convinced him how well they were pleased with what had been doing. The reply to this was, that the judgment formed was extremely just, that the reasons were popular as well as right, and that the House of Commons when left to judge of the measures only would approve, but that the leaders there had taken such personal aversion to him, the D——, that he was no longer able to carry on business. That therefore it was absolutely for his M. service, that he should have leave to resign, and it was his earnest request that his Majesty would entrust his affairs in the hands of Lord Gr(anville), who was the only person in England who would carry them on with ease and honour to his M——.

Thus things stood when I left London on Saturday. At such a crisis it is most important that Lord Gr. (Granville) and his Lieut., Mr. Fox, should find themselves disabled to undertake what the D. of N. refuses. I have therefore sought out Dr. Hay [2] and secured him

---

[1] The Treaties with Hesse and Russia for the subsidies.

[2] George Hay, LL D., and M.P. for Stockbridge. He was Principal of the Arches Court of Canterbury, and Chancellor of the Diocese of Worcester. He was afterwards in Parliament for Newcastle-under-Line, and in 1774 was made Judge and President of the High Court of Admiralty, and knighted. He died in 1778.

in the strongest manner. But I have done more. I have read such a lesson to the D. of B(edford) about the necessity of declaring with violence against the Subsidies as the certain means to ruin the D. of N., that he is convinced of it, and declares as loud as anybody. Encouraged with this, or rather to produce this, I entrusted him with such parts of Mr. P.'s conversation with the D. as were proper, and particularly his firm declaration to oppose all measures which tended to enfeeble our efforts in America to draw the war to another quarter. He took the whole exactly as I wished, fell into the strongest panegyrics on Mr. P.'s virtue and abilities, saw the immediate destruction of the Duke of N. if nobody was weak enough to interfere, hoped in God no one of his friends, particularly Mr. F., would attempt it. Having got thus far, I clinched the whole with drawing forth a message in form from him to Mr. P., *approving in the strongest terms* of what had passed, and assuring him of all his support *in such measures as he Mr. P.* should think fit for the extirpation of the common enemy, and *for the support of himself,* who he was sure was *the only man* who had virtue and abilities enough to retrieve the affairs of this country.

I communicated to him no part of the report to the —— and only the most proper parts of the conversations at Powis House, but told him that it was *reported* the D. of N. threatened to resign in case the R(ussian) subsidy was not carried. And now let Mr. F. and the Duke of Cumb. come to him and welcome. The Duchess (of Bedford) said Lord and Lady Temple talked of coming to pass a day or two at Woburn[1].

[1] It will be seen by the following letter, that Lord Temple did pay a visit to Woburn.

Let them go immediately and talk as Lord Temple
can talk.   I am on the road to Bath, hastening to Mr.
P. as fast as I can.   I propose returning in a fortnight.
In all situations, I am most affectionately yours,

T. P.

MR. POTTER[1] TO EARL TEMPLE.

(About the middle of October, 1755.)

WHAT shall I say to your Lordship of this man[2], or
rather what will you believe of him?   Will you believe
him to be a man of honour, and sense, and even dignity?   I protest I do; and I even think I can account
for all that coldness which appeared to you, without
attributing it to any other but a manly motive.   When
I came home, I found that unusual civilities had been
shown in my absence to my son; and when I presented
myself, I found a most welcome reception, a countenance of ease, and a freedom of communication.   When
the visit was paid to the wife and the company that
were with her, he followed me to the door of the drawing-room, as if he expected I should speak in private;
and on my whispering that I would take some other
time to trouble him with a few words on business, he
pressed eagerly into the next room, and listened to me
with the greatest attention.

I began with alluding to some conversation which had
passed in the drawing-room, and saying that I was one
of the speculatists who had been to town on purpose to
look about; that I found the scene highly interesting,

----

[1] This letter is neither signed nor dated; it is, however, unques-
tionably in the handwriting of Mr. Potter, and its contents evidently
refer to the date to which I have ventured to ascribe it.

[2] The Duke of Bedford.

though in a different way from what it was when I saw
him last; that the hopes we had then entertained of
seeing this country immediately freed from the administration of the most contemptible of men were blasted
in the very manner he himself had suggested, by Fox's
eagerness for place and power, as he had now most
effectually secured him in his office, perhaps for life.
He interrupted me with eagerness: " Did not I tell you
so? If you remember, I said the very thing, that if I
had been the privy counsellor and bosom friend of the
Duke of Newcastle when Mr. Pitt had so virtuously
and so honourably refused his support, I would have
advised him to have offered any terms whatever to Fox,
who perhaps might be *unwary enough* to accept them,"
and it seems he has done it. I answered, 't is true he
has done it, whether through unwariness, or whether
through that thirst of power and money which I remembered likewise he had observed to be Fox's character-
istics, I could not tell; but the thing was done, and
those whom he had extolled for their virtue and firmness
were now likely to fall the victims of it. I added that I
found Lord T. (Temple) had been at W. (Woburn),
and had signified to him Mr. Pitt's feelings of that full
and explicit approbation of his conduct which he had
commissioned me to deliver (to this he assented with
a nod); but that I found Lord Temple alarmed, and
Mr. Pitt much more so, at some representations which
had been made to him of a conversation that had
passed, the beginning of the summer, between Mr. Pitt
and Mr. Fox at Lord H.'s (Hillsborough's?), and that
he had disapproved of the part Mr. Pitt then took.
He told me it was true; that the day after I had seen

him, Mr. Rigby[1] came down to him from Mr. Fox; that Rigby was in the greatest agitation from the imagination that all cement between Pitt and Fox was broke, for that Fox had told him the reason of his taking this part was, Mr. Pitt's having declared in that conversation more than once that he would have nothing more to do with him. That he had asked whether he, Mr. Pitt, had anything to object to him or his conduct since they had acted together; whether he had assumed too much, or behaved improperly; to all which Mr. Pitt answered, no; he was perfectly satisfied with his behaviour, which had been open, and that of a gentleman, but that (a very remarkable expression, and which could not be mistaken) they were upon different lines, possibly, and he hoped they would prove, convergent; but their ground at present was so different, that he could not go with him either into Court or Opposition. This conversation I own, says he, did make a great impression upon me; I could not doubt the truth of it, because I have an opinion of Fox's honour so far as to think he would not lie; and yet that Mr. Pitt should bluntly and without provocation tell Mr. Fox that he would neither go with him into Court or Opposition did exceedingly dissatisfy me.

I told him that no one, I believed, could give a better account of that conversation than myself, as Mr. Pitt had

---

[1] Mr. Rigby came into Parliament for the borough of Tavistock, under the patronage of the Duke of Bedford, and when his Grace became Lord Lieutenant of Ireland, in 1757, Mr. Rigby was appointed Chief Secretary, and he held at the same time the office of Master of the Rolls, in Ireland. His letters in the *Bedford Correspondence*, show how intimately he was in the confidence of the Duke, up to the time of his death in 1771.

given me an account of it long before Mr. Fox had thought it right to make any use of it; that I would not determine whether Mr. Fox would lie, but I was sure he would most egregiously misrepresent, and that he had given a most astonishing instance of it in this report of that conversation; that I would deal with him very frankly, and speak with great confidence to him. I had been one of those whose inclination as well as principles had led me to consider the Duke of Newcastle as the great object of opposition; that with this view I had been solicitous to forward every junction which was likely to contribute to his destruction; that it was visible to all the world that a union of Mr. Pitt and Mr. Fox must (as in effect it had) be the coup de grâce to him; that in the course of forming this union, and during its continuance, I had watched the turns of Mr. Pitt's mind, and that nothing could be clearer than it was of all ideas of rivalship, or of private animosity, but that Mr. Pitt's sagacity, as well as his Grace's, had discovered in Mr. Fox's temper that eagerness for power which inspired a doubt of his firmness on trying occasions; that the suspicion was but too often increased by Mr. Fox's conduct; that it was apparent he was always pursuing a private rather than a joint plan. I then went through the history of the whole session, beginning with the attack on Murray touching Ireland, and ending with the Regency: that all these things together had filled Mr. Pitt's mind so full of suspicions, that, as I thought a man of honour ought always to do, he had resolved to open himself fully to him; that he had done so in this conversation, in which, far from approving the whole of Mr. Fox's conduct, he had told him all I had recapitulated, as reasons which made it impossible that any union could continue; that nothing could be so absurd as a union where only one side was bound, and that Mr. Fox had ever kept in reserve an implicit obedience to the commands of the Duke of Cumberland, whose soldier Mr. Pitt was not, and whose commands might, at the end of a campaign, counteract all that had been jointly done; that, therefore, till Mr. Fox could call himself sui juris, and could agree to walk with Mr. Pitt either in the paths of Court or Opposition, as should be found most expedient, no union could subsist, nor was it to any purpose they should meet to embarrass each other; that if Mr. Pitt did use that remarkable expression *that they were on different lines,* he used it with great justice, because Mr. Fox never would stand upon the straight line which led to the end in view, but would have deviations and stops of his own.

He appeared extremely satisfied with the account, and said the story was perfectly natural, and the observations on Mr. Fox's conduct during the course of the session just; but, says he, it is the easiest thing to pervert conversations, and each man may make his own account plausible; that therefore he thought it was but justice, before he determined his opinion, to hear what was said on each side, which he hoped to have an opportunity of doing, as he would go to town the end of this month for five days, and return hither for a week, and then go to the meeting of Parliament; that Fox had sent to him the strongest assurances that he came in with a view to strengthen himself in the Closet, and to undermine the Duke of Newcastle; that he had come in against all the efforts both of the Duke of Newcastle and Lord Chancellor, by the influence of the Duke of Cumberland.

I told him this was very inconsistent with all the

declarations both of the Duke of Newcastle and Lord Chancellor, who expressed to every one who would hear them their high satisfaction not only in the assurances Mr. Fox had given them, but in the candour of his conduct since; that one way or other, Mr. Fox's conduct was unjustifiable, for if he really meant to support the Duke of Newcastle, he betrayed his friends who wished to oppose him, and if he really meant to undermine him, he was the villain who smiles in your face and stabs you to the heart. Yes, but says he, Fox insists he has made no promise, except that he will do the King's business. However, I think on the whole as you do, that Fox's acceptance has been precipitate and ill-judged; that he has saved the Duke of Newcastle, who, without his acceptance, was absolutely undone; that Fox could have run no risk in standing out, as Mr. Pitt had refused first, and as, if the Duke of Newcastle fell, he stood first in the graces of the Closet; that he might have refused now with much more safety than he did a year and a half since, and as he lost no favour then, he could have lost none now.

My next business was to get some information of his opinion as to the subsidies. I therefore said, that for my own part, nothing could have given me more real concern, for besides that not only the great end of my life, the destruction of the Duke of Newcastle, was defeated, but Fox, for whom I had a real respect, and who even now had shown me a very particular civility (relating to him the occasion), had taken so unpopular a point, that he would undo himself with mankind, for that however he might flatter himself, the idea of a continental war, and subsidies, was in the minds of mankind the same, and though he might get a majority for a day, he would feel the weight of that day while he lived.

He then asked me how that would go in the House of Lords, and what part the Duke of Devonshire [1] would take. I told him the Duke of Devonshire was in the country, and I had not seen any one who had seen him lately, but that I imagined there was not the least reason to doubt but that he would appear the very first day of the session, to enter his protest. Why, to tell you the truth, says he, I do not chuse to tell people in general the part I shall take, because I want to see whether confidence cannot be restored; but as to the subsidies, it is as you say, a war on the continent or not, and a war in Germany, the most dangerous part for us. As to ourselves, to be sure, we can't send a man, because there is no place for him to rest his foot; but if we are to hire armies to defend Hanover, *which is not attacked*, where will be the end of it? 'Tis lighting the candle at both ends with a witness. Besides, suppose it should be attacked, why should it not share the fate of other countries? If it should be ravaged, other countries have suffered the same fate without being undone, and I own I should think that this country, pursuing the war in its own way, would be bound, whenever they came to make peace, to insist on full reparation for those allies that are attacked *en haine*.

The only war we can carry on is a sea war, and an American one, though that we have done hitherto like pirates, rather than a great nation.

---

[1] William, third Duke of Devonshire. He died on the 5th of December following.

You know, I suppose, that they intend to make this subsidy as palatable as possible, by declaring they mean not to renew the subsidies of Bavaria and Saxony, and that they even will not renew this of Hesse, unless the French are in possession of Hanover. I told him I would not thank any man of 72 for a promise he was to execute when he was 76 or 77. As for the Russian, that, Lord Granville says, is completely executed, and for 25,000*l.* more than Sir Charles Hanbury[1] was commissioned. There was a dispute of 50,000*l.*, and Sir Charles has split the difference. I asked him the sum to be paid, and the number of years. He said Lord Granville had not informed him, and he did not chuse to be inquisitive. Upon the whole, says he, before I resolve on the part I shall take, I will go to town for five days, as I told you, the end of the month ; for since Lord Temple was here, I have not seen a creature to inform me of anything, nor do I at all know the bottom of things.

I suppose I shall see Mr. Rigby in a day or two here, who will bring me some message from Mr. Fox ; but when I go to town I hope I shall see both Mr. Pitt and Mr. Fox. I told him I was sure Mr. Pitt would call on him the moment he knew he was at leisure to receive him, for that he had nothing more at heart than to be set right in his opinion, and that he had even pro-

---

[1] Sir Charles Hanbury Williams came into Parliament for Monmouthshire, in 1733, and uniformly supported the administration of Sir Robert Walpole. He was made a Knight of the Bath in 1746, and soon after appointed Envoy to the Court of Dresden. He was also for a time Minister Plenipotentiary at Berlin, and, subsequently, at St. Petersburg, where he concluded a convention with the Empress of Russia. A very entertaining account of him, and a description of his Embassies, will be found in the Appendix to the second volume of Horace Walpole's *Memoirs of King George the Second.*

posed coming down on purpose to Woburn, if Lady Hester's situation had permitted him.

Mr. Pitt shall have notice from me of his journey; but quære whether it might not be right for Mr. Pitt, if possible, to tell his story first.

12 o'clock Monday night.

THE EARL OF HOLDERNESSE[1] TO MR. GRENVILLE.

Whitehall, November 20, 1755.

SIR,—I have the King's commands to acquaint you that his Majesty has no further occasion for your service as Treasurer of the Navy; I should be glad of a more agreeable occasion of assuring you of the truth and regard with which I am, Sir,

Your most obedient humble Servant,
HOLDERNESSE.

THE EARL OF BUTE[2] TO MR. GRENVILLE.

November 20, 1755.

DEAR SIR,—I have been unfortunately out till now, and my servants had not the sense to bring me your letter and Mr. Pitt's where they would have been of use.   I

---

[1] Robert D'Arcy, fourth Earl of Holdernesse, at this time Secretary of State; he had previously filled several diplomatic appointments. At his death in 1778, the Earldom became extinct, but his Barony of Conyers devolved upon his only daughter, who married Francis Godolphin, afterwards Duke of Leeds, in whose family that Barony is now vested.

[2] John Stuart, third Earl of Bute, subsequently so well known as the favourite minister of George III. He married the only daughter of Lady Mary Wortley Montague, by whom he had a numerous family. Lord Bute died in 1792.

must tell you, my worthy friend, what I should have wished you would have told me on such an occasion; 'tis glorious to suffer in such a cause and with such companions; in times like these, the post of honour is a private station.   I own I from my heart congratulate you, and I am proud to call a man of your distinguished character my friend; for well may this be the prelude only to what your merit loudly calls for.

Most entirely yours, &c.,
BUTE.

EARL TEMPLE TO LADY HESTER PITT.

November 20, 1755.

MY DEAR LADY HESTER,—I cannot defer till to-morrow morning making a request to you, upon the success of which I have so entirely set my heart, that I flatter myself you will not refuse it me.   I must entreat you to make use of all your interest with Mr. Pitt to give his brother Temple leave to become his debtor for a thousand pounds a year 'till better times[1]: Mr. P. will never have it in his power to confer so great an obligation upon, dear Lady Hester, your most truly affectionate brother,   TEMPLE.

LADY HESTER PITT TO EARL TEMPLE.

Pay Office, November 21, 1755.

I DO not find, my dear and generous brother, that having had time to reflect calmly upon your goodness

---

[1] Lord Temple's generous gift was made upon the occasion of Mr. Pitt's dismissal from the Paymastership of the Forces.

has made it easier for me to express what I feel upon it. On the contrary; and therefore I must content myself with saying that my gratitude is like the occasion that inspires it, great indeed. I made no difficulty of conforming to your desire that I would use my interest with Mr. Pitt, because my own love for him makes me a judge of the pleasure you would receive from his acceptance of such a testimony of your friendship. I should have had little hopes of prevailing in such a cause if I had not known how strongly the joy and pride of being obliged to you would operate upon his mind. Believe me, my dear brother, that will still be, notwithstanding our situation, the circumstance from which we shall derive our greatest satisfaction.

Judge if you can how my heart is affected by being, not the sharer only, but the means, of your proving in so noble a manner your affection for a person dearer to me than myself. You make me the happiest woman in the world, so that to avoid ingratitude, I must forgive your having laid me under an obligation to those who, in turning us out, have furnished the occasion of so much joy to me.

I write in my bed, for I could not longer contain the overflowings of my heart, nor defer assuring my dear brother how highly I am his obliged and most affectionate Sister,   HESTER PITT.

EARL TEMPLE TO LADY HESTER PITT.

(November 21, 1755.)

I AM infinitely happy, my dear Lady Hester, in your having proved successful with Mr. Pitt in a matter in which my heart was so deeply interested: this proof of his kindness and friendship to me is the only remaining one that he could give me. I receive it with all possible gratitude, and will call upon you and him very soon, to tell you how unalterably I am your most affectionate Brother. T.

LADY HESTER PITT AND MR. PITT TO EARL TEMPLE.

(November 21, 1755.)

THE affection and generosity of my dearest brother affects me so strongly, and in so many various ways, that I find no words to express the sentiments with which my heart is filled, nor am I literally in a situation to write any farther.

(*The remainder of this letter is in the hand-writing of Mr. Pitt.*)

The heart of one brother does not overflow more with nobleness and affection, than that of the other does with the warmest, quickest, deepest sentiments of love and gratitude. Your most endearing proceeding touches and moves my mind even to a distress of the sweetest kind. How decline, or how receive so great a generosity, so amiably offered? I am little better able to hold the pen than Lady Hester. We are both yours more affectionately than words can express. We could have slept upon the Earl of Holdernesse's letter; but our hearts must now wake to gratitude and you, and wish for nothing but the return of day to embrace the best and noblest of brothers.

MR. PITT TO EARL TEMPLE.

(November 22, 1755.)

WORDS are not made to express the sensations of my heart on the kind and noble friendship which my dear Lord Temple pours upon us, but as silence is impossible, though language is ineffectual, I will say in a word, that I am more yours than my own, and that I equally love and revere the kindest of brothers and noblest of men. Ever, ever, your devoted,

W. PITT.

MR. PITT TO MR. GRENVILLE.

(December, 1755.)

LORD Temple is of opinion, and I am now as much so, that it is best not to move an amendment to the appropriation. I think we may, with as much effect, assert our insular plan, by declaring that we mean to enable his Majesty to defend the dominions of England, and not to lay foundations for continent operations. I think this the rather, because under the words of last year's grant, any troops taken for various eventual purposes, provided the defence of England be one of them, are now continued within the appropriation. Si quid novisti rectius istis, I will do as you would have me.   Tuesday night.

MRS. GRENVILLE TO MR. GRENVILLE.

(December 23, 1755.)

I BELIEVE you must content yourself, my dearest love, to know nothing by this post but what relates to your

own fireside, for since your going, I have seen nobody
able to give me the least information that I can depend
upon, but if the card table to-night furnishes me with
any materials, they shall be added in a postscript.

* * * * * * *

The news of the day is, the Speaker having been
detained in his chair expecting Mr. Hume Campbell's[1]
writ to be moved, he having told the Speaker yesterday
that it would happen to-day, but after having waited a
considerable time Lord Marchmont[2] was consulted, and
having said he had heard nothing upon the subject from
the Duke of Newcastle, the House was adjourned, and
Mr. Hume remains in statû quo.   Lord Sandwich[3] and
Mr. Ellis[4] have kissed hands for the third of the Vice-
Treasurership.   Lord Sandys is unprovided as yet.

Mr. Dodington[5] kissed hands yesterday.

There has been a report in town to-day that the Duke
of St. Alban's[6] had shot himself as he was going to Italy,

[1] Brother to Lord Marchmont, and at this time M.P. for Berwick.
He was made Lord Registrar of Scotland.   He died in December,
1760.

[2] Hugh Home, third Earl of Marchmont.   He died in January,
1794, and the peerage became *dormant.*

[3] John, fourth Earl of Sandwich.   Upon the resignation of the
Duke of Bedford, in 1748, he became First Lord of the Admiralty,
and was soon after employed to negociate the peace of Aix-la-Chapelle.
He was subsequently Secretary of State, and again First Lord of the
Admiralty.   He died in 1792.

[4] Mr. Welbore Ellis, afterwards Lord Mendip.   In 1763 he became
Secretary at War, and many years afterwards Secretary of State for
the Colonies.   He died in 1802, aged 89.—See a character of him in
Walpole's Memoirs of George the Second, vol. ii. p. 142.

[5] " That so often *repatrioted* and *reprostituted* Dodington is again
to be Treasurer of the Navy."—*Walpole Correspondence,* vol. iii.
p. 180.

[6] George, third Duke of St. Alban's.   The report was unfounded.
He died in 1786.

but it is not credited, and nobody knows whence the report arose.

Lady Temple is here, and has just told me that Henry is arrived from Bath ; he had drank tea with her, and complained heavily of the time he had passed. Mr. Pitt and Mr. Potter set out this morning as they intended : Henry met them upon the road.

Once more adieu! my dearest Love.

MR. PITT TO MR. GRENVILLE.

Bath, January 3, 1756.

MY DEAR GRENVILLE,—A thousand thanks to you for imparting to me, with your own hand, the happy event in the family. My warmest felicitations attend you and Mrs. Grenville, who, I hope, is as well able to bear the intrusion of the very affectionate compliments of her friends, as Lady Hester was at the same period of her progress through the straw. Another Grenville, that is, another Englishman [1], who will one day love and help to serve his country, is a most seasonable recruit to the age.

I heartily and joyfully welcome this little honest Briton into a degenerate world, and accept him as a happy omen, not only of the new year, but of a better

---

[1] Mr. Pitt was a true prophet upon this occasion. He refers to the birth of a child who afterwards became the Right Honourable Thomas Grenville, and who, having reached the patriarchal age of ninety-one, died in December, 1846. This venerable and most excellent person did indeed " love and help to serve his country." He has immortalized his name and memory by his bequest to the Trustees of the British Museum, for the use of the British nation, of one of the most splendid libraries ever formed by a private gentleman.

and nobler order of times to come. My health, which you remember so kindly, is pretty well, indeed, quite so, the remains of a cold excepted. Potter is better, and gains ground every day. W. PITT.

MR. POTTER TO MR. GRENVILLE.

Prior Park, Saturday, January 3, 1756.

DEAR SIR,—Mine are not congratulations of form. They proceed from a heart warmly interested in everything which affects your happiness.

Mr. Pitt has just communicated to me the highly agreeable news of Mrs. Grenville's safe delivery. I rejoice that more Grenvilles are born, but I rejoice much more that those of that name whom I love and honour receive an addition to those comforts which their own virtues will increase into the greatest blessings. You will serve the public in a private station by assisting Mrs. Grenville in the task for which you are both peculiarly fitted, the educating those who are to be the supports of the public. In every station your country will be your debtor. So will your friends. It is my pride to rank myself under that class, and it is my comfort that some little sameness of disposition has contributed more to bring me into the number of them, even than my pride. I shall imitate you when I can, and where I cannot I am contented to admire you.

T. P.

MR. PITT TO MR. GRENVILLE.

Sunday, March 21, 1756.

THE pain in my face and ear is so much more troublesome that I would avoid, if I could, an unnecessary trip to town to-morrow. I therefore beg you will be so good to let me know by the bearer, who is ordered to return to-morrow morning very early, whether Sir George's inflexibility holds out, and the tax on plate[1] is to be forced upon us to-morrow. I am at present muffled up with flannel, but will come up (unless much worse) accordingly as your note shall inform me. Lady Hester is very well, and hopes to see you some time or other.   W. PITT.

MRS. GRENVILLE TO MR. GRENVILLE.

April 20, 1756.

I AM happy to hear, my dearest Love, that you got safe to Wotton; for notwithstanding all your boasts about the practicability of the country, I think the roads must be such as to make utter safety rather a piece of good luck than a certainty, for we have had a deluge of rain either night or day, and sometimes both, since you went out of town.

. . . .

---

[1] The tax upon plate formed part of Sir George Lyttelton's Budget, as Chancellor of the Exchequer: a sum of five shillings was to be levied for every one hundred ounces, as far as four thousand ounces, and all persons were to enter the amount of their plate at the Excise Office. It produced, says Horace Walpole, but 18,000*l.*

Lady Exeter[1] has made a will, by which she has left all her fortune, consisting of 70,000*l.*, to Lord Exeter, for his life, and afterwards to Mr. Tommy Townshend[2], according to her father's desire. Her distemper was the same as Lady Granby's[3], a St. Anthony's fire, which struck in and seized her brain. I heard yesterday that the Bishop of London withdraws his pretensions to the interruption of the Duke of G——'s road[4], so that it is once more confidently said that the Duke of Bedford will be defeated.

The news of the town is that there are fresh proposals of peace just imported, so advantageous that we shall certainly accept them. There is a Prince of Nassau, a sovereign just arrived, who is much admired for his beauty, and a Morocco Ambassador, as much admired for his great politeness (though he does not speak a word in any known language); he gives the preference to Lady Caroline Petersham[5] before Lady Coven-

---

[1] Wife of Brownlow, ninth Earl of Exeter, and sole daughter and heir of Horatio Townshend, third son of Horatio, first Viscount Townshend. She died on the 17th instant.

[2] Grandson of Charles, second Viscount Townshend. He was made a Lord of the Treasury in 1765, and in 1782 Secretary of State; he was soon after created Baron and Viscount Sydney, and died in June, 1800.

[3] Lady Francis, daughter of Charles Seymour, sixth Duke of Somerset; she married the Marquess of Granby, in 1750, and died in 1760.

[4] Now called the New Road, leading from Paddington to the City. It was considered to be very advantageous to the Duke of Grafton's property, but as it was intended to pass near the back of the gardens of Bedford House, it was objected to by the Duke on account of the dust it would make, and of some proposed buildings which would interfere with his prospect. Bedford House stood upon the site of what is now Bedford Place, Bloomsbury Square, and was taken down about fifty years ago.

[5] Lady Caroline Petersham was the daughter of Charles, second

try[1]; he says she is a glorious creature, and handsomer than either of his three wives. The Duke of Richmond[2] has put the Prince of Nassau in possession of his house at Whitehall during his stay in England; they went yesterday together to Newmarket. The Duke of Cumberland is gone there, but is to stay but two days. I met Mrs. Admiral West[3] at Lady Cobham's on Sunday; she had then had no letters from the Admiral, and therefore gives no credit to the reports of their being put back into Plymouth.

Postscript.—From the most *genuine* authority, news is just come that the French sailed from Toulon the 9th, with twelve ships of the line, six frigates, with 16,000 men on board, three months' provision, and the Duke of Richelieu at their head; this is a stolen march,

---

Duke of Grafton, and wife of William, Viscount Petersham, who succeeded his father the 8th of December, 1756, and became second Earl of Harrington. She died in June, 1784.

[1] Maria, eldest daughter of John Gunning, Esq., and wife of George William, sixth Earl of Coventry. She died Sept. 30, 1760, of consumption, and her death was the subject of some beautiful lines, by Mason :—

> "Think of her fate! revere the heavenly hand
>   That led her hence, tho' soon, by steps so slow!
> Long at her couch Death took his patient stand,
>   And menaced oft, yet oft withheld the blow;
> To give reflection time with lenient art,
>   Each fond delusion from her soul to steal;
> Teach her from folly peaceably to part,
>   And wean her from a world she loved too well."

[2] Charles, third Duke of Richmond, K.G. He married in April, 1757, Mary, eldest daughter and co-heir of Charles third Earl of Ailesbury. He was sent Ambassador to the French Court, in 1765, and in the following year made Secretary of State. He died in 1806.

[3] Admiral Temple West was a nephew of the late Lord Cobham, being the second son of his eldest sister, Maria Temple, who married Dr. West, and afterwards Sir John Langham. Admiral West married Frances, daughter of Admiral Sir John Balchen. He was for some time M.P. for the borough of Buckingham. He died in 1757.

as the Government here expected no such attempt till the 20th; they are gone to Minorca[1]; all faces here lengthen upon it, and the greatest face of all could not forbear to take the same dimension. This is my friend and first intelligencer that has waylaid me that you might hear the news.

The news in the paper of the French ships taken is true.

MR. ELLIOT[2] TO MR. GRENVILLE.

May 25, 1756.

YE fields and woods, my refuge from the toilsome world of business! I know it well, Wotton is a perfect Paradise; who would live in London, or think of the public, who may enjoy undisturbed his plantations, his

----

[1] This is the expedition which Admiral Byng encountered at Minorca, and with which he so unfortunately declined to engage.

[2] Mr. Gilbert Elliot, second son of Sir Gilbert Elliot, of Minto. He was M.P. for Selkirk, and afterwards for Roxburghshire, and third baronet upon the decease of his father. In December, 1756, he was made a Commissioner of the Admiralty Upon the retirement of Lord Bute, in April, 1763, the Duke of Newcastle writes to Mr. Pitt:— " My Lord Bute and Mr. Fox have taken good care of their friends. A second reversion of so considerable an office as Justice Clerk of Scotland, with that which he has already of Keeper of the Signet of Scotland, a place worth 1500l. per annum, for life, seems to me to be an ample reward for Mr. Gilbert Elliot, who has also an employment of Treasurer of the Chambers, worth between two and three thousand pounds per annum." Sir Gilbert Elliot had considerable poetical talent; he was author of a beautiful pastoral song, mentioned in the notes to Scott's *Lay of the Last Minstrel*, beginning—

> " My sheep I neglected: I broke my sheep hook,
> And all the gay haunts of my youth I forsook."

In the *Bedford Correspondence*, vol. iii. p. 52, Sir Gilbert is said to have died in 1782, but other authorities state that his death occurred in 1777.

children, and his chicken-yard! Yet I must congratulate with you, that only one Peer[1] was found to speak
against a militia. Earl Stanhope[2] opened the debate,
professing his love to mankind, his devotion to the public; then took a solemn oath that, if the Bill passed, he
would accept of any commission, however low, and never
retreat from any enemy, so help him God! As he
began with an oath, he ended with a prayer.

Lord Granville spoke next; declared it was a hot
day, he would not overheat himself, nor the Lords;
the Bill was impracticable nonsense, a shoeing-horn to
faction; ridiculed the manner it passed the Commons;
he was against all militias, especially this unamended
Bill.

My Lord Chancellor[3] spoke an hour; though no
friend to foreigners, a friend to *a* militia, though an
enemy to this Bill; it was a violation of prerogative,
inconsistent with a commercial country; these were his
two points. He proved the first by asserting Clarendon
and Southampton had desired prerogative in the Militia
Act, the 14th of Charles II.; this Bill a direct repeal
of that Act, by making the consent of Parliament
necessary to call out the militia; then a panegyric
upon the King, a devout wish that his reign might be
long, and his crown not descend to an excellent young
prince, tarnished by this law. The second point: this
country consists of merchants, artificers, and country
gentlemen, all to be defended by an army; warlike ideas
incompatible with trade; in twelve years, three hundred

---

[1] John, Lord Granville.

[2] Philip, second Earl of Stanhope; died 1786.

[3] Philip Yorke, first Earl of Hardwicke, became Lord Chancellor
on the death of Lord Talbot in 1737. He resigned the seals in 1756,
and died on the 6th of March, 1764.

thousand men would be disciplined, &c.—d—— the post: the division 59 to 23[1]. The rest next post-day.

MR. G. ELLIOTT TO MR. GRENVILLE.

London, May 27, 1756.

MY DEAR SIR,—When warm from the debate of Monday, I intended to have wrote you a circumstantial account of it; I am now glad I was prevented; it is indeed not worth recording. My Lord Temple and Lord Halifax exhausted the subject on the side of Militia, and my Lord Chancellor's argument against the Bill was worthy of so great a man, one who declared that day he was no prerogative lawyer. He, too, is a friend to militia; his idea is, that it ought to consist only of 30,000 men; a fixed revenue for their pay, not to be annually voted; to depend solely on the Crown. The consent of Parliament to their being called is no doubt a violent encroachment upon prerogative. How could the House of Commons entertain so wild a project? At any time it would have been absurd, much more so under the present auspicious Administration.

This hint, it is devoutly to be wished, will be adopted next session. The accounts from abroad are very favourable; we have not indeed beat the French fleet, but Byng is very safe; he had not passed the Straits the 28th of last month. There are letters that mention the *Warwick* man-of-war being taken by Monsieur Perrier's squadron near the Leeward Islands. The merchants, who are easily alarmed, say that there are

---

[1] The Militia Bill was rejected.

near two hundred merchant ships that must now be in the power of the squadron. The letter which gives rise to this piece of news came to Gordon of Argyll Street, who has an estate in that part of the world, and for that reason the letter deserves little credit. When I leave this place is the most uncertain thing in the world; my horses, however, are set out, so I flatter myself I am already upon the road. I admired Mrs. Grenville all this winter for her strength of mind and superior understanding, but I now find she has a womanish fondness for lawns and green fields, and cannot live without her children. I love her the more for those infirmities, but I am sorry to say I admire her less. My wife begs her best respects to Mrs. Grenville; she would wait upon her at Wotton, but every day she is from her children, to be sure, she is miserable.

With regard to *other matters*, they stand, I believe, just where they did when you left London. Sir Dudley Ryder[1] dead, his patent not past; Murray, it is said, will succeed him; I know nothing authentically of it. The House adjourned this day for three weeks. The King looks well. I passed all yesterday with Lord Bute, whom I found deeply affected with the death of Bothwell, his old tutor, to whom, more from habitude than on any other account, he was much attached.

I hardly expect to hear from you; when once I go over to Scotland, on me the curtain of intelligence must drop: yet should I be pleased to hear how spring the tended plants, how blooms the shrubby grove.

---

[1] Sir Dudley Ryder, Lord Chief Justice of the King's Bench, died suddenly on the day that the Attorney General had prepared a warrant for his creation as Baron Ryder of Harrowby. After much negotiation, he was succeeded in his office by Murray, the Attorney General, who became Baron Mansfield.

On Monday the Prince and Princess go to the country. The Speaker's speech[1] was a good one, and popular. I stood up to move, or at least to express my wish, that it might be printed, but was stopped, because it seems you can only speak upon the question of adjournment. Ever, dear Sir, &c.   GILB. ELLIOT.

EARL TEMPLE TO MR. GRENVILLE.

Thursday, June 3, 1756.

DEAR BROTHER,—I desired Miss Banks to send to Mrs. Grenville such an account as I then knew of what alarms the whole town, and I fear will disgrace, if not ruin, this country.

The letter is from Monsieur de la Galissionière[2] to the Intendant of the Marine, transmitted in a copy from the Spanish Minister at Paris, to Mons. D'Abreu[3] here: it says, that on the 17th the *Gracieuse* frigate was dispatched for intelligence, which brought back an account of the English fleet which appeared in sight, I think, on the 18th, the French going out to meet them; that Byng[4] might have engaged them all the 19th with advantage, but did not seem to care for it. On the 20th Mons. de la Galissionière got the wind of him

---

[1] See Parliamentary History, vol. xv. p. 769.
[2] The Admiral in command of the French Fleet.
[3] The Spanish Ambassador in London.
[4] Admiral John Byng, fourth son of George Viscount Torrington. He had been appointed to the command of the Fleet sent out for the protection of Minorca; but having failed in the relief of that island, Byng returned to Gibraltar, and the French took possession of Minorca. Upon his arrival in England, Byng was tried by Court Martial, and, having been found guilty, was shot on board the *Monarque*, in Portsmouth Harbour, March 14, 1757.

for a very little while, it shifting in our favour very soon; that the engagement began, and lasted betwixt three and four hours, but was never general; that we attacked his rear, which was so closed that we could never penetrate; that none of our ships continued long engaged; that all the French officers behaved well; and that our fleet was out of sight on the 21st. The number of killed on board the French, I think 35, wounded 100 and I don't know how many.

These particulars I learnt from one who had read the letter, and though I may be mistaken in some little circumstance, I think I tell you pretty near the whole that I heard, and as I heard it.

We think of leaving London on Tuesday, but our motions are not always of the most certain and determined nature, therefore if Wotton continues in our scheme, you shall hear beforehand. Very late—good night. Many kind loves.

The French twelve ships of the line, with three frigates. The English thirteen, with five frigates. This news came yesterday.

MR. PITT TO MR. GRENVILLE.

Hayes, June 5, 1756.

My dear Grenville,—I know not how you hermits of Wotton may be furnished with news, or whether the printed papers will be filled with an event that will fill your hearts as it has ours.

The squadron under Mr. Byng has, after a slack and poor distant cannonade, retired from before M. Galissonière's squadron, which last is returned to its station before Mahon. Byng is gone to Gibraltar, and if his own account does not differ widely from that of the French, where he ought to go next is pretty evident. He is said to have had one ship more of the line, and to be superior in men to the French. Tyrawley[1] is dispatched to Gibraltar, to take the command of that place in the room of Fowke[2]. I dread to hear from America. Asia perhaps may furnish its portion of ignominy and calamity to this degenerate helpless country; for it is not yet quite certain where that cloud, Mr. Perrier, will burst. Quæ Regio in terris nostri non plena doloris? It is an inadequate and a selfish consolation, but it is a sensible one, to think that we share only in the common ruin, and not in the guilt of having left us exposed to the natural and necessary consequences of administration without ability or virtue. The villagers of Hayes rejoice at the good accounts of the inhabitants of Wotton, great and small. They hope the last rain has showered verdure over the walks to match the pastures of Bucks. Lord Temple goes to Stowe, Tuesday; Prince of Nassau[3] and who not, very soon. This is all at present from the most affectionate brother and sister of Hayes.

---

[1] James O'Hara, second Lord Tyrawly, succeeded his father in that title in 1724, having been previously created Lord Kilmaine, for his eminent services during Queen Anne's wars. He was a general in the army, and had filled high diplomatic appointments. He died in 1774.

[2] General Fowke was deprived of his regiment also, for disobedience of orders in refusing a regiment for the relief of Minorca.

[3] Upon the occasion of the Prince of Nassau's visit to Stowe, Lord Temple wrote some verses in praise of his beauty, and Lady Temple an acrostic on the same subject, but neither of them are worthy of quotation.

MR. POTTER TO MR. GRENVILLE.

Bath, June 11, 1756.

THOUGH the use of pen, ink, and paper is in the most positive terms forbidden, I shall trespass a little to answer your most friendly enquiries. Yet perhaps my answer will not give you much satisfaction, except from the assurances you may receive that I am yet alive, and that while I am so, my sincere respect, and let me say affection, to you and Mrs. Grenville must continue unchanged. I am still at Bath, and cannot even guess when I shall be able to leave it, though within these three days I begin to feel my forces a little recruited.

I have suffered much, and have been reduced to the very last extremity.

The gout, which had received in London such formal and full possession of my chest, seemed resolved not to be dislodged, and the repeated attacks between that and the Bath water, had almost laid the scene of action desolate. But for the present the Bath water is triumphant. My carcase is indeed miserably ravaged and harassed, and my sole business for this last fortnight has been to repair and recruit it.

The attempts of the last three days have been more successful than those which preceded, and if the same success continues, I shall flatter myself that in a few weeks I may get into my great chair at Ridgmont[1].

As to public affairs I have long considered myself as a traveller of short continuance, and therefore feel no other emotions than the greatest pity for those whose

---

[1] Mr. Potter's seat in Bedfordshire.

hearts are not yet quite so abandoned, as to be callous to the public infamy and public misery which has already begun to overwhelm us.

You may talk of pursuing your private happiness, and of shutting your eyes to those horrid scenes. But it is in vain : you are too nearly engaged, your stake in the public stock is too great to suffer you to be indifferent, and yet all efforts will be fruitless. Nothing but a miracle worked by the hand of the Almighty can turn aside the impending perdition.

Have you wrote to Dr. Hay? The newspapers have told you that he is turned out from the office of King's Advocate. What zeal is this for the public, and how intently are the thoughts of the Ministers engaged on the successes of the French.

Adieu! my dear friend; continue to me your regard, and recommend me to that of Mrs. Grenville.

THO. POTTER.

MR. PITT TO MR. GRENVILLE.

Hayes, June 16, 1756.

MY DEAR GRENVILLE,—When I parted with Lord Temple, I understood you would see him at Wotton in his way to Stowe, and by that means be as well equipped with the news of the times as I am here.

I conclude you will have met before now, and that nothing would remain for me to impart if I had the pleasure of a walk with you upon the solitary banks of your sylvan river. As to quo sit Romana loco res, I am almost as far from the hearing of it in our own suburban village, as you are in the midst of your quiet wide-spread lawn and deep embowering woods. I hear, however, from Rumour, that clouds gather on every side, and Distress, infinite Distress, seems to hem us in on all quarters. The same weak infatuated conduct that begat this distress seems determined to increase and multiply it upon our heads. We are as helpless and childish as ever, and worse still; if any among the ministry are disposed to be men, I hear they would be madmen; for the regret is that we have no continent war. So much for those at the helm; the Passengers, the City of all denominations, are in alarm, and think the ship sinking.

I am in most anxious impatience to have the affair in the Mediterranean cleared up. As yet nothing is clear, but that the French are masters there, and that probably many an innocent and gallant man's honour and fortune is to be offered up as a scapegoat for the sins of Administration.

The treatment of West[1] in particular is, without example, unjust and cruel; for as yet nothing appears but that he may be, not only blameless, but most meritorious. I am persuaded he will come out of this persecution with honour.

We go to-morrow to Ealing to pass a day or two, and from thence to Pinner. Lady Hester is still, thank God, very well, and little Hester[2] a very growing

---

[1] Admiral Temple West, " whose behaviour," says Walpole, " had been most gallant, was soon distinguished from his chief, and was carried to court by Lord Anson. The King said to West, ' I am glad to hear you have done your duty so well; I wish everybody else had.' "—*Memoirs of George II.*, vol. ii. p. 228. Admiral West died in 1757, being then one of the Lords of the Admiralty.

[2] Mr. Pitt's eldest daughter, afterwards married to Charles third Earl of Stanhope. She died in 1780.

personage in bulk and in favour, not to say in understanding.

May health and happiness attend all your paths.

W. PITT.

MR. PITT TO MR. GRENVILLE.

Pay Office, June 23, 1756.

MY DEAR GRENVILLE,—We returned this morning
from passing two or three days with Jemmy at Pinner,
and find in our way to our village the following news of
this day : a letter from Barcelona of the 1st of June
says, that that day a Lieut. Basset arrived there from
Admiral Byng with dispatches to the Admiralty from
before Mahon, where he had cruised ever since the
action of the 20th, which had ended by the French
running away and not appearing again. The Lieutenant
left the Fleet the fourth day after the action, and was
seven days in getting to Barcelona. Byng, he said, intended to disembark his troops the day he left him, in
consequence of a Council of War he had called, finding
the French did not return.

We are just getting into our post-chaise. Lady Hester
and I could not enjoy this good news with a clear conscience if we had not given our dear friends of Wotton
their share in it.

We are both well, and hope to have the pleasure of
embracing you as you go to Petworth.

W. PITT.

MR. PITT TO MR. GRENVILLE.

Aylesbury, Tuesday, July 13, 1756.

DEAR GRENVILLE,—Lady Hester and I are just
setting out for Stowe, and find it no small difficulty to
turn our steps from one wished-for object, Wotton, to
another of the same description, at so much a greater distance.   But among various reasons that have regulated
the priority of our visit to Stowe, the consideration of
passing the rough road between that place and Wotton,
but once, has had no small share.

Lady Hester has borne her journey well.   I left
London all in alarms, the French being embarking at
Dunkirk.

We propose staying a week at Stowe, and are so unreasonable as to hope it may not be impossible that you
and Mrs. Grenville may think the road thither less
formidable than we do, and that we shall have the pleasure
of being together there, before we are at Wotton.

Adieu! I hope for a very short time.   W. PITT.

———

MR. PITT TO MR. GRENVILLE.

Hayes, August 20, 1756.

DEAR GRENVILLE,—Concurrent causes have occasioned my silence about our intended expedition to
Ridgemont: first, a letter from Potter informed me of
his intentions to be in town, and to see me at Hayes
about the 15th instant.   A second, which I have received
a day or two, tells me he is obliged by business to defer
his journey to London for ten days.   Thirdly, and as
conclusively as the last of many reasons for not firing on

the enemy, the want of guns, I have been utterly unable to move for this ten days, by a very awkward, uneasy, but not hurtful malady, nor am I yet able to use my accustomed exercise. News I never attempt to write, and indeed the public papers of the same date always reach Wotton sooner than the Hayes à la main could do. General Fowke's trial has had its nine days, in the wonder of mankind: how monstrous, either the conviction or the punishment! Utrum horum: my own opinion is fully formed, as to that alternative, on a mature consideration of the several orders, and I declare that no consideration can make me find in the General wilful disobedience to a clear positive order; but at most, innocent error concerning the ill-explained intentions of Government. We are all well here (errors as above excepted), and intend that our little colony shall, God willing, receive its increase in the pure air of our village; a better world to introduce youth to, than the great world—that least and most despicable of all little things. I hope your own happy world (and let me call it ours) is in perfect health. Wotton, with all these showers, must be more than green; as we say his *Most Christian*, her most verdant Majesty must look like the Queen of all Pastures. I suppose the Bridge white, and from my couch it enlivens everything about it: deep shades of oak, softening lawns, and tranquil waters, like a lively smile lighting up a thoughtful countenance. I am growing poetical, and shall talk Phœbus very soon, so adieu.

W. PITT.

MR. POTTER TO MR. GRENVILLE.

London, Saturday, September 11, 1756.

DEAR SIR,

. . . .

I have seen Mr. Pitt and Lady Hester; they both appear in perfect health.

The point disputed between Lord Temple and you is not yet clear to my satisfaction: as yet I have not been able to consult any authorities, but what I have seen inclines to your opinion.

There is much talk of an expedition, but the Ministers, I hear, deny there is anything in agitation. Two hundred transports are now in pay, artillery is preparing, and six or eight thousand slings (such as bargemen use to tow their boats, and with which soldiers draw cannon when horses cannot be used) are ordered forthwith. It is said, too, the Hanover troops are in motion. Some think the Ministers mad enough to attempt the retaking Minorca at this season. Others suppose it is calculated merely to stop the current of clamour, by pretending to do something.

The King of Prussia has certainly taken possession of Leipsic, and published his manifesto against the Elector of Saxony. Nothing is talked of but the high spirits of Mr. Byng and the Duke of Newcastle, though I was told this morning that his Grace, being on a visit a few days since to Lady C. Pelham [1], was somewhat alarmed at the indignation of the Greenwich mob, who saluted his Grace with dirt, and humbly proposed to his coachman to drive towards the Tower.

---

[1] Lady Catherine, widow of the Right Hon. Henry Pelham.

This morning I heard the whole city of Westminster disturbed by the song of a hundred ballad-singers, the burthen of which was, " to the block with Newcastle, and the yard-arm with Byng." Their music alarmed my devotion enough to draw from me many a hearty Amen. I repeat it again here, and as I think it very probable that a letter from me to you will be opened at the Post Office, in order to inform his Grace what my dispositions to him are, I will subscribe my name in capitals. It is then no other than that of his determined enemy, and your determined and very affectionate friend,   THOMAS POTTER.

MR. PITT TO MR. GRENVILLE.

Hayes, October 10, 1756.

DEAR GRENVILLE,—Lady Hester is as well as can be in her situation, after being delivered of a son[1] this morning, who is also well. She had a sharp time, but not longer than two hours and a half.

There was notice enough to have Hunter and all comforts about us. My joy, my dear Grenville, will so easily be imagined by one who experiences so many, that I will rather commit it to your thoughts and feelings than to my own words. Dear Lady Hester is so happy with her offspring, that her spirits would easily run away with her, if not beyond her strength, at least beyond the seasonable discretion of the sagest of the Sybils, Mrs. Tyson.

Mrs. Grenville, I am sure, and perhaps you, will excuse my talking nursery: the young man meets with

---

[1] Afterwards John, second Earl of Chatham.

general applause for stature and strength : Nurse Creswell looks with satisfaction, and Nurse Long with envy, upon his quality and quantity. He is, however, as they flatter me, without appearance of heaviness, notwithstanding his size. I hope to have the satisfaction of adding soon a good account of Lady Hester in the critical time of her confinement.

I hope this will find all Wotton in perfect health.

I am, &c.   W. PITT.

(In the handwriting of Earl Temple.)

MINUTES upon Memory of a Paper dated October 15, 1756, laid before the KING by LORD GRANVILLE from Mr. FOX [1].

SOME months ago Mr. F. told the D. of N. that he believed Mr. P. would not be induced to come into the K. service, at any rate without being S. of St. ; and that if that was his M——y's pleasure, Mr. F. was ready to resign. Lord Bar—, ten days ago, came to Mr. Fox, to put him in mind of that conversation, and said that if the D. of N. thought it could be done without offending Mr. F., he would make an offer of it to Mr. P. the next day. To which Mr. F. said he thought it extremely right, and that he was perfectly willing ; that Mr. F. now hoped that negociation with Mr. P. was in great forwardness, being the only thing could be of service in his M. affairs ; that Mr. F. found his credit in the House of Commons sensibly diminished for want of authority there, and therefore, as he found it impossible to carry on the King's business, begged his Majesty's leave to resign it ; and that if his Majesty thought him worthy

---

[1] See *Harris's Life of Lord Hardwicke*, vol. iii. pp. 69, 76.

in that arrangement of any inferior employment not of the Cabinet, he was ready to accept it, and would support the King's measures to the utmost of his power, and give his best assistance thereto.

LETTER TO LORD CHANCELLOR
(inclosing the above paper).

I SEND you the inclosed paper, as it has probably given you the trouble of coming to town from Wimpole. At the time of Mr. Pelham's death I saw the impossibility of the plan then proposed; and when I took the seals in consequence of his Majesty's orders, I obeyed them with the greatest unwillingness. How I have behaved since, both to the King and the D. of N., I leave to the D. of N. to relate. I hope now the negociation is in great forwardness with Mr. Pitt, as it is the only party the King can take for the service of his affairs. I feel no resentment: if I had any ambition, the course of last summer would have completely cured me of it, and all possible resentment must be over with my ambition. I could speak to the D. of N. upon this subject with as much ease as any other man whatever. Some things, about the time of Mr. Pelham's death, made me angry, which I do not care to call to mind. I think it of consequence, as I cannot be of any further service to the King's affairs, that I should resign immediately, that it may not look like a struggle for power. I do not only say that under that arrangement I will support, but I will do it to the utmost of my power, and in any station I will support the King's measures in Parliament to the utmost of my power, except the measure of governing the House of Commons under the D. of N., which I need not mention, because the impossibility of it excepts itself.

This paper delivered to the D. of Bed., Marl., Waldegrave, Devonshire, &c.

Two or three subsidiary treaties concluded, not shown to F. to this day.

Lord Bute says Fox submitted to have the business of his office done by Holdernesse.

Resign.

MR. WILKES TO MR. GRENVILLE.

St. James's Place, October 16, 1756.

DEAR SIR,—After the two spirited pamphlets which I had the honour of sending to you by the last post, I own I feel some reluctance in inclosing the present vile political trash. It is indeed of the very worst kind, for it is a number of Gazettes printed together in an 8vo. pamphlet. I have, however, religiously observed your commands and have sent it, but I really pity you, who have to wade through so much dirt, and thank Heaven it is well over with me. The public indignation is rising very strong against Lord A., and Byng has now everywhere some warm advocates, from an idea I hope of his innocence, at least a less degree of guilt, and not from the natural inconstancy of this, and I believe every other country. *Poor Byng* is the phrase in every mouth, and then comes the hackneyed simile of the *Scapegoat*.

I have wrote this post to my tenant Dell, to give all possible dispatch to the survey, estimates, &c., he is preparing.

I return into Buckinghamshire the week after next, only for two days, but one of them I give to the feoffees of Aylesbury, and I hope at that meeting to settle with them the affair of the Stone Bridge Road, so far as my dominions extend; and I take myself to be one of the most powerful princes of your country. I hope to live to say rather of *your county;* for though we Bucks have been nobly represented at Naples, we have been most scurvily represented at Westminster.

The letter to Mr. Pitt I could not send to the post till Thursday noon; for my coach broke down with Mr. Freeman and myself between Berkhampstead and St. Alban's, our honours were laid in the dirt, and we forced to do penance there all night.

We moralized much how chequered life is, and thought it contrasted well with the agreeable evening we had spent at Wotton the day before.

I have not yet received the necessary informations to regulate the assize, &c. of bread: as soon as I hear, I must beg your advice and assistance.

Every *brochure* shall be regularly sent to Wotton. I wish I could be of any real service to you here: it would be the greatest pleasure to me, for I am, with gratitude and esteem, &c., &c.   JOHN WILKES.

I beg my respectful compliments to Mrs. Grenville.

MR. PITT TO MR. GRENVILLE.

Hayes, Sunday, October 17, 1756.

DEAR GRENVILLE,—I received this morning a letter from Lord Chancellor, dated yesterday, at Wimple: his Lordship desires, with civil excuses, that I will give him the meeting on Tuesday next, in the forenoon [1]. Though

---

[1] See an account of the conference and negotiation with Mr. Pitt, in Harris's *Life of Lord Hardwicke*, vol. iii. p. 77.

I expect our conference will be short and final, considering the negative I go resolved to give to any plan with the D. of N. at the head of it, as well as to any proposal for covering his retreat, in case he wishes to retire from being Minister; yet as it is impossible to be sure, in the present state of things, how far his Majesty may be brought to open his eyes, I beg of you, as I do of Lord Temple, to be in town Tuesday evening, at my house in Brook Street, where I may receive your lights and final determinations as to any ulterior conversations with the Court, should they be proposed.

I am resolved to go to this conference without previous participation with Lord B. I will report the issue afterwards: this, I trust, you will think right. We are all well, and most affectionately yours and Mrs. Grenville's.

LORD HILLSBOROUGH TO MR. GRENVILLE.

North End, October 26, 1756.

MY DEAR SIR,—I was very much disappointed, when I came to your house yesterday morning, to find a letter only. "Think," says Queen Dollalolla, "what must be the sun's surprise rising to see the vanished world away. How greater far the wretched wife's, when stretching forth her arms to fold thee fast, she folds her useless bolster in her arms!" You make up a little for this bilk, however, in so kindly pressing us to make use of one of your bolsters on Friday, but if we do it that night, we shall be forced to leave it on Saturday, because I, who am an excellent courtier, must kiss the Princess's hand and the fair Augusta's on Sunday. We therefore resolve to be with you on Tuesday next, if that be agreeable to Mrs. Grenville and you; but if it is not, we beg you to let us know, and we will come on Friday, though but for a day.

I have ventured to contradict what I heard yesterday reported in town, that Mr. P. had insisted upon Seals for himself; Lord Lieut. of I. for Lord T.; Paym. for you, and something else for J—— ; in short, to make a family Administration. I am sure that this is false; and I thought I, being penetrating, saw the design of propagating such a report. Be all this as it will, though I am no Cato, I do from the bottom of my heart sigh, " O ! my country ! "

Lady Hillsborough[1] sends you and Mrs. Grenville her best compliments; I hope she will honour me so far as to accept of mine.

I am sorry you will not be a Minister, for I might then find my account as well as gratify my inclination in being, My dear Sir, &c., &c. HILLSBOROUGH.

MR. CHARLES JENKINSON[2] TO MR. GRENVILLE.

Bond Street, November 15, 1756.

SIR,—I was at your door a few days ago to pay my respects to you, and I imagined I should yesterday have

---

[1] Sister of James, first Duke of Leinster, and first wife of Lord Hillsborough. Their eldest daughter was the Marchioness of Salisbury, who was unfortunately burnt at Hatfield House, in 1835.

[2] Afterwards first Earl of Liverpool. This very eminent gentleman, so distinguished for his talents and for the political influence which he exercised during the greater part of the reign of George III., was indebted for his success in public life to the introduction of Mr. Grenville, at whose recommendation he became Private Secretary to Lord Bute, and in Mr. Grenville's Administration he was made Secretary to the Treasury. His numerous letters to Mr. Grenville in this

met you at Court, when I should have troubled you with an affair which I am now obliged to make the subject of a letter. I am conscious how unreasonable I am in what I am going to propose, but as I do not mean to trouble you with an application, but only to beg that you would represent a case for me, I hope you will pardon the freedom I take.

Upon some mention that Lord Harcourt[1] made of me to Lord Holdernesse, the latter was so good as to employ me both at his own house and in the Secretary's Office, without any profit or emolument to myself, but with the design alone of instructing me in foreign affairs and the business of that office, and qualifying me for anything of which my friends might hereafter think me worthy; and as it is commonly supposed that Mr. Pitt will dismiss Mr. Amien[2] and Mr. Digby[3], who

collection, show the unreserved and confidential intercourse which existed between them for many years. He came into Parliament for Cockermouth, in 1761, and was a Lord of the Admiralty in 1766, and a Lord of the Treasury in 1767, being then Member for Appleby. He was also for a time Secretary at War, and President of the Board of Trade. He was elevated to the Peerage as Baron Hawkesbury, in 1786, and advanced to the Earldom of Liverpool, in 1796. He died in December, 1808, in the 80th year of his age. The title became extinct by the death of his son, the late Earl, in 1851.

[1] Simon Harcourt, second Viscount and first Earl of Harcourt. He was for some time Governor to George III., when Prince of Wales, and he was sent Ambassador to demand the hand of the Princess Charlotte of Mecklenburgh Strelitz, in marriage, for George III. In 1772 he was made Lord Lieutenant of Ireland, and in 1777 he was accidentally drowned in the park at Nuneham, his seat in Oxfordshire.

[2] Claudius Amyand, Under-Secretary to Lord Holdernesse, as Secretary of State, and M.P. for Sandwich. In December, 1756, he was made a Commissioner of the Customs.

[3] At this time M.P. for Ludgershall. He succeeded his brother as seventh Lord Digby, on the 30th of November, 1757, and was advanced to the British Peerage in 1790, by the title of Earl Digby. He died in 1793.

are Under-Secretaries in the Southern Province, and perhaps Mr. Rivers, who under the name of Interpreter of Southern Languages, has also acted as an Under-Secretary, I should think it a high honour to serve Mr. Pitt in either of those employments, and should be obliged to you if you would only mention my name and situation to him, in case he should want anybody in those stations. I mean on this occasion not to use any kind of interest to which I cannot pretend, but so far only as the representation of the case, and the little experience I may have acquired in the Secretary's Office, by serving as a volunteer in it, may recommend me; and as to my political sentiments, or any other qualifications of which it would be improper to speak myself, I must refer you to Lord Harcourt. Excuse this trouble from,

Sir, Your most obedient humble Servant,

CHARLES JENKINSON.

LORD HARCOURT TO MR. GRENVILLE.

Cockthrop, near Witney, November 21, 1756.

SIR,—Whatever may be the effect of your generous and friendly endeavours to serve Mr. Jenkinson, it is impossible for me not to take the earliest opportunity of thanking you for so extraordinary an instance of your goodness to a young man, whom you have already laid under an everlasting obligation.

The awkward situation I have been in has made it impossible for me to serve him, though I have wished to do it, because I know he is a very deserving man. If he should be so fortunate as to succeed to the employment you have recommended him to, I should hope

that his abilities and application will recommend him to
Mr. Pitt. But whether Mr. Jenkinson does, or does
not succeed, yet your uncommon goodness to my friend,
and the great regard which you have shown me upon
this occasion, will make me ambitious of deserving your
friendship, on which no one can set a higher value than,

Sir, &c., &c.   HARCOURT.

MR. JENKINSON TO MR. GRENVILLE.

Bond Street, Tuesday (November 30, 1756).

SIR,—I send you with this some papers which I drew
up at the latter end of last summer for the use of Lord
Harcourt, upon a subject [1] which has of late been
thought of great national concern: I will beg of you,
therefore, to honour them with your perusal, and if you
would favour me with your opinion upon them, whether it
may be of service at present to commit them to the press
as they are, or with any alterations, or whether I should
throw them wholly into the fire, it will be acknowledged
among the many other favours I have received from you,
by Sir, your obedient Servant,   C. JENKINSON.

EARL TEMPLE TO THE DUKE OF DEVONSHIRE [2].

4 o'Clock, December 1, 1756.

MY LORD,—I am much concerned to hear that some
words now stand part of our Address to which there are

---

[1] Mr. Grenville has endorsed this letter as referring to a Pamphlet
about the Militia. The Pamphlet was published by Mr. Jenkinson,
about this time; it is entitled, *A Discourse on the Establishment of a
National and Constitutional Force in England.*

[2] The Duke of Devonshire was now first Lord of the Treasury,

the highest exceptions; I mean that part in which we are to thank His Majesty for bringing over his Electoral troops, the various improprieties of which are so striking, that it seems the whole Cabinet, at which I had the great misfortune of not being able to attend, unanimously declared against them [1]. It imports me so much to take a public part against them, that if it be possible for me at any rate, I will go down to the House of Lords to-morrow, and lay my thoughts before them in the fullest and clearest manner; and if I should not be able to do it then, I will take the first opportunity I can of dis-culpating myself and my own honour. This is a very unfortunate step at the outset, and such a one as Mr. Pitt and I judge will tend to the speedy dissolution of a system of which I cannot make a part longer than I am able to prove myself consistent with myself.

I feel very unhappy at being obliged to give your Grace this trouble, but it is very unfit for me, in my present state, to attend so much to business as to write even thus much, but I cannot resist such sensations, and I am sure I owe it to justice, and to the frankness

---

[1] Lord Waldegrave, in his *Memoirs*, p. 89, alluding to this part of the Address, describes it as " a compliment of mere decency, His Majesty having ordered them over at the request of both Houses of Parliament. But the new chief of the Admiralty (Earl Temple) was of a contrary opinion; he came, as he told the Lords, out of a sick bed, at the hazard of his life (indeed he made a most sorrowful appearance), to represent to their Lordships the fatal consequences of the intended compliment. That the people of England would be offended even at the name of Hanover, or of foreign mercenaries; that the thanks pro-posed might raise suspicions that a total change of measures was not intended, which would break that harmony and union now so happily established. He added many other arguments of the same kind, with-out mentioning the true reason of his disapprobation, namely, the Duke of Devonshire's having added this compliment without consulting him."

and sincerity your Grace has always treated me with, to apprize your Grace of my intentions the very first moment I can.

Excuse the confused manner of my writing, and be assured that I am, with the highest degree of respect and esteem, My dear Lord, &c., &c.   TEMPLE.

MR. JAMES GRENVILLE TO MR. GRENVILLE.

(December 2, 1756.)

I SEND the King's Speech inclosed with my copy of the Address. The former I must beg the favour of you to let me have early to-morrow morning, as I have no other copy of it, and must show it to Sir John Phillips [1] about ten o'clock. Nothing made a bad figure at the meeting, in my opinion, but the change in the line of battle, from Lord Granby [2] to Mr. Sandys [3]; an immense fall by way of anticlimax.

Mr. Yorke [4], I find, has been wearisome and loquacious, and no more: but of this no farther than just between us.

THE DUKE OF DEVONSHIRE TO EARL TEMPLE.

London, December 2, 1756.

MY LORD,—My time was so much taken up last night that it was impossible for me to acknowledge the receipt

---

[1] Sir John Phillips, afterwards M.P. for Pembrokeshire; he died in June, 1764. His son was made Lord Milford, in the Peerage of Ireland.

[2] John, Marquess of Granby.

[3] Edwin Sandys, M.P. for Bossiney.

[4] Charles Yorke, second son of the Earl of Hardwicke.

of your letter. I am very sorry to find your Lordship
has such difficulties in regard to the words proposed in
the Address to thank His Majesty for bringing over his
Electoral troops. I could have wished them out, because I think there is an impropriety in thanking the
King for bringing over his troops, and taking no notice
of their going back at a time when the danger is very
near as great : on the other hand, your Lordship will
forgive me if I own that I do not see any great objection
to merely thanking the King with having complied
with the advice of his Parliament.

Your Lordship is, however, most certainly the best
judge where you think your own honour concerned;
and I shall only add, that it will give me great concern
to see a system that I flattered myself might be a means
of preserving this country, and restoring it to a state
of tranquillity, demolished upon a point of this sort.

I am, with great truth, my dear Lord, &c.

DEVONSHIRE.

MRS. GRENVILLE TO MR. GRENVILLE.

Saturday, December 4, 1756.

. . . .

THE times have been a little feverish, as you will find
from Mr. James Grenville, who, I hear, intends to make
part of his journey this evening, after the House of
Commons, if no new event happens to prevent him,
but lest any should, I will not omit telling you that
Mr. Pitt did not kiss hands yesterday. A report prevailed that the Address of the Commons was to be

altered, corresponding to that of the Lords[1], which made it necessary for him to go down to the House and suspend accepting the Seals, but the motion was not made, and I hear he takes them to-day, if no extraordinary step again puts it off.

A spurious copy of the King's Speech has been carefully circulated, I hear, both in town and country, and the Lords were summoned this day to deliberate upon it: some of the printers or hawkers have been taken up[2]. I have taken great pains to get one to have sent you, but have been unsuccessful. Mr. Pitt is not quite so well to-day as he has been. Duke Hamilton[3] is better. I will carry my letter in my pocket till the last moment, in order to fill it with anything I can pick up, though I do it with less ardour, as you will hear everything from your brother.　.　　.　　.　　.　　.

Mr. Pitt[4] has kissed hands, was received very graciously, and all the others have likewise kissed hands, except Potter[5], who I fear is ill; but for all farther accounts I refer you to Mr. James, who will arrive to-morrow, but is not yet set out.

[1] The clause of thanks for having sent for the Hanoverians, which had been inserted in the Address from the Lords. " Mr. Pitt," says Walpole, " went angry to Court, protesting that he would not take the seals if any such motion passed: it was sunk."

[2] George II. said that if the printer was to be punished he hoped the man's punishment would be of the mildest sort, because he had read both, and, as far as he understood either of them, he liked the spurious speech better than his own.—*Waldegrave's Memoirs*, p. 89. The spurious Speech was burnt by the common hangman, in Palace Yard, on the 8th of Dec., 1756, in the presence of the Sheriffs, &c.

[3] James, sixth Duke of Hamilton, married the beautiful Elizabeth Gunning. He died January 17, 1758, and his widow was remarried to Colonel Campbell, afterwards Duke of Argyll.

[4] Mr. Pitt kissed hands this day for the office of Secretary of State.

[5] Mr. Potter had been appointed Joint Paymaster of the Forces.

MR. PITT TO MR. GRENVILLE.

(December 12, 1756.)

THE Bill proposed to be moved to-morrow is, to quarter the Hessian troops during their *continuance here*, and *until their departure*. I understand you will find the country gentlemen quite for it. George Townshend[1] is eager for it. You need not fear the stay of the Hessians here[2]. You might depend that I should not have given into this matter, if I had not seen the ground clear. The Court, perhaps, rather look on this step as a slur than as a favour. Good night. Ever yours,

W. PITT.

EARL TEMPLE TO MR. GRENVILLE.

Tuesday, December 14, 1756.

DEAR BROTHER,—Will you be so kind as to call here[3] to-morrow morning, that Mr. Cleveland[4] may explain to you some matters relating to the 55,000 men which are to be voted to-morrow? Hay and Elliot[5] are

---

[1] Afterwards Viscount Townshend.

[2] " Mr. Pitt is not yet able to attend the House, therefore no inquiries are yet commenced. The only thing like business has been the affair of preparing quarters for the Hessians, who are soon to depart ; but the Tories have shewn such attachment to Mr. Pitt on this occasion, that it almost becomes a Whig point to detain them. The breach is so much widened between Mr. Pitt and Mr. Fox, and the latter is so warm, that we must expect great violences."—*Walpole Correspondence*, vol. iii. p. 262.

[3] At the Admiralty ;—Earl Temple was now first Lord.

[4] Secretary of the Admiralty.

[5] Dr. Hay and Mr. Gilbert Elliot had been made Commissioners of the Admiralty, and not yet re-elected. " Mr. Fox," says Walpole, " has already skirmished his borough (of Stockbridge) from Dr. Hay, one of the New Admiralty." Fox writes to the Duke of Bedford, " I have set up my Lord Powerscourt at Stockbridge, and will certainly keep out Dr. Hay there." Dr. Hay was, however, re-elected.

out of Parliament, so the Treasurer of the Navy [1] will please to protect his affectionate brother,   TEMPLE.

MR. PITT TO MR. GRENVILLE.

Wednesday, December 15, 1756.

DEAR GRENVILLE,—I desire you will tell Mr. Legge [2] and Lord Barrington [3], that I strongly recommend to him to keep the words, the *said* foreign troops, and to adhere inflexibly to maintain the Bill throughout, relative only, and confined to the exigency that demands the immediate provision, referring the consideration of the general policy of foreign troops at large, to its proper and only time and place, the approaching Mutiny Bill.

This ground I know to be so tenable, that Fox's attempt to gravel us will be baffled, and his *strong sense*, as White's may think it, concerning Dutch, &c., to come in summer, the poorest stuff that ever was uttered.

I wish I could put on a shoe to hear you to-day.

Your ever affectionate   W. PITT.

MR. POTTER TO MR. GRENVILLE.

Prior Park, January 6, 1757.

DEAR SIR,—I have heard of Lord Temple and Mr. Pitt: the first tells me he is in perfect health, and the latter that he is in a fair way of being so. But I hear

---

[1] Mr. Grenville had succeeded Bubb Dodington as Treasurer of the Navy.

[2] Now Chancellor of the Exchequer.

[3] Now Secretary at War.

nothing of you and Mrs. Grenville, and yet there are none in whose happiness I am more interested. If you can spare a minute, use it to gratify my impatience on that subject. As to myself, I am a little patched up by the waters; for aught I know, I may lay up stock enough of health to last in London for one whole week. More than this it is chimerical to expect. Mr. Pitt commands me to protract my stay 'till he sends for me, and he has engaged that he or you will give me notice of the first day on which business is expected. When I receive this intelligence I shall be glad at the same time to receive a hint of the particular business likely to be agitated. I shall hold myself in the readiness of a Prussian soldier, to march at a minute's warning. Would to God my arm was as strong as my heart is willing. Do me the favour to peruse the inclosed memorandum. The request is not a great one, and, for reasons which hereafter I will tell you, must be complied with. I had rather it should be done on your letter to the Comm^r. of Portsmouth, than on one from the Admiralty. Your faithful and affectionate,

THOS. POTTER.

I have taken a house in Hanover Street.

SIR HENRY ERSKINE[1] TO MR. GRENVILLE.

Pall Mall, April 1, 1757.

DEAR SIR,—You wish to know the occurrences of the times, and after all the bustle which we have had, you will be surprised to hear that those who told us we had

[1] Sir Henry Erskine, M.P. for Crail, &c., and a Lieut.-Colonel in the Army.

no Administration, have not been able to make out the representation of a ministry[1]. 'Tis doubted whether or not Lord Egremont[2] will accept of being Secretary of State; most people say he has refused: he is gone to Petworth. His Royal Highness the Duke set out this morning for Germany. The command of the forces is left with Sir John Ligonier. All our friends have, I believe, resigned. You will ask about Charles Townshend: I cannot learn if he is amongst the number of the resignees, but I have reason to think he has not as yet the honour of that distinguished body. The City talk of making Mr. Pitt the present of his freedom. There is a terrible combustion there. The new, or, if you please, the future Administration, are trying if they can get the money, but they have not as yet proposed their terms. Mr. Dodington, 'tis said, is to be Treasurer of the Navy. Mr. Fox is to be First Lord of the Treasury, and Chancellor of the Exchequer after the Session is over; and Lord Hillsborough is to succeed Charles Townshend if he makes room for him. But many sensible people seem to think the Administration will go no farther than it has gone. The Duke of Newcastle is at Claremont, and to continue there 'till Parliament meets.

Lord Dupplin[3] was told at first by Mr. Fox, that he

---

[1] See *Walpole Correspondence*, and Notes, vol. iii. p. 281.

[2] Charles, Earl of Egremont, was eldest son of Sir William Wyndham, by Katherine, second daughter of Charles, Duke of Somerset. He succeeded, by special remainder, to the Earldom of Egremont, upon the death of his uncle, Algernon, Duke of Somerset. Lord Egremont married Alicia Maria, daughter of George, Lord Carpenter. He was Secretary of State when he died suddenly in August, 1763.

[3] Thomas Hay, Viscount Dupplin. He was at this time M.P. for the town of Cambridge. He soon after became Chancellor of the Duchy of Lancaster, and was appointed Ambassador Extraordinary to

was to have his Lordship's employment, and afterwards
wrote him a letter that His Majesty had dispensed with
his taking it at least at present. His Lordship is
angry, and gone to the country. Even down to Lord
Barrington, all Ministers, and under Ministers, are
gone into the country for the holidays. The Minister-
makers at Arthurs' are gone to Newmarket, and there
is such a scarcity of members that I begin to be afraid
of walking the streets lest the press-gang for Ministers
should seize me and force me into office.

Please to present my respects to Mrs. Grenville.
The enclosed print is new : you, perhaps, may understand, though I don't. I have, &c., &c.

H. ERSKINE.

EARL TEMPLE TO MR. GRENVILLE.

(April 4, 1757.)

DEAR BROTHER,—Little did you expect to be called
from all the dirt of Wotton to the cleanly and delect-
able operation of resigning an honourable and lucrative
employment, yet such is your hard fate.

Before you can receive this, I shall, like another
Damien, be hanged, and drawn, and quartered, after
having been kept alive upon the rack for some days.
The black funereal Earl of Winchilsea, succeeds me[1],
accompanied by Lord Hyde, Sir W. Rowley, Admirals
Boscawen and Mostyn, Hamilton and Sandys[2]. Sir F.
Dashwood has had it offered to him, and Forbes they

Portugal, having succeeded his father as eighth Earl of Kinnoul. He
died in 1787.

[1] As first Lord of the Admiralty.

[2] See *Walpole Correspondence*, vol. iii. p. 281, *note*.

meant to have, but the King would not hear of it. Elliot by a kind indulgence may likewise stay, if he pleases. Further than this is not yet settled, at least as we can learn. I am to receive my letter of dismission to-morrow. The D. of N., it is said, remains as you left him. What to-morrow will produce, and to-morrow, and to-morrow, I know not: I only know that all the friends mean to throw up I believe on Thursday, so you may be in town early enough for so delightful a function. How this has come to pass and so forth, you know almost as well as I do; perhaps your brother Egremont has writ you this most terrible news by Saturday's post, and then what I tell you has not even novelty to recommend it. The world is at a gaze, and, when they wake from their astonishment, I fancy the new-fangled nonsense will go to pot. Love to Mrs. Grenville, and, my dear Treasurer of the Navy, good night.

EARL TEMPLE TO MR. GRENVILLE.

Friday, 12 o'clock (April 8, 1757).

DEAR BROTHER,—I kept your servant 'till now in order to be the better able to satisfy that curiosity which is as inseparable from a country life as it can possibly be from a town one. My journal is as follows :—On Tuesday Lord Holdernesse came to me with the dreadful tidings, much offended himself at not being let into a word of this matter 'till the day before; the enemy expected this would bring on a general resignation, and the whole upon a personal footing ; but we were wiser, to the great surprise and concern of our antagonists : so, behold, on Wednesday night, Lord Holdernesse performs, in person, upon the body of Mr. Pitt the same operation as upon mine. Yesterday Jemmy resigned, and, to my great grief, Mr. Potter, who I think has been too precipitate ; though I must tell you that on Wednesday Mr. Fox informed Lord Dupplin that he was to kiss hands as Paymaster General next day, which, however, has not happened.

Legge gives up his seals this morning. The Admiralty now in possession are Winchilsea, Rowley, Boscawen, Martyn, Carysfoot, Sandys, Elliot, that is our Elliot, who has declined, and his place to be supplied by Hamilton[1], if the borough of Petersfield says yea.

Your brother of Egremont is, I believe, destined to be another Pitt. In this state matters now stand. The Duke of D. to continue till the end of the session. Lord Mansfield to hold the Exchequer Seals, as Lord Chief Justice Lee did before[2].

Offers without end to the Duke of Newcastle, who not only stands his ground, but I have now the utmost reason to think that his union with us is as good as done, in which case Foxism must go to the devil, which that it may, is the sincere prayer of your most affectionate brother upon this very good day, commonly called Good Friday.

As for your own resignation, it may keep cold till your return. Love to the coachfull. The freedom of the City in a gold box is thought of for Pitt: the clamour very great.

---

[1] William Gerard Hamilton, so well known by the sobriquet of *Single Speech*, at this time M.P. for Petersfield.

[2] It is usual for the Exchequer seals to be committed to the care of the Lord Chief Justice of England, until the new Chancellor is appointed.

Rapacious Fox has got the reversion of Dodington's Irish place for his life, and his son's. Peerages, it is said, for Digby and Shelburne.

The Duke not gone.

Lord Hardwicke out of town. Anson eager against the new system, &c., &c.

MR. GRENVILLE TO THE EARL OF HOLDERNESSE.

Wotton, April 9, 1757.

My Lord,—I beg the favour of your Lordship to represent to His Majesty in the most dutiful and respectful manner my humble request that he will permit me to lay at his feet my commission as Treasurer of the Navy, with which His Majesty was graciously pleased to honour me. The present situation of the public affairs sufficiently explains the reasons of my giving your Lordship this trouble, and makes it unnecessary for me to detain you any longer than to assure you that I have the honour to be, with the greatest regard,

My Lord, &c., &c.   GEORGE GRENVILLE.

THE EARL OF HOLDERNESSE TO MR. GRENVILLE.

Arlington Street, April 11, 1757.

Sir,—Having laid your letter, by which you desire leave to divest yourself of your office of Treasurer of the Navy, before the King, His Majesty has directed me to acquaint you that he is graciously pleased to accept of your Demission. I am, &c., &c.

HOLDERNESSE.

MR. HORACE WALPOLE[1] TO MR. GRENVILLE.

Arlington Street, May 13 (1757).

DEAR SIR,—I flatter myself that you have goodness enough for me, to excuse the liberty I am now taking.

The ridiculous situation of this country for some months drew from me yesterday the inclosed thoughts[2], which I beg you will be so good as to run over and return.

As it certainly was my intention, so it has been my endeavour, to offend no man or set of men: it most assuredly was my desire to give no umbrage to you or your friends, and therefore I will beg you freely to tell me if there is the least expression which can be disagreeable to you or them.

The paper is a summary of melancholy truths, but which, as my nature is rather inclined to smile, I have placed in a ridiculous light. If it should not displease your good heart, or should divert Mrs. Grenville for a moment, I should be happy; but I must beg the return of the inclosed copy, as I go out of town early to-morrow.

I am, &c., &c.   HOR. WALPOLE.

MR. JENKINSON TO MR. GRENVILLE.

London, June 30, 1757.

DEAR SIR,—I cannot deny myself the pleasure of wishing you and Mrs. Grenville joy upon the final con-

---

[1] On the death of his nephew, in 1791, he became Earl of Orford; or, as he sometimes styled himself, "Uncle to the late Earl of Orford." He died in 1797.

[2] I had stated that these "Thoughts" were probably never printed. They are, however, to be found in the 4to edition of Horace Walpole's Works, vol. i. p. 205, under the title of a "Letter from Xo Ho, a Chinese Philosopher at London, to his friend Lien Chi at Pekin."

I have to express my obligations to the Right Honourable John Wilson Croker, who has had the kindness at the last moment before

clusion that was yesterday put to our confusions, when Mr. Pitt kissed His Majesty's hand upon being again possessed of the seals; and I hope and trust that his superior genius will be able to keep the various links of this chain together, and, like the Jupiter of Homer, by having hold of one end of it, he will be able to properly direct and support every part of this system.

We have no news since the accounts received on Monday of the Duke's having passed the Weser, and the small loss sustained in his retreat; but I wish that he may not soon be driven further back into the Electorate by the superior force of the French.

We have also to-day a report that the Empress Queen has recalled Coloredo[1] without taking leave, but I know nothing certain about it, and from the improbability of the affair, I suspect the truth of it. I beg my respects may be presented to Mrs. Grenville, and I have, &c., &c.

CHARLES JENKINSON.

MR. JENKINSON TO MR. GRENVILLE.

London, July 1, 1757.

DEAR SIR,—Very soon after I wrote to you on Thursday night we received by the Flanders mail the first account of two very disagreeable pieces of news— that of the Prince of Bevern being defeated by Marshal Daun, and that of Prince Charles with a considerable body of troops having broke out of Prague and defeated that part of Marshal Keith's army that opposed him: and this news has since been confirmed by the Dutch

publication to point out the error into which I had fallen, and thus enable me to correct it.

[1] The Austrian Minister.

mail, and by a letter from Mr. Mitchell[1]: I need not trouble you with the particulars of these unhappy disasters, the papers are possessed of the greatest part of them; the King of Prussia acknowledges the bravery of his troops, and imputes the ill success to his own rashness, and indeed his uninterrupted successes seem to have inspired him with too great an opinion of the infallibility of his troops, which induced him to make this fatal attack upon the Austrians, who were in a very strong post, fortified with all the art of Marshal Daun, who, I find, is so much esteemed for his knowledge in the science of war, as to be at the head of the Military Academy at Vienna; we wait with impatience for a farther account of this affair and of its consequences; there have been various reports to-day of there having been a second action to the advantage of the Prussians, and some letters from Holland mention it, but there is no authentic account come of it, and I fear there is very little credit to be given to it.

I must also add that what I mention of Coloredo's departure is true, he having applied for a pass for that purpose.

After this public news permit me to mention something domestic which will surprise you. Mr. Fox is to be opposed at Windsor by Sir James Dashwood, and there is so much danger that they have sent for the Duke of Marlborough[2] express about it.

---

[1] The British Minister at Berlin.

[2] George, second Duke of Marlborough, K.G., a military officer. He distinguished himself at the battle of Dettingen. He was subsequently appointed to the command of an expedition against the French Colonies. He died of a fever, in October, 1758, at Munster, in Westphalia, whither he had gone in command of the British forces, under Prince Ferdinand of Brunswick.

I ask pardon for troubling you with the perusal of three tedious pages, and for presuming to send these scraps of news to you who receive so many more particulars from so much better hands; but I know not what impulse drives me to lay hold of the most trifling occasions of showing the sense I have of your favours, and of convincing both yourself and Mrs. Grenville how very much I am and ever shall be, &c., &c.

CHARLES JENKINSON.

MR. JENKINSON TO MR. GRENVILLE.

London, July 9, 1757.

DEAR SIR,—I am extremely obliged to you for the letter with which you was pleased to honour me, and for your indulging me in the pleasure of giving you still further trouble.

This day a mail arrived from Holland, but it brought no letters directly from Bohemia; all the accounts we hear are from the Hague, which much diminish the action of Kaurzim, and reduce the sally from Prague absolutely to nothing. There being no letters directly from the King of Prussia makes it probable that he is busily engaged in marches, and that he is resolved as little as possible should be known of his defeat until he had done something to retrieve it.

The news from the Duke is that the French have not as yet passed the Weser; that they threaten much and do but little; that they talk of attacking His Royal Highness, but that he is so posted that he does not apprehend so much from them; and your judgment is certainly right, that the success of the Austrians will not make the French accelerate their motions.

The town has speculated much both yesterday and to-day upon the Government having taken up 15,000 ton of transports; various, as you may imagine, are the opinions of the uses that are to be made of them, but every one expects and hopes that they will be employed upon some action of vigour.

I should ask your pardon for sending you a wrong piece of intelligence in my last letter, but being told by the Marlborough family that Sir J. Dashwood was to stand at Windsor, I thought I might rely on such intelligence : Bowles, however, was the man ; he had most of the independent on his side, and most of the Beauclerc interest. Fox spent as much money as he could in so short a time, but carried it at last by a great majority. I am satisfied that the Duke of Newcastle and his friends wished most sincerely that he might not succeed.

I had agreed with Lord Harcourt to meet him at Nuneham on Saturday or Sunday next, that we might go over to Wotton together ; but I presume that the same cause which prevents your stirring from home will make it inconvenient for you to see any one, so that I suppose his Lordship will now put it off till after the increase of your family.

Between sun and dust we pass a wretched time of it at present in London ; I presume you must feel some ill effects from it in the country, and I fear the sun has diminished the beauty of your lake by his late potations. As the weather, however, has grown hot, the political world seems to have cooled, and mankind seem in general to be in tolerable temper : I hope most sincerely that they may long continue so, and that a summer of success may add glory to Mr. Grenville's family, and security and content to the public. I beg my respects to Mrs. Grenville, wishing her a boy or a girl as she may like best, and for the sake of the world that it may be as like her as it can be. I have, &c., &c.

CHAS. JENKINSON.

MR. JENKINSON TO MR. GRENVILLE.

London, July 19, 1757.

DEAR SIR,—On Saturday last the Duke of Marlborough, Sir John Mordaunt, Generals Conway and Cornwallis, were sent for up to town to receive their orders; the three last are to have commands in the designed expedition; twelve regiments it is said are designed, three only as yet have received their orders, viz., Lord Home's, Hodgson's, and one whose name I forget; these are all of the Chatham department, and are to march from thence to-morrow to embark. There are also four horse transports taken up, which are designed, I suppose, principally for carrying the officers' horses, and those of the Artillery.

The French try to alarm us with bad news from America, and of their having defeated our fleets there; I believe we need not, however, be apprehensive of this; more credit may perhaps be given to a report that the several French fleets that left Europe this spring, having met at a general rendezvous, had proceeded to block up the port of New York, where they detain Lord Loudon, and prevent his going out to meet Holbourne. It is not supposed, however, that they have troops enough on board to do any mischief by landing; but the worst misfortune seems to be that when Holbourne comes to their relief, it is doubtful whether he may have force sufficient to ascertain success, unless the French should have left some of their men-of-war at their islands for the protection of their commerce. A large reinforcement, however, under Mr. Boscawen, is supposed by this time to be not far from America. A French East Indiaman taken by some privateers, of which you will see the particulars in the papers, is supposed to be worth two hundred thousand pounds.

This day we received a mail from Holland, and some letters from thence say that the French have passed the Weser, but there is no account come as yet directly from the Duke : I forgot to mention that the troops designed for the expedition are to assemble on the Isle of Wight, and it is said that the dispositions of most of the camps are to be changed.

We were alarmed last night with what we thought was an earthqake. I felt a very severe shock as I was sitting at my lodging, but it proves to have been a powder-mill blown up near Epsom. I have, &c., &c.

CHARLES JENKINSON.

MR. JENKINSON TO MR. GRENVILLE.

London, July 21, 1757.

DEAR SIR,—You will be glad to hear that all our apprehensions in relation to Lord Loudon[1], and all the French pretences to victory, are without foundation : yesterday the New York packet arrived, and brings word that Lord Loudon had sailed out of that port with ninety-one sail of transports and five men-of-war, and that they were

[1] Commander-in-Chief of the British forces in America.

out at sea proceeding with their voyage with the greatest
prospect of success; and that Lord Loudon (as he had
wrote word before) had detained the packet boat until
he could send this account; and as it is supposed that it
could not be many days after this that he must have
joined Holbourne, and as any French fleet coming from
the Islands must have probably been to the southward
of him when he left New York, and as our fleet must
continue advancing on to the northward, it is to be
hoped that there is not the least reason to fear their
meeting each other, till our fleet becomes so strong as to
make such an event desirable.

A large train of Artillery, consisting of cannon as
high as 24-pounders, is embarking; platforms for batteries, and even hay for the horses that were to draw
them, are also put on board, and the public seem to be
extremely pleased with the secrecy and spirit of this enterprise. I have, &c., &c.   CHARLES JENKINSON.

MR. JENKINSON TO MR. GRENVILLE.

London, August 4, 1757.

DEAR SIR,—I have had the honour of both your
letters, and should have answered the first sooner
if I had not been absent for a few days from London.

I left Lord Harcourt at Nuneham on Tuesday, where
he proposed to stay until to-morrow, but when he
meant to return I cannot tell: he usually spends four or
five days there in every fortnight, and as I have let him
know of your intention to wait on him, I am sure he
will hurry his return there, and will send a servant over

to Wotton to let you know it. I am only sorry that the uncertainty of his being there will prevent my being able to meet you there, especially if it should be on Monday or Tuesday next, as it will be impossible for me to know it time enough.

To make one amends, however, for this loss, I shall wait on you at Wotton with Lord Harcourt, who will take, I know, the speediest opportunity of returning your visit, and who is determined to trouble you for two or three days when he comes, and had directed me, when I left him on Tuesday, to find out when Mrs. Grenville would be well enough to make it agreeable to you to see us.

I must now be the transmitter of ill news. On Tuesday an account arrived to Baron Munchausen[1], from Hanover, of the French having attacked the Duke, and forced him to retreat. There are no letters come as yet from the Duke or any of his people, which makes us think the defeat the worse, and the confusion the greater: the letters from Hanover say that there are 800 Hanoverians killed; as to the loss of the other corps, it is not known. The Hessians are said to have behaved well. The Duke sent to Hanover to let them know that they must take care of themselves, as he was no longer able to protect them. Colonel Keppel is so ill in Hanover that he will be taken prisoner; the rest of the Duke's family are well. We wait hourly for more particular accounts of this affair[2] and its consequences, though Heaven only knows in what way they are to get at us.

Boscawen is extremely angry upon his being sent for

---

[1] The Hanoverian Minister.
[2] The Battle of Hastenbeck.

home : he has also received a letter of dismission ; he complains that this is a private pique of Mr. Pitt's, and assigns as the cause thereof his opposition to the Navy Bill : he talks in short like a man who has lost a good cruise, and wants to raise a disturbance ; but whether it will go so far as to make him resign his seat at the Admiralty Board I cannot as yet find out.

Believe me, &c., &c. CHAS. JENKINSON.

MR. JENKINSON TO MR. GRENVILLE.

London, August 9, 1757.

DEAR SIR,

. . . .

We had yesterday letters from the Duke of the 29th ultimo. The action was not decisive as we at first apprehended ; the loss does not exceed 1200 men, and it is hoped that His Royal Highness may, on a proper occasion, be able to put his fortune to another trial. He continues with his right to the Weser, and when he is forced to quit that river he will, I suppose, cross over to Stadt, and pass the Elbe there.

Between you and I a great many people complain here of the Hanoverians not doing their utmost to defend their country : their not having raised any irregulars, or disciplined any of their people at a time when troops of that sort must have been of great service in distressing the French, and hindering their advances. The French have done a very unusual thing in recalling their general, Marshal d'Estrées, in the midst of a campaign ; the cause assigned for his disgrace is, that he being a great friend of Marshal Belleisle had shown some countenance to his son, the Duke de Gisors, in preference to the Prince of Soubize, upon which the latter, both jealous and angry, has constantly represented Marshal d'Estrées as dilatory, and not pushing the war with the vigour that he ought, to Madame Pompadour, in whose favour the Prince of Soubize has the honour to be ; and this all-powerful lady, under this pretence, has got this disgrace cast on M. d'Estrées, and has transferred Marshal Richelieu into his command. A letter is come to a merchant of Bristol from a place near Halifax, giving an account of the arrival both of Loudon and Admiral Holbourne at that place, and of the latter having had the success to take transports containing 1000 French troops. This we hope to be true, though it does not come immediately from Halifax itself, and though there is no letter for the Government.

What a long letter have I wrote you, and how is your goodness to me repaid with torment to yourself. I will presume, however, to add one observation, though they are commonly the dullest part of dull letters. I fear that the change the French have made in their generals will prove to our disadvantage, for Marshal Richelieu, to justify the choice and alteration that has been made, will probably push on the war with the greatest vigour, and there seems to have wanted that alone to have made their superior force already more successful. I have, &c., &c.   CHAS. JENKINSON.

MR. PITT TO MR. GRENVILLE[1].

St. James's Square, August 11, 1757.

DEAR GRENVILLE.—The calamitous state of affairs has brought several distressful questions on the carpet among the King's servants here. My colleagues have declared for sending a body of British troops to Germany to reinforce the Duke. This, together with other inadmissible measures, has been (thank God) effectually withstood, but such has appeared, to my judgment, the exigency of things since the loss of a battle, and of the Electorate in consequence, that I have advised a present supply in money, in order to provide for a melancholy and cruel interval, till Parliament shall meet, lest the beaten army retired, and still retiring under the Duke, should want the necessary for a temporary subsistence. In this view a warrant is directed on the million for 100,000*l.*, and one for 20,000*l.* to the Landgrave, now a fugitive at Hamburgh, with the princess[2] his daughter, lodged in an inn, and without provision for a table.

This concession I have judged advisable to make upon the grounds of a fatal necessity, to the best of my understanding quite irresistible.

I wish extremely it could have been in my power to have consulted you, as I intended, before I took the step; but the moment of decision pressed upon me in such a manner as to render that impossible.

I trust that you and Lord Temple will be of opinion,

---

[1] See Mr. Grenville's reply to this letter in the *Chatham Correspondence*, vol. i. p. 243.

[2] Princess Mary, fourth daughter of George the Second, married in 1740, to Frederick Prince of Hesse.

upon fully weighing the whole extensive consideration, that I have not done wrong. My own lights, such as they are, assure me I have made the only tolerable option, in so violent and urgent a crisis ; but, be that as it may, your disapprobation will render me unhappy. My affectionate compliments to Mrs. Grenville, and joy to hear she and the young lady are so well. I am ever, &c., &c. W. PITT.

CAPTAIN GEORGE BRYDGES RODNEY[1] TO MR. GRENVILLE.

Dublin, before Rochelle, September 23, 1757.

MY DEAR FRIEND,—Hearing the present expedition was a plan of our Friend's[2] was the great motive that induced me to be upon it, notwithstanding the very ill state of health I have been in for some time past, in hopes I might contribute something towards making his Administration what I most sincerely wish it to be.

I have the pleasure to acquaint you that the beginning has been successful. On the 21st we made the land, but it being thick weather the pilots would not take charge of the ships, which obliged us to anchor in the sea, between the islands of Rhè and Oleron. On the 22nd, late in the night, we got into the Road of Basque, and this morning Vice-Admiral Knowles with

---

[1] George Brydges Rodney, descended from an ancient family long settled at Rodney Stoke, in Somersetshire, and a very distinguished ornament of the British Navy. In 1762 he was made a Vice Admiral, and created a Baronet, January 22, 1764. In 1782 he obtained a complete victory over the French fleet, commanded by the Admiral Comte de Grasse, for which service he was elevated to the Peerage on the 19th of June in that year, by the title of Baron Rodney. He died in 1792.

[2] Mr. Pitt.

his squadron, had orders to attack the island and citadel of Aix. Captain Howe, in the *Magnanime*, led, and behaved with such cool and steady resolution, as has (most justly) gained him the universal applause of Navy and Army; notwithstanding the enemy kept a constant fire from several batteries for thirty minutes, he never returned a shot 'till such time he anchored his ship within fifty yards of the fort, and then kept so terrible and continual a fire for thirty-five minutes as drove them from their batteries, and obliged them to submit before the other ships of the squadron could get into their stations; but that you may not be led into a mistake concerning the other ships, I must acquaint you that they were ordered to keep half-a-mile astern of each other, to give time for anchoring and to prevent confusion.

General Conway is in possession of the citadel, and I hope to-morrow morning we shall be able to land the army in an advantageous place, a number of proper officers being this night employed in reconnoitering the shore for that purpose. Rochelle will likewise be bombarded this night or to-morrow morning. Accept this as a token of the very sincere respect I shall always bear you, and believe me to be, &c., &c.   G. B. RODNEY.

CAPTAIN RODNEY TO MR. GRENVILLE.

Dublin, off the Isle of Aix, September 29, 1757.

DEAR SIR,—The hasty letter I wrote to you on the 23rd instant, and the account I therein gave you that further operations would immediately succeed the taking the Isle of Aix has proved without foundation, the time that should have been employed in execution having been mis-spent in holding Councils of War. At last 'tis concluded to return, I hope with approbation, the Isle of Aix being certainly a very considerable conquest, not only in regard to its strength (which was one of Vauban's best forts), but likewise as it will for the future prevent the enemy from assembling their convoys in this port.

I have the pleasure to assure you, that the scheme for taking this place and Rochfort, will, if inquired into, bear the strictest examination, and prove to the whole world, 'twas wise, prudent, and well-timed. I shall conclude with assuring you I am most sincerely, &c., &c.

G. B. RODNEY.

MR. ELLIOT TO MR. GRENVILLE.

October 6, 1757.

THOUGH we have letters this day from the Fleet, I can hardly promise to give you any satisfactory account of their proceedings. Upon the 23rd they entered the Basque road, which is very safe, and sufficient to contain the whole fleet and merchantmen of England. The *Magnanime*, Captain Howe, and *Barfleur*, Captain Greaves, attacked very gallantly the fort upon Aix; in half an hour after their ships were placed, they silenced its guns and carried the place: they made 600 prisoners, and have destroyed the fortifications.

They suffered little themselves, except in their masts and rigging, though the fort mounted 30 guns. This action was performed on the 25th. The Admirals in the mean time sounded the coast, and found two landing-places, near the mouth of the river, which they declared to be very practicable : from the 25th to the 28th Councils of War were held : a disposition was once made in order to land, but in the issue it was resolved not to land, but to return to England : we don't hear any enemy appeared. They seem to have thought that though they might land with safety, yet it might be hazardous to get off again in case they were pressed. They also seem uncertain whether the ditch, which is the only fortification on one side of Rochfort, was wet or dry; in the first place they think it could not be forced, in the other it might be.

The Fleet is daily expected. Thus ends the expedition.

MR. JENKINSON TO MR. GRENVILLE.

Whitehall, October 6, 1757.

DEAR SIR,—My negligence has been so great in respect to yourself that I am almost ashamed to ask your pardon ; and nothing but the presumptuous confidence that I have in your goodness could make me do it, and, to confess the true cause of my fault : all the while the mysterious business of the neutrality was transacting, between unwillingness to send you uncertain intelligence, and the diffidence I had of every piece of news I heard concerning it, I delayed writing from post to post, until I at the last found myself in the scrape I am at present in.

Having thus made my confession, I shall beg leave to inform you, that the Fleet under Sir Edward Hawke is arrived off the Island of Rhè, and the troops are landed on a little island called l'Isle d'Aix, where the large men-of-war that go up to Rochfort leave their cannon and military stores. This news came first by the Flanders mail, and has since been confirmed by the way of Holland; it is said that our troops found no opposition in their landing there, and that they have since that been equally successful in passing over to the Continent; that there are no troops of any consequence in that part of France, and that there are about two thousand men in Rochfort.

You were surprised I do not doubt at the unexpected retreat of the Russians: the cause of it is not as yet known, and among the various ones that are conjectured at, the most probable seems to me that they are under some alarm from the Turks.

We expect every hour to hear something of consequence from the King of Prussia, and if he should be successful against the Prince of Soubize, as one really flatters oneself that he will by means of Marshal Lewkald's army, he should be able to so far reinforce his troops in Silesia as to give a check to the Austrians, what a surprising revolution this would be in his favour, after all the desertions he has met with.

I beg my compliments to Mrs. Grenville, and hope that after all my negligence you will permit me to subscribe myself, &c., &c.

CHAS. JENKINSON.

Have you seen the comet[1]?

---

[1] The comet now visible was declared by Dr. Bradley not to be the comet whose return, at this time, had been predicted by Dr. Halley. The latter, however, did appear at the beginning of the year 1759, and was visible in England for some months. Its revolution being performed in about seventy-six years, it appeared again in 1835.

MR. JENKINSON TO MR. GRENVILLE.

Whitehall, October 8, 1757.

DEAR SIR,—Penitents for a short time are always very good, and sometimes, perhaps, a little troublesome; though I may incur the censure, I cannot help acquainting you that we are all here both surprised and concerned at the return of our Fleet without doing anything of consequence[1]. I know not what Sir Edward Hawke's account is of this affair, but the contents of Sir John Mordaunt's letter I understand to be, that after two of our ships had silenced the enemies' batteries on the island of Aix, and though found stronger than we expected, it was surrendered to us; that then a Council of War was held to fix on a proper place to land the troops on the Continent, and that such a place was there determined on, and that after that another Council of War was held, to consider whether they should land or no, and that this was then determined in the negative, and that they should return home. All this is past comprehension, and we are at a loss to assign any reasons for such conduct, and by what I can find, the King, the Administration, and the public, are equally surprised and concerned at it. We wait with patience the arrival of the Generals in town, to hear what causes they can produce for what they have done, or rather for what they have not done.

[1] The sudden return of the Fleet from Rochfort was the cause of great discontent, and it was not imputed by the people generally to the misconduct of the officers. It was considered that this pacific disposition was only a preliminary for the Convention of Stade, and to get better terms for Hanover. It was reported that an express had been sent after Hawke, and that immediately, in consequence of it, orders had been given not to land the soldiers.—*Chatham Correspondence*, vol. i. p. 277.

Our accounts from Germany give us to understand that the Russians continue still to retire with precipitation, though as yet we know not the cause of it.

The King of Prussia has not as yet attacked the Prince of Soubize, and we fear from thence that he has met with some unexpected difficulties. I have, &c.

CHAS. JENKINSON.

MR. JENKINSON TO MR. GRENVILLE.

London, October 11, 1757.

DEAR SIR,—I had the favour of your obliging letter yesterday, and I now send you what farther particulars I have been able to pick up of the late unhappy miscarriage.

Sir Edward Hawke, who is come to town, disculpates himself, and says that he was always ready to have performed his part, and to have lent the sailors that were to have assisted the land forces in the assault upon Rochfort. I do not find that they pretend to say that they found the coasts stronger or any ways different from what it was represented to them before they left England; and what is remarkable, Captain Howe went in his yaul to the coast, landed there with an officer and two sailors, and each with a musket in his hand walked above two miles up the country, entered into several of the houses, gave an alarm to a little fort that fired upon them, but saw no troops, and returned, without any obstacle, to their yaul; and Colonel Clerke, who was the principal engineer, said in my hearing to-day, that he saw no troops on the coast; and yet, after all this, the only excuse that I can hear alleged for a delay of six

days, and for coming away at last, was the difficulty of
landing; and when they cannot pretend to say that there
was anything that could prevent them, they urge that
there might be troops concealed, which might not have
discovered themselves till they were sure of destroying
them.   But all this might as well have been supposed
at Spithead, and upon as good foundations.   Alas! Sir,
this affair will make us the ridicule of all our neigh-
bours, and by what I have heard Foreign Ministers say
to-day, I am confident it is the subject of many a face-
tious dispatch this evening; and when one considers the
uneasiness of the better sort of people at home, and the
readiness of the lower sort to rise on every occasion, I
own the prospect makes one tremble.   Happy are you,
Sir, that have a subject that can call off your thoughts
from these reflections.   We have no news from Germany: it is imagined that the Duke must be landed,
though we have not heard of him.   I have, &c.

CHAS. JENKINSON.

I hear that the King gave Sir Edw. Hawke a good
reception, and Sir John Mordaunt an indifferent one.

CAPTAIN RODNEY TO MR. GRENVILLE.

Dublin, Portsmouth, 13th October, 1757.

DEAR SIR,—As I find the Post Office has thought
proper to detain the letters that were sent from the
officers of the Fleet employed on the late expedition, I
fear those I did myself the honour to write to you have
met with the same fate; not that I shall be least concerned at what was contained in them, as I can prove

every assertion to be truth; neither can I ever be brought to think but that the most sanguine expectations might have been answered, had the spirit of His Majesty's instructions been vigorously and speedily executed. This from him who longs to hear how yourself and family are, and who is with real sincerity and respect, dear Sir, &c., &c.,   G. B. RODNEY.

MR. JENKINSON TO MR. GRENVILLE.

London, October 18, 1757.

DEAR SIR,—I had yesterday the honour of your obliging letter, and can most sincerely assure you that I take a great pleasure in executing any commands that you are pleased to give me; but before I tell you any more particulars of our unfortunate armament, I must acquaint you how difficult it is to get at the detail of facts with any certainty, for I have already heard different officers tell the same fact in so different a manner, that no allowances could bring both relations within the bounds of truth. As to Mr. Howe, I find that all agree that he, the principal Engineer, and two more, were ashore, that they were near Fort Fouras, that a sentinel challenged them, and fired upon them, but the distance is at present very much disputed, and though the first story I sent you I heard from very good authority, I am now told that Howe says they did not go above 400 yards. I find it also acknowledged as true, that though by Mordaunt's orders it appears that he intended they should land immediately upon their coming upon the coast, yet that he then called a

Council of War, which sat no less than sixteen hours;
and that after all this, during the next five days, no preparations were even made for landing, none of the
cannon or stores were got into the cutters, neither
were the very mantelettes fixed to the boats that they
were to land in, 'till so late on the 29th that they had
hardly time to do it; on that night also, the General
quitted the *Ramillies*, and went aboard the *America*,
designing to land themselves from her, and it was from
some resolution they took there, that they ordered the
troops back to their transports. As to what passed in
the Councils of War it is difficult as yet to know, as
Cornwallis is not yet come to town, and Conway came
but the day before yesterday. I find however that they
consisted of the admirals and the senior captain, and
the general officers, and the senior colonel, which was
Howard. I believe it is also certain that Conway protests
that he was for landing both at the first, and also on the
29th; and if his friends are to be credited, he thought
the scheme very practicable; and by a letter I have
received from a person who has seen several of the
regiments since their landing, I find it to be the general
opinion of the officers that the scheme would have succeeded at first, but think it would not have done on the
29th. The number of French troops that were on the
coast is a point that is very little agreed on: I have
seen no one that pretends to say that they saw any
camps, but an officer has assured me that he saw some
regiments exercising on the shore, as well horse as
foot; and yet accounts from France say that all the
force they had was six regiments of Gardes des Côtes,
and two of regular troops, of all which, two regiments
were at Rochelle, two at Fouras, and four at Rochfort:

it is also affirmed that the King of France said at his levée: "By this time the English are in possession of Rochfort, and it will cost me thirty millions of livres to repair the injury they will do me;" the sum seems rather extravagant. I do not hear a word of batteries on shore, but they saw them every day enlarging their works at Fort Fouras. The point the generals rest their defence on, is the difficulty of retreating to their ships, in case there had been a superior force; but to this it is answered, and universally allowed, that if they had taken Fouras, they might have retreated in defiance of any number of troops, and they might have made a trial of what they could do there, before any troops could come to attack them: this fort was weaker towards the land than the sea, so that it was the business of the land forces rather than the sea, and yet the pilot engaged to run a ship so near to the fort as to batter it with success if they would venture her being run ashore: this fort once taken, it was thought that nothing would then oppose them up to Rochfort.

Having been so tedious upon this unhappy affair, I will mention what I have yet to say in as few words as possible. You heard perhaps on Saturday night, or else permit me to surprise you with telling you now, that the Duke[1] has resigned all his employments: the cause is, the displeasure of the King upon account of his conduct in Germany, but what has particularly passed between the King and him since his return I know not.

We hope that the King of Prussia will show the French that they are to be beaten; but if he does not, we cannot think that they will besiege so very strong a

---

[1] The Duke of Cumberland.

place as Magdeburgh so late in the year with 16,000 men in it. I have, &c. C. JENKINSON.

MR. ELLIOT TO MR. GRENVILLE.

October 18, 1757.

I SEND you, my dear Sir, the reasons of the Navy Board, which I had copied a great while ago, and, as you rightly conjectured, forgot to transmit to you. I wrote to you last post a long letter upon the expedition, which I had the prudence to throw into the fire. I cannot yet venture to trust my pen with that subject: I can only say that after having carefully perused the Councils of War, letters, &c., and also held many conversations upon the subject with those who were present and privy to all that passed, I still remain unable to comprehend the reason why nothing was attempted. I can make no doubt but the commanding officers have two great a regard for their character not to attempt the clearing up this hitherto unexplained proceeding.

The resignation of a great personage is at present the general topic.

CAPTAIN RODNEY TO MR. GRENVILLE

Portsmouth, October 19, 1757.

DEAR SIR,—Yesterday I was favoured with yours of the 13th, from Wotton, and imagined you was in the country, by my not having the honour to hear from you sooner, as I waited with some impatience at this important crisis, having a great deal to communicate to you, had time permitted me to have seen you (but for an hour) in town, which I was fully determined to do, had you been in London; now 'tis too late, as Sir Edward Hawke is come to Portsmouth, and we sail to-morrow or next day at farthest.

The author of the detracting pamphlet called the " Genuine Account," has mixed truth with falsehood; but as to the dissension at the Councils of War (if any), he cannot be a judge, unless 'twas from the extraordinary length of them, which made people conclude that variety of opinions prevailed therein. This, I can assure my friend, that though he will find my name to the first Council of War, 'twas on this single point only, viz., that Rochfort could not be taken by escalade, if *pallisadoed, or a wet ditch.* This opinion of mine was grounded upon the opinion of all the generals and engineer, that no place *so provided* could be taken by escalade. As I was totally unacquainted with the nature of land attacks, I hope you will think I was obliged to depend upon the judgment of those who were supposed to be masters of their profession; but I must beg you will take notice that I was far from the opinion that Rochfort could not be taken or destroyed by other methods, or that the troops should not land; for, from the first to the last, I continued firm in that resolution, nor could I ever see any cause to alter it.

What will be your surprise when I tell you that the Isle of Aix surrendered the 23rd, at two o'clock in the afternoon, and the Council of War (which ought to have been held that moment, if necessary) was not summoned 'till the 25th. To me it appeared astonishing, as by my letter to you of the 23rd you will know what I thought ought to have been done instantly; and so certain did it appear to me at that juncture, that I had prepared all the boats and troops on board the *Dublin*, to be ready at daylight to obey the signal, which I expected would then be made for landing the troops[1]. What infatuation prevented our taking that happy opportunity when the enemy were totally unprepared to dispute the landing, I am as yet at a loss to know.

The malicious reports, propagated with a design to mislead the minds of people, are without the least foundation of truth[2], the *Viper* sloop of war being the only vessel that brought despatches during our stay in the road of Basque, which despatches were published in the Gazette of the 13th instant. Vide Mr. Pitt's letter to Sir Edward Hawke.

I could say much more to you on the propositions I made to the Commanders-in-Chief, in regard to distressing the enemy by taking the Isle of Oleron, if they would not land on the main; but as my opinion was not then regarded, and as I should be unwilling to fall in your esteem by talking of myself, I shall conclude this long epistle with assuring you that I am most sincerely, Dear Sir, &c., &c.   G. B. RODNEY.

P.S. I have the pleasure to tell you my health is restored; hope you and all your family are perfectly well. On my return from this cruize I hope to see you, when you shall know the whole of this unhappy affair.

---

[1] See Captain Rodney's letter of Sept. 23, *ante*, p. 207.

[2] The alleged secret pacific instructions before mentioned. Horace Walpole and Lord Chesterfield refer also to these reports, which were evidently very current at the time.

CAPTAIN RODNEY TO MR. GRENVILLE.

Portsmouth, 21st October, 1757.

FORGIVE me, my dear Sir, for being thus impertinent in troubling you with my letters, but as you were pleased to tell me you should always be glad to hear of every occurrence that happened in the Fleet, I cannot help telling you the surprise that an alteration in the command of the Fleet destined on the present cruize occasioned, as it seems to bear the appearance of reproach, and points out as delinquents the junior Admirals that served on the late expedition.

Yesterday they received orders to remain at Spithead, to make room for Vice-Admiral B—s—n to command in the second post. We cannot refrain from thinking that avarice has in a great measure been the motive to these alterations, and that the good of the public must be subservient to private emolument ; for can it be possible to imagine that two Admirals are sufficient to command thirty sail of the line, when the unhappy man[1] who suffered last spring laid his misfortune to the want of a third officer, and the enemy we are now in hopes of meeting have three at least.

The hope of prize-money, and the unwillingness to have others partake with them, seems to have banished true honour from the breast of those who ought to prefer it to every other consideration, and contributes likewise to discourage officers in general, as it contributes to prevent their promotion to that rank they hope (by their services) to obtain.

Forgive me, my dear Friend for thus unburdening my bosom to you, and you alone, who I am well assured

[1] Admiral Byng.

have the honour of your country at heart, and must sincerely despise those whose minds are so very corrupt, that, even in a military capacity, they can prefer wealth to honour.

I cannot refrain from making you acquainted with an anecdote worth your notice, as it will more clearly give you an insight into men. On a *certain* expedition the Commander-in-Chief applied to the Admiralty to appoint him a first Captain, that he might be better enabled to perform the important service he was going to execute; their answer acquainted him that the Order of Council ordained that Admirals commanding twenty sail of the Line should always have two Captains, but that his fleet was composed only of sixteen. The present Fleet is composed of thirty sail, but neither has the Admiral applied, or the Board thought proper to appoint a first Captain. The motive you can guess when I tell you the first Captain ranks and shares as a Rear-Admiral.

However I make no doubt but we shall give a good account of the enemy, if we are so fortunate to meet with them, and hope I shall ever prove myself worthy the friendship you are pleased to honour me with, and am, Dear Sir, with the utmost sincerity, &c., &c.

G. B. RODNEY.

P.S. We are now getting under sail.

MR. WILKES TO MR. GRENVILLE.

Great George Street, Saturday,
October 22, 1757.

DEAR SIR,—I wished extremely to have paid my compliments to you the two last posts, but I found it impos-

sible. Ever since I have been here I have been surrounded with Milton's evil spirits, beseeching and besieging me. This is my first hour of leisure, which I
most cheerfully dedicate to you ; as cheerfully as an
honest man can enjoy life in the present public calamity.
There is the most general discontent I ever knew, and
every person I converse with, of all parties, seems to be
under the dread of something very terrible near approaching. Party is almost annihilated, and we all look
up to the holy Theban band, as alone capable to avert
the impending ruin. The City will take the lead, and
will address the Throne. Great interest is making to
ward the blow, but it will be ineffectual. The publication of Mr. Pitt's letter [1] has done him infinite service,
and mankind do justice to his singular merit. The
truth is now generally known, and the saddle laid on the
right Ass. We are much diverted here with a plain
blue coat, and a modest uncockaded hat; only we are
apprehensive that the French will take this opportunity
of invading us, now we are deprived of our great
General [2]. Poor Britain ! and yet scarce one of her
sons seems sensible of so important a loss. Hawke has
been frequently in the city, and has sent his banker and

---

[1] To Sir Edward Hawke and Sir John Mordaunt. It was said that
Sir Edward had secret instructions to return to England by the end of
September. Mr. Pitt's letter directs that notwithstanding any such
instructions he is to continue with the Fleet such a further time as
may be necessary for the completion of the intended operations, after
which they are to return in the manner before directed. See a good
account of the Secret expedition in the *Gentleman's Magazine* for 1757,
p. 456.

[2] An allusion to the Duke of Cumberland, who had resigned all his
employments on the 15th instant, in consequence of his cold reception
by the King, after having concluded the Convention of Stade, or, as
it is oftener called, the Treaty of Closter Seven.—See *Walpole's Memoirs
of George the Second*, vol. iii. p. 60.

others to the Exchange, who have abused Mordaunt in the grossest terms. "Mordaunt fills the trump of fame, Gazettes are crowded with his name," &c., &c., the whole from Swift will make an excellent parody for Monday's balladins.

If I can get a printer to venture his ears, you shall have it at Wotton.

Lord Lincoln[1] proposes to send for Clive[2] from the East Indies, as we have not one fighting man here. I beg my compliments to Mrs. Grenville, and am with the sincerest gratitude and respect,

Dear Sir, your most obliged humble Servant,

JOHN WILKES.

MR. JENKINSON TO MR. GRENVILLE.

Whitehall, October 22, 1757.

DEAR SIR,—I send you what few circumstances I have been able to pick up, since I troubled you last, relative to our unfortunate expedition. A very sensible officer told me that he thought he very soon saw that General Mordaunt[3] had lost himself, and that the world

---

[1] Nephew and heir to the Duke of Newcastle. His mother was Lucy, daughter of Thomas, Lord Pelham, and sister to the Duke of Newcastle and Mr. Pelham, and he married his cousin Catherine, daughter and co-heir of the latter. She died July, 1760. He succeeded to the Dukedom by special remainder, in 1768, and died in 1794.

[2] Captain, afterwards Lord Clive, who was now at the commencement of that splendid career in India, which has since immortalised his name. "One of those extraordinary men," says Walpole, "whose great soul broke out under all the disadvantages of an ugly and contemptible person."

[3] Walpole gives a somewhat similar account of Mordaunt at this time. "Mordaunt had been remarkable for alertness and bravery, but

was mistaken in his character; that he grew peevish; that he talked of the affair they were going about as a very sharp piece of work, and particularly on the night they were to debark. He said that he believed that it was the greatest attempt that England had made since the days of Edward the Third. General Conway also by no means answered the idea that had been entertained of him, though he was better than the other two; and it is remarkable that not one of the generals went out to reconnoitre the shore all the time they were off the coast, until about five hours before they were to debark, when Conway went. The distance that Captain Howe and Colonel Clerk walked on the shore was two miles, as I sent you word at first; the last of these gentlemen told me so himself just now. The same person assured me that there was no occasion to have stopped to have taken Fouras, and that after taking Rochfort, for facilitating their retreat, they might have sent a couple of battalions for reducing Fouras, which would have been sufficient. In short, this gentleman, who was the only Englishman upon the expedition who had been before at Rochfort, and of course was the only person that knew anything of the matter, is clearly of opinion that the attempt was easy to be executed.

I have the pleasure also to inform you that the world here is totally satisfied with Mr. Pitt, and the publication of his letter[1] has thoroughly wiped off the scan-

was much broken both in spirit and constitution, and fallen into a nervous disorder, which had made him entreat, last year, not to be sent to America, lest it should affect his head, and bring on disorders too familiar to his family."—*Memoirs of George the Second*, vol. iii. p. 46.

[1] See *ante*, p. 223, *note*.

dalous aspersion that had been published in relation to the recall of the Fleet.

We expect every hour an account of the death of the Empress of Russia[1], she having been taken so ill, that there was not the least hopes of her recovery.

The Duke has kept retired in an ill humour at Windsor, until this day, when he came to town on account of the celebrity[2].

The Hanoverian Regency and His Royal Highness are very much displeased with each other. There is no talk of giving away his regiment.

I forgot to mention that when Conway was presented, the King spoke to him, but he did not to Cornwallis[3]. I have, &c.
                                        CHAS. JENKINSON.

MR. JENKINSON TO MR. GRENVILLE.

Whitehall, October 27, 1757.

DEAR SIR,—By a Cartel ship, arrived from Calais, we have an account that the plague had broken out at Lisbon, and that orders had been given to prevent the entrance of the ports of France to any ships that come from that most unfortunate city. Though we hope that this affair is not quite so bad as it is represented, yet our ministers have been very busy all last night and to-

---

[1] The Czarina did not die before 1762.

[2] The Coronation-day.

[3] Colonel Edward Cornwallis, brother to Lord Cornwallis. He was M.P. for Westminster, and a Groom of the Bedchamber. Walpole says of him, that he was " as cool as Conway, and as brave, and indifferent to everything but to being in the right. He held fame cheap, and smiled at reproach." He died in 1776.

day, considering of proper regulations to prevent its being communicated to this kingdom.

A commission is to be given to Sir John Ligonier to command the Army; and this circumstance, as well as others, makes me think that there is no probability of a reconciliation between His Royal Highness and the King, and, indeed, the friends of the former are extremely angry with the latter; they say that he has a mind to throw the blame of the loss of the Electorate upon His Royal Highness, and they talk in rather an indelicate manner on the occasion. I have, &c.

CHAS. JENKINSON.

MR. PITT TO MR. GRENVILLE.

Hayes, October 29, 1757.

DEAR GRENVILLE,—I can begin this short epistle by imparting the happy news of the alarming report concerning Lisbon being disproved, letters having come from that place of as late a date as the 14th, which mention nothing of any distemper raging there. Our glad tidings, my dear Grenville, are confined to the class of negatives; and when so spoiled a game as the public affairs will produce any actual positive good, God knows.

Our fleets are abroad, and those of France, I believe, all out of their ports. The King of Prussia keeps the field, and his cause is still alive. An event or two may yet change the gloomy prospect. Immense expense I see is unavoidable, and the heavier load of national dishonour threatens to sink us with double weight of misfortune. But I will leave this melancholy theme to

Q 2

your meditations, instead of troubling you with mine, though pernoctant nobiscum peregrinantur, rusticantur.

The purpose of my letter was to desire the pleasure of your company at dinner on the King's birthday, in case you are not promised to the Duke of Newcastle, or elsewhere. I understand you propose leaving Wotton about the 6th of November, and by that day, according to Lord Temple's sarcastical Chronicle, it will be as much as you can do to disengage. Proud of his gravel as of the Appian Way, his Lordship does intimate that you are knee-deep in the delightful scenes of Wotton. I will still figure to myself far other things, and suppose not the mud nymphs, but the fair-haired naiads claim your rural hours. I conclude your bridge is finished, and is really, with its accompaniments, delightful: we pass ours, namely, that of Westminster, as frequently as we can. We see our little people and draw the village air by snatches at most. My health by this help, thank God, holds out, under constant unpleasing labours. Hayes most affectionately greets Wotton collectively. Your ever affectionate brother, W. PITT.

MR. JENKINSON TO MR. GRENVILLE.

Whitehall, October 29, 1757.

DEAR SIR,—I have the pleasure to acquaint you that yesterday brought us letters from Lisbon, which make not the least mention of the plague, from whence we conclude that the news of it must have been false, though it has left us at a loss to think how the French could be deceived in it, as it is hardly to be supposed that they meant purposely to deceive us.

I met this day a French gentleman whom I knew about three years ago, and who had been five years an officer in the marine of France. He told me that he had been at Rochfort, and he gave me a detail of the fortifications of that place, agreeing exactly with what Col. Clerk says of it, that it is enclosed only with a single wall, that it has a dry ditch, and that it may be approached by land without taking Fouras, &c. This evidence I thought was of some consequence, as there is a Mons. Bonneville who pretends to have been at Rochfort, whom Mr. Conway took with him, and who contradicts the account that Clerk gave of the place, and on whose opinion it is thought the Generals a good deal relied.

I hope another week will give me the pleasure of seeing you in town. I have, &c. CHARLES JENKINSON.

While I was writing my ears were saluted with the cry of a ballad on the Ditch of Rochfort, which I send you.

MR. PITT TO MR. GRENVILLE.

St. James's Square, 4 o'clock (November 15, 1757).

THE King of Prussia has gained a complete victory over the Prince Soubise, near Weisenfels, in Saxony. The battle[1] was the 5th of November. 4000 French killed, but 600 or 800 Prussians killed and wounded ; of the latter, the King's brother, Prince Henry, wounded slightly in the shoulder. Cannon, standards, colours, drums in abundance. The King of Prussia in full pursuit of the enemy, towards the *Unstrut*, a deep and

[1] Of Rosbach.

rapid river. Richelieu said to be retiring with precipitation from Halberstadt. Prussian army 20,000 men. Soubise's, including troops of the empire, 50,000 men. Heaven be praised for this great event! And now to dinner with a better appetite.

EARL TEMPLE TO MR. GRENVILLE.

Stowe, November 24, 1757.

I AM very glad, my dear brother, to hear from all parts so happy a confirmation of the King of Prussia's unexampled success : it is an event that will cost France very dear, but I think too we shall not come off cheap; however, it is, perhaps, our last stake. I intend to be in town on Tuesday evening or Wednesday morning, pay my affectionate duty at the birthday, join, in all human probability, my affirmative yea to the anniversary ode in prose on Thursday, and then return to the *gravel* of Stowe 'till after Christmas. Many observations occur upon all the glorious, and all the infamous events, of this year: I will trust none of them to paper. I will only send my affectionate compliments to Mrs. G., &c.

EARL TEMPLE TO MR. GRENVILLE.

Tuesday, December 13, 1757.

DEAR BROTHER,—Jemmy charitably sent me the certain account of the Prince of Bevern's complete victory; the Austrians were Soubised, and I waited with impatience to enjoy all the Gazette particulars of last Saturday. No Gazette! but behold a d——d extraordinary one from Brussels : lying, impudently false as that paper is generally, I am a little staggered from so many circumstances, and wait in the most painful anxiety 'till to-morrow night, unless some charitable Parson in the neighbourhood should relieve me from my doubts by his intelligence, before.

CAPTAIN RODNEY TO MR. GRENVILLE.

Dublin, at Spithead,
Wednesday morning (March 15, 1758).

DEAR SIR,—I have deferred writing to you till General Amherst[1] was come, because I would not give either my friends or enemies reason to imagine I was unwilling to go anywhere His Majesty's service required. The moment I was made acquainted that Mr. Pitt had desired the *Dublin* might supply the place of the *Invincible*, with pleasure I got her ready for sea ; my friend the Governor has acquainted me with the motive of her being ordered.

As a friend I may say to you, that as an officer I feel myself injured by the Admiralty in being ordered to serve in America as a private captain, when a junior captain has so considerable a command in that part of the world ; and for what I know we may chance to meet, which must render it very disagreeable to me, as I know but of one alternative, either his broad pendant

---

[1] General Amherst distinguished himself at the several battles of Dettingen, Fontenoy, Lauffeldt, and Hastenbeck. He was now appointed by Mr. Pitt to the command of the expedition against Louisbourg. He was subsequently made a Knight of the Bath, and created Baron Amherst, and a Field Marshal. He died at the age of 81, in 1797.

being struck, or my being in honour obliged to resign : but I hope our destination will be far distant from each other.

I presume you know that I am solely intrusted with the estate and concerns of the Compton family[1]: the young man comes of age the latter end of the summer, and as 'twill be necessary I should be at home to settle his affairs, I must beg your interest with our common friend that my ship may be ordered home when the service is over she was sent on.

I need not acquaint you with my reasons for desiring the Commander-in-Chief may have such orders. You know him : you remember the Navy Bill[2], you know his resentment, and in case a squadron should be ordered to winter in that part of the world, if he thinks it will be disagreeable to me, I know if left to him my ship will be one that stays. Excuse this trouble, and believe me to be, &c., &c.   G. B. RODNEY.

P.S.—The wind, which has been so long easterly, is now shifted to the west, but if moderate, nothing shall prevent my sailing.

MR. JENKINSON TO MR. GRENVILLE.

London, March 28, 1758.

DEAR SIR,—A messenger arrived yesterday from Mr. Lorenzi, the King's Electoral Minister at the Hague, who brought an account that Prince Ferdinand had

---

[1] Captain Rodney had married Jane Compton, sister to Spencer, eighth Earl of Northampton. She died in 1757.

[2] He had been Member for Saltash, and he probably alludes to a vote he had given in Parliament contrary to the wishes of Lord Anson, who was now First Lord of the Admiralty.

gained a victory over the French; but there were some circumstances in this intelligence that soon made us believe that the whole of it was not true, and by the mail, which is since come in, we find that the French have certainly evacuated Hamelen, and continue to retire, and that there have been some great and successful skirmishes, but I fancy no general action. We are, however, still very ignorant of the particulars of everything.

We also wait with impatience for some account of what has passed in the Mediterranean: even the French accounts seem to allow that we had some advantage, but just what, we know not. Upon seeing our fleet, Duquesne made a signal to his ships to fly and disperse, and in consequence thereof the *Pleiade* is got into Toulon, but she did not know what is become of her companions.

The new bishops kissed hands to-day: Secker for Canterbury, Hume for Oxford, and Yonge for Bristol[1].

I am extremely obliged to you for your kind wishes that I was at Wotton, and I can sincerely assure you that my own wishes are there also, and I should never want fine weather to make that place or your company agreeable; but as I consider myself at present as serving an apprenticeage, I am unwilling to play until my time is out. I have, &c.,　　　CHAS. JENKINSON.

CAPTAIN RODNEY TO MR. GRENVILLE.

Dublin, at Vigo, March 29, 1758.

DEAR SIR,—I dare say you will be surprised at receiving a letter from me dated at this place, but when

---

[1] Dr. Thomas Secker had been Bishop of Oxford; Dr. John Hume was translated from Bristol; and Dr. Philip Yonge had been Canon Residentiary at St. Paul's.

you learn the cause, I flatter myself you will not be displeased.

On the 21st instant, being in the latitude of 49.00 degrees, about twenty-five leagues to the westward of Ushant, I fell in with and took a French ship called the *Montmartel*, from the East Indies, bound for Brest; he is about five hundred ton, loaded with coffee, but of no force. As the wind was southerly, my officers would fain have had me seen him into Plymouth, from which port we were about twenty-four hours' sail; but as I considered the consequence of the service I was ordered on, and that the General who was to command was on board my ship, I did not hesitate a moment in sacrificing my private interest to the public welfare, and therefore made the best of my way to the southward, which is the passage I am ordered to take, but it proving little wind, I did not make the coast of Spain 'till yesterday, and the prisoners being very sickly, I thought it prudent to put them on shore, and see the prize into Vigo, where I hope their Lordships will favour her with a convoy, as she is very valuable.

If my conduct in this affair meets with Mr. Pitt's and your approbation, I shall be happy, and you may depend that no time shall be lost from prosecuting my voyage with all the dispatch imaginable. I beg you will present my respects to Mrs. Grenville, and when you see them, to the good people who lately favoured me with their company at Portsmouth. I beg you will permit me to assure you that I am with real respect and sincerity, dear Sir, &c., &c.   G. B. RODNEY.

P.S.—I sail to-morrow if the wind permits.

MR. JENKINSON TO MR. GRENVILLE.

London, April 4, 1758.

DEAR SIR,—By the last accounts, from Germany, it is very plain that the French have no design to make a stand on that side the Rhine, and some of them have already begun to pass it at Dusseldorf; they have also totally evacuated the Pays de Hesse, Prince Henry of Prussia having advanced into that country to drive them out of it. I am apt to think they will take care to secure Guêldres and Wesel. We have sent Brudenel's regiment to garrison Emden. I understand, also, that the King of Prussia has declared that he will accept £500,000 of us; so that I suppose we shall next week have the state of public affairs open to the House of Commons. I do not hear that as yet there is any account come from the Mediterranean, and yet I cannot help flattering myself that we have at least taken two of their men-of-war.

It is generally now said that the Bill of Habeas Corpus is to be thrown out of the House of Commons[1]. I am very certain, however, that they at least intend to attempt it.

I fear that you must feel very sensibly this cold weather after the dog-days of the last week. Lord Holdernesse has been very much out of order ever since Saturday with a cholic. I have, &c., &c. CHAS. JENKINSON.

[1] The Habeas Corpus Bill passed the House of Commons, but was rejected by the House of Lords, after long debates.

MR. JENKINSON TO MR. GRENVILLE.

May 13, 1758.

DEAR SIR,—We received yesterday the melancholy account that the *Prince*[1] had taken fire at sea, and that the ship, with above half the crew, were burnt; but that Admiral Broderick, who was on board her, and the Captain, were among the saved.

We also received yesterday an account that De la Clue[2] was got back to Toulon, and that they are going to disarm those ships.

We have at present nothing very particular from the Continent, but that the King of Prussia continued still advancing in Moravia. I have, &c., &c.

CHAS. JENKINSON.

COUNTESS TEMPLE TO EARL TEMPLE.

May 13 (1758).

I AM heartily glad to hear you are so well, though I am in low spirits myself, for our poor little friend, Ben Bathurst's son, who I am afraid is no more. Broderick's ship by some accident took fire, and it was with great difficulty he saved himself.

I desired Lady Hester Pitt to get me what information she could, as soon as I heard of this accident, and I have sent you the note she sent me last night. The King has expressed great concern at it; he has been ill

---

[1] The *Prince George* had about 780 souls on board, of which it was true that more than half were drowned, and the ship burned to the water's edge.

[1] The French Admiral.

of a cold and kept his bed, but is better again. I was at Leicester House last Thursday: I met with great civility from the Princess, and she said many kind things of you, which always pleases me best.

I am sorry to hear you have company; as you have so many things to do, and so little time, I believe you could have spared it.

. . . .

I am, your most affectionate little Wife,

A. Temple.

MR. JAMES GRENVILLE TO MR. GRENVILLE.

Friday, June 9, 1758.

My dear Brother,—Though I have desired Mr. Elliot to write the particulars of the good news which arrived very late last night, I cannot help felicitating you upon the landing of our troops in Cancale Bay.

The troops were detained unluckily two days by a calm between the Islands, and though this must have taken off part of the surprise, and have given notice, yet no troops were got to oppose the landing.

Probably Lord Anson has alarmed the coast towards Brest. The passage of the Rhine is said to have been the finest operation that ever was executed. Cancale Bay is seven miles from St. Maloes.

MR. JAMES GRENVILLE TO MR. GRENVILLE.

(June, 1758).

Last night the express arrived about 12 o'clock from St. Malo. The troops reimbarked on the 12th without loss.

They found the place stronger fortified than they expected: the ground all round very much cut and difficult. Some prisoners gave intelligence of a body of forces not far from them, which as they said might amount to about ten thousand men. Several difficulties and circumstances relative to the securing a retreat prevented, it is said, the army from being able to march and meet them in a collected body; and upon the whole view of things, it was judged right to reimbark, which was executed with great order and safety.

One man only was shot by the enemy, two by our own people for marauding.

This is the amount of the loss on our side. All the enemies' shipping in the harbour are burnt and destroyed, amounting to one hundred vessels of all sorts, among which one 50-gun ship, I forget which, one or two 36-guns, and some privateers. This was performed by the light horse and volunteers, supported by a brigade under the command of General Waldegrave[1]. The troops are not returned yet. Friday, 2 o'clock.

MR. JENKINSON TO MR. GRENVILLE.

London, June 13, 1758.

DEAR SIR,—Though we have at present no public news to send you, I cannot help filling a page or two with the account of a very extraordinary trial which happened yesterday, I mean that of Dr. Hensey[1]. He

---

[1] Younger brother of James, Earl of Waldegrave; he succeeded to the title in 1763, and died in 1784.

[2] Florence Hensey, Doctor of Medicine. He was found guilty and sentenced to death, but afterwards reprieved, and in a few months pardoned.

was convicted on the clearest evidence which the case would admit of (and which could only be circumstantial) of having carried on a correspondence with the enemy; he himself first applied to France to be employed in this way, and all the wages they gave him was about 100*l.* a year; there was found among his papers the very instructions the enemy had given him on the nature of his correspondence, several of their letters to him scolding him for not sending good intelligence, and the various directions he was to make use of.

One letter was found that ordered him to write in lemon juice between the lines of an ordinary letter; and even these letters had been discovered at the Post Office by holding them to the fire, and yet after all this the French were so dissatisfied with his correspondence, that they reduced his annuity to 50*l.* a year, and they sconced him a guinea for every post-day that they did not hear from him; and yet after all this hard treatment, he says in one of his letters, that he would do them this service, though they paid him nothing, as he did it out of principle and love of the cause. This poor wretch received a good education in Louis XIV.'s College at Paris, and afterwards took a degree at Leyden, and by some of his letters appears to have been a man of sense.

I congratutate you on the unexpected success of our little expedition to Africa, and I hope we shall soon hear of St. Malo's being in our possesion.

I go out of town for a few days on Thursday, I will trouble you with another letter as soon as I come back.

I have, &c., &c.   CHAS. JENKINSON.

THE REV. MR. COTTON[1] TO MR. GRENVILLE.

From on Board the *Princess Amelia*,
at Anchor in Gabreuse Bay, June 20, 1758.

SIR,—I might justly be deemed ungrateful if I neglected any opportunity to acquaint you with the various
occurrences of a public nature since I sailed from England for Halifax, where I arrived the 8th of May, and
by the 28th we were joined by all the troops and ships
of war (except the *Vanguard*), and had the good fortune to meet General Amherst, in the *Dublin*, going in
as we came out of Halifax harbour, who immediately
went on board the Admiral's[2] ship, and proceeded with
us, and by the 2nd instant we came to an anchor in this
bay, and the day following all the transports (except
two or three) came to an anchor, and the necessary disposition for landing the troops was made on the 5th and
6th; but the thick fog and great surf prevented from
accomplishing the design; but on the 8th the troops
were again in the boats by three o'clock in the morn,
and at sunrise our frigates were hauled in nigh the
shore to cover the landing, on which the enemy began
with throwing shells, and our frigates commenced their

[1] Mr. Cotton was at this time Chaplain on board the *Princess
Amelia*: an appointment for which he was probably indebted to Mr.
Grenville.

[2] Admiral Boscawen, and General Amherst, with a fleet of one
hundred and fifty sail, and fourteen thousand men, had appeared before
Louisbourg on the second of June, and, by the end of July, made
themselves masters of the place. Boscawen's rough courage was fully
known before: Amherst was a cool sensible man, whose conduct, now
first experienced in command, shone to great advantage, and the activity of spirit in Wolfe, who accompanied him, contributed signally to
the reduction of the place.—*Walpole's Memoirs of George the Second*,
vol. iii. p. 134.

fire upon the enemy's entrenchments, upon which the boats made in for the shore, and our fire from the frigates was wholly disregarded by the enemy, until our boats had got within half-musket shot of them, and then they began an incessant fire with cannon and musketry, which at first obliged our boats to retire a little; but they soon rallied again, and made the shore and landed, which the enemy perceiving left their entrenchments to us.

They were entrenched for above a mile, and had in that place from seven hundred to a thousand men, besides four or five hundred more posted at every place where there was any prospect of our landing, having cannon from 24-lb. shot to 3-lb., as also 7 and 10-inch mortars. Notwithstanding all these our troops behaved with the greatest spirit and resolution, zealous to surmount all dangers that they were inevitably exposed to, from the advantageous position of the enemy; and when they beheld the intrepidity of our officers and soldiers, climbing up the rocks where they judged it impracticable to land, they were struck with astonishment, and soon after turned their backs upon us.

We have killed and made prisoners between two and three hundred, and some of them (besides a few deserters from the garrison) have entered into our marine service; they are Germans, and highly dissatisfied at their being sent to Louisbourg.

We had the misfortune to lose in landing the Captain of Highland Grenadiers, and one of the Lieutenants. Several of the officers of the Army and Navy were wounded, and some soldiers and sailors; the killed, wounded, and drowned, does not amount to one hundred.

Since our landing the enemy have deserted the Grand

and Lighthouse Batteries, destroying them and throwing the cannon into the water.

They have made two or three unsuccessful sallies from the town.

We have blocked up in the harbour five or six two-deckers, and an equal number of frigates and store-ships ; and last evening General Wolfe, who has taken possession of the ground adjacent to their lighthouse, opened several batteries on the shipping, and obliged them to haul in close to the town, though even now they cannot well get out of the reach of Mr. Wolfe's cannon and shells, and by Sir Charles Hardy's being at anchor before the mouth of the harbour with an equal force, it is judged impracticable for them to get out, unless a violent storm should favour them.　Some of our cruizers have, within this day or two, brought in a French frigate of 30 guns, bound to Canada from Louisbourg, having got out before Sir Charles was at anchor there.

The greatest zeal and ardour has appeared in the Admirals and Generals to do their utmost to execute every scheme for reducing this place, and I doubt not it will shortly be attended with the desired success.

July 2nd.—I was in hopes by this time to have acquainted you that our batteries had been opened and belaying upon the town ; but I believe the great difficulty in making the roads to draw the cannon, and taking possession of the eminences adjacent to the town, and erecting redoubts to prevent being dislodged by the enemy, are the chief points that have retarded the Army from battering the walls.

The enemy within these few days have sunk the *Apollo*, and two or three store-ships at the mouth of the harbour, not to block it up entirely, but to render the entrance so narrow that it will make it more difficult for our ships to go in if they are at last obliged to storm them by sea and land.

The Island Battery is in some measure rendered useless by one that General Wolfe opened upon it from the Lighthouse side.

The enemy continue a very warm fire upon our troops in their approaches upon this side, though the loss is as yet comparatively nothing, notwithstanding their frequent sallies, which, upon the whole, prove ineffectual.

All the accounts that we have yet received from General Abercrombie are, that the troops that are to proceed with him against Crown Point were marched for Albany above a month since, and that it was expected Mr. Abercrombie would have an army exceeding 20,000, and that General Forbes, with eight or nine thousand men, is marched against Fort du Quesne on the Ohio, in General Braddock's route, and we impatiently expect to have good tidings from those quarters.

These, Sir, are the most material occurrences worthy notice, and I hope you will pardon the liberty I have taken in troubling you with so long a letter, and that in my next I shall have the satisfaction to acquaint you with the success of His Majesty's arms here and elsewhere in America, as there is no reason at present to doubt but that Louisbourg will in a few weeks be subjected to the British Crown.

I still flatter myself that you will continue me an object of your favours, and that upon my return I may rely on your interest with the same freedom for my future preferment, as I did for what I now enjoy. I am, honoured Sir, with the greatest respect, &c., &c.

NATH. COTTON.

P.S.—I forgot mentioning that by all accounts the Garrison consists of about five battalions of *Regulars*, which, with the inhabitants, amount to near 4000, and not many more or less.　　　　　　　　　　　　　N. C.

MR. PITT TO MR. GRENVILLE.

Tuesday, June 27, 1758.

I HAVE just time to send, my dear Grenville, the joyful news that Prince Ferdinand has beat the French near Creveldt, the 23rd instant : victory complete, but no officer yet arrived with the particulars. All the King's generals safe, and but about 500 men on His Majesty's part killed : we are sending twelve squadrons of English cavalry to this glorious school of war, and I hope to share a sprig of Germanic laurel very soon.

We are all joy here, as you will be at Wotton. My affectionate compliments wait on Mrs. Grenville. I am ever, &c., &c.　　　　　　　　　　　W. PITT.

MR. JENKINSON TO MR. GRENVILLE.

London, June 27, 1758.

DEAR SIR,—We have at last received our mail from Holland ; they brought us word that Prince Ferdinand had advanced, and that the French had retreated before them, and this morning an express arrived bringing the joyful news that the two armies had come to an action, and that the French were totally defeated, having lost all their cannon and baggage. This great event happened on the 23rd. We are here full of rejoicings.

I write this amid the sound of cannon, bells, and marrow-bones, which are loudly expressing their joy, and I suppose as soon as it is dark we shall have illuminations. I understand that four English regiments of Dragoons, and one of Horse, are going to join the Hanoverian army.

We hear from the King of Prussia that though the siege of Olmutz does not go on very fast, yet that they have no apprehensions of its being relieved, so that the point is secured.

I congratulate you and Mrs. Grenville on these great successes.

Not only the fortune of England, but, in my poor opinion, her real intrinsic power, seems to be gaining the ascendant; and I cannot but think that any one who had well considered the state of the debts and finances of France, at the end of the two last wars, and had observed how all her resources were then exhausted, might have foreseen that she could not long be able to pay her armies in this war, and consequently that she could not be well served by them : what should we think of our own situation if the preservation of our country depended on the arrival of two or three ships with treasure? and yet a Comptroller-General of France has acknowledged, in his Mémoires, that his country was once saved by such an event; and the treasure, though the property of private persons, was seized by the Government. I am, &c., &c.

C. JENKINSON.

MR. JAMES GRENVILLE TO MR. GRENVILLE.

Thursday morning, June 29, 1758.

I was not in town when the news of the victory[1] arrived, so you happened not to hear from me. The particulars with regard to numbers killed, &c., were not arrived last night from Prince Ferdinand; but, upon the best accounts to be got from the officer who brought the express, it is thought that the King's army has lost from 500 to 1000, and the French to the extent of perhaps 8000.

I am told it was said in full circle that there are not better troops in the world than the Hanoverians when they have a good general at their head : that the greatest obligations are due to the King of Prussia for giving Prince Ferdinand to that army : that Prince Ferdinand loves that army, and the troops adore Prince Ferdinand, &c.

Politics are much as they were, and in some particulars very good.

P.S. What is material is, that the reinforcement of 15,000 men expected by the French had joined their army the day before the battle. It is thought their full force in the field was about 60,000 men.

MR. ELLIOT TO MR. GRENVILLE.

July 4, 1758.

OUR expedition, my dear Sir, arrived safely at St. Helens, on Saturday evening; the Volunteers got to

[1] The battle of Creveldt.

town on Sunday; the Duke of Marlborough, Lord George[1], and Howe this day. They looked into the Bay of Caen, prepared to attack Cherbourg, but the wind changed, and water and forage were near exhausted; both these articles were ready at Spithead to put to sea, and before this time are on board. But new circumstances require new councils. The transports are ready at Gravesend to receive 1800 horse, the first division of the body destined for the Rhine. Nothing important from the Continent. The French retire to Cologne: Olmutz not taken. We have letters from Boscawen, dated Halifax, May 27th: he sailed next day with the troops. The other operations in America advance, though with no great rapidity: another battalion of Highlanders ordered. We sent directions to the Navy Board about the new method of paying the seamen, but have not as yet got their report. I believè they must be roused by more than one letter upon this subject. Our transport account will exceed all imagination this year.

Marshal Belleisle mourns over his son[2], who is dead of his wounds: several other noble families have suffered, besides the nameless vulgar. Believe me, &c.

GILBERT ELLIOT.

---

[1] Lord George Sackville, a younger son of the first Duke of Dorset. Having returned from St. Maloes with the Duke of Marlborough, they set out together immediately for the army in Germany.

[2] The Duc de Gisors, who was killed at the battle of Creveldt. "He was recommended to me," says Walpole, "when he was in England: I knew him much, and thought as well of him as all the world did. He was graver, and with much more application to improve himself than any young Frenchman of quality I ever saw. How unfortunate Belleisle is, to have outlived his brother, his only son, and his hearing!" Marshal Belleisle died at Versailles in January, 1761, aged 78. He had been Minister and Secretary of State to the French King, for the War Department. He left nearly the whole of his very large fortune to the King.

MR. ELLIOT TO MR. GRENVILLE.

July 10, 1758.

THE landing of the troops at Cancale Bay, six miles from St. Maloes, tallies very exactly with Prince Ferdinand's passing the Rhine; and these two pieces of news are not ill supported by the accounts we have this day from the coast of Africa.

The several French forts, settlements, and storehouses on the River Senegal, with a rich booty, consisting of merchandize of various kinds, gold, gum, &c., are now in the possession of the English : ninety-two pieces of cannon, seven vessels, and several prisoners of some note, besides the prejudice done to the French East India Company, all contribute to enhance this success.

The scheme was formed and conducted by the Admiralty, and executed by ships and marines only.

Notwithstanding this success, so extraordinary, and manifested in every different quarter of the world, many people are so malignant as to assert that this auspicious ministry, which plan so wisely, and conduct their enterprises with equal dispatch and secrecy, is composed of the most jarring and unaccording principles. As Dryden expresses it—"Gods war with gods, and jostle in the dark."

Others, still more profane, ridicule Habeas Corpus, and still persist in the old opinion that an Alderman of London is inferior to a Peer of England. All this, with a little philosophy, one can bear; but when they rise a note higher, and talk contemptuous of the Navy Bill itself, then, indeed, patience can hold no longer; yet upon this happy day, which quietly closes the end of every week, all animosities are laid aside—no Treasury, no Admiralty, no House of Commons, even St. James's is deserted ; Alderman and Peer alike dine at their villa every Saturday : in short, we conquer every principle but habit, which suppresses even faction, and combats Nature herself. If you are happy in the country I rejoice at it; and yet you have no great merit—serenity, Mrs. Grenville, an Italian sky, and the blandishments of your little favourites. I beg you will flatter me, and own I have some merit, who feel myself happy, in spite of smoke and inconsistency.

SIR RICHARD LYTTELTON TO MR. GRENVILLE.

Ealing, July 22, 1758.

MY DEAR GRENVILLE,—Your brother James lay here last night in his way to Butleigh, and, as he set out very early this morning, I am charged to write a few lines to you upon the news from Moravia, that you may not be too much cast down with the accounts in the papers, which are all of them Austrian, either from Vienna or Bruxelles; though I am afraid the Prussian affairs go ill enough, as by a letter which Jemmy received from Mr. Pitt (which I have sent to your brother), he says that the siege of Olmutz is raised; his words are these, viz., the news of the day is very unfavourable, but as yet the whole is reducible to this single fact, that the siege of Olmutz is raised. I apprehend nothing very decisive has happened, nay the motives of raising the siege are unknown. Reports are various, all exaggerated certainly, most probably false, being Austrian and French.

Yorke[1] writes that the King of Prussia had assembled his whole army at Littau: if this be true, there will probably be an action, and all may be well, and better than before. He adds, Louisbourg is despaired of in France: God send us a good account of it, and that soon.

You know, my dear George, that Bligh[2] is at last the Commander-in-Chief for the Expedition. Prince Ferdinand calls out loudly for its sailing; he asks it even at the expense of some diminution of the forces to be sent; him nothing, he says, can serve him so effectually. Pitt, I hear, is well pleased with his new General: Clarke and Fitzmaurice go with him as Lieut. General and Adjutant General (Deputy as I suppose), as they can have no pretence to the rank of Colonel.

I have been lame for a long time, but as I begin to recover strength, projects arise in my mind, and I begin to think of going either to Harwich to bathe in the sea water made warm, or to take a fortnight of the Tunbridge waters, and then for Stowe and Wotton; but perhaps I may not go to either water place, but get to Wotton and Stowe the sooner; at all events I shall, God willing, find myself at Stowe about the 20th of next month, when Lord Lincoln, Viry[3], &c., are to be there. The Duchess[4] joins with me in kindest compliments to Mrs. Grenville, and declares I shall not go alone, be it when it may, to Wotton, so you may expect

[1] Sir Joseph Yorke, British Minister at the Hague.

[2] General Bligh was appointed to the Expedition against Cherbourg. Walpole speaks of him as " an elderly man, of no talents, brave, but in every other shape unfit for the destined service."

[3] The Sardinian Ambassador.

[4] The Duchess of Bridgewater, his wife.

to be troubled with us. Adieu, my dear George, your ever affectionate brother,   RICHARD.

MR. JENKINSON TO MR. GRENVILLE.

London, July 22, 1758.

DEAR SIR,—I did not write to you by the last post on account of our ill success in Moravia, as we had then only the accounts of our enemy, which we were willing to give as little credit to as possible. Yesterday, however, the mails arrived from Holland, and we find the news but too true, that the siege of Olmutz is raised. Our intelligence from thence contradicts all that the Austrians have published of the King of Prussia's having lost a great number of men in his retreat, and very much diminishes the pretended success of taking the convoy, and that with a great deal of reason : we having received even here an account a few days before, that part of that very convoy got safe to the Prussian Camp on the 28th, which the Austrians pretend to have taken on the 30th. We have also from Holland another reason assigned for the raising the siege, which was that the King had found that it became necessary for him to detach a part of his army to oppose that body of the Russians that are advancing towards Silesia. This, indeed, was probably one inducement to it, though it is certain that he had found the enterprise much more difficult than he had expected, for the enemy being able to flood the country for a great way round, made it very difficult to invest it; and the vigilance of M. Daun[1] caused great distress in relation

---

[1] The Austrian General.

to forage and convoys. Nothing of certainty is yet I believe known of the detail of this affair, as there are no letters from Mr. Mitchell[1], or from Moravia. We must, however, I am afraid, allow that his Prussian Majesty has missed his blow, and that like last year his first project for the campaign is defeated. I am, &c., &c.   CHA. JENKINSON.

SIR RICHARD LYTTELTON TO MR. GRENVILLE.

Cavendish Square[2], Friday night, 12 o'clock,
(July 28, 1758).

MY DEAREST GEORGE,—I will not for ever send you bad news, and though I am but just come to town from Lord Baltimore's, have seen nobody, and am more than half-a-sleep, yet I will tell you what I verily believe, to make you some amends for my last letter, and by way of thanks for the very kind one I have just received. I verily believe, then, that that astonishing man the King of Prussia has gained another victory, still more glorious and decisive than the last; I could talk of magazines fallen into his hands, of thousands upon thousands killed and taken; I could talk of letters from Prince Henry to Prince Ferdinand, of letters from Prince Fer-

---

[1] Mr., afterwards Sir Andrew Mitchell, K.B. He was appointed Envoy Extraordinary and Plenipotentiary to the Court of Berlin, in 1756, and remained there, with the exception of a short interval, until 1771, when he died. His papers and correspondence are deposited in the British Museum. A selection from them has been recently published, and some interesting letters addressed to him will be found in Sir Henry Ellis's Collection of *Original Letters*.

[2] At the corner of Harley Street: the house which was successively in the occupation of the Princess Amelia, Mr. Hope, and Mr. Watson Taylor.

dinand to Prince Louis, I think his name is, at the Hague; of a thousand circumstances related by a thousand and ten thousand mouths, coming from almost as many different quarters, and all agreeing; but I have told you enough for one that really knows nothing, who arrived this evening and goes to-morrow for about three weeks to Harwich, having left his good wife at Woodcote; but yet one thing more I must tell you, that I believe the Admiralty believe that Louisbourg is taken, with certain men-of-war in the harbour, and that the advice boat that should have brought the account is taken by the enemy.

MR. JENKINSON TO MR. GRENVILLE.

London, August 10, 1758.

DEAR SIR,—We have this day the agreeable news that our troops under General Bligh are landed at Cherbourg, and have by a vigorous action repulsed a body of 3000 Horse and Foot, who opposed their landing: this service was done by the Guards and Grenadiers of the Army, who received three fires, before they returned it, but then made their attack with so much vigour, that the enemy, after a considerable loss, retreated. We had ourselves but about 20 men either killed or wounded. We have also taken two cannon, and one pair of colours: this happened on Monday, and on Tuesday morning the whole force began their march towards the town.

Our news from Germany is not so good. The Prince of Soubise's army is raising contributions in Hanover.

I have, &c., &c. C. JENKINSON.

THE REV. MR. COTTON TO MR. GRENVILLE.

Louisbourg Harbour, *Princess Amelia*,
August 10, 1758.

SIR,—I hope my thus troubling you with frequent letters will be overlooked, as I am very desirous to acquaint you with every material circumstance relative to our affairs in America that is worthy your notice.

In my last of the 27th of July, I had the satisfaction to acquaint you of our troops taking possession of Louisbourg that day, and the Garrison were obliged to surrender prisoners of war, and towards the close of it I added a list of the loss the French have sustained in their marine, since our investing this place, and that we had an imperfect account of the success attending General Abercrombie at Lake George, which was true, though since the enemy have obliged him to retreat, which was occasioned in the following manner, viz., after our troops had landed within four miles of Ticonderago (the French fort) they met with no opposition but what they surmounted without any great loss (except that of my Lord Howe)[1], and some of our scouting parties intercepted an express from M. Montcalm[2] to the General, whom he had detached with 3000 men to the German flatts, ordering him to return back to reinforce him (Montcalm) at Ticonderago; and our reconnoitring parties told Mr. Abercrombie that the French were very busy in completing their entrench-

---

[1] George Augustus, third Viscount Howe in the Peerage of Ireland. He was only 34 years of age at the time of his death. His brother, the Commodore, succeeded to his title.

[2] Marquis de Montcalm, Commander-in-Chief of the French forces in America. He was killed at the siege of Quebec.

ments about the Fort, and appeared confused; upon this, and the intercepted letter, the General thought it advisable to attack the enemy without loss of time, which he did, and found them too well prepared to receive him, and that their trenches were completed, and after returning to the attack twice or thrice, he found it impracticable to force their trenches, and was obliged to retreat with the following loss, viz., of regular troops, 464, officers and private men, killed: 29 missing, and 1117 wounded, making a total of killed, missing, and wounded—1610.

Provincials or Americans: 87 killed, 8 missing, and 240 wounded—total, 333.

This, Sir, is the consequence of that action; had I the liberty to make any remarks, I might say that had our troops the day after our landing in this island, agreed on forcing the enemy under fire of their cannon, I doubt not we should have met with the same fate, but it has been otherwise with us, and I am full of opinion that had our troops towards Lake George secured themselves on their first success, and made their regular approaches, they must have succeeded, for if upon the batteries being opened they would not capitulate, then would have been the time to storm after the breaches were made, and we had better known their strength and situation, and not when we were ignorant of both; for if our Army then had entrenched themselves, the French would find it very difficult to drive back above 16,000 men, unless they had a much superior force, which I am sure they could not have.

This freedom, I hope, Sir, you will pardon, for I would not be understood to mention a word derogatory from the character of the General or Officers employed in that affair, and the foregoing is the result of what I have collected of the matter, and we are not without hopes they will make another attempt which will prove more successful.

The prisoners here are embarking for England, and will sail the beginning of the week under Convoy of His Majesty's ships *Terrible, Northumberland, Burford, Dublin, Kingston,* &c., which I hope will arrive safe.

Our troops are gone to take possession of the island of St. John's, where I hope they may meet with no opposition. I have, &c., &c.　　　　NATHL. COTTON.

MR. JENKINSON TO MR. GRENVILLE.

London, August 14, 1758.

DEAR SIR,—I congratulate you on the farther success of our arms on the coast of Normandy. Cherbourg has surrendered to the terror of our arms, for the enemy abandoned it before we could make them feel the force of them. We have taken in it 80 pieces of cannon, and about 27 merchant vessels; but I will not dwell on particulars, as you will have them from better hands, and as you receive them also this night in the Gazette. I will only observe what is contained in a private letter, which is, that the consternation since the first landing is so great, that there was not then a man in arms within four leagues of Cherbourg, and yet there had been at first reports spread that the enemy had 20,000 within a few miles of them, which upon experience was found to be so totally false; a report, however, of this kind would, I doubt not, have made some of our Generals quit the enterprize, and they would afterwards have urged it as a serious article in their defence.

There is only one officer wounded, that is Mr. Cocks[1]; his wound is the shoulder, but not dangerous.

We have this day, also, a piece of good news from the Rhine. The French detached about 8000 men to take a magazine at Ries, and to get possession of our bridge on the Rhine at Emmerick, and so prevent the junction of the British troops that are now marching from Embden; this would have been a great stroke, especially since Prince Ferdinand has taken the resolution to transport the war upon the Meuse; His Highness, however, provided against the evil, and detached a body to oppose the French, which had defeated them totally, taken 12 pieces of cannon, and killed 700; the bravery of two Hessian battalions is on this occasion highly celebrated; they marched up to the battery, and took it without ever firing their muskets. I have, &c., &c.

C. JENKINSON.

EARL TEMPLE TO THE DUKE OF NEWCASTLE.

Stowe, August 16, 1758.

MY LORD,—My brother Jemmy, who is this moment arrived, informs me of the very obliging part your Grace has acted with regard to procuring a step to Lord Braco[2]

---

[1] Nephew of Lady Hardwicke. He was scarcely recovered from this wound, when he was killed at the battle of Zorndorff. He was a volunteer, and had a fortune of seven thousand pounds a year.

[2] William Duff, Esq., had been created Baron Braco of Kilbryde in the Peerage of Ireland, in 1735, and was this year advanced to be Viscount Macduff and Earl of Fife. He died in 1763.—See *Bedford Correspondence*, vol. iii. p. 346.

in the Irish Peerage. Your Grace's proceeding upon this matter not only lays me under great obligation to you, but gives me a welcome and kind proof of that friendship which I so much wish and mean to cultivate with you and yours.

I wait with impatience for the pleasure of seeing Lord Lincoln this evening : if your Grace's affairs could have permitted you to have been one of the party, it would have added greatly to our joy : however, your health, and that of your Duchess, will not be forgotten, nor will it be drank with more sincerity by any man in the kingdom than by, my dear Lord, your Grace's most affectionate and obedient humble Servant,   TEMPLE.

MR. JENKINSON TO MR. GRENVILLE.

London, August 18, 1758.

DEAR SIR,—I had the honour of your letter on Monday, and have now the pleasure to acquaint you that your wishes are accomplished by the success of our arms in America. This morning, Captain Edgecomb, and Captain Amherst[1], brother of the General, arrived with the joyful news of the taking of Louisbourg on the 27th of last month, after forty-nine days of siege ; the garrison are prisoners of war, and consists of 5637, of which 2667 are sailors; their wounded and sick are 500. We have taken in the place 220 pieces of cannon, and 18 mortars ; and in the port we have taken one ship of 74 guns, and 4 frigates ; and two ships of 74 guns, and two of 64 are burnt, one of 74 is blown up, and one of 50, and two frigates are sunk by the enemy.

[1] Captain William Amherst. He died in 1781.

The fire of the enemy during the whole siege was prodigious, but not being well appointed did not very great execution; we lost 20 men at the landing and 500 at the siege, of which 13 are officers, but none above the rank of captain.

I congratulate both you and Mrs. Grenville on this very good news. I have no doubt but that it will convince our enemies of our superiority in America, and hope it will bring about an advantageous and honourable peace. I shall send this letter to the Post Master at Thame, and order him to send it over by a messenger to you; you will by that means have the news a day sooner, and therefore I hope you will approve of what I do. I have, &c., &c. CHAS. JENKINSON.

THE DUKE OF NEWCASTLE TO EARL TEMPLE.

Claremont, August 19, 1758.

MY DEAR LORD,—I had yesterday the honour of your Lordship's most obliging letter.

I am extremely happy that I have been able to do anything that may shew my real regard and attention to your Lordship and your family, and how desirous I am upon all occasions to do what may be agreeable to you, and sincerely to deserve the friendship with which you honour me.

My heart was so full with the joyful news which we received yesterday morning of the taking the Islands of Cape Breton and St. John's, with everything that belongs to them, in the most masterly and complete manner, as appears by the Capitulation published in the Extraordinary Gazette, that I had immediately sent it to your Lordship by express, if Mr. Pitt had not told me that he had already done it.

Allow me, my dear Lord, to congratulate your Lordship, and all my good friends at Stowe upon this great event; an event which does so much honour to the King, the nation, and to those who have the honour to be in His Majesty's service, and which cannot fail of having the best consequences: and it must be a satisfaction to us all to see the bravery and conduct with which the King's officers and troops, both by sea and land, have acted upon this occasion; and, indeed, the Capitulation does in my opinion great honour to those who made it, for there is nothing omitted which could be wished or hoped for. There is great reason to think that Prince Ferdinand, in his present situation, and after his junction with the Duke of Marlborough, will find himself more at liberty, and be in a better condition to disappoint the views of the enemy, and of their two armies, than he has hitherto been. I wish I could say the same as to the King of Prussia's situation.

I must also congratulate your Lordship upon our success at Cherbourg, where the General and Commodore have done most excellently well. We have for some days been in expectation of more news from France, and I this moment am told that it was said in London this morning, that an express was come in with more good news from Commodore Howe[1]; but

---

[1] By the death of his brother at Ticonderago, on the 5th of July, he was now the fourth Viscount Howe. In the previous year he had been sent, under Sir Edward Hawke, to make an attack on the French coast. Captain Howe commanded the *Magnanime*, in which ship he battered the fort on the isle of Aix, until it surrendered. He became subsequently still better known as Admiral Howe. He was made an Earl in the Peerage of Great Britain, in 1788, and K.G. in 1797. He died in 1799.

I yet know nothing either of the truth of the report, or of what may be come. I beg my best compliments to my good friend Count Viry, my brother Granville, my Lord Lincoln, and all the good company at Stowe. If I might presume, I would accompany the Duchess of Newcastle's best compliments to your Lordship and my Lady Temple, with the addition of mine to her Ladyship, and the assurances of the utmost respect and regard which I have always had for her.

If Mr. George Grenville be with you (which I don't know), I beg he would accept my compliments also, and congratulations upon this good news. I envy my Lord Lincoln the pleasure and advantage of waiting upon your Lordship at Stowe. Nothing but my necessary attendances at this time should have prevented my taking a place in the chaise.

Tell Viry that if the Queen of Spain[1] should not recover, he knows what *we* wish, and he should think what steps he should take towards it. I hope to have the pleasure of seeing your Lordship at Claremont some time this summer, and am, with the most affectionate respect, my dear Lord, &c., &c.

HOLLES NEWCASTLE.

MR. PITT TO MR. GRENVILLE.

August 22, 1758.

MY DEAR GRENVILLE,—You have so kindly and warmly felt my joys on the happy event of Louisbourg, that you will share my present grief for the repulse and

---

[1] The Queen of Spain died on the 27th of August, in her 47th year.

great loss of the troops under General Abercrombie, at Ticonderago, of which the enclosed Gazette contains the whole and true account. I own this news has sunk my spirits, and left very painful impressions upon my mind, without, however, depriving me of great hopes for the remaining campaign. The troops deserve all applause: the provincials share the honour. The General attempted willingly, bravely, and unfortunately, and took his part well under his misfortune. Bradstreet is sent on an expedition to the Lakes of the greatest importance[1]. Forbes, by a letter of the 10th of July, was at Carlisle, some miles west of the Susquehanna, and 100 miles on his way to Fort Du Quesne. Amherst will be felt, I trust, wherever he goes, perhaps even to Quebec, though the season be far advanced for such an operation. The loss of Lord Howe afflicts me with more than a public sorrow. He was, by the universal voice of army and people, a character of ancient times: a complete model of military virtue in all its branches. I have the sad task of imparting this cruel event to a brother that loves him most tenderly, because he has himself all the same virtues. I must take my leave of you, being overwhelmed with business. I will not despair of seeing you at Wotton, though I must depend every day on the events thereof.

I cannot finish without telling Mrs. Grenville how sensibly I feel her letters to Lady Hester on the happy event of Louisbourg. I am, &c., &c.   W. Pitt[2].

[1] Colonel Bradstreet took Fort Frontenac, and General Forbes Fort Du Quesne.

[2] Mr. Grenville's reply to this letter is printed in the *Chatham Correspondence*, vol. i. p. 338.

MR. JENKINSON TO MR. GRENVILLE.

London, September 2, 1758.

DEAR SIR,—I have the pleasure to transmit to you the agreeable news of a great victory[1] which the King of Prussia obtained over the Russians in the meadows of Cüstrin, on the 25th of last month. As soon as His Prussian Majesty had brought back his army into Silesia, he marched with a reinforcement to assist Count Dohna, and having joined him he immediately attacked the Russians, who were carrying on a terrible bombardment against Cüstrin, which had reduced the town to ashes, without doing any harm to the citadel, which being situated on the embouchure of a little river into the Oder, is so surrounded by waters as to be almost impregnable. The battle began about nine in the morning, and lasted the whole day. The Russians have

---

[1] The battle took place at Zorndorf, within six miles from the fortified town of Cüstrin. In this sanguinary conflict the Russians, under the command of General Fermer, numbered more than fifty thousand, while the Prussians, under Frederick, were thirty-two thousand, with one hundred and seventeen pieces of cannon. In no battle during the whole war was so much blood spilt as in this, for neither party would give or accept quarter. The King acknowledged with a sigh that the Russians were easier to kill than to conquer. The Russians laid claim to the victory, as well as the King. Fermer sent couriers to his Empress with intelligence of the happy event which cost him a great part of his army, and the results of a whole campaign. He asserted in corroboration of his claim that he had kept the field of battle, and one of his own general officers confirmed the assertion, with this remarkable observation in addition, that " those who kept the field were either killed, wounded, or drunk." The Russians in general, however, fought with the greater obstinacy for their intoxication, and exasperated as were their antagonists; the battle was for this reason the more sanguinary, for the confusion was aggravated in a frightful degree by the want of discipline in the Russian soldiers, who had seized on the spirituous liquors belonging to the sutlers.—See *Campbell's Court and Times of Frederick the Great.*

lost 15,000 men, three Lieutenant Generals taken, their cannon, and their military chest; this last I should fancy is no great prize.

The Prussians have lost about 3000, and General Calder is wounded: the King himself is perfectly well. These are all the particulars I know, and I should hope that His Majesty will have no farther trouble with these Russians, who, when they are once beaten, are not, I should imagine very easily kept together; and I think it looks probable that His Prussian Majesty may extricate himself this year, as he did the last, and beat his enemies by piecemeal.

We are going to have the cannon that were taken at Cherbourg, and the colours taken at Louisbourg, fixed as a trophy for some time in Hyde Park. I am, &c., &c.　　　CHAS. JENKINSON.

The above account comes from Berlin, from whence it was transmitted to the Hague, and so here.

MR. JENKINSON TO MR. GRENVILLE.

London, September 7, 1758.

DEAR SIR,—Last night a further account arrived of the victory of the King of Prussia over the Russians, which makes it more complete than was at first imagined: the number of the enemy killed are made now to amount to 18,000; six Generals are taken; General Brown was also a prisoner, but refusing to accept quarter, was either killed or terribly wounded. On the Prussian side the loss, both in killed and wounded, does not amount to above 1600. Upon the whole, from te general representations that have as yet been received of this affair, there never was anything more complete ; the Russian army was almost annihilated, and may be considered as nothing in the scale of our enemies for the future.

I hear also that an account is come that General Amherst, upon hearing of the unfortunate affair at Ticonderago, had resolved to transport a large part of his troops on the Continent to reinforce Abercrombie.

Yesterday the colours that were taken at Louisbourg were carried in procession to St. Paul's : the mob was immense on the occasion, and it has contributed very much to heighten popularity.

Since I wrote the above I have seen these farther accounts of the Prussian Victory. Brown was certainly killed in the manner above mentioned : besides the killed there are 1700 prisoners; the military chest taken contained 200,000*l.* The King of Prussia computes his loss at 560 killed, and about 1000 wounded ; two Generals are killed, two of the King's Aides-de-Camp, two Generals are also wounded. The King says that Dohna is pursuing the enemy, from whence it is concluded that he is going himself to Silesia.

The occasion of obtaining the victory is said to be principally owing to General Seidlitz and the Cavalry.

The Russian Foot behaved prodigiously well ; whole regiments were killed without leaving their ranks. Galitzin, a cousin of the present Russian Minister, and Chernikow, a near relation of the last, are two of the Generals that are prisoners. These particulars, with what I have mentioned above, is the whole of what is arrived, except some unintelligible circumstances which cannot be reconciled with the more authentic ones. I forgot to say that the number of cannon taken are seventy-five.

I had yesterday the honour of your letter, and I am extremely obliged to you for the kind invitations you have been again so good as to give me to wait on you this summer at Wotton; I own myself ashamed that I have not as yet fulfilled my promise, and I am sorry I should still have some affairs that keep me here. I confess I am no shooter, but I should want no other inducement but yours and Mrs. Grenville's company to bring me : but we will talk more of this when you come to town, when I hope you will let me have the honour of waiting on you. I have, &c., &c.

CHAS. JENKINSON.

MR. JENKINSON TO MR. GRENVILLE.

London, September 14, 1758.

DEAR SIR,—I have the pleasure to acquaint you that our troops have once more landed on the Coast of France, and this time without the least opposition. They debarked in the Bay of St. Lunerre, which is about three leagues to the westward of St. Malo's, which they were to have attacked; but the weather was so bad whilst they were there, that the fleet could not act, so they were forced to abandon their design. They have, however, burnt about twenty ships and destroyed some batteries, and they are now marching upon the coast to another bay, to which the fleet is gone round, and where the troops will reimbark as they shall find it prudent.

By the last letters from Pologne we hear that General Fermer is making a fine retreat with the remains of the

Russian Army; that he has shown himself in his present distresses to have a great knowledge in his profession; and that he chuses such strong camps, that the Prussians who are in the pursuit have not dared to attack him; the slaughter, however, of his army in the battle proves to have been even greater than was imagined: there have been buried 19,000 bodies in the field of battle, and the number of cannon taken amount to 108. I have, &c., &c.   CHAS. JENKINSON.

EARL TEMPLE TO THE DUKE OF NEWCASTLE.

Stowe, September 18, 1758.

MY LORD,—The death of the Earl of Carlisle[1] having occasioned a second vacancy in the Order of the Garter, your Grace will allow me to express my desires to be included in the next promotion, if His Majesty shall think me worthy of that honour from the rank I hold in his service[2].

I cannot, to be sure, be insensible to the many marks I have had the misfortune to receive of His Majesty's displeasure, arising from the suggestions and misrepresentations of my enemies, who at the same time led His Majesty into many difficulties from which your Grace, in conjunction with our common friends, has had the honour and satisfaction in a great measure to deliver him. From that happy union many signal benefits have been derived to the King and to the nation; and I have for my share, at least, the pleasure to reflect that I have

---

[1] Henry Howard, fourth Earl of Carlisle. He died on the 4th instant. He had been made a Knight of the Garter in March, 1757.

[2] Earl Temple was now Lord Privy Seal.

not been wanting in zealous endeavours to promote and cement it. If I ask my own heart, I cannot but trust that your Grace will employ your best offices to dispose His Majesty's mind to give me, after so many mortifications, this honourable mark of his Royal condescension and goodness. But whether I attain it or not, a just sense of my own honour, and the dictates of my own conscience, will equally direct me to support all measures which appear to me conducive to the true interest of the King, and the real service of my country, fighting for her last stake. I shall, however, think that I was wanting to myself and to my own situation, if I did not, with all possible respect, lay these my wishes at His Majesty's feet.

To your Grace I will make no professions ; you are certainly well enabled to judge and decide whether I have or have not been wanting in proofs of my friendship and good wishes to you. Upon that foot I take my leave of this matter, and have only to add the most affectionate assurances of the great respect with which I have the honour to be, my Lord, your Grace's most obedient and most humble Servant, TEMPLE.

EARL TEMPLE TO THE EARL OF LINCOLN.

Stowe, September 19, 1758.

MY DEAR LORD,—I am returned to Stowe delighted with my excursion, and penetrated with all the kind marks of friendship and partiality with which your Lordship honoured me. In my expressions of love for Oatlands[1]

---

[1] Oatlands, near Weybridge, in Surrey, celebrated for its grotto and gardens. It was the residence of Henry, Earl of Lincoln.

and the inhabitants thereof, Lady Temple desires to claim and assert her whole share, and I will accordingly with pleasure add it to mine, which taken together with that of the rest of my family, is the best return I can make your Lordship and my Lady for all your favours: I only wish I had it in my power to make a better. In one of our conversations upon a certain matter[1], I expressed an unwillingness to your Lordship to put my friends under any difficulties upon my account, which I still feel; and I did not care in a party of so much pleasure to mix up anything of my own situation that was not agreeable to me; but having more than once considered over this matter since, which your Lordship must imagine I have turned in my mind frequently before we touched upon it at Oatlands, I have taken the resolution of writing a letter to the Duke of Newcastle upon it, a copy of which my brother George will show you, and I think his Grace, who knows the *mollia tempora fandi*, will, if he pleases, dispose our Royal personage properly; but whatever may be the result of it, or indeed of any part of my political situation, it never can, nor ever shall in its consequences, produce the least diminution in my warmly affectionate friendship and honour for your Lordship; and I will ever have such a guard upon myself as never deservedly to forfeit what I really value more than any favour I have to ask of Ministers or Courts, I mean the satisfaction of being thought, and really proving myself to be, with infinite esteem and respect, my dear Lord, your most devoted, &c., TEMPLE.

---

[1] Alluding to his application for the vacant Garter, and apparently very conscious of the King's extreme disinclination to confer it upon him.

MR. JENKINSON TO MR. GRENVILLE.

London, September 23, 1758.

DEAR SIR,—Though I imagine that this letter will get to Wotton before you, as it will contain no news, but will only relate to what we talked on while you was in town, the delay will be of no consequence.

I have since I saw you begun to put the materials together for my Treatise[1], and I find I should soon complete it, if it was not for the distress I am in for want of books, out of which I am to make my quotations: for though the English are very great politicians, they have I believe fewer books on Public Law, or anything that relates to Foreign Policy, than any other nation in the world. What particularly distresses me on this occasion is, that I find it absolutely necessary to complete my argument, that I should quote some of the best writers on the point of Natural Law; the Duke of Newcastle's letter only refers to them, and to do no more than that again, would be unsatisfactory, especially as I shall be so extensive on the other points. I have ordered all London to be searched for the books I want, and I have sent for two of them from Holland. I shall set them down at the bottom of this, that if you should have any of them yourself, or know of any one that hath a collection of books of this sort, you would be so good as to assist me: they must be somewhere in

---

[1] The Treatise was entitled, "A Discourse on the Conduct of Great Britain in respect to Neutral Nations during the present War." It was published during the present year, and was held in considerable estimation as a performance of great solidity and import: it was translated into several languages. Mr. Jenkinson was eminently conversant with the Laws of Nations, and the principles and details of Commerce.

England, since they were quoted by the lawyers in the above-mentioned memorial.

These delays will make me longer in finishing of it than I could wish, but this advantage will follow, that I shall be able to send it complete to you for your correction, and after all I shall get it printed by the meeting of the Parliament, and it would not be read much before. I hope to receive as soon as you conveniently can, the anecdote you promised me. I am, &c., CHAS. JENKINSON.

Loccenius de Jure Maritimo, lib. ii., cap. 4, sec. 12.

Voet de Jure Militari, c. 5, No. 21.

Heineccius de Navibus ob Victuram vetitarum Mercium commissis, cap. 2, sec. 9.

Bynkershoek Quæstiones Juris Publici, l. i., cap. 14, per totum.

Zouch (an Englishman) de Judicio inter gentes, pars 2ᵈᵃ, sec. 8, n. 6.

I should not think it necessary to quote all these, Heineccius, Bynkershoek, and Zouch, especially as I can add Puffendorff and Grotius.

MR. JENKINSON TO MR. GRENVILLE.

London, September 30, 1758

DEAR SIR,—I had last night the honour of your letter. I have very fortunately met with the greatest part of the authors I wanted: I sent down to Oxford for the old ones, and had the passages transcribed; and the new ones, and particularly Bynkershoek, I have picked up in London. All I want is Heineccius; I shall send to Holland for him. I have all his books but this particular tract. His History of the Roman Law is the best law book I ever read, and much exceeds anything of the same kind that Sir Matthew Hale has done in our law. I wait still for another authority or two more from Oxford, and I shall then set to work heartily and soon finish what I intend.

We expect every hour some news from Saxony. The King of Prussia and Marshal Daun are so near that they cannot well avoid coming to action.

We have at present great debates in town in relation to the conduct of General Bligh[1]. The military men fall very foul of him, and Colonel Clerk and Lord FitzMaurice suffer very much as his advisers; in short, there is much of party in this affair, as there always will be in unsteady Administrations.

The King has seen my Lord Howe, but not General Bligh, and this gives the greater weight to the clamour.

I am, &c., &c.   CHAS. JENKINSON.

EARL TEMPLE TO THE DUKE OF NEWCASTLE.

Stowe, October 1, 1758.

MY LORD,—I am obliged to your Grace for the honour of your letter, and for the assurances you give me of your favourable dispositions to promote my wishes in every instance in your power.

Far be it for me to think of adding to the difficulties and distractions of the times, by entering into com-

---

[1] In the disastrous affair at St. Cas, near St. Malo's, where the troops under his command were forced to re-embark, with very considerable loss.

petitions upon such a subject; I therefore avoid all reasonings upon it. Thus much only let me say to your Grace, that I found myself under the disagreeable circumstance of being obliged to state myself as a candidate for this mark of distinction[1], lest a real reluctance to mention myself shall hereafter be assigned as the reason for passing me over. In that light I was induced to write to you, and I hope I did it in terms the most respectful to the Crown, as well as friendly to your Grace. The promise of including me in the next promotion whenever the King shall be pleased to make it (which is the thing I asked), would undoubtedly be subject from many causes to many contingencies; but my mind was certainly disposed to give more than its full weight to the importance of the object, if attained, from the proof your Grace would thereby give of your real desire to cultivate the union of the connected Administration so necessary for the good of the public, which is my great and only favourite object. I am, with the highest respect, my Lord, &c., &c. TEMPLE.

THE REV. MR. COTTON TO MR. GRENVILLE.

Princess Amelia, Louisbourg Harbour,
October 24, 1758.

SIR,—Since my last, of September 27th, wherein I had the satisfaction to annex the account of Colonel Bradstreet's success on Lake Ontario, and that it was conjectured he would proceed further, but it was thought more prudent to desist, and for him to make a speedy return, as a superior force was expected upon

---

[1] The Order of the Garter.

the Lake from Canada, which might in some measure
have frustrated the good effects that the reduction of
Frontenac will produce, and accordingly be made the
best of his way towards Albany, after he had destroyed
the fort, magazine, ships, &c.

Since Mr. Amherst's junction with General Abercrombie we are ignorant of what has passed, though
nothing material had happened the 9th instant; but it
is expected they will repass the Lake again.

As to General Forbes, we have lately received accounts from him, which inform us that Major Grant,
of the Highland regiment, being detached from the
main body with 800 men, marched from Loyal Hannon
(distant 42 miles from Fort du Quesne), and got to
the Fort September 13th, and towards evening burnt
all their block-houses, and ruined their outworks without any opposition, and having made a disposition of
his little army, he remained with about 400 men, within
300 yards of the Fort, while the others took post at
some distance, and soon after the sun's rising, September 14th, the enemy rushed out of the Fort, to the
amount of a thousand, and attacked him; on which
the other parties hastened to his relief, and upon their
coming up found Major Grant and his troops almost
defeated, and by the superiority of the enemy they
were obliged to retreat, leaving behind 300 officers and
men killed, wounded, and taken prisoners, and the
others rejoined the General after being harassed by the
enemy for some miles.

Major Grant was among those left behind, and what
will be the further consequence of this enterprize time
must shew, though it is surprising to think that we
should attack with 800 men a place that 7000 or 8000

were marching against; and in all probability, if this advance body had avoided coming to an action 'till the main body had come up, and employed their time in reconnoitring all round the Fort, there can no doubt be made but they must have reduced it, for the Fort itself cannot well contain more than four or five hundred men, whereas there was upwards of a thousand in it, and they must have been obliged to make their escape, as undoubtedly the Indians would, if they perceived the whole army before the Fort; but the enemy having reconnoitred our troops in their march, knew very well our strength, and their own superiority, which encouraged the savages to remain, otherwise they never would have been able to have prevented their going away.

We still hope that the army will proceed, as the same express advises us that the troops were in high spirits, and only waited the second convoy of provisions.

These are the only material occurrences since Mr. Boscawen's leaving us, and whatever is worthy your notice I shall be very careful to transmit by every opportunity. I am, &c., &c.   N. COTTON.

EARL TEMPLE TO MR. GRENVILLE.

Monday (November, 1758).

DEAR BROTHER,—Jemmy and Elliot came here on Saturday night, and return to-morrow. The eloquence of the first, and a letter from Mr. P., have prevailed upon me, in conjunction with your second thoughts, not to put myself in the wrong in the opinion of my best friends. I, therefore, go for the birth-day[1], but write it

[1] On the 10th instant.

not to town. Silence has hitherto been predominant; whether anything, and what, will pass on Wednesday at the Treasury, I know not. No fresh news from Sir Richard. Potter exceedingly ill. Ever your most affectionate, with many loves, &c., &c.

MR. PITT TO MR. GRENVILLE.

Mr. PITT begs Mr. Grenville's succour, being so overwhelmed with business himself, as not to have time to draw the Address.

If Mr. Grenville be returned to town, and will be so good to be in St. James's Square *before seven*, Mr. Pitt will be infinitely obliged to him. The Address must be drawn by to-morrow morning, 10 o'clock.

Sunday, ½-past 4, November 19th, 1758.

MR. PITT TO MR. GRENVILLE.

(November 19, 1758.)

THIS instant returned from Mr. Speaker, past eleven. In case the Parliament be opened by Commission, as in 1736–7, the only difference is that the Address to the King is carried by the Privy Council, and the King is thanked *for the speech delivered by your Majesty's commands.*

Be so good to return the draught of the speech to-morrow morning.[1]

----

[1] Parliament met on the 23rd.

Bury Street, Friday morning,
(December 15, 1758.)

DEAR SIR,—Since I was with you I have seen Mr. Legge. He was so kind as to repeat what you had mentioned to me. He approved of the sort of thing which you recommended me to apply for, and he engaged to point it out himself to the Duke of Newcastle, and to urge, as strongly as he was able, the propriety of it. He was so good as to say that he looked upon it as a public concern, and that he should urge it under that idea. He made only this addition to your plan, that as I had been two years about Lord Holdernesse, and was considered by him as belonging to his office, he would ask it as a salary to be given to me on that account by warrant, and this to cease if it should ever be thought proper to employ me abroad.

All this I thought proper to send to you by a letter, as the necessity of going to Newcastle House prevents my attending you in person, and I have already had too many proofs of your kindness to doubt, that if you can forward this affair by yourself or through any one else, before you leave town, you would, even without an application, do it.

If the Duke of Newcastle could not be brought to consent to the point above mentioned, or something of the same sort, Mr. Legge then proposes the other alternative of a Commissioner of the Stamps, or some such office. I have, &c., &c.   CHAS. JENKINSON.

THE DUKE OF NEWCASTLE TO EARL TEMPLE.

Newcastle House, December 18, 1758.

My Lord,—I have the honour and pleasure to acquaint your Lordship, that I this day proposed to the King, that your Lordship should succeed the late Duke of Marlborough as Lord Lieutenant and Custos Rotulorum of the County of Bucks, which His Majesty was pleased to agree to, and I have spoken to Mr. Pitt to prepare the necessary instruments accordingly. I should not have deferred it so long, but that I thought that out of civility, I should first acquaint the present Duke with it, which I had not an opportunity of doing 'till this morning. I am, with the greatest truth and respect, my Lord, &c., &c. Holles Newcastle.

MR. JAMES GRENVILLE TO MR. GRENVILLE.

December 19, 1758.

Dear Brother,—I shall certainly obey your commands to the utmost of my power, but when the unnatural father leaves his own child to the mercy of the times, what zeal or endeavours can be found sufficient to supply so great a defection. The million was granted yesterday. The Admiralty laid in their claim for a farther demand if it should be found necessary before the end of the sessions. Mr. Chancellor insists upon one of two things, either that they shall ask the whole that in this abstracted possibility of things can come to be demanded between this and next Christmas twelve-month, or take upon themselves the case of any accidental deficiency: for break in upon the course he will not at any event.

We meet to-morrow; you shall hear farther what passes. Adieu. Ever yours, &c.   J. GRENVILLE.

EARL TEMPLE TO MR. GRENVILLE.

Tuesday, 4 o'clock, (December 19, 1758.)

THE younger brother of a Lord Lieutenant, if he behaves well, may possibly hope for an humble commission some time or other in the Militia. Last night I received a letter, civil, melancholy, and gentlemanlike, from the Duke of Newcastle, telling me that he had that morning named me to the King. This morning I waited upon his Grace in a civil, melancholy, and gentlemanlike mood. It was not his fault he said if everything I wished was not done: he explained and excused about Lord Mansfield[1]. I touched not the other subject, but decently took my leave: for a considerable time I believe. My reception of the most *distinguished* kind when I kissed hands: you know rumpatur quisquis rumpitur invidiâ.

I know no news, but that by the accounts of this day

---

[1] Lord Mansfield's influence in the Closet was now increasing; and being aware of the King's dislike to Lord Temple, he probably did not endeavour to remove it. A few months before this time, when the King had given him full powers to negotiate with Pitt and the Duke of Newcastle, Lord Mansfield stated that the King insisted Lord Temple should have no employment which required frequent attendance in the Closet.

it is probable the Princess of Orange¹ is by this time no more.

Sir George Lee's² death was most sudden.

Love to your poor melancholy, confined, tyrannized wife, and unhappy babes. Yours most affectionately, T.

Sir C. Williams³ is again confined. Mr. Pitt is this morning again confined by his old companion, and I hear has taken to a great shoe.

EARL TEMPLE TO THE DUKE OF NEWCASTLE.

(December 20, 1758.)

MY LORD,—I am extremely sensible to the great honour his Majesty is pleased to do me in appointing me Lieutenant of the County of Buckingham.

I am very happy in any mark his Majesty conde-scends to give me of his Royal goodness, and shall ever most humbly and gratefully acknowledge it.

I have many thanks to return to your Grace for

¹ The Princess of Orange died on the 12th of January following. She was the eldest daughter of George the Second, and was married to the Prince of Orange in 1734. Since the death of her husband in 1751, she had been Gouvernante during the minority of her son. In Lord Hervey's *Memoirs of George the Second* are some amusing details respecting this Princess and her husband.

² He died the day before the date of this letter, in his 64th year.

³ For some time past his health had rapidly declined, and his head was occasionally affected: towards the end of the following year he relapsed into a state of complete insanity, and died on the 2nd of November, aged 50. Sir Charles Hanbury-Williams is remembered principally for his sprightliness of conversation, ready wit, and agree-able manner, and for his poetical effusions, which were principally of a political and satirical character, often very closely bordering upon the extremes of licentiousness.

naming me to the King. I am, with the greatest respect, &c. Temple.

MR. JAMES GRENVILLE TO MR. GRENVILLE.

December 20, 1758.

Dear Brother,—The solemn conference between
Proud Treasury and Lordly Admiralty was held according to appointment.

The poor Orphan bill had the good fortune to find a
charitable friend or two, notwithstanding the defection
of its great founder; and from the weakness of its enemies, as well as from the zeal of its advocates, it passed
its time tolerably well. I went to school and endeavoured to get my lesson as well as I could from the moment I received your commands. I think I learned
enough to speak about it with the appearance of seeming to know something of the matter.

Elliot, Forbes, Hunter, Hay[1] were more able and not
less cordial friends. In short, the only vivacities that
made their sallies from the enemy, were certain blunt
thrusts and hints from Lord Anson about desertion and
unmanning the fleet, seconded by a gruff brightness or
two from Admiral Boscawen upon the same topic. Upon
the whole it was concluded that the 2,170,000*l.* granted
on the head wages would sufficiently answer the purposes of the bill, and satisfy all the probable, if not
absolutely all the possible, demands upon that head before next Christmas twelvemonths. If more should
appear to be wanting upon a nearer view of things towards the end of sessions, a farther application might

---

[1] All Lords of the Admiralty.

then be made, but it was agreed by all present that the sum already granted would, upon the most probable conjecture, suffice.

I have a statement in writing for you which is too long for me to insert here; I reserve it for your contemplation upon your coming to town. I am at present in too good company, and have upon my back my too fine clothes, and in my head a certain glass of too cheerful wine, to be fit for writing more accurately. I am, &c., &c.

J. GRENVILLE.

MR. JENKINSON TO MR. GRENVILLE.

London, December 26, 1758.

DEAR SIR,—I could not deny myself the pleasure of writing to you, though I have really nothing new to send you. The principal news we expect is from Holland, where the ferment is uncommonly great, and the health of the Princess Gouvernante is so very precarious, that the worst of news is to be expected. In short, the interested views of their merchants have obtained so great an influence in the republic, that I much question whether we shall be able to avoid coming to a rupture without giving up such of our rights as may be considered, perhaps, as too great a price for their friendship. The affair will at least require to be managed with the greatest delicacy and understanding.

In the morning after I had received the kind letter with which you was pleased to honour me, I saw the Duke of Newcastle, who gave me as good a reception as I could expect, and told me he should be glad to do anything for me; and I hear privately that he has spoken very warmly in my favour.

I had not, however, a proper opportunity, and therefore did not choose to enter into particulars. I have waited, indeed, for the effects of Mr. Legge's negociation; but I have been a little surprised that, after all which had passed between you and him, and after what he had in consequence of that promised to me, he has not yet spoken a word to the Duke of Newcastle about me. I have seen him three times since, and upon his not mentioning anything to me about it, I spoke to him. He confessed he had not as yet spoken—seemed to raise more difficulties about the affair than he had done at first—and seemed also to expect that the Duke should speak to him first; but, however, he then promised again expressly that he would open it to his Grace. I have not, however, as yet heard anything from him. I doubt not but he has good reasons, but this delay puts my whole affair at a stand during this delicate conjuncture. I hope, however, it may be capable of being recovered when my friends come to town: some comfortable provision on this occasion would make me the happiest man in the world, and would satisfy either my avarice or ambition. I shall tell you that Lord Hardwicke, who gave Lord Parker leave to introduce me to him, paid me personally compliments in such a manner that I think he would have promoted my interest if I could ever have gotten my affair once put in motion.

My Discourse is at present out of print, and I do not venture to publish it again 'till Lord Holdernesse comes to town, or signifies otherwise to me what he would have me do with it, to whom I have written on the occasion. As to the point of the Aggression, besides the manner of arguing, with which you was so kind as to furnish me, I think I can still strengthen that point with another topic ; for as we have formally made the requisition, and they have never returned any answer, the time of the execution of the Treaty coming to exist, there is from that instant a breach of it. We are not to suppose the objection 'till they make it, and may act therefore as if there was no objection at all, and whatever they may urge at present, it cannot concern what is past. I should tell you that a majority of the Province of Holland have, upon another occasion, declared as the aggressors, and they were willing to return an answer, but not in positive words declaring us the Aggressor, to the requisition we made; but as neither of these resolutions ever passed the generality, it cannot be considered as an act of the States.

There is another Pamphlet published on the same as mine, by a Proctor of Doctors' Commons. It is written in a dry unentertaining manner, but it contains many good materials; has hit off several new topics of argument, and has a good deal of merit.

I congratulate you on the Government's having at last acted properly in honouring Buckinghamshire with Lord Temple as Lord Lieutenant.

CHAS. JENKINSON.

MR. JENKINSON TO MR. GRENVILLE.

London, December 28, 1758.

DEAR SIR,—I find, since I wrote to you, that Mr. Legge has spoken to the Duke of Newcastle. I cannot tell precisely what answer His Grace gave him, as I have not seen Mr. Legge, but I believe it was favourable, though he (Mr. Legge) adds, that he has not yet been able to fix the particular employment with His Grace, but that he will not leave soliciting 'till he has done it. This is what Mr. Legge wrote on Saturday last in a letter to Lord Harcourt, from whence I transcribe it, but I can hear nothing farther from him at present, as he is out of town, and does not return until the meeting of the Parliament.

We have no news. The prisoners of St. Cas are arrived: one unfortunate man, a Mr. Grant, a Lieutenant of Grenadiers, is left behind, having killed an Irish officer in the French service, and who in the last rebellion was in the service of the Pretender. He was reduced to this unfortunate step by the insolency of the Irishman, who added to abusive language at last a stroke with a sword over the head: the affair happened at Boulogne, and the other English officers, before they left that town, drew up a strong representation of the case to be sent to the French Ministry, who, it is hoped, will order Mr. Grant to be released, especially as the Governor of Boulogne joined also to represent the affair favourably. I am, &c., &c.　　　CHAS. JENKINSON.

MR. JENKINSON TO MR. GRENVILLE.

London, January 2, 1759.

DEAR SIR,—I had last night the honour of your very obliging letter: your goodness to me in assuring me of your application when you come to town in my favour, is more than I could possibly expect, and demands my most grateful acknowledgments. Your interest at all times would be both of credit and service to me, but it will be of the utmost use at present, when it appears as if there was wanting only a steady and active friend to give motion (as it were) to those good dispositions, which they who dispose of His Majesty's favours pretend at present to bear towards me, and which without such a one would end I fear in fair words, without any real benefit to me.

I send you by this post several large packets: three of them contain the pamphlet I mentioned; one other and this, contain the argument of aggression which I have deduced more at length, though not as yet wholly to my satisfaction.

I hope you will honour it with your perusal, and add farther obligation in giving me freely your opinion on every part of it: besides any deficiency in the argument, it is not quite worded as I would have it, but I had not leisure to alter it.

Lord Holdernesse hath sent me orders to publish another edition of the Discourse[1] as soon as possible. I have therefore given orders for it, and I shall make several corrections in it. I should be glad, therefore, if you could return me these papers with your opinion on them by the post on Sunday.

I set out to-morrow for Oxford to vote for a Chancellor[2], but shall come immediately back again. If

---

[1] "Discourse on the Establishment of a National and Constitutional Force in England." The first edition was published in 1756.

[2] The Candidates were John Fane, Earl of Westmoreland; George Henry Lee, third Earl of Lichfield; and Richard Trevor, Bishop of Durham. Lord Westmoreland, who was elected, is described by Horace Walpole as "an aged man of gravity and dignity, married to a Cavendish, and formerly so attached to the House of Hanover, that he commanded the very body of troops which King George had been obliged to send to Oxford, to teach the University the only kind of passive obedience which they did not approve. But having fallen into

Lord Westmoreland's and Lord Lichfield's parties should continue divided, it is thought the Bishop of Durham may succeed, but the success of the last depends solely upon the separation of the former.

Lord Harcourt, who is at present at Nuneham, comes to town with me upon my return, which will be Saturday or Sunday, as most suits his Lordship.

We have no news: the Princess of Orange is said to be out of danger, but there are such strange accounts come over of the infirmities she is subject to, that I think her health is very little to be depended on.

I have, &c., &c.   CHAS. JENKINSON.

MR. JENKINSON TO MR. GRENVILLE.

London, January 11, 1759.

DEAR SIR,—I had the honour of all your packets on Monday, and am extremely obliged to you for the assistance you have been so good as to give me in relation to the most difficult of all points, the Aggression. I have been considering of it ever since. From the many hints you have been so good as to send me, I have no doubt I shall be able to show, that to enter into little cavils on account of the first Aggression, is contrary to the spirit of the Guarantees; but I fancy we must not make use of

the intimacy of Lord Chesterfield and Lord Cobham during the opposition to Sir Robert Walpole, his regiment was taken from him, and his resentment, which was not so versatile as theirs, had led him to imbibe all the nonsensical tenets of the Jacobites. They wanted a representative, and he was a comely one. The choice accordingly fell on him, after Lord Lichfield, who divided the Tories, had flung his interest into that scale, to prevent the election of the Bishop."—*Memoirs of George the Second*, vol. iii. p. 167.

any arguments which arise solely from the circumstances of the time when the Treaty of 1678 was made, as this was not then a new Treaty, but only a copy of an old one between France and the States; and for the same reason it seems improper to give any interpretation of the Treaty as subsisting now between England and Holland, which would not equally have holden between France and Holland when the same Treaty subsisted between them. I think, however, the point may be sufficiently proved without all this. I have several other observations to make, which are too long for a letter, but which will serve for conversation, when you come to town. I will draw out the affair against the time I see you; and as the point is of so very great importance, I think it will be best to show it to one or two of the Ministers, before I venture to publish it.

I came to town with Lord Harcourt on Sunday; Dr. Hay, who had been down to Oxford to poll as well as myself, joined us on the road. Lord Lichfield's party joined that of Lord Westmoreland, the day before the Election: if this had not happened, the Bishop would have been chosen, as he had a great majority of either of the others separately. I found the University in much better temper than I expected; the friends of Lord Lichfield and Lord Westmoreland had so much exhausted their rancour upon one another, that they had very little left for any one else.

I have a suspicion that Dr. Hay has a mind to offer himself for Member for the University, and I should not think it impossible but he might succeed.

One odd thing happened whilst we were there; that Beckford came and entered himself of Baliol College (of which he was formerly a member), and it is thought he intends to take his degrees regularly. We have not the least news, there have been no mails for this fortnight. Conway sets out to-morrow.

I have, &c., &c.   C. JENKINSON.

MR. JENKINSON TO MR. GRENVILLE.

London, January 18, 1759.

DEAR SIR,—Though this letter may possibly arrive at Wotton after you have left it, as I have gotten a piece of news or two to send you, I will still venture to write it.

A certain account is arrived that the French have abandoned Fort Duquesne, and that our troops had no other trouble than to take possession of it. This is surely a great proof of the internal weakness of the French in that part of the world, and seems to me, on that account, to be a more acceptable piece of news than if it had been taken after siege.

This event appears to have been known some time before in France. It is also confidently asserted (and by what I hear I believe with truth) that Mons. Bussy, who was employed by the Court of France in England about eighteen years ago, is arrived lately in London. The cause of his coming creates great speculation, and it is said that a person of that consequence could not arrive without some proposals of importance.

The last news from Holland brought so bad an account of the Princess of Orange that it is thought she must be dead by this time. I have, &c., &c.

CHAS. JENKINSON.

MR. JENKINSON TO MR. GRENVILLE.

London, April 7, 1759.

DEAR SIR,—So much has passed between Lord Holdernesse and myself upon my own affair since I saw you, that it would be impossible to recite the whole of it in a letter; I will keep, therefore, the particulars until I have the pleasure of seeing you; and I will endeavour only to give you a general idea of it.

When I first saw his Lordship the morning I spoke to you, I found him very much discomposed by the letter he had received the night before from Lord Harcourt; he seemed to impute this principally to me, and he was particularly offended with a part of it, where he was told that he had given me the strongest assurances that I should be Under Secretary in case of a vacancy, and that I had told my friends of it. He seemed at first to deny this, and by very passionate expressions to make me afraid to avow it. I followed your advice in keeping myself both from passion or reproaches, though there was the justest occasion for both. I told him, however, that there was not a word said in Lord Harcourt's letter which I meant to disown; and though I would not presume to keep him to his promise, yet I must beg him to recollect the assurances he had twice given me: I then calmly mentioned the time, the place, and the words in which he made them, and I then added that I repeated these with no other view but to confirm the truth of what was said in the letter: and I said that as to my having mentioned these to my friends, I did it to show the just reason I had to confide in his Lordship at a time when many wondered that some provision was not made for me, and this I thought he would not disapprove of. He then confessed the truth of all I said, and dropping all warmth in respect to myself, he at once changed his plea, and said that he would have given me the vacant employment if the Duke of Newcastle would have given the least thing in the world to Mr. Fraser, his private Secretary, but as the Duke of Newcastle had used him ill in that, he was obliged to make a remove in his office, that he might provide for Fraser. I then took up the conversation again, and after urging my pretensions as well as I could in a general manner, I added that I was particularly unfortunate that the Duke of Newcastle's ill usage of his Lordship had been the cause of my not having what he intended to give me, since his Grace had on the other hand urged as a reason for not having given me a pension, that he (Lord Holdernesse) meant that I should succeed to Mr. Wallace.

These words were hardly out of my mouth when he fell into the greatest fury rather than passion, oftentimes saying, *I know what you say is true, the Duke of Newcastle has used me shamefully ill; thank God, a person was by when all that passed on this occasion between the Duke and myself was said; it was all in the presence of Lady Yarmouth*[1]; *but I will have an éclaircissement with*

---

[1] Amelia Sophia de Walmoden, the reputed mistress of George the Second, by whom she was created Countess of Yarmouth for her life: at her decease in 1765, the peerage therefore became extinct. Archdeacon Coxe, in his *History of the Pelham Administration*, speaking of Lady Yarmouth, says that " she became the principal channel of communication between the King and his ministers, and from her acquaintance with his Majesty's temper, she knew how to introduce memorials, petitions, letters, and recommendations at the proper season; and thus not only relieved the King from personal importunities, but the ministers from the necessity of frequently irritating their

him on this point: I know not how it is, but those per-
sons with whom I first came into power have of late be-
haved strangely to me, and how cruel it is that they thus
force me in my own justification to discover it.

Astonished at all this, I affirmed what I said was
truth, that I should not have mentioned it unless I had
had your permission, and that much the same thing had
also been said to Lord Portsmouth[1]; he replied, that I
need not affirm it, for he knew of himself that it must
be true: he then concluded, that he would do the utmost for me, and that he would deliver in a paper to
Lady Yarmouth containing my pretensions, and would
get her to give it to the King. He would not tell me
what he meant precisely to ask, but bade me come to
him now more constantly than usual, as he should have
something now every morning to say to me, and desired
me to acquaint Lord Harcourt that he should be glad to
see him, but not until the beginning of the week, as
some new matter would by that time have arisen. I then
left him in very good humour, at least with myself. He
went down to Court, and from Court came up to wait on
Lord Harcourt, but did not find him at home. You
know already what had passed that morning between
Lord Harcourt and the Duke of Newcastle, so I do not
repeat it.

On Friday morning I saw Lord Holdernesse again:
he immediately called me in: he told me that he had

Royal master, by making applications which they knew would be disagreeable, but which the affairs of state rendered necessary."

The circumstances described by Mr. Jenkinson corroborate the observations of Coxe, and show the influence exercised by Lady Yarmouth
in the appropriation of places and pensions.

[1] John, second Earl, father of the present Lord Portsmouth.

had an éclaircissement with the Duke of Newcastle before Lady Yarmouth; that the Duke had said that he had been misunderstood in respect to the words it was pretended he had used; but, Lord Holdernesse added, notwithstanding that, I know what you said was true; but, continues he, as to yourself, the Duke said before Lady Yarmouth that he had engaged to get you a pension according to your desire, and added, that if the Duke set himself thoroughly to it he did not doubt but it would succeed, as from what had passed between them, the Duke would be able to assure the King, that there would be occasion to employ me in another way so soon, that the King would be charged with it but a very little time. Soon after this, Lord Portsmouth came in to Lord Holdernesse: in conversation upon me the latter repeated what he had said before to me, and added that he would add all his influence to bring the point to bear; assured him of his great regard for me; that he approved of my conduct in particular upon the present occasion, tried to convince Lord Portsmouth that the Duke of Newcastle's ill-usage of him in respect to Fraser was a sufficient reason for his not complying with his assurances to me, and then added that as there must necessarily be a congress soon for a Peace, that there was no doubt but I should in that case be the Secrétaire d'Ambassade.

This morning I saw his Lordship again, when he told me that the Duke of Newcastle had not spoken to the King yesterday, but that he had engaged before Lady Yarmouth to return an answer by the middle of the week.

I hope you will excuse this very long tale; I shall leave you to make your own reflections upon it. If there is any sincerity in all that is passed, I think I shall succeed. Whatever, however, the success may be, I am equally obliged to you for the great pains, and the very kind and friendly part which you was so good as to take in it. I had the pleasure of seeing this morning the two children you have left behind you; they are both very well. We have not the least news, though we are in the greatest expectations: the Mail of Friday is not yet arrived. I am, &c., &c.   CH. JENKINSON.

As this letter contains what it would not be proper that it should be known, I shall seal it with a wafer first, and wax over it, that it may not be opened without our knowing it.

MR. JENKINSON TO MR. GRENVILLE.

London, April 10, 1759.

DEAR SIR,—By the mail which arrived last night from Holland, we have an account that the Hereditary Prince of Brunswick had advanced upon the army of the Empire, and, with two squadrons of Prussian Horse, had destroyed two regiments of the troops of Wirtemberg, one of Infantry and one of Cavalry, and that he was now driving the remainder of that army back into Franconia.

Prince Ferdinand is at Fulda, but no action hath as yet happened between any part of his troops and those of the French. Lord Granby and General Mostyn was got up to the army, and it does not appear that the French army upon the Rhine are likely to make any motion to disturb the operation of Prince Ferdinand. This is, I believe, all the news.

As to my own affair, nothing as yet is done in it. I did not indeed expect that the Duke of Newcastle would speak before to-day, but think it probable that he will do it this morning, and this news is come fortunately enough to put the King into a good humour. I have the greatest reason to think that Lord Holdernesse finds himself very much embarrassed, but in his behaviour to me he is much more full of attention than usual.

I am, &c., &c.   CHAS. JENKINSON.

It is said in town, that Lord Waldegrave is going to marry Miss Maria Walpole[1].

MR. JENKINSON TO MR. GRENVILLE.

London, April 12, 1759.

DEAR SIR,—Though we are at present without any foreign news, I could not help troubling you with a letter, that I might send you the account of a decision which was this day given in a second Dutch appeal. The case was a very strong one : it was that of a Dutch ship coming directly from St. Domingo with a cargo confessed to be the property of the French. The Lords Commissioners have in this case confirmed the decision of the Court of Admiralty, and have condemned both ship and cargo; but they have in this, as in the former instance, avoided any mention of the Treaty, and they have considered the ship, in this case, as an adopted

---

[1] James, second Earl of Waldegrave, K.G., and some time Governor to George, Prince of Wales. He was married, on the 15th of May following, to Miss Maria Walpole, second daughter of Sir Edward Walpole. Lord Waldegrave died of small-pox, on the 13th of April, 1763. His widow was re-married to William Henry, Duke of Gloucester, brother of King George the Third.

French ship, proved to be such from several particular circumstances, and as such no object of the Treaty, and on this principle they have founded their instance.

The Lords present were Lords President, Hardwicke, Mansfield, Harcourt, Berkeley, Sandys, Falmouth, Cholmondeley, Duke of Argyll, and Mr. Legge. Pratt[1] and Hay were for the captors; both did well, particularly Pratt in his reply. Mr. Yorke[2] gave us again a very long discourse, and as much laboured as his former.

I hear nothing further yet about my own affair; but I see what I know not how to interpret. His Lordship of Holdernesse, notwithstanding all that has passed, shews such particular attention to me at present, as if I was the master of his affections, and that he had conferred some great favour upon me. These Ministers are certainly most inexplicable beings!

The three Dutch Commissioners[3] are arrived; but they have not as yet been with any of the Ministers, or appeared at Court, though they have been in town ever since Monday night. I am, &c., &c.   CHAS. JENKINSON.

MR. JENKINSON TO MR. GRENVILLE.

London, April 17, 1759.

DEAR SIR,—I had the favour of your letter last night. I have no news in return to send you. The

---

[1] Sir Charles Pratt was now Attorney-General, and afterwards Lord Camden, and Lord High Chancellor.

[2] Mr. Charles Yorke: at this time Solicitor-General.

[3] Their instructions were to insist upon the release of certain Dutch vessels which had been taken, and to adhere to the Treaty of 1674, with respect to contraband articles. Walpole, in noticing their arrival, writes to Sir Horace Mann, " The Dutch Deputies are a proverb for their dulness."

Duke of Newcastle has not as yet spoken to the King, and Lord Holdernesse, on the other hand, delays still to fill up his office. His Lordship told me to-day that he would put the Duke in mind of speaking just as he went into the King's closet, but as I have not heard anything this afternoon, I presume his Grace has not spoken.

The Dutch Deputies were introduced this morning to the King, and I suppose they will now immediately begin their negociation. Your remarks are certainly just in reference to their coming at this juncture, and I am convinced that in case the appeal which was last tried had been given in favour of the claimant, it would have produced consequences of which the Government would have reason to repent.

What I have heard of the Brest Fleet is that the French have undoubtedly a great many ships in that harbour, but whether they could man them or fit them for sea was the doubt. It is commonly, however, supposed that Boscawen's orders for the Mediterranean are countermanded, and that he is now gone only to the Bay.

The last Mail brought nothing new from Germany. Every one almost is gone to Newmarket except Kitty Fisher, who is descended to Lord Poulet's[1], in Devonshire, to whom it is doubted whether she is to become wife or mistress.

The young Duke of Marlborough[2] is lately come

---

[1] John, second Earl : he died unmarried in 1764.

[2] George, third Duke of Marlborough. He had recently succeeded to the Dukedom. He married Caroline, only daughter of John, fourth Duke of Bedford, and died in 1817. His mother was Elizabeth, daughter of Thomas, Lord Trevor.

to town, and by the advice of his mother has flung himself totally on Lord Harcourt to direct his conduct in the County of Oxford, and this with such circumstances as makes me think that Fox has no great influence over him.   I am, &c., &c.   C. J.

MR. JENKINSON TO MR. GRENVILLE.

London, April 19, 1759.

DEAR SIR,—The Dutch Deputies have begun their negotiation ; as preliminary conditions, prior to any farther agreement, they have demanded an extrajudicial release of all the ships which have already been taken, and that some further security shall be given them for their trade to their own colonies.   If these points are granted them, they are then willing to enter into some agreement upon the future interpretation of the Treaty of 1674, and to confine the privileges of it to Europe only.

These are such proposals as cannot possibly be complied with, and there seems indeed to be such a storm rising, that it will require the greatest prudence in the Ministers of his Majesty to conduct themselves through this affair.

The only other piece of news which we at present enjoy, is that Capt. Barrington[1], in a 64-gun ship, has taken a French ship of 60 guns.   I know not the name of either of the ships, or the particulars of the action.

A Treaty of Marriage between Lord Waldegrave

---

[1] A younger brother of Lord Barrington, afterwards an Admiral : he died in 1800.

and Miss Maria Walpole is completely agreed on. I am, &c., &c. CHAS. JENKINSON.

MR. JENKINSON TO MR. GRENVILLE.

Bury Street, April 24, 1759.

DEAR SIR,—We received this morning an account that Prince Ferdinand had attacked the army of the Duke of Broglio, which was entrenched at Bergen, a village not far from Hanau, and that he had been repulsed.

There is no relation of this affair as yet directly from the Prince, and indeed all that we know is very confused and inconsistent. The French account you will see in the papers.

There are letters also from Mr. Hunter, at Munster; these make our loss to amount to no more than 1100. It is universally agreed that Prince Isenburgh[1] is killed; the British troops which were there, as they consisted only of Cavalry, could have little concern in an affair of entrenchments, and have therefore suffered but little. The French are said to have evacuated Hanau. You see how very contradictory all this is. It is certain that this event has prevented the execution of the plan which Prince Ferdinand designed; but I question whether the affair, considered exclusively of that, will turn out much to our disadvantage. I have, &c., &c. CHAS. JENKINSON.

[1] It was true that Prince Isenburgh was killed in this battle at Bergen, and that Prince Ferdinand had failed in his design; but he was enabled to make a safe and judicious retreat to a place called Winkeden.

MR. JENKINSON TO MR. GRENVILLE.

London, May 24, 1759.

DEAR SIR,—The only authentic news I have at present to send you relates to a Dutch cause, which was this day tried before the Lords of Appeal. The ship was clearly Dutch, and bound from Amsterdam to St. Eustatia; the cargo outward bound was of a suspicious nature, consisting of provisions and gunpowder, and at St. Eustatia she took on board some coffee, which the Captain swears to be Dutch property, and other goods which came undeniably from the French islands, and to the property of which the Captain would not swear; there was also great irregularity in the ship's papers, there being no Charter Party, and several of the Bills of Lading not being signed.

Upon consideration of these particulars, their Lordships have sentenced *that the ship and coffee whose property is attested, be released, and that the claimant be admitted into the proof of the property of the rest of the cargo.*

You will see by this that their Lordships have come nearer to a determination of the existence, or at least interpretation of the Treaty, than they have done yet, for though the ship is avowedly Dutch, they have clearly given to understand, that if the cargo should even in part appear to be French, they will condemn it.

I was ordered myself to attend one of the Dutch Deputies to the Council; he appeared very well satisfied with the method of the proceedings, and when the sentence was given, he did not show any displeasure, though I will not be sure that he will be contented with it.

We have at present no other news, though we have the justest reason to be in expectation of it. Prince Henry's army and the army of the Empire must soon come to some decision. Prince Ferdinand's troops marched out of cantonment the 16th ; some event must soon arrive in consequence of all this.

There are reports flying this day about the City, that Mr. Moore has had some success at St. Pierre, in Martinico. All, however, which the Government knows of this affair amounts to this, that by a ship just arrived from Jamaica, it appears that a vessel had arrived there from the Leeward Islands, giving an account that Guadaloupe having completely surrendered, Mr. Moore and the forces were sailed away to Martinico, but what their design was was not known. I am, &c., &c.   CHAS. JENKINSON.

MR. PITT TO MR. GRENVILLE.

Hayes, Monday, May 28, 1759.

DEAR GRENVILLE,—I have the joy to acquaint you, that Lady Hester was safely delivered of a boy[1] this morning, and that mother and child are, thank God, in as good a way as can be.

Lady Hester, sends her love to you and Mrs. Grenville, and we both assure ourselves that our news will not be unwelcome. I send this by Monday's post, trusting that it may reach a day sooner. I am ever, &c., &c.   W. PITT.

[1] Afterwards the celebrated Statesman, William Pitt.

MR. JENKINSON TO MR. GRENVILLE.

London, May 29, 1759.

DEAR SIR,—I know of no event of any importance to send you. The account of the progress of the army of Prince Henry is printed in all the papers. We have, as yet, no direct intelligence that he is gotten to Bamberg, but we credit the Brussels news, which says that he is.

This was the first great object, as the magazines of the army of the Empire were lodged in that city; but we imagine that his Highness means now to advance still farther into Franconia.

I do not find that the Dutch Deputies are dissatisfied with the last decision. Lord Granville spoke for the first time in the Council upon this cause. He told the Lords, that he did not approve the method they followed of making so many distinctions in their decisions. He said he thought they had better speak out at once their sentiments upon the Treaty, since he was sure they would be reduced to it at last.

I should have mentioned before, that Prince Ferdinand is moving down the Lippe towards the Lower Rhine, and has left General Imhoff to command in Hesse, while, on the other hand, Monsieur de Contades is marched to join Broglio's army on the Maine, and has left Mons. d'Armentiers to command in his place. The French army is said to be in a very ill condition, no less than five regiments of Horse being laid up with the glanders.

Notwithstanding all that is said in the papers, I do not find that the French fleet is as yet come out, or even ready as yet to come out. I have, &c., &c.

C. JENKINSON.

THE REV. MR. COTTON TO MR. GRENVILLE.

Louisbourg, June 1, 1759.

SIR,—I did myself the honour last year to transmit to you as particular accounts of the good and bad success attending the British armies in this part of the world, as I could procure in my situation ; I flatter myself that I did not incur your displeasure, and hope that the doing myself the same honour this year, will meet with your approbation, as I am fully sensible that your desires are equally great to hear further accounts of the flourishing state of the English, and the decline of the French, and I shall, in as few words as possible, give you the true state of affairs in America, which are as follows : viz.—

Admiral Saunders arrived at Halifax the beginning of May, at which time Admiral Durell sailed for the River St. Lawrence, and if the ice did not prevent him, was to make the best of his way with eight sail of the line, and a frigate or two, to the Isle of Bie, and higher if possible to that of Coudres, the former of which is between sixty and seventy leagues, the latter ninety ; and in all probability, let him anchor at either of the aforementioned places, he will effectually prevent supplies passing them for Quebec, unless the enemy should force him with a superior naval armament, and then he has nothing to do, but to conquer, or be conquered ; and lest the French should attempt the River after him, Admiral Saunders with the remainder of the fleet and army will sail to reinforce him in a very few days, and to push the operations up the river with the greatest vigilance, and from the martial spirit that appears in our Admirals, and Generals, and Troops, there is a great prospect of success; and I know but one thing that may defeat our hopes, which is, that in case the French should judge their possessions all at stake, and that it is most prudent to make the strongest opposition at the capital, I cannot but fear· that we shall meet such a superiority of numbers to our army, as will be sufficient to overpower us, and oblige a retreat; for I think it so tender a point with them, that either they must (on our safe getting up the river) make the best terms for the whole, or a very forcible opposition, which will be before we take possession of the ground, and compel us to dispute every inch with them; and if they have the numbers they ought to have, and can, they may by one or frequent engagements reduce our troops, so as that courage and bravery must submit to superiority of numbers, and nothing else.

If General Amherst should meet with the desired success to the westward, and push his conquests to Montreal, it will greatly facilitate the river expedition, and weaken their strength at Quebec; and I hope to have the satisfaction towards the close of the campaign to send you the agreeable account of the reduction of both the above-mentioned places, and at present can surmise nothing that will frustrate the designs, unless it is the defeat of one of our armies, which will enable the enemy to reinforce as their service may require.

When our fleets join, we shall make twenty-one or two sail of the line, besides frigates, &c., and hope it will be a naval force sufficient to keep the enemy at a proper distance if they should send out a fleet into these parts; though, if they should send out a fleet upon this coast while ours is up the river, they might create some confusion, and if they pushed with vigour, reduce some of our settlements.

As to the state of the army, I am not so knowing to that as to be so particular in its strength, though the whole, marines, &c., will not exceed 8000 effective men, and by appearances, are as complete for the service as the like number in any part of the world; and it is to be hoped that the navigation up the River will be such as will favour their designs as soon as can be well expected.

The winter in this part has in fact been very severe, and in my passage to this place, I met with vast quantities of ice, that as the wind sets out or in to this harbour, fills it in such manner as renders it almost impracticable for boats to pass and repass from the ships to the town.

It has been Admiral Durell's and Governor Pownall's[1] pleasure to keep me going from Halifax to Boston, three or four times the winter past, to settle the terms between them relative to the engaging of seamen to enter into his Majesty's service, to enable the fleet that wintered at Halifax to put to sea this spring; and it was attended with such success, that before I left Boston, there were 250 sent down to Admiral Durell, and it is expected that more will enter.

Although Admiral Durell did not sail for the river 'till after Mr. Saunders's arrival, yet I believe the severity of the season, in the great body and islands of

[1] Thomas Pownall, at this time Governor of South Carolina. He had been Lieut.-Governor of New Jersey in 1755, and in 1757 Governor of Massachusetts Bay. He will be hereafter mentioned in these volumes.

ice that are now in the Gulph, will prove fatal to some
of the honest seamen, for it is very difficult to believe
all, unless one is an eye-witness of it, and made sensible
by the intenseness, which is more than can be conjectured, and at this season of the year.

We have not heard a word from Admiral Durell
since his departure; the *Alcide* and *Stirling Castle,*
which were ordered to reinforce him, on their way to
him fell in with a store-ship from France, took and
sent her in here, laden with powder and clothing for
Quebec, burthen 200 tons, and came out, as they say,
with two more and two frigates on the King's account,
which I hope will meet with the same fate.

I shall take particular care to be as accurate in my
accounts as is possible, and never presume to insert anything more than I am satisfied can be depended upon,
and I hope on my return to England to have the honour
of your countenance and patronage.   I am, &c., &c.

NATHANIEL COTTON.

MR. JENKINSON TO MR. GRENVILLE.

London, June 14, 1759.

DEAR SIR,—I have the pleasure to acquaint you that
Colonel Clavering[1] is arrived from Guadaloupe, and
brings us the agreeable news of a total surrender of that
Island to us.   I have seen very little relating to this
event as yet, and the Government has as yet published
nothing concerning it, so that I am not able to send you

---

[1] Colonel Clavering brought letters to Mr. Pitt from the Hon.
General Barrington and Commodore Moore, containing full details of
these events, which were afterwards published in the *London Gazette.*

any particulars. I do not find, however, that we have had any loss except what has happened from sickness. I congratulate you on this piece of good news, as I think in every respect of importance.

The next place from whence we are to expect news is the Pays de Hesse. Here the French are making the greatest efforts, and by this means to advance at last into Saxony.

The armies of Maréchal Contades and the Duke of Broglio are joined, and if we mean to defeat their designs, I should think an action must soon ensue.

Some ships are sending to the Mediterranean to re-inforce Boscawen.

Lord Harcourt saw the Duke of Newcastle a few days before he left town: his Grace then assured him that he would certainly do my affair; but when I saw him a few days ago, he then told me that there was an intention of sending me abroad immediately, and he wished that I might succeed. This was, I have no doubt, only a pretence to account for his not having as yet accomplished the other request. Lord Harcourt intends to write to him again; I wish I could get his Grace to accomplish this affair, as I am heartily tired of my long attendance, and want very much to be out of town. I have, &c., &c.　　　CHAS. JENKINSON.

MR. PITT TO MR. GRENVILLE.

Hayes, June 23, 1759.

DEAR GRENVILLE,—Lady Hester and I feel a most sensible satisfaction from the more favourable accounts of your dear children, and we trust that a very little time longer will not leave the least room for any anxiety. Our little tribe are, thank God, in perfect health, the last arrived of which is the subject of a request which father and mother desire to make to you, and which they trust you will easily pardon them for troubling you with, from a certain fellow-feeling which all true promoters of christenings must have for one another. We hope that you will do us the honour to be godfather to our boy, and if you are so good to grant us that favour, care shall be taken of your proxy.

Lady Hester, who walks abroad with more courage than conduct, joins in all affectionate compliments and best wishes for Wotton.

We expect every moment news of a general action in Hesse: the expectation is big with inquietudes, but hope predominates. I am ever, &c., &c. W. PITT.

MR. JENKINSON TO MR. GRENVILLE.

London, June 26, 1759.

DEAR SIR,—I have not for some time troubled you with a letter, in hopes of being able to transmit to you some news of importance, and the near approach of the two armies of Prince Ferdinand and Marshal Contades seemed likely to have afforded that opportunity, but the accounts which were yesterday received from Holland say that the Prince is retired to Lipstadt. There are no letters by the last mail from the army, but if the above circumstance is true (as I believe it is), there will be no action for some time.

The only particular that is worth sending you is a

very silly action of Lady Coventry[1], who having been insulted in the park, Sunday was se'nnight, the King heard of it, and said, that to prevent the same for the future he would have a guard. Upon this foundation her ladyship ventured boldly again into the park on Sunday evening, but she was attended with two Sergeants of the Guards in front, with their halberds, and no less than twelve followed her. The whole guard was ready to have turned out if there had been occasion, and the Colonel of the Guard in waiting kept at the proper distance : with this ridiculous parade she walked there from 8 of the clock to 10 ; and as all this could not prevent the mob from having curiosity, some impertinent things were still uttered, though at some little farther distance, and some of Fielding's men that attended took up the most troublesome. I am, &c., &c.

                                        CHARLES JENKINSON.

MR. JENKINSON TO MR. GRENVILLE.

London, July 3, 1759.

DEAR SIR,—Though the progress which the French are enabled, by the superiority of their numbers, to make on the Continent is not the most agreeable news, and makes the world in general apprehensive that they will again get possession of Hanover, and retain it as a deposit in case of peace ; yet our accounts from every other quarter are as good as we could wish. A frigate yesterday arrived from Saunders, bringing an account that he with the fleet, and the troops under the com-

---

[1] Maria Gunning, Countess of Coventry, so celebrated for her beauty.

mand of Mr. Wolfe[1], sailed from Louisbourg on the
3rd of June, and were proceeding in their voyage towards Quebec.   All the letters also agree that the
troops were in remarkable health and spirits, and that
everything there bore a favourable aspect.

There are letters, also, this day from Sir Edward
Hawke, saying, that he had looked into Brest Water,
and that there were neither so many ships there, nor
those in so much forwardness as had been reported.

I have, &c., &c.   C. JENKINSON.

SIR RICHARD LYTTELTON TO MR. GRENVILLE.

Ealing, July 7, 1759.

MY DEAR GEORGE,—It was not 'till Thursday that
Lady Bute told us of Master Grenville's illness.   You
know how sincerely the Duchess and I interest ourselves
in whatever concerns you and Mrs. Grenville, you will
therefore believe the anxiety we are under for your
sweet boy, and how much we long to hear of his being
out of danger, and that you are free from your fears in
regard to him.   God send him a speedy recovery.

Letters from our gallant friend Rodney received yes-

---

[1] General Wolfe had been appointed by Pitt to the command of the
enterprise against Quebec. Walpole, in his *Memoirs of George the
Second*, has accurately described the character of Wolfe as " a young
officer who had contracted reputation from his intelligence of discipline,
and from the perfection to which he had brought his own regiment.
The world could not expect more from him than he thought himself
capable of performing. He looked on danger as the favourable moment that would call forth his talents." The same author speaks of
Admiral Sir Edward Hawke as " a man of steady courage, of fair
appearance, and who even did not want a plausible kind of sense : but
he was really weak, and childishly abandoned to the guidance of a
Scotch Secretary."

terday at the Admiralty, give an account of his having
begun his operations against Havre with good appearance of success; that his shells had twice set fire to the
town and stores, and seemed to take place amongst the
boats, but with what success was not precisely known
(as I apprehend), and that he was at the time the sloop
left him closely engaged with some batteries. I have
had no account from authority, but this intelligence I
have just received from a person who saw his letter.

I know little what passes in my retirement, but some
things I have lately heard of do not delight me greatly.
Lord Ligonier[1], you must long since have heard, has
got the Ordnance, but what of that? I have heard of
private audiences, and presents of hock and sausages—
't is strange, the *produce of Westphalia*—'t is strange,
but I hear 't is true : well! all 's well that ends well, say
some folks. God send good success to Rodney, say I,
and then I shall neither fear the French nor a new G.
'T is hot work at Havre, and at Quebec too, by this
time. Good success to Wolfe and Townshend[2] is my

---

[1] Lord Ligonier was appointed to succeed the Duke of Marlborough
as Master General of the Ordnance.

[2] Brigadier General George Townshend, afterwards Lord Townshend. He was associated with Wolfe in the expedition against Quebec.
Upon the death of Wolfe, and General Monckton being wounded,
Townshend assumed the chief command at Quebec, and signed the
articles of capitulation. He was accused of attempting to appropriate
to himself the honours of the conquest; and it is certain that in his
letters to Pitt, immediately after the battle, he said nothing in praise
of Wolfe. He was soon afterwards very bitterly attacked by the
writer of a letter, which was published under the title of a *Letter to an
Honourable Brigadier General*. This production attracted considerable
attention, and was the cause of Townshend challenging Lord Albemarle
as the friend of the Duke of Cumberland, at whose instigation he
believed the Letter to have been written. I shall abstain from any
further allusion to this Letter at present, as I shall have occasion to
say more upon that subject, when I treat of the Authorship of the
Letters of JUNIUS.

toast also.   Our kindest compliments to Mrs. Grenville. Adieu.   Yours, &c., &c.   R. L.

MR. JENKINSON TO MR. GRENVILLE.

Bury Street, July 7, 1759.

DEAR SIR,—I was extremely sorry to hear by your letter last night of the ill state of health of Master Grenville.   I do not wonder at your great concern, and I partake myself most sincerely of it; but I hope that Providence, at least for the parents' sake, will on this occasion spare the child.   I am in the utmost distress for poor Mrs. Grenville.

If public news would not on this occasion look like impertinence, I should inform you that letters were yesterday received from your friend Mr. Rodney, which give an account that he had bombarded Havre de Grace, that he had set it on fire in several places, that some of the flat-bottomed boats had been burnt, that the fleet still continued the bombardment when the Express came away, and that they could not therefore as yet precisely know the loss of the enemy.

I might also add that an account was this morning received that some of the French were landed in Kent, and orders began to be given out in consequence, when about two hours after another account arrived, saying that the former was all a mistake,   I have, &c., &c.

C. JENKINSON.

MR. JENKINSON TO MR. GRENVILLE.

London, July 17, 1759.

DEAR SIR,—As I am sure you are convinced how sincerely I grieve and condole with you and Mrs. Grenville for the loss[1] you have so lately sustained, I will not contribute by the use of many words to renew your own sorrow on this melancholy occasion.

I will rather endeavour to divert it, and as you are a Captain of Militia, I will first tell you that the Norfolk Militia passed this day in review before the King, and in the opinion of every one made a very good appearance. Lord Orford[2] marched at the head of them as Brigadier-General, having a Commission given him for that purpose.

The cap of their Grenadiers was of an uncommon shape ; they are like the Devils' caps on the stage, and one of each pair of colours is black, with the arms of the county upon it. The King appeared very much pleased, and Lord Orford seemed justly proud thus to have 1200 of his countrymen following him for the defence of his country.

Prince Ferdinand is retreated to Osnaburgh. He left the passage to Hanover open to the French, but they did not choose to enter : the truth is they were afraid to leave our army in the rear, which was what the Prince wanted ; but they are resolved, if they do enter Hanover, to drive our army into it before them.

Boscawen sends accounts that there are preparations at Toulon which will make the French fleet equal in number to his own. I am, &c., &c.   C. JENKINSON.

---

[1] The death of their eldest son, Richard Percy Grenville, about seven years of age.

[2] George, third Earl of Orford, grandson of Sir Robert Walpole. He was Lord Lieutenant of Norfolk. The review of his regiment of Militia took place in Hyde Park, and is mentioned with great satisfaction by his uncle, Horace Walpole (*Correspondence*, vol. iii. p. 463); and also by Mr. Pitt, in the *Chatham Correspondence* (vol. ii. p. 4).

MR. PITT TO MR. GRENVILLE.

Hayes, July 21, 1759.

My dear Grenville,—I should attempt in vain to give expression to the sentiments of my heart for you and Mrs. Grenville, nor is consolation to be offered but by the hand of Time, aided by the very source of your present just affliction, parental tenderness for the dear gifts of Heaven which remain ; and may that protecting Heaven preserve them to you, and both of you to them, to each other, to your family, and friends! I learn with infinite satisfaction that your health and Mrs. Grenville's has been able to support itself. Give every attention to that article I beseech you, for without competent strength of body, vain are the efforts of the strongest and wisest minds.

I will not resign the hope of a run, some day this summer, to Wotton, for the health and comfort of which I form the sincerest unceasing wishes. I am ever, &c., &c.

W. Pitt.

MR. JENKINSON TO MR. GRENVILLE.

London, July 26, 1759.

Dear Sir,—I am obliged to leave town, and be thereby deprived of an opportunity of transmitting you intelligence just at a time when news was likely to arise that was worth sending; besides what might be expected from the West Indies, the armies on the Continent are at present placed in such a situation that events must probably have already happened which will determine not only the fate of this campaign, but also of the war. The cause of my going out of town is to attend a brother who has lately had the Small Pox very bad, and is going into the country to recover his health. I set out therefore for Hampshire to-morrow morning: I shall stay, however, as little time there as possibly I can, that I may return again to town to hunt a certain Minister[1], who never does a favour with a good grace, and must fairly be run down if you mean to have him accomplish any promise he has made to you.

Lord Harcourt has again written to him in a more serious and urgent manner than can be imagined consistent with that great kindness with which he has always indulged me, but it has as yet produced no effect. Every time I see his Grace he still repeats to me the same promises. His own people, *West* and *Jones,* have put him in mind of it, but all will not as yet bring him to a performance. I shall follow, however, the advice of my friends, and continue to pursue the blow, though it is the most irksome and ungenerous task I was ever engaged in in my life.

Anything directed to me at Winchester will find me. I am, &c., &c.   C. JENKINSON.

MR. JENKINSON TO MR. GRENVILLE.

Winton, August 6, 1759.

DEAR SIR,—The only things worthy of observation in this place are the French prisoners, and a regiment of Militia. The number of the first amounts at present to 3600: they consist of all nations: there are some even Turks, many Irish, and a few days ago a Militia-man of Wiltshire discovered his own brother. They are con-

---

[1] The Duke of Newcastle.

fined here in a house which belongs to the Crown, and
which was begun by Charles the Second for a palace, and
stands upon a very high spot of ground, where a castle
before stood that belonged to the famous Sir William
Waller. Adjoining to this has been railed in a large
piece of ground, where the prisoners are let out in the
day to air themselves. They complain very much of the
French Government for having withdrawn its allowance
from them: many of them have offered, as I am told, to
enter into our service, and some were accepted, but they
behaved themselves so very ill that they were remanded
to prison. They have established a sort of Police
among themselves, and try and punish all that are guilty
of little thefts and other crimes. It appears from this
how naturally men form themselves into civil societies.
They keep up also some forms of religion, assembling
every morning to sing their matins, and in the evening
their vespers. The regular life they are obliged to lead
preserves them uncommonly healthy, though they are so
very ragged that they have very little to cover themselves from the inclemency of the weather.

The Militia of Wiltshire are here to guard them, and
went on Saturday into camp. Lord Bruce[1], who commands them, discharges his duty in a manner that does
him honour. Lientenant-Colonel Northey and Captain
Beckford are also very assiduous. They are a finer body
of men than the Norfolk Battalions, but not under so
good discipline. The Warwickshire Militia, which was
marched as far as Salisbury with a design to have been
encamped also here, are countermanded. Lord Denbigh[2],

---

[1] Thomas Brudenell, second Baron Bruce, afterwards Earl of Ailesbury. He died in 1814.

[2] Basil Feilding, sixth Earl of Denbigh. He died in 1800.

upon hearing what was to be their destination, flew immediately to town and represented the indignity that was offered to his corps in appointing them to the guard of prisoners, so that for this, or some other reason, their destination is altered.

I am very much obliged to you for your kind wishes in relation to myself : the treatment I have received on this occasion gives me the greatest concern, as it places me in a situation, which of all others I was most desirous to avoid ; however troublesome I might be to other people, I hoped never to become so to those who were truly my friends, and I always flattered myself that at least, by industry and good intentions, I might render any application they should make in my favour not very difficult, as I was always resolved it should be reasonable ; but in the present case I have not only been a trouble to my friends, but have also brought a disgrace on them, since in favour of me they have been refused a request, which on such an application has usually been granted to the lowest and least deserving of beings ; and though their kind endeavours were backed and supported by the good inclination of the public in general, yet in the present instance it has availed nothing, and his Grace of Newcastle is resolved upon the present occasion to show the plenitude of his power, and that no circumstance or consideration shall oblige him to perform even a promise, where, at the same time that he passed his word, his inclination was not with it.   I have, &c., &c.

CHAS. JENKINSON.

THE REV. MR. COTTON TO MR. GRENVILLE.

Princess Amelia, Isle Madame, August 27, 1759.

SIR,—The following is a copy of my letter to you, dated August 10th and 15th, Isle Madame, which was put on board His Majesty's ship *Diana* for conveyance, and is as follows, viz. :—

In the beginning of June last, I took the liberty, Sir, to send you as true a state of affairs in America as I could then procure, and I hope it arrived safe in His Majesty's ship *Nightingale*, who sailed from Louisbourg for England, June 10th, and in that letter I hinted that I feared but one thing, which might defeat our hopes in this quarter, which was that the enemy might assemble such a body of troops at Quebec as might check the ardour of our army in making themselves masters of the place, and by their superiority in numbers oblige us to dispute every inch of ground, and of consequence reduce our numbers and make us retreat. This has in part been the case, and is as follows, viz. :—

On the 31st of July a disposition was made to land and force the enemy from their trenches, which was attempted; but the enemy's superiority, and orders not being duly observed, a retreat was beat, and well executed, with the loss of 65 men only, and between 200 and 300 wounded and brought off. Notwithstanding which the cannonade and bombardment has been continued from the other side of the river upon the town with great spirit and vigour, that the houses in the lower town are well nigh consumed by the shells, and carcasses beat down by the shot.

Brigadier Murray, with 1200 or 1300 men, is above the town, besides the following ships of war, viz. :— *Sutherland* and *Squirrell*, under the command of Admiral Holmes.

Brigadier Monckton commands at Point Levy, on the south side of the River, opposite the town, where are the cannon, and bomb batteries, which incessantly play upon the town.

Brigadier Townshend is with General Wolfe at the falls of Montmorency, where they have a number of cannon, mortars, &c., and from thence have annoyed the enemy in their trenches, as they are to a man entrenched.

The above has been, and still is, the disposition of the army, except frequent detachments sent out, which bring in women and cattle.

There is scarce a day passes but skirmishes happen, and loss sustained on both sides.

As yet we have had no authentic accounts from General Amherst, though from what we can collect from prisoners and deserters, success has attended his army, and we are in hopes he will join us or send a reinforcement; if he should not, it is thought another attempt will be made to force their trenches, and if that should not succeed, they hint as if the greatest part of the army will winter at Isle Coudre, and, before they go to their cantonment, will procure all the stock and necessaries that the country and their security will admit of; after which they will consume the houses and standing corn, so as effectually to distress the enemy the ensuing winter. His destruction has already begun at St. Paul's Bay, Goore Cape, and contiguous, and I suppose will be executed, ere long, each side the river, and upon the Isle of Orleans.

Admiral Saunders has hoisted his flag on board the *Stirling Castle*, and is with 8 or 9 ships of the line, besides frigates, &c., at the West end of Orleans, in the Bason which is formed by that end of the island and Point Levy, and within sight of the town.

The enemy, Sir, have attempted once again to burn our fleet and transports, by fire ships and their fire stages, which fortunately proved ineffectual to that purpose, and done us little or no damage. The form of their fire stages is the putting several timbers together, very nigh a square, upon which they put their combustibles, linking 70 or 80 of them together, and tow them till they come nigh the fleet, and then turn them adrift; but by the vigilance of our boats, which, by means of their fire grapnels, tow them clear of the ships, and oft times on shore, to the no small mortification of the contrivers of them.

Admiral Durell, Sir, has the command of 8 or 9 of the line at the Isle Madame, or East end of Orleans, about six or seven leagues from Mr. Saunders, where he lays commodiously moored, to prevent a French fleet from coming to the assistance and relief of Quebec, if they should attempt it.

Two ships more lay at Coudre, and one at Isle of Bec, so that we shall be soon advised if an enemy's fleet should enter the river.

Admiral Holmes, as I noticed before, commands above the town. This, Sir, is the disposition of the fleet, which has happily got up the River, with scarce a misfortune attending them or the transports.

I wish, Sir, I could with an equal degree of certainty ensure the conquest of Quebec and the country, as I did of Louisbourg last year, and I am well satisfied, if General Amherst should join, we must meet with success ; but if he should meet with opposition and impediments sufficient to prevent this much-desired junction, I can say that, without assuming to myself too great a knowledge, I shall not go down the river disappointed. From my first knowing the plan of operations, I could not forbear saying that the land force was insufficient, if the enemy did as they ought, and must be expected they would do, and I found my opinion was singular, and was obliged to be silent.

And even now, Sir, I cannot forbear saying that I think the army was rather tardy in attempting the enemy's trenches, for they had four weeks, after our troops got up, to strengthen their works and call in the peasants, which they did, and to a very good degree, so that as we did not attempt them at first, we should have delayed 'till we had certain accounts of Mr. Amherst's motions, and perhaps, by such time, the enemy would have been tired out, and Vaudreuil and Montcalm would have thought it prudent to send a part of the inhabitants to gather in the harvest, which is now the case in those parts, where it is risking a detachment too much to send and molest them.

This, Sir, I communicate without the least design of prejudice to Admirals or Generals, and purely, Sir, for your amusement, and I hope soon affairs will bear a more favourable aspect.

The disposition of the ships, Sir, I conclude will depend on the fate of the place. I very much fear, Sir, the reason of our ill success, will not originate wholly in the superiority of the enemy as to numbers, but in some unrevealed causes subsisting among ourselves, which I hope the conquest of the place will suffer to lay unnoticed[1].

28th August, 1759.

Since the foregoing a detachment from our army have been down the North shore almost to Cape Torment, at the East end of Orleans, and have burnt all the houses and barns between the Cape and the Falls of Montmorency, and it is expected that the South shore and the Isle of Orleans will soon suffer the same fate.

Admiral Holmes and Brigadier Murray joined the army on the 26th instant, and from them we have the following account: that in their excursion above the town they have burnt a large Magazine, with clothing, provisions, &c.; that they had frequently small skirmishes with the enemy, and have taken some prisoners, from whom, and by letters found with them, we learn that Brigadier Prideaux has succeeded in taking Niagara, though he lost his life, together with the second in command, who we supposed to be Colonel Haldiman; that upon General Amherst's approach the enemy had abandoned and destroyed Ticonderago and Crown Point, and retired to St. John's, where he is closely pursuing them, and are in hopes he will have it in his power to reinforce us here. This, Sir, is the account from the prisoners and the letters; I cannot but wish the truth, as it has

---

[1] Evidently an allusion to the difference of opinion which was supposed to exist between Wolfe and Townshend, and perhaps some others of the officers, with respect to the plan of operations before Quebec. In the pamphlet entitled *A Letter to an Honourable Brigadier General*, already mentioned, Townshend is particularly charged with opposing, both in public and private, the intentions of Wolfe, as well as protesting in form against the last desperate, but eventually successful, attempt, in which his life was sacrificed.

the air of probability, and gains credit amongst us, and the channel in which I have it is so good, that its falsity must originate with the prisoners, in order to blind us more effectually, which, as things are circumstanced, I cannot think to be the case.

As to the cannonade and bombardment, it has been continued on the town with the same violence as at first, that it is now but a scene of ruin and destruction.

We still continue to maintain our posts as usual, and shall find it equally difficult to gain a footing between the Falls of Montmorency and the River St. Charles, as the enemy are so strongly entrenched.

The wind has not yet favoured the *Lowestoff* and *Hunter's* going above the town. I have the honour, &c., &c.   Nath. Cotton.

N.B. The *Lowestoff* and *Hunter* passed the town the 28th, in the evening, without any other damage than one man killed and two wounded on board the latter.

P.S. This is to come by the *Rodney* Cutter, Captain Percival.

September 6, 1759.

We have the confirmation of the enemy's destroying and abandoning Ticonderago on the 26th of July, and the melancholy news of Colonel Roger Townshend[1] being killed the day before by a cannon-ball.

That Colonel Haldiman was attacked in his entrenched camp at Oswego, by 1800 French and Indians, and that he obliged them to retreat and leave him.

As also, that our troops had besieged Niagara, and the enemy had offered to capitulate on the honours of war being granted, but were refused; and it is reasonably thought that we are long before this in quiet

---

[1] Fourth son of Charles, third Viscount Townshend.

possession of the Fort, on our own terms. That Brigadier Prideaux was killed by the bursting of one of our cannon or mortars.

A detachment from General Wolfe's army is come down to burn and destroy whatever they can on the South shore.

General Wolfe has moved his camp from Montmorency, and is gone above the town with 5000 men. Two days ago four men arrived from General Amherst, and left him at Crown Point. What we are to expect from him, and what will be the issue of this campaign, I do not presume to say, as the purport of General Amherst's despatches is known only by Brigadier Generals and Admiral. I am, &c., &c.   N. C.

MR. JENKINSON TO MR. GRENVILLE.

Bury Street, September 6, 1759.

DEAR SIR,—I came to town but a week ago, and should have written to you before, if anything had occurred worth your notice. Our Mails from Holland arrived at last this morning: there are no letters as yet from Mr. Mitchell, or any direct accounts from the King of Prussia, but it is certain that Marshal Daun, to improve the Russian victory, is advancing with his army towards Berlin; that Prince Henry is following him; that upon this account the King himself is drawn nearer his capital; that His Majesty's army is brought again into tolerable condition, and that it does not as yet appear that the Russian army has advanced over the Oder. All the forces, however, of His Prussian Majesty, and his enemies, are drawing now towards a point, and he may probably fight in the sight of his capital, both for his crown and his life.

The last accounts from Prince Ferdinand are of the 23rd: the French were then at Marlborough, but it is thought they have since quitted it. Lord Granby had then taken the command of the British forces. I do not find that Lord George [1] is yet come to England, and he has not been heard of at the Hague, or anywhere on the road.

I hear nothing yet, of any consequence, of the King of Spain's death [2]. I have, &c., &c.   C. JENKINSON.

THE REV. MR. COTTON TO MR. GRENVILLE.

Isle Madame, *Princess Amelia*, September, 20, 1759.

SIR,—I have the satisfaction to acquaint you that through the smiles of Providence, we are in safe and quiet possession of Quebec, and in the following manner, viz.—

On the 3rd instant General Wolfe decamped from Montmorency, and soon after proceeded above the town with nigh 4000 men, and continued in a moving posture 'till the 12th, when towards night he went up the river in boats with the tide of flood for several leagues with his little army; and the enemy on shore, observing his motions, marched their army up also, thinking he would attempt landing towards the Trois Rivières.

When the tide of ebb made, he silently dropped down with all his boats 'till he came within a few miles of the

---

[1] Lord George Sackville.

[2] Ferdinand the Sixth, King of Spain, died on the 10th of August, in his 46th year.

town, when he landed early in the morning, the 13th, with very little opposition, and about 10 o'clock the armies had a close and warm engagement, and the enemy was entirely routed. Their army consisted of 7000 men, regulars and irregulars, and the loss they sustained was the Marquis of Montcalm, who they carried off the field of battle, and he died of his wounds at Quebec the same evening. Two Brigadiers General killed, one Colonel, two Lieutenant Colonels, five Majors, besides Captains and Subalterns, and 1200 or 1500 men killed and wounded.

Our loss consists of General Wolfe being killed on the field of Action; Brigadier Monckton, Colonel Carleton, and Major Barré[1] wounded, but on the recovery; about sixty officers killed and wounded, and 500 men.

It has been as glorious an action on our side as Annals can produce, for we pursued them into town, and since have been preparing to open our batteries; but the ships dropping up to the town with the tide, they judged it more prudent to capitulate, and we are in possession of Quebec.

What terms have been granted I cannot say, as I have not seen the Articles, but I hope they will every way be beneficial to the British interest.

I hope soon to have the honour to pay my compliments to you in England. I have, &c., &c.

NATH. COTTON.

---

[1] Major, afterwards Lieut.-Colonel, Barré was so severely wounded in the face that the sight of one eye was totally destroyed. Soon after his return to England, Colonel Barré came into Parliament for Wycombe, under the patronage of the Earl of Shelburne, and he became distinguished in the House of Commons by the vehemence of his oratory. He was Adjutant General to the Forces, Governor of

MR. JENKINSON TO MR. GRENVILLE.

Bury Street, September 22, 1759.

DEAR SIR,—The Mail of yesterday brings us an account that the Castle Marbourgh was surrendered, and the Garrison prisoners of war; and that General Wunsch, who was sent to the relief of Dresden, and arrived too late to effect that, had attacked a large body, consisting partly of Austrians and partly of the army of the Empire, and had totally defeated them. We have no accounts directly from the King of Prussia, but the Berlin intelligence seems, I think, to be favourable. He holds his enemies at bay, and that alone will, I believe, be sufficient to make them retire soon for want of subsistence.

The French have kept a body of troops embarked in their ports for these last ten days, but they have not ventured to come out, though the wind has been as favourable as they could wish, if they meant to do anything.

Lord George Sackville's reputation is at present, I think, lower than ever, since the publication of his letter [1] to Colonel Fitz Roy, and his answer to it, and the Declaration of Captain Smith: the facts which are there brought to light are thought to make against him. I have, &c., &c.   C. JENKINSON.

The Duke of Newcastle made a very long speech a his meeting on Wednesday, giving a detail of the

---

Stirling Castle, and, in the Duke of Grafton's Administration in 1766, he was appointed to be one of the Vice-Treasurers of Ireland. He survived until the year 1802.

[1] Lord George Sackville's letter, and Colonel Fitz Roy's reply, will be found in the *Gentleman's Magazine* for 1759, p. 417.

war, and the causes of it. He subscribed £500, the two members for the county £100 each.

EARL TEMPLE TO MR. WILKES.

October 2, 1759.

MY DEAR SIR,—Though I do not pretend to be as infallible a lawyer as Lord Chief Justice Willes, nor even as Lord Chief Justice ——, yet if I am to use the forbidden weapons in Law, common reason and common interpretation of words, I cannot figure to myself the least foundation for Mr. Attorney Bull's exemption[1]. His writ of privilege sets out with mentioning a custom in the Court of King's Bench from time immemorial, &c.

Now I apprehend that we are to act under a modern written law, establishing a mode of modern militia which has no respect whatever to the former, and where Parliament has itself specified the only exemptions, even of Peerage itself; if we look into the words of those exemptions we shall find none under which attorneys are comprehended. They cannot surely style themselves *Peace* Officers, and submit to come after constables. But indeed the writ of privilege seems to put it upon nothing but immemorial use: but why may not they, as well as Members of Parliament, nay Mr. Speaker himself, be obliged to find at least a substitute? the tax on that profession would not be very severe. Thus much for common reason. As to law, you had better

---

[1] Bull was a Buckinghamshire Attorney, who had claimed the privilege of exemption from the Militia, merely, it seems, because he was an Attorney!

take a ride over to the lawyer of our family, Mr. George Grenville, by whom it may be best to be directed. Not that this point should by any means be given up, if it can be maintained, and in all events I do not see that you are at the next meeting bound to proceed, but adjourn till a further time without insisting upon his being sworn in, by which means we may have leisure to procure more full information. We have a power, to be sure to discharge, at any time, upon reasonable cause, but reasonable cause will not appear to me to mean an exemption of any class of men not exempted by the express words of the law.

Having now finished writing grim ——, believe me to be ever, devout Sir! your faithfully devoted,

TEMPLE.

I see the name of Wilkes in the papers, is it any relation of yours?

———————

EARL TEMPLE TO MR. GRENVILLE.

Sunday night (Nov. 4, 1759)

THE sagacious Mr. Nugent informs me that we great Personages of state are to attend His Royal Highness [1] to the House of Lords the first day of the sessions.

You may perhaps be able to inform yourself authentically of Lord Bute, how that matter stands, for if my absence should be taken ill, I will certainly put the swift four-footed steeds to my post-chaise on Monday.

I have at last condescended to send a short card to the Duke of Newcastle, to tell him I cannot wait upon

———

[1] The Prince of Wales took his seat on the first day of the meeting of Parliament.

him at dinner on the King's birthday, which, considering all things, is just what he might expect, and feel himself entitled to.

If you think Mr. T. Grenville[1] is of a proper age for the reversion of a Clerkship in my office, it may be as well for me to dispose of it before the waves run so high as to overwhelm it, in which case I would have you send for my Secretary Wilson, at the Privy Seal Office, to inform you of precedents, which when you let me know, I will act accordingly, only if it be any favour, and not a strict matter of right, I cannot ask it. Adieu, ever most affectionately yours,   T.

MR. PITT[2] TO EARL TEMPLE.

Tuesday, November 13, 1759.

MY DEAR LORD TEMPLE,—Whatever steps my affection for you has prompted me to take, without your leave, relative to a matter where your person is concerned, rather wants forgiveness than deserves such kind thanks.

---

[1] Mr. Grenville's second son. He had not, at this time, quite completed his fourth year! If the reversion of a Clerkship in the Privy Seal Office was conferred upon Mr. Thomas Grenville, it is certain he never performed any of its duties.

[2] In reply to a letter from Lord Temple, in which he thanks Mr. Pitt for having asked the King to confer the honour of the Garter upon him. Lord Temple's letter will be found in the *Chatham Correspondence*, vol. i. p. 438, where it is dated (but, as I think, in error) " *October* 13th;" and " Tuesday Morning." Mr. Pitt's reply is correctly dated, " Tuesday, November 13th," the day on which the Parliament met. On the following day Lord Temple resigned the Privy Seal, but resumed his office on the 16th, at the command of the King, and with a promise of the Garter, conveyed to him through the medium of the Duke of Devonshire.

It would be a great presumption to suppose, had my wish succeeded, that my consideration alone had procured that success, but as it has failed, I have a satisfaction which I trust your friendship will indulge to me, that is, that the repulse is mine, and consequently, infinitely less sensible to, my dear Lord Temple's ever most affectionate Brother, W. Pitt.

Can you call this morning? I am not able to come to you, having a pain in my jaw.

THE EARL OF BUTE TO EARL TEMPLE.

Wednesday (November 14, 1759).

My dear Lord,—Need I tell you that your Lordship's letter surprises me exceedingly: need I assure you that I interest myself too much in what regards you, not to be extremely alarmed at the reasons that could have produced this resolution[1], and the more so, that from the high opinion I have ever had of you, I am certain they must be of the greatest import: if you will take the trouble of calling this evening at seven, or any other hour if that prove inconvenient, I will be ready to receive your commands.

I have the honour to be, my dear Lord, your Lordship's most obedient humble Servant, Bute.

(*The following Memorandum is in the handwriting of Lord Temple.*)

" The Duke of Devonshire commissioned by the King.
" November 15, 1759.

" Lord T. is sensible of the honour the King does him

[1] Probably the announcement of his resignation of the Privy Seal.

in restoring him to his good opinion ; that as His Majesty is again pleased to express his desire that he should return into his service, he is ready to obey His Majesty's commands.

" His Majesty being graciously pleased to destine the Garter for Lord T., he will think himself highly honoured with it, as a public and most distinguished mark of His Majesty's favour and protection."

THE DUKE OF DEVONSHIRE TO EARL TEMPLE.

Devonshire House, November 15, 1759.

My Lord,—Your Lordship is very good to me, and does me a great deal of honour. I shall be extremely glad to see you this evening, either here or at your own house, which we may fix at Court. I hope you are persuaded that I can have no view in troubling your Lordship, but to do whatever I think essentially necessary for the King's service and the public, and to show the regard with which I am, &c., &c.　　　Devonshire.

MR. JENKINSON TO MR. GRENVILLE.

Bury Street, December 25, 1759.

Dear Sir,—I had the honour of your letter yesterday: I will set about the revisal of what I showed you immediately. I can at any time have it ready at a week's notice for the perusal of any one, whenever you think it proper that it should be produced. I hope to free it from the objections to which you thought it liable, particularly in relation to the head of Jealousy in Neutral Powers, which I shall argue and explain more

at large. I shall lower every part of it, where there is
the least appearance of presumption, and to take off any
objection which may after all appear in that respect. I
shall alter its title, and call it no longer *a Memorial,*
which implies its being written for a Minister, but *a
Discourse,* which may be supposed to be written only for
the perusal of friends, and this will leave me the liberty
of arguing the point with the more freedom, and of
dressing my thoughts in the manner that may best recommend them. I shall continue to collect all the
materials I can, that may be of use both for the
formal and essential parts of the Treaty. I would,
however, just mention, as far as you may think any of
these to be of use, whether it might not be proper to
suggest (if you have not done it already) that I am
possessed of such materials, and have drawn up such a
paper; for as I shall not mention it to any other of the
King's Ministers, if my paper or materials can be of
any service, is it not proper that one at least should
know it?

I am very much obliged to you for the kind offer of
your service to make this affair turn to my advantage:
I shall refer that consideration to yourself and the rest
of my friends, and shall wholly confide in their judgment and zeal on the occasion: I only hope that they
will take in the whole of my pretensions, and consider
how many years I have been in the service of the public
without the least emolument. I saw the Duke of Newcastle on Tuesday as I intended. Lord Portsmouth
had a very brisk conversation with him about me, so
that I could not put in a word myself. He vowed, however, to both of us, in the most solemn manner, that he
would fulfil his promise to me, but when Lord Ports-

mouth urged him to fix the day, he burst from him saying, *why won't you let me do it my own way?* The resistance of His Grace to the uncommon applications that have been made in my favour, where the object is so small, when all his own people are with me, and he has so often and so solemnly passed his word himself, affords matter of reflection. But, whatever the cause may be, it is rather uncomfortable to depend upon such a man. There is a pamphlet published on the subject of a Peace[1], which is a good deal talked on: it is imputed to Lords Chesterfield, Bath, and Egmont, but it is surely beneath either of them. I send it to you, however, that you may judge of it; I think that it comes from not a very common hand.

When you come to town, I wish, if it was agreeable, that you would bring Père Charlevoix with you: you mentioned, also, that you did not know whether you could not furnish me with a short statement of our rights in relation to Tobago: if you have such a thing in your power, I should be glad if you could let me have that, before you come to town.

I know of no public news, but what is in the papers. On last Friday night, Lord George Lenox[2] and Lady

---

[1] It was entitled *A Letter to Two Great Men* (meaning the Duke of Newcastle and Mr. Pitt) *on the Prospect of a Peace, and on the necessary Terms,* 1759. It has been often attributed to Dr. Douglas (afterwards Bishop of Salisbury), Lord Bath's Chaplain. There is a detailed account of this pamphlet in the *Gentleman's Magazine* for 1759, p. 585; and Walpole speaks of it as " a Plan for the Peace, much adopted by the City, and much admired by all who are too humble to judge for themselves."

[2] Lord George Henry Lenox, eighth son of Charles, second Duke of Richmond, married Lady Louisa Ker, daughter of William, Earl of Ancram, eldest son of the Marquess of Lothian. Lord George had been Aide-de-Camp to the Duke of Cumberland in 1757, and he also served in the expedition against the coast of France, in 1758.

Louisa Ker set out together for Edinburgh to be married. The Duke and Duchess of Richmond accompanied them. Lord George had before made his proposals to Lord Ancram, who would not consent, and desired his daughter to stay at least 'till she was of age, which is in less than a twelvemonth, but love got the better of duty. I have, &c., &c.   C. JENKINSON.

MR. JENKINSON TO MR. GRENVILLE.

London, December 29, 1759.

DEAR SIR,—I really mistook what you said to me about the paper of Grain. I thought you said it would be time enough about twelfth-day to have it, when Lord Harcourt came to town, which made me not write to him about it. I have written, however, this post.

I am very much obliged to you for your advice about what I am writing : modesty and firmness are the two points I shall have in view : I shall draw no conclusions myself, but shall do all I can to make others draw them. I will do all I can to make it please my friends : I am very much of your opinion in relation to the only motive that will operate on the *vis inertiæ* of the Duke of Newcastle : I have long thought that Force is the only true way of working, and by the alarm I can visibly distinguish that any application on my affair always puts him into, I am convinced that it would succeed.

I wont repeat to you the news you will see in all the papers. The King of Prussia seems likely at last to recover Saxony. I wish he may begin the next campaign well. I am apprehensive he will not be able to recruit the troops he has lately lost.

Lord Howe was very graciously received at Court. The ships in the River Villaine cannot be destroyed, but it is thought they must suffer by lying there.

It is said that the Irish riots[1] are totally at an end.

You may depend upon it, that the pamphlet I sent you was Lord Bath's. He very near owns it. It is very much cried up. I have, &c., &c. C. JENKINSON.

MR. JENKINSON TO MR. GRENVILLE.

London, January 8, 1760.

DEAR SIR,—I trouble you with a letter, though I have no news to send you.

Everything is in the greatest agitation in Saxony, but there is nothing decisive. The King was still at Freiburg when the last messenger came from him. The Hereditary Prince was then so near the King that the whole affair is probably before now determined.

Our King has expressed great disapprobation at the sending of this detachment from the army of Prince Ferdinand, and it has been feared that he was in danger of being attacked, but from what has passed I think that danger seems to be diminished. All the accounts talk of the cold that has been abroad with horror.

I go on with my work, but do not overhurry myself, as I do not see that the appearance of a Peace approaches. I shall hope, however, to have arrived at that part which relates to the neutral islands by the

---

[1] They were in consequence of an apprehension that an Union with England was in contemplation by the Houses of Parliament.—See Mr. Rigby's letter to Mr. Pitt in *Chatham Correspondence*, vol. i. p. 468.

time you come to town, when I shall trouble you for the materials we have mentioned.

I have, &c., &c.   C. JENKINSON.

EARL TEMPLE TO THE DUKE OF DEVONSHIRE.

January 31, 1760.

MY LORD,—The Duke of Newcastle, your Grace knows, has informed me that he had moved His Majesty to confer upon me the great honour of the Garter, in pursuance of his most gracious destination of it for me, but that the King had refused it at present "as a work of supererogation," adding, that he had promised it only at the end of the sessions, at which time he would do it. Your Grace well knows how much I declined from the beginning acquiescing under conditions of any sort, and how little I can reconcile my mind even to the appearance of them.

As your Grace was commissioned by His Majesty to make me the offer, I take the liberty of troubling you to lay me at his feet, and in the most humble manner to inform him that I now find myself under the necessity to decline accepting it, since His Majesty no longer leaves me any room to flatter myself that I am to receive it "as a public and most distinguished mark of His Majesty's favour and protection."

Happy, however, that I had it in my power to do a pleasure to the King, which he at that time condescended to think essential to his service, it is my duty, and I have no merit in it, to continue to exert my best endeavours to serve His Majesty, and to extricate my country from the perils which still surround it. I may, however, with great respect, persist in indulging the wish that I had been allowed to give proofs of my zeal for His Majesty's safety and glory out of his service.

I am, with the most sincere esteem and regard, my Lord, &c.　　　TEMPLE.

THE DUKE OF DEVONSHIRE TO EARL TEMPLE.

Devonshire House, January 31, 1760.

MY LORD,—I take for granted Mr. Pitt has acquainted you with what passed, which I flatter myself will have effectually removed any doubts that might have arisen in your Lordship's breast. I hope to have the honour of seeing you to-morrow morning, any time after ten that is most convenient to your Lordship, when I will faithfully relate to you what has passed.

I hope you excuse my not waiting on you personally this morning, but being obliged to go to all the courts I really had not time, and I had sent to Mr. Pitt before I received your Lordship's letter.

I saw the Duke of Newcastle at the Treasury, and informed him of His Majesty's intentions, which, to do him justice, seemed to give him great pleasure, and now your Lordship is at full liberty to acquaint your friends[1]. I sincerely congratulate you on this event, and am, my Lord, &c., &c.　　　DEVONSHIRE.

[1] The King had at last consented to bestow the Order of the Garter upon Lord Temple. " It is well known that George the Second, who, though he generally yielded to Ministerial violence or importunity, yet manifested often great reluctance, and even ill-humour, in his manner of compliance on these occasions, strongly disliked Lord Temple. Being, however, compelled, in consequence of political arrangements very repugnant to his feelings, to invest that nobleman with the Order of the Garter, the King took so little pains to conceal his aversion,

THE DUKE OF NEWCASTLE TO EARL TEMPLE.

Newcastle House, January 31, 1760.

MY DEAR LORD,—I have too much real pleasure in the justice which His Majesty has this day done to himself and to your Lordship, to delay one moment expressing my sense of it. I have long most ardently wished that His Majesty would do what was so right for his own honour and interest.

My wishes are now completed, and I am extremely happy. I most sincerely congratulate your Lordship upon it, and am, with the greatest truth and respect, my dear Lord, your most obedient and most affectionate humble Servant,   HOLLES NEWCASTLE.

THE EARL OF BUTE TO EARL TEMPLE.

Tuesday night (February, 1760).

MY DEAR LORD,—I congratulate your Lordship very sincerely on the mark you have received of His Majesty's favour ; situated as you are, you could, in my opinion, have no competitor. I have given my noble friend so many strong proofs of unlimited friendship on every occasion that appeared to me material for his interest and honour, that I hardly think it necessary to mention the satisfaction I have in this feather. I have the

both to the individual and to the act, that instead of placing the ribbon decorously over the shoulder of the new Knight, His Majesty, averting his head, and muttering indistinctly some expressions of dissatisfaction, threw it across him, and turned his back at the same instant in the rudest manner. . . . .
The aversion of George the Second towards Lord Temple, originated partly in personal, but more from political motives and designs."— *Wraxall's Historical Memoirs*, 8vo, 1836, vol. i. p. 129.

honour to be, my dear Lord, very sincerely and affectionately yours,   BUTE.

MR. ELLIOT TO MR. GRENVILLE.

Admiralty, Monday evening (March —, 1760).

MY DEAR SIR,—I came so late this day from Kensington that I found everybody had been acquainted with the late action before it came to my knowledge. Nothing can so much increase the satisfaction I feel on this occasion as the very cordial and friendly part you take in what more immediately concerns my brother[1], and consequently me, on this fortunate event. If it had not been for your friendship, he might not so soon have been in the way of doing so much credit to himself and his friends. Believe me ever yours most affectionately,

GILB. ELLIOT.

MR. JENKINSON TO MR. GRENVILLE.

London, May 17, 1760.

DEAR SIR,—The mail arrived this day has brought no news from the army, and there is no intelligence from any other parts.

I understand that Mr. Pitt has got a fit of the gout that confines him.

When you have read the papers you took with you into the country I should be glad (if you could do it with convenience) that you would send them to town.

---

[1] Captain Elliot, with three frigates under his command, had captured the French squadron under Thurot, after they had sailed from Carrickfergus, where they had made a descent upon Ireland, levying contributions, and carrying off the Mayor and some of the principal inhabitants. Thurot made a gallant defence, and was killed in the action.

I will then add to them such other materials as I have since collected, I will mould them into the best form I am able, and I will finish the other parts of the designed plan. You would, however, oblige me very much if you would take the trouble of giving some sketch of your opinion of them, as they appear to you at present. I am, &c., &c. C. JENKINSON.

MR. JENKINSON TO MR. GRENVILLE.

Bury Street, May 24, 1760.

DEAR SIR,—I have received the letter with which you have honoured me ; I don't doubt that the parcel is come safe, but when I sent just now to your house your servant was out, so that I have not yet received it.

As you are so kind as to be solicitous concerning it, I will write to you again on Tuesday.

The favourable opinion you are so good as to entertain of these papers is very flattering to me. I should want judgment very much myself if I did not always rely upon yours, and however it may be biassed in the present case, as it is a proof at least of your friendship, it does not give me less pleasure.

I am also very much obliged to you for the trouble you have taken in making observations on the several parts of it : these will be of the greatest service in the alterations I propose to make.

As to the general observation you make in respect to what should be added concerning the opinion of France, this is what I mean to do, as the second part of the question I proposed to discuss : it was the delicacy of this part of the question which has made me so long delay the execution of my design. To have said little of it would not have completed properly my design, and, on the other hand, to say too much would be dangerous.

I hope, however, I have at length hit off a method that will free me from all embarrassment. I shall give a history of the French policy in respect to their Colonies on the Continent, from their first establishment to the negotiation of the last Commissaries, from which it will appear that the Fisheries were the principal object which made those colonies valuable ; that if they should lose this, the profit arising from the trade of the Peltry is not equal to the support of the Colony, especially if we should be admitted to any farther share of it ; and that they have not any other staple commodity established there ; in a word, that Canada, without her Fisheries, is, in their own opinions, hardly worth their acceptance, and if their Fisheries could be otherwise secured to them, they will have little occasion for the former. This will appear to be the opinion of all the great persons who have governed the Colonies.

I shall show also that the opinion of Mr. Silhouette[1] and the French Ministry was, that our disputes should be determined on the very same *principle* which I have principally endeavoured to establish as the pivot on which the negotiation should turn. This seems to be all the light which can be thrown on this part of the question, and is indeed decisive, unless it can be supposed that the French Ministers have very lately changed their opinions, and have discovered that all their predecessors were mistaken.

I shall then, as the third part of the question, treat

---

[1] The Controller General of the Finances in France.

of the opinion of Neutral Nations.   My ideas of this I
will mention when I see you.

I shall greatly alter, also, and add to what I have
already put on paper, and shall explain with greater
precision the great points of national law, and the grand
motives which should direct our measures, that it may
not be possible to shake this, which is the basis of all
our reasoning.

I ask pardon for troubling you so much on this
subject, but I was willing you should turn my ideas in
your mind before I have the pleasure of conversing with
you in town, and indeed I had nothing else to say.

The intelligence from North America is that our
success in those parts is certain.

The Spanish Ambassador is not yet come to town.   I
shall settle with you with pleasure the time I am to
wait on you at Wotton.   The last bell rings.   I am, &c.,
&c.   C. JENKINSON.

MR. JENKINSON TO MR. GRENVILLE.

London, June 19, 1760.

DEAR SIR,—Though I know little more of the action
near Quebec than what is in the papers, I could not
deny myself the pleasure of writing to you.   We all
here blame Mr. Murray, and are not at all satisfied with
the reason he assigns for leaving the town to attack the
enemy.   He says, as I hear, that if the enemy got possession of the Heights of Abraham, the town was not
defensible; but we wonder then, why he did not entrench
himself there, and defend it by the force of his artillery,
with which he was very well supplied, and the French
very ill; so that we cannot conceive, as long as our force

was complete, how they could have any hopes of taking the town.

As it is, however, I understand that there are no expectations that it can be saved, and, indeed, I am told that Murray himself gives little reason to hope it. The relief from Amherst is certainly impossible, and I do not think that he has ever shown activity enough to make one hope that he would make an attempt vigorous enough, even if there was a mere chance of success [1].

How unexpected and unfortunate all this is! and how it has marred all our schemes of peace.

I propose to myself the pleasure of talking all this over with you, some day in the end of next week, and shall hope to have the pleasure of being of the party with you and Mrs. Grenville, over to Nuneham, as soon after as shall be agreeable to you. I know it will give great joy to Lord and Lady Harcourt, and the time you mentioned when we talked of it in town, will be very agreeable to them. I am, &c., &c. C. JENKINSON.

THE DUKE OF NEWCASTLE TO EARL TEMPLE.

Claremont, July 9, 1760.

MY DEAR LORD,—Your Lordship will receive from your House, a card, desiring the honour of your company here, on Wednesday next, the 16th instant, with the Spanish Ambassador [2].

You have flattered me with the hopes of coming, and I hope it will not be inconvenient to you, though I am

---

[1] The French were, however, soon after compelled to raise the siege and make a precipitate retreat, leaving their artillery behind them.

[2] The Count de Fuentes, recently arrived.

sorry to give you the trouble of coming so far, but the honour and obligation will be the greater.

I wish I could send to your Lordship any good news; I am persuaded I should have been able to have done it before this time, had not Prince Ferdinand's great plan of possessing himself of the strong post where Marshal Broglio now is, been disappointed; by what accident we don't yet certainly know, but hitherto it is attributed to some fault or mistake in General Imhoff.

We have not yet the particulars of the defeat of General Fouquet's corps[1]. I doubt, however, the loss has been very great, and that the distress of the King of Prussia will be so great, that nothing but himself could surmount. I most heartily wish that even His Prussian Majesty may be now able to do it, surrounded as he is with such numerous enemies.

I must have the pleasure of finishing my letter with congratulating your Lordship upon the great and almost unexpected event of recovering Quebec, and turning the loss entirely upon the French. Everything looks well in that part of the world.

The Duchess of Newcastle begs her best compliments to your Lordship and my Lady Temple, to whom I beg the honour of mine. I am, with the greatest truth and respect, my dear Lord, &c., &c. HOLLES NEWCASTLE.

THE DUKE OF NEWCASTLE TO EARL TEMPLE.

Claremont, July 19, 1760.

MY DEAR LORD,—Allow me to return you my sincere thanks for the kindest and most agreeable letter

---

[1] Near Landschut: a desperate fight, in which six or seven thousand Prussians were killed, and many pieces of artillery fell into the hands of the Austrians, whose victory cost them 5000 men.

which I ever received. I was so proud of it that I
could not avoid showing it to our two good friends, my
Lord Lincoln and Mr. Pitt, with whom I had the pleasure to drink your Lordship's health. We were very
lucky in the weather, and, without a compliment, wanted
nothing but your good company. Mr. Pitt was extremely
good and agreeable, and was here by twelve o'clock.
Claremont put on its best looks. The Duchess of Newcastle, who sends her best compliments both to your
Lordship and my Lady Temple, lamented extremely
the want of your Lordship's company; I believe she had
some *message* to send to her friend, my Lady Temple.

I wish I could yet send your Lordship some news
from Germany.

Everything still remains in our army as it was. I
think neither army looks likely to attack the other, in
their present situation, though Prince Ferdinand will do
his utmost to draw M. Broglio out of his strong post.
The late fatal disappointment happened, by all accounts,
from a disobedience of orders in General Imhoff, upon
which subject a very proper letter has been wrote to
Prince Ferdinand.

I beg my compliments to Lady Temple, and am, with
the greatest truth and respect, my dear Lord, &c.

HOLLES NEWCASTLE.

MR. PITT TO EARL TEMPLE.

Tuesday, July 22, 1760.

MY DEAR LORD,—As no accounts but that from
Monsieur Maubert, of the events of the 10th instant,
has appeared in our papers, I cannot leave you under
the anxiety which even so unauthorized relations may

create. Be assured then, my dear Lord, that the thing is of no material consequence to the sum of things; our loss not exceeding in killed and wounded and prisoners above 500 men. The English dragoons, a few squadrons, Bland's and Howard's, are covered with glory. Griffin, with two regiments of foot, greatly praised. This prelude, however, to the general action, which is supposed over by this time, is not a pleasing one, and we count the minutes with much pain, 'till news arrives of our fate. Three Battalions of Guards embark for Germany, we hope, by Friday or Saturday.

I trust your Lordship will approve this sudden and perhaps somewhat bold measure. The cloud hung heavy, spirits began to droop; dignity, energy, and éclat were to be added to our operations: or retro sublapsa referri *Res* Danaum: not a moment was to be lost, and I stand responsible for the event: may Heaven send it prosperous! If the news be happy, I hope to embrace your Lordship at Stowe about the middle of next week.

An absolute refusal from Turin. I have just finished another despatch, as a last effort to save our respectable friend, whose heart is almost broken.

I am, ever, &c., &c.   W. PITT.

Lady Hester is at Hayes and very well. My affectionate compliments to Lady Temple.

THE DUKE OF NEWCASTLE TO EARL TEMPLE.

Claremont, August 2, 1760.

MY DEAR LORD,—The warm and affectionate concern which your Lordship so sincerely shows for the

great and irreparable loss[1] which I have had, and for
the miserable object of it, my dear Lord Lincoln, will
ever be remembered by me and mine with the utmost
gratitude and affection.   It did not surprise me, though
it greatly pleased me and honoured me: I knew what the
impulse of your heart would be upon an occasion where
so many of your friends were so deeply affected and concerned, and particularly the poor dear unhappy man
himself.   Be assured, my dear Lord, no returns can
ever be wanting on our parts.   The poor dear Duchess
of Newcastle feels every line of your letter, and indeed
every one is too expressive, not to make the greatest impression.   We both join in our sincere compliments and
thanks to Lady Temple, Mr. J. Grenville, Mr. Henry,
and Mrs. H. Grenville : the Duchess of Newcastle begs
also that you would accept hers.

Poor Mrs. H. Grenville little imagined, when we
both had the pleasure to be there last Thursday evening, that this fatality would come upon us so soon.   I
never saw the poor dear creature gayer or more cheerful in my life.   Your Lordship knew her, by the just
character you give of her, and that must be a melancholy satisfaction to all her friends.   Poor dear man !
he is inconsolable, and indeed I can't attempt to say anything to alleviate his loss in any degree : I am afraid he
will even, if possible, feel it more when his passion
shall be abated.

I thank God he is tolerably well in his health, though
much heated and agitated.   He was blooded plentifully,
and that step will secure him from any fever, from his
anxiety and distress.   The children, I thank God, are

---

[1] The death of Lady Lincoln.   She was near her confinement, and
died in convulsions after three hours' illness.

extremely well. Whenever dear Lord Lincoln can admit of any comfort, or indeed of hearing anything with that view, I am sure the very tender love and concern showed by your Lordship, and a very kind letter which I immediately received from Mr. Pitt upon this occasion, will give him the greatest comfort, and, if anything can, some relief. I shall watch the first opportunity of acquainting him with it. Give me leave to add a circumstance which, I flatter myself, will give your Lordship some pleasure, as well from the thing itself as from the person who conveyed it to me.

When I waited upon the King, he was most extremely compassionate and gracious upon what he knew I suffered : and then told me, *I know* Mr. Pitt has talked in the properest manner to Lady Yarmouth upon your subject. He hopes you will not suffer it to prejudice your health. I see everything in this that is pleasing and flattering to me.

I am, my dearest Lord, &c., &c.

HOLLES NEWCASTLE.

THE REV. MR. COTTON TO MR. GRENVILLE.

Princess Amelia, Plymouth Sound, August 5, 1760.

SIR,—I have once more the happiness to arrive safe at this place, and beg leave to assure you that it affords me no small satisfaction to know, that our cruizing on the French coast for the last four months has had the desired effect, in effectually preventing the enemy from sending any ships or succours to their East or West Indies from the ports of Rochelle and Rochfort, for there still remain the same ships in those ports when we left the station, as upon our going there in the Spring, and even one of the Enemy's frigates, which has long waited an opportunity to go for their West Indies, now lays above the Isle of Aix.

During our cruize we have anchored several times in Basque road, and sent a flag of truce to the Isle of Aix; and on its return was informed, that the few inhabitants received them very courteously, and there was not a soldier on the Island, nor any works of defence executed or carrying on; and upon the genteel supply of vegetables which they sent us, the truce left them in quiet possession.

We left Quiberon 31st ultimo, at which time Mr. Boscawen remained in much the same position he has done the whole season, with a few ships to guard the Bay. Admiral Geary was to sail soon after us, for his old station off Basque, where we left the following ships, viz., *Duke, Prince, Newark,* and *Adventure.*

Before we left the Bay, Captain Hervey[1] in the *Dragon,* with the *Conqueror, Brilliant, Venus,* and a Cutter or two, had been sent to attempt the conquest of the Isle of Groa, a small fortified island that commands the entrance into Ports Louis and L'Orient, but it proved unsuccessful; why and wherefore pertains to the assailants to make known to the world, though it is whispered that neither His Majesty's ships or men were to be risked in executing the plan, which is a new method of attempting conquests, and may be attended with beneficial consequences to the British interests when it is more fully known: but the reason I assign for its failure may be this: Mr. Hervey having cruized

[1] Augustus Hervey, a younger son of John, Lord Hervey. His name will frequently occur hereafter in these volumes.

off that port, has once and again been insulted from the coast, on which he has stood nigh in shore, silenced the enemy's fire, landed, and thrown their cannon into the sea: this success might give him hopes of becoming masters of the Isle of Groa at the same easy rate, and having communicated his design to Mr. Boscawen for his approbation, obtained leave to make an attempt in case he could do it without risk to men or ships; and the result has shewn it impracticable, unless he brought a ship or two to cannonade the batteries more effectually than one of the frigates did, otherwise he must lay the design aside, which I believe is the case, and thus Sir, ends this little, grand, feasible scheme.

This is the sum and substance of what I can at this time transmit; there are too many obvious remarks to be made, upon what is too visible in Quiberon Bay, and I shall never more be surprised at the immoderate increase of the National Debt, when there is seemingly so great a want of economy.

In my letter of the 10th of May last, I intimated how easy and practicable it was to become masters of any of the Islands in Quiberon, which may be as easily accomplished now as then; and if there was no other advantage than that of the supply of water, would be more than a balance for the small degree of risk our men or ships could run; for the number of transports now employed as victuallers, exceeds by one half what the service demands or requires, and I am sure the numbers would be much diminished by having a supply of water from an island, which is now brought to the fleet from Plymouth.

As, for instance, there is one transport ship laden with water (from which we had a supply), that came to an anchor about the middle of March last, and at the time we took our water from her, the Master declared the amount of his pay and ships was but very little less than 2000*l.*, which I think too much evidences the want of that economy which will tend much to establish the national interest, and prevent the too just clamours of an injured people.

My thoughts and reflections sue your well known candour, if judged premature. I have the honour to be, &c. NATHANIEL COTTON.

EARL TEMPLE TO MR. GRENVILLE.

October 4, 1760.

MR. PITT has desired me, my dear Brother, to send to you for your perusal these very important papers: what the decision at the Court of Spain will be I know not, but Jemmy tells me, who came here yesterday, that the Duke of N. and Lord H. admire to the highest degree the very manly, temperate, and able answer which has been given to the matter of the two very extraordinary memorials[1]. You will be so good as to send them back by the bearer.

The very wet weather has hitherto interposed such a gulph betwixt the Cormorant and us, that we must wait 'till the crows have picked up the dirt, and till your gravel is dry.

Many kind compliments to all Wotton from all Stowe. Your most affectionate. TEMPLE.

[1] See *Parliamentary History*, vol. xv. p. 1018, &c.

Bury Street, October 11, 1760.

DEAR SIR.—I arrived in town on Wednesday last, and found it full of nothing but good news. I passed my time after I left you, some part at Sir John Cope's, but much the greater part at Nuneham. My Lord Harcourt obliged me to employ my leisure hours in perfecting those purposes which you know I had in hand. I have totally new modelled the work, have added to it new thoughts and new materials, and, as far as I have gone, have made it as perfect as I am able. I have finished the two parts that relate to ourselves and to the enemy : what relates to the neutral powers I have not yet finished. But, after all, I am very unwilling to produce it, and had rather that it should rest in my own bureau.

The last fault I would willingly be thought guilty of is presumption, and I am apprehensive that my very attempt shall be thought presumptuous, though the execution is (as it ought to be, and as I hope mine is) modest. When you, however, come to town you shall see it, if you will do me that honour, and judge of it.

There are as yet, I believe, no steps taken towards a Peace : I suspect, however, that there will be soon, for reasons that I cannot explain by letter, and I fancy that an opportunity may before then be given me, of producing my papers in a manner that may make the production of them less improper than it would be otherwise. I am forced to speak mysteriously. Whatever may be the issue of this affair, which is very important to my own interests, I can only say that I mean well.

We have nothing new to-day from Germany; yesterday brought us an account that the Castle of Cleves had surrendered, and that the Hereditary Prince had got his heavy cannon up to Wesel; but there was no account then of any motion in Broglio's army. It is what Broglio will now do that every one here is very anxious to know.

I hope that Mrs. Grenville continues to enjoy perfect health. I was glad to hear from Mr. Lloyd[1] that she was so at the time he left Wotton. I should have been over there again myself, before I came to town, if Lord Harcourt had not kept me prisoner, as some booksellers do their poor authors when they want them to finish copy already paid for. But I have lately had an opportunity of knowing of your healths, which I believe you don't suspect. I had not been long gone from Wotton, before Mr. Deska admitted me into the number of those he favours with his correspondence, and I have had from him variety of politically poetic letters. He has drawn from me one in answer, and I believe I must send him another soon; pray don't betray me to my correspondent.

There is added a Battalion of Guards to the troops that were ordered before on the Expedition[2]. It is said that Kingsley is to command them. Keppel leads the squadron out, and when it comes to the Bay, it is to be under the command of Sir Edward Hawke.

I am, &c., &c.   C. Jenkinson.

[1] Probably Philip Lloyd, afterwards Dean of Norwich. He was at this time tutor to Mr. Grenville's children. He died in 1790.

[2] Extraordinary preparations were made for this Expedition, which was, however, countermanded in December following, and the troops disembarked.

MR. PITT TO MR. GRENVILLE.

St. James's Square, October 18, 1760.

DEAR GRENVILLE,—I have waited many a tedious day for the arrival of news from the armies, in hopes to have sent you something better than my best thanks for the favour of your obliging letter, but no public news arriving, I have still some of a private nature to impart which will give you pleasure, which is, that our two girls may now be considered as convalescent.

The Address of the City of London [1] will speak for itself, and I believe you will think that it speaks loud enough to be heard at Paris, to the no great satisfaction of the Controller-General, and the whole tribe of Financiers. How it was heard at Kensington you need not be told, as the Address is big with a million in every line. Were it able to produce an advantageous peace it would be most happy : next to that, such generous and warm assurances of supporting the war, cannot but give the highest satisfaction to Government.

I don't know your resolution about coming to town, but if you shall be, at the Birth-day [2], and the Duke of Newcastle has not secured you, you will do me great pleasure if you will dine with me that day.

I am ever, &c., &c. **W. PITT.**

MR. PITT TO MR. GRENVILLE.

Thursday, past Four o'clock (November 13, 1760).

DEAR GRENVILLE,—I send you with this the King's speech, as it will be submitted to His Majesty; perhaps

[1] Upon the taking of Montreal.

[2] The King did not live for another birth-day. He died suddenly, on the 25th instant.

A A 2

some mention will be thrown in of the late glorious event of the King of Prussia's victory[1].

I should have desired of you the favour to call this evening, if an early meeting of the Cabinet at St. James's to-night had not rendered it impossible.

You will already guess the request I have to make to you; it is, that you will be so good to draw the Address: my moments are literally so filled that I am unable to do it myself, nor would the thing be so well done, if I was able, in point of time, to set about it. I trust your answer will be favourable, and that the work will not be of a disagreeable nature to you. I will only add that you cannot oblige me more.

I am ever, &c., &c.   W. PITT.

MR. JENKINSON TO MR. GRENVILLE.

(November, 1760.)

SINCE I left you I have seen Lord Bute. Granby continues indisposed, so that he has not been with Lord B. Shelburne[2] has given hopes that by means of some of the little agents he can employ he shall be able to make the Rutland family[3] acquiesce in some expedient between what he desires and what is offered. I have in general but little opinion of these operations;

---

[1] The battle of Torgau, where the Austrians, under Marshal Daun, were defeated by the King of Prussia.

[2] John, Viscount FitzMaurice, made Earl of Shelburne in 1753, and in May, 1760, he was advanced to the Peerage of Great Britain, by the title of Baron Wycombe. He died in May, 1761.

[3] The Duke of Rutland was Lord Steward at the accession of George the Third. He was, soon after this time, made Master of the Horse.

though they have often more success upon a necessitous man, as Granby is, than others. I am convinced, however, that neither party will push affairs to extremities, so that it will end well at last, though the manner how cannot yet be determined.

Since Bamber Gascoyne was with you he has been with Lord Bute, calling upon him to give him all his support[1]. He has desired him to write a letter to Lord Rochford. Lord Bute does not think it proper for him in his present situation to do it, but desired me to suggest it to you. Observe, that Lord Rochford is one of the *King's pensioners.*

I hear that Lord George Sackville has been at court[2], and that the King was civil to him. I have much to say to you on this head, which has, I find, already created a clamour, and may possibly create still more, which makes me extremely sorry for it.

[1] He was probably making interest to represent the borough of Malden, for which he was elected in the new Parliament. Lord Bute had succeeded Lord Rochford as Groom of the Stole.

[2] This circumstance marks the probable date of this letter. The King held a Levée early in November. Horace Walpole, writing on the 13th of that month, says : " For the King himself, he seems all good-nature, and, wishing to satisfy everybody, all his speeches are obliging. I saw him again yesterday, and was surprised to find the Levée-room had lost so entirely the air of the lion's den. The Sovereign don't stand in one spot, with his eyes fixed royally on the ground, and dropping bits of German news; he walks about and speaks to everybody." Lord George's appearance at Court, at the invitation, as was supposed, of Lord Bute, gave great offence to the Ministers of the late King, and those who had the conduct of the war, and the clamour it created was probably the cause that Lord George subsequently spent several years in retirement.

COUNTESS TEMPLE TO EARL TEMPLE.

Tuesday, January 6 (1761).

AN express arrived yesterday morning from the Bath to notify the death of poor Lady Jane[1]; but what is still more shocking, poor Lord Harry Beauclerc[2] died last night in a fit at 11 o'clock: he had been ill some time of a violent pain in his breast and stomach by intervals.

You have heard a story of a cook who is become Lord Aston[3], and the Roman Catholics allow him a hundred a year. My Lord Bute went from the King to the Duchess of Norfolk, to say that His Majesty could not hear of a peer in that distress, though of a different religion, without contributing to his maintenance; therefore had sent by Lord Bute two hundred pounds, to be disposed of to Lord Aston in the manner she thought proper. The Duchess sent to the man; was afraid to tell him the whole at once for fear of turning his head, but mentioned only one hundred. Is this true? says the man; then I beg you will give me leave to run directly to my mother and my master to tell them the news. I should add, that Lord Bute told her Grace this was to be continued every year out of his Privy Purse, which she told the cook Lord. God bless you, this is all I can pick up to divert you.   A. T.

[1] Lady Jane Coke, sister to the first Duke of Wharton.

[2] Fourth son of the first Duke of St. Alban's. He was a Colonel in the Army, and, at the time of his death, M.P. for Thetford.

[3] Probably Philip, the sixth Baron, who is described in the Peerages as the " *great-great-grandson of the late Lord's great-great-great-grand uncle.*"

THE EARL OF BUTE TO MR. GRENVILLE.

Wednesday (February 11, 1761).

DEAR SIR,—You will receive a letter from Lord Holdernesse, notifying the King's pleasure with regard to the Cabinet[1], which is all the form used, and it will be proper for you to acknowledge the receipt of it, and to desire Lord Holdernesse to lay you at the King's feet, and return your thanks, &c. Let me congratulate you, my worthy friend, on this additional honour; may I see many added to it.

I am, with the utmost regard, &c., &c. BUTE.

MR. JENKINSON TO MR. GRENVILLE.

Bury Street, March 24, 1761.

DEAR SIR,—I hope that by the time this letter will get to you all your trouble and fatigue at Buckingham[2] will be at an end.

I have ten thousand thanks to return you for my present situation[3]; I am absolutely in love with Lord Bute; his goodness shows itself to me more and more every day. I have mentioned to him all you ordered me; he daily laments that you are going to take yourself out of active business in the House of Commons, where your abilities and influence might be so serviceable to the King and the Public[4]. If there should be

---

[1] Mr. Grenville was now a Cabinet Minister, and he still retained his office of Treasurer of the Navy.

[2] His re-election for the borough.

[3] Under Secretary to Lord Bute as Principal Secretary of State, in which office Lord Bute had just succeeded Lord Holdernesse.

[4] At this time Mr. Grenville was desirous of becoming Speaker of the House of Commons, on the retirement of Mr. Onslow.

any important news, he has ordered me to send a messenger down to you. He does not take the seals till to-morrow. There is a messenger arrived from Prince Ferdinand this morning. Cassel still holds out. The enemy in it is much stronger than was expected. Broglio is at present advancing, and will, I think, attack Prince Ferdinand, and I know that the other will not decline it, so that an action will probably determine the issue of this whole affair.

I have had a most afflicting piece of news since I saw you. My poor brother is dead in Hesse; fatigue has killed him. What adds to my concern is, that I cannot hear any particulars of his death. The account of it is come in a letter of Prince Ferdinand to Lord Ligonier, an honour which makes the loss the more affecting.

But not to dwell on this melancholy subject, Lord B., partly at my earnest request, has declined to take Mr. Wallace as my colleague, but he is so good as to mean to do something for him. He has taken in his stead a very able, worthy, good man[1], who before served in the same capacity Lord Townshend and Lord Harrington. You may imagine that his choice must be very agreeable to me. I shall hope to hear from you and to receive your commands. I am, &c., &c.

C. JENKINSON.

MR. JENKINSON TO MR. GRENVILLE.

Whitehall, March 26, 1761.

DEAR SIR,—The Earl of Bute took the seals yesterday, and all the other changes took place of course.

---

[1] Mr. Edward Weston, the " *tééraire vieillard*," who was afterwards so ferociously attacked by Junius for his supposed *Vindication of the Duke of Grafton.*

His Lordship intends to remove his office. I have this day taken for that purpose a great house in Cleveland Row, just opposite to what were the Duke's apartments[1]. His Lordship intends to do there all his business, and to see all his company; and his Lordship, among his other acts of goodness, has been so good as to assign me a particular apartment in it where I shall live, and be always at hand. I will trouble you to tell my friend Lloyd that I will get him, when he goes to Oxford, to send my books up to town, as I am now likely to be settled, and to have a proper place to receive them. His Lordship has also ordered me to communicate all things of importance to you, as between you and myself, though the circulation does not extend to you. When you come to town we will settle the nature of the correspondence.

We have at present no news, but there is great probability that there will be a battle in Hesse for the decision of the great affair. The public symptoms of peace are not so strong as when you left town, but yet I do not think it far off. I have, &c., &c.

C. Jenkinson.

Though I suppose that your election is over, yet as it may not be known at the Post Office, I shall put my name at the back of this. Don't think that I am playing the Secretary of State.

MR. JENKINSON TO MR. GRENVILLE.

St. James's, May 21, 1761.

Dear Sir,—All that has happened since I wrote you last is that a Courier has arrived from France,

---

[1] Duke of Cumberland's, and still in the occupation of the King of Hanover, as the present Duke of Cumberland.

saying that M. Bussy[1] cannot be at Calais till the 25th, but at the same time giving the strongest assurances that no political reasons, but such only as are of a private nature, are the cause of this delay. It is determined therefore that Mr. Stanley[2] shall not go from hence till the 25th, and a letter with this answer is sent to the Court of France.

There is also this day arrived advice from Belleisle. Everything goes on there very well, though not very expeditiously. Their heavy cannon is landed, and they have erected one battery. The enemy had been able to throw no succours into the place, and they had contrived to send but one small boat with intelligence to the Continent. None of our reinforcements are as yet arrived. I am, &c., &c.   C. JENKINSON.

MR. JENKINSON TO MR. GRENVILLE.

St. James's, May 28, 1761.

DEAR SIR,—I send you all the news we have from the Continent by the last mail in the enclosed bulletin.

We have this morning had letters from Belleisle. They inform us that the reinforcements were not yet arrived, but notwithstanding the siege went on very well. The enemy had fired a great deal of late, but it was not doubted but in a few days our fire would become superior to theirs; and I have heard from a private hand, but from good authority, that our batteries would be higher than their parapets, and would of course com-

---

[1] The French Minister appointed to negotiate the Preliminaries of Peace.

[2] Sent to Paris for the same purpose on the part of England.

mand all their works; and if so, the place must very soon surrender.

M. Bussy is not yet come, but is hourly expected. I am engaged by Lord Egremont to meet you at dinner on Sunday.   I am, &c., &c.   C. JENKINSON.

MR. JENKINSON TO MR. GRENVILLE.

St. James's, June 9, 1761.

DEAR SIR,—You will receive by this post a précis of what arrived by the Dutch mail yesterday, which amounts in fact to nothing.

Since you left town we have no intelligence from Belleisle.

Bussy saw Mr. Pitt this morning. He held to him a language very different from what he had held to Lord Granville. He said that we by our answer had broken the conditions of peace, which the Duke of Choiseul had proposed, and that he was not therefore bound by it. He talked to Mr. Pitt in all other respects in the same manner he had talked in his two first conferences with him, and he has in fact at last dispatched his courier; so that we shall wait now till his return, before we hear anything more. I suspect that he is at some work or other. I know he has been with ordinary people that write for newspapers. As soon as anything occurs you shall certainly hear from me.

I am, &c.   C. JENKINSON.

MR. JENKINSON TO MR. GRENVILLE.

St. James's, June 11, 1761.

DEAR SIR,—We received yesterday morning further accounts from Belleisle. They say that everything was prepared to batter in breach, and that it was not expected, when the breach was once made, that the enemy would stand an assault; so that we shall soon probably hear of the place having surrendered.

Great complaints are, however, made here at present of the want of skill in our general and his engineers, as it is certain the place with proper management might have been taken much sooner.

I am afraid that Bussy is at some trifling work. I have reason to think that he did not dispatch his courier 'till to-day at noon, though he said he should send him the night before last. He has not seen any of our ministers since Tuesday.

I am, &c., &c. C. JENKINSON.

MR. JENKINSON TO MR. GRENVILLE.

St. James's, Saturday, 12 at night, June 13, 1761.

DEAR SIR,—I send you enclosed an account of the good news we have just received of the surrender of the Citadel of Belleisle, and beg leave to offer you my congratulations upon it.

Yesterday a messenger arrived from Stanley. The conversation of the Duke de Choiseul appears by that to differ very much from that of Bussy.

The Duke de Choiseul disavows Bussy's delay in the strongest manner. He is transported with the idea of a

separate Peace. He agrees to the terms of the uti possidetis, but seems to wish for the proposed epochs, or to
have the others proposed by us.

As to compensations, he expressed a desire that we
should make the first offer, but did not insist. He dis-
approves of the Austrian alliance, and said, *that* was
owing to Bernis. He said he believed that Belleisle
was taken, but made slight of it, and added that he had
ordered Bussy to illuminate his house upon it. Stanley
is to be introduced to the King of France.

This is the chief of what had passed last Wednesday
when the despatches are dated. I could say much on
this if I had time for reflections.

I received to-day your letter. I rejoice at the good
news you send me of the improvement of Master Grenville's health. I beg you will believe that I am highly
sensible where you are so nearly concerned.

I showed your letter to Lord Bute, who directed me to
say many kind things to you. He said he had some engagements for Crown livings, but bid me put him in
mind of Mr. Butler.

I shall talk to him more on it in a day or two. I send
you enclosed a Parliamentary Case. I have no doubt of
the point, and yet should be obliged to you for an answer
to it, that I may be sure in the advice I give Sir James
Lowther, who seems to rely very much on me in all his
public concerns. I am, &c. C. JENKINSON.

MR. JENKINSON TO MR. GRENVILLE.

St. James's, June 16, 1761.

DEAR SIR,—I received yesterday the favour of your
letter acknowledging the receipt of mine by express, and

I did not fail to acquaint Lord Bute with your congratulations on the occasion, who expressed himself extremely obliged to you on that account.

I remember very well that you foresaw what appears by the dispatch of Mr. Stanley: I wish I could give you a more particular account of that dispatch, but, I know not for what reason, Mr. Pitt endeavours to keep from us here everything that he can, so that I have not read this dispatch, but only know the contents of it, from what I have been told. There is, however, besides the letter on business, another giving an account of the state of the Court, which describes the King of France as melancholy and dejected; the Dauphin as hated on account of his attachment to the Jesuits; and the young Pretender (who appears, it seems, at length to be at Paris) to be always drunk[1]. It mentions also that the Duke de Choiseul has obtained a degree of favour superior to Madame Pompadour, so as in fact to use her ill.

The same messenger who brought these dispatches from Mr. Stanley, brought others also from the Duke de Choiseul to Bussy, and yet, notwithstanding this, and what Stanley has related, Bussy waited on Mr. Pitt on Sunday morning, and held the same language as before, and even added, that as Belleisle was now taken, he was to demand as a preliminary article, before they proceeded to treat on anything else, that that Island should be surrendered. He would not illuminate, as Choiseul says he had ordered him, and held a language very un-

---

[1] " The Pretender continues to be perpetually drunk: the other day he forced a Cordelier to drink with him as long as he possibly could: at last the Friar made his escape, which the other resented so much that he fired with ball from the window at him: he missed him, but killed a cow that was passing by."—*Private Letter from Mr. Stanley to Mr. Pitt*, July 12, 1761.

friendly and sour. This has surprised very much, as being diametrically opposite to all that Choiseul had said, but it seems to me to imply two things: the first is, that M. de Choiseul has a mind to draw the negociation to himself: the second is, that Bussy is personally indisposed to this country. This I have long thought, and I am now convinced of it. The Council sat to-day on the affairs of peace, &c. The next post I will let you know what they have determined.

You will receive at the same time with this the précis of the Dutch mail arrived to-day, but, as you will see, it contains nothing.

I am obliged to you for the opinion you have sent me.

I am, &c.   C. JENKINSON.

MR. JENKINSON TO MR. GRENVILLE.

St. James's, June 18, 1761.

DEAR SIR,—Since I saw you I have perused Stanley's dispatch, and shall be able to show you a copy of it when you come to town. It contains, however, nothing more than what I have already sent you. I think, indeed, that the abstract Lord Bute made of it was to Stanley's advantage; for in general the dispatch is very ill drawn, and though he has upon the whole acted properly, yet it is in a very odd manner. It is the first dispatch in which I ever saw metaphysical reasoning. I cannot help, however, observing one thing, which is that the Duke de Choiseul[1] is a more sensible and able

---

[1] "The Duc de Choiseul, though he may have his superiors not only in experience of business, but in depth and refinement as a statesman, is a person of as bold and daring a spirit, as any man whatever in our

man than the world has generally represented him to be. He treats with a great degree of gaiety and laughter what is trifling in business, but whatever is of importance strikes him very strongly, and he immediately lays hold of it.

This appears very evidently upon the present occasion. He has a good deal of pride, and it is evident Mr. Pitt has not known how to treat that, but otherwise it is evident that he is agreeable and explicit in the manner of doing business.

Bussy holds still the same conduct as before : either he must be a very bad man and an enemy to this country, or the French Ministry use him very ill; both which are perhaps true in part.

After having given to you this preface of the general state of affairs, I will now acquaint you with what has been determined by the Council upon them. They were very fortunately unanimous and full of good

---

country or in his own. In his military professions, though bravery is far from uncommon among the French gentry, he was always distinguished. It has been his constant maxim to play the whole for the whole in the Cabinet. As soon as the Cardinal de Bernis admitted him into a share of administration, he took a very decided resolution to have all or nothing. Madame Pompadour has ever been looked upon by all preceding Courtiers and Ministers as their tutelary deity, under whose auspices only they could exist, and who was as much out of their reach as if she were of a superior class of beings; but this Minister is so far from being in subordination to her influence, that he seized the first occasion to deprive her, not of an equality, but of any share of power, reducing her to the necessity of applying to him, even for those favours that she wants for herself and her dependants. He has effected this great change, which every other man would have thought impossible, in the interior of the Court, not by plausibility, flattery, and address, but with a high hand, with frequent railleries and sarcasms, which would have ruined any other, and, in short, by a clear superiority of spirit and resolution."—*Mr. Stanley's Private Letter to Mr. Pitt*, Aug. 6, 1761.

humour, and the resolution they have taken has been a wise one. As the Duke de Choiseul has called upon us to propose new epochs, we have proposed them: for Europe, the 1st of July; for the West Indies and America, the 1st of September; for the East Indies, the 1st of November. You should observe that this is the same gradation which they observed in their epochs, so that the only difference is in the commencement between the 1st of May and the 1st of July. But we have added to this proposition these conditions, first, that the Peace, as it regards ourselves, shall be separate and distinct from whatever is concluded at Augsburgh; secondly, that there shall be something signed and agreed to before the 1st of August, otherwise we are to be no longer bound by these propositions; thirdly, whatever captures are to be taken, are not to be comprehended in the general terms of the *uti possidetis;* fourthly, to promote the work of peace, we propose at once to enter into compensation for the island of Belleisle; and lastly to call upon them to propose whatever compensation, exclusive of all this, they may think necessary. This is the abstract of what will be sent tomorrow to Stanley, to propose to the Duke de Choiseul.

I will reserve what I have to say on these propositions, and on some private affairs, 'till the next post. I am, &c., &c.   C. JENKINSON.

MR. JENKINSON TO MR. GRENVILLE.

St. James's, June 20, 1761.

DEAR SIR,—I have nothing new to acquaint you with by this post, than that a messenger is despatched to

Paris with instructions to Mr. Stanley conformable to what I mentioned to you in my last, as having been agreed on by the Cabinet Council. This resolution of the Cabinet seems indeed to me to be the wisest that has hitherto been taken: it has put the negotiation once more on its right basis, from which I wish, for the good of this country, it had never been removed; and the paper in which Mr. Pitt has explained the King's ideas on this occasion is very well drawn. This paper has also been translated and read to Bussy, who continues still to hold the same contradictory language as before.

I have the pleasure to acquaint you, that from an exact return taken of our army in Germany on the 1st of this month, it amounted to 91,000 men, of which 12,000 were sick; but this last number included those who by sickness were likely to be confined only for a few days, those whose sickness was likely to be of any continuance not amounting to above 4000 men. I am, &c., &c.   CHAS. JENKINSON.

MR. JENKINSON TO MR. GRENVILLE.

St. James's, June 23, 1761.

DEAR SIR,—I write principally to-night to acknowledge the receipt of your letter of the 21st instant, and to declare my entire agreement with you in what you say therein. Several of the points on which you require an answer were answered in my letter of Saturday. Choiseul says that Bussy's instructions are conformable to what he says himself to Stanley, and that *Bussy is horrified with Mr. Pitt's presence*[1], which makes him act in the manner he does. This is *ridiculous*. I have not time to write at length to you to-night, but if anything material occurs you shall have a long letter from me on Thursday.

I am happy to hear that you are coming to town. If you see anything inconsistent in my letters you will have the goodness to impute it to hurry of business. I cannot trust any one to take a copy of what I write to you, and really my memory is not sufficient, among a multiplicity of affairs, to recollect what I wrote the post before. I am, &c., &c. C. JENKINSON.

MR. JENKINSON TO MR. GRENVILLE.

St. James's, June 25, 1761.

DEAR SIR,—The negotiation between us and France grows so full of events and so embroiled, that it is diffi-

---

[1] In one of Stanley's " *most secret* " letters to Mr. Pitt, he says, " M. de Bussi was originally Private Secretary to the Duc de Richelieu, who is the nearest relation and dearest friend of the D'Aiguillon family. His son, the Duc de Fronsac, is contracted to their heiress. I have observed that both the young Duchess and the Dowager speak of him with uncommon regard, and even affection. The Duc de Choiseul found him an old experienced *Commis*, established in his office, and barely kept him there; he was nominated Minister at our Court, before the expedition against Belleisle was even thought of here. . . . . . When the Duc de Choiseul informed me of the awe with which he was struck by you, he said he was not surprised at it, ' *car le pauvre diable trembloit de peur en partant ;* ' he was so much frightened that he wrote for a passport to return ; the Duc showed me this request in his own hand. The Duc was with the King at Marli when he received it. His reflection upon it was, ' *Apparemment, Sire, qu'il a deplû a M. Pitt, qui l'aura fait sauter par les fenêtres:* ' I replied, ' *Je n'aurois pas trouvé bon dans ce cas de faire la même gambade par manière de représailles.* ' He appeared to me to talk of this imaginary leap with great coolness."

B B 2

cult and even dangerous by letter to give any account of it. This makes me the more desirous that the time was come when we might converse together in town. It will be sufficient to say that Choiseul has transmitted conditions of peace under the greatest injunctions of secrecy, with which even Bussy is not to be acquainted, and none of our own Ministers but those who are trusted in the utmost confidence. Upon these the Council sat yesterday, and determined that a counter project should be returned to it. They have not ultimately determined what it shall be, but they are to sit upon it again to-morrow.

Thus far, however, I may now say for certain, that Canada is to be ours; Choiseul has already consented to this. The fisheries are to be left to France, but not Cape Breton. France is to evacuate Westphalia. Goree is to be restored. Senegal is to be ours. The other parts of the scheme are not ripe, but from all appearances we shall have a Peace very soon; I think a cessation of arms in less than a fortnight.

Pray take the utmost care of this letter. Lord Temple is in town.

Stanley has sent the strangest dispatches that were ever seen. I am, &c., &c.   C. JENKINSON.

MR. JENKINSON TO MR. GRENVILLE.

St. James's, June 27, 1761.

DEAR SIR,—Lord Bute asked me to-day when you would be in town; I told him in about ten days. He then answered, as that is the case, I will not send a messenger, otherwise I should, with an account of all that has passed in this memorable week; he seemed unwilling to trust the post.

I will, however, just venture to say this, that there was a Council yesterday, which lasted as long as that on Wednesday, and to-day a courier is gone with a long dispatch to Mr. Stanley, containing our ideas on a Peace: we insist on all Canada, including Cape Breton, and the islands of Senegal and Goree; Dunkirk to be destroyed; Minorca to be restored; the neutral islands to be left wholly neutral, or an equitable partition of them. These are sine quâ non. All the rest is left to Stanley to negotiate with. But in such case France is to evacuate all the possessions of our allies in Westphalia and on the Rhine. This is the sum total of what is determined.

I shall long to talk with you upon it when you come to town. I am, &c., &c.   C. J.

MR. JENKINSON TO MR. GRENVILLE.

St. James's, June 30, 1761.

Dear Sir,—I had yesterday the favour of your letter, and am glad to hear of the safe arrival of mine of the 25th.

I have nothing to send by this post, but that Bussy has received a courier, but he has not as yet offered anything new in consequence of his arrival. He acknowledges that the courier left Paris, after they had received there the proposals contained in the Memorial of Mr. Pitt, but he says that the Duke of Choiseul thought them of too great consequence not to take time to consider of them. The truth is that he certainly waits for an answer to his *note*.

There is a great appearance on the coast of France of fitting out flat-bottomed boats, insomuch that Pitt gives credit to something being intended, but I can hardly believe it myself. I live in hopes of seeing you soon in town. The scene thickens every hour. I am, &c., &c. C. JENKINSON.

MR. JENKINSON TO MR. GRENVILLE.

St. James's, July 2, 1761.

DEAR SIR,—I wrote to you last night by Lord Bute's order, and sent my letter by a messenger, who was to carry the summons for an extraordinary Council that is to meet on Wednesday. What the design of this Council is I protest I don't know. It is the only secret I have known since I have been in office. It is certainly, however, not of the deliberative kind, as the whole Privy Council is summoned, but it is for some declaration which the King is to make there. The conjectures which we form here are all of the same domestic kind. We have no news relative to peace.

I have, &c., &c. C. JENKINSON.

MR. PITT TO MR. GRENVILLE.

July 2, 1761.

DEAR SIR,—The extraordinary summons you will have received for a Council on Wednesday next, the 8th instant[1], sufficiently marks, by the urgent terms in which it is conceived, the intention that all Privy Coun-

---

[1] At this Council the King announced his intended marriage with the Princess Charlotte of Mecklenburgh-Strelitz.

cillors within reach should attend, and I make no doubt
that your own prudence would have determined you to
be there; but lest any accidental engagement should
happen to stand in the way, I have thought you would
not disapprove a hint that your attendance on that day
is highly necessary. The King will be personally present in the Council, and I shall be very sorry, sure
that you will be so too, if anything prevented your
attendance.

Wotton must be delightful this fine weather, and the
navigation enchanting, with gales breathing hay to fill
your sails. My best compliments attend Mrs. Grenville,
and sincerest wishes for the health of Wotton.

I am ever, &c., &c.   W. PITT.

MR. JENKINSON TO MR. GRENVILLE.

St. James's, July 14, 1761.

DEAR SIR,—The dispatches of Mr. Stanley were safely
delivered to me by the person to whose care you committed them. You will see by the two bulletins which
have been sent to you all the news we have received
since you went out of town.

The late manœuvres of the armies in Westphalia have
been very wonderful. We have no further letters from
Stanley, and there has been no meeting.

Pitt and every one seems to me not to know what to do.

Lord Bute has written a very firm letter to the Duke
of Bedford, and has declared in it that he will not consent to a peace which shall leave to the French any
even *civil possession* on the shores of Newfoundland.

I have mentioned to his Lordship what you directed me

He seemed to wish that you would have been contented with the answer he had already given you. Whether he has written to you himself I don't know, but he did not give me any orders.

I am, &c. C. JENKINSON.

MR. JENKINSON TO MR. GRENVILLE.

St. James's, July 21, 1761.

DEAR SIR,—As the public papers will contain all we know of the taking of Pondicherri and Dominica, I will say no more on this subject than just to wish you joy of these great and important events.

Amidst all our rejoicings yesterday we received at length a courier from Stanley. He brought letters from Stanley, and a memorial from the Duc de Choiseul. Stanley's letters consist in a great measure of apologies for his own conduct, and are evidently in answer to some Mr. Pitt had written to him, giving him a sort of reprimand. He still, however, continues to speak more favourably of the French measures than they deserve.

As to the Mémoire, it is in many respects a strange one: it proposes even worse conditions than have been hitherto offered. It insists on Cape Breton; it mentions nothing of Nieuport, Ostend, and Dunkirk, and insists upon keeping possession of Wesel and the King of Prussia's possessions on the right. This has disgusted Lord Bute very much, who has been endeavouring, for the last three or four days, to spirit up the Dukes of Newcastle, Devonshire, and Bedford, to something vigorous. The Council met to day; what their resolutions have been I do not yet know, but they sat but a short time, and I believe they were unanimous, and their opinions conformable to Lord Bute's. I will write to you again by Thursday's post.

I am, &c.   C. JENKINSON.

LADY HESTER AND MR. PITT TO MR. JAMES GRENVILLE.

Wednesday, July 22, 1761.

RENEWED Praise and Thanksgivings to the Almighty, my dearest Jemmy, for fresh tidings of happy glorious success from the most interesting quarter[1]. Duke Ferdinand has obtained a complete victory over both the Marshals, with a very little loss.

My heart at once jumped to our dear little Captain[2], of whose safety I trust there is not the least doubt, the loss being so small, and no names named. Sure this will bring you to rejoice with us from your retreat; if not, we can do nothing greater for you. Lord Temple is in town. All is triumph. All is joy.

Captain Wedderburn came away at 12 o'clock the 16th and left the Hereditary Prince still engaged and pushing the enemy.

(The remainder of this letter is in the handwriting of Mr. Pitt.)

The French, after a long and brisk cannonading, ran away in the most infamous manner. Some of their best corps throwing away their arms. We have already taken

---

[1] The battle of Kirch-Denckern, in which Marshal Broglio and the Prince de Soubise were defeated.

[2] Captain Grenville, of the Coldstream Guards, second son of James Grenville. He was afterwards M.P. for Buckingham, and a General officer.

three thousand, with many cannon. But four officers killed. *The Captain* no doubt covered with glory, but we know not further particulars.

On the same side of this paper it is not worth while mentioning that we have taken a French 64-gun ship in the West Indies.

I have the joy to tell my dear James that the officer arrived saw Captain Grenville, after the action, perfectly well.

MR. JENKINSON TO MR. GRENVILLE.

St. James's, July 25, 1761.

MY DEAR SIR,—I sit down at one of the clock in the morning, after one of the heaviest days of business I ever had in all my life, to trouble you with a short letter. I am sorry that you had not the late good news so soon as I could wish, but I thought the first short bulletin we published of it was not worth the sending by express, and I had some suspicion that we had given it out in too high a strain, which afterwards proved, and the only papers which could give any real information in the affair were kept so long at Court, that it became useless afterwards to send an express with them.

I wrote, however, by the post, and ordered the Postmaster to send it directly over to you. I have regularly transmitted to you since what we have hitherto known of this affair, and I send you now what is come in by a messenger and mail just arrived. I should also inform you that Colonel Beckwith is come in with the trophies that were taken, and I am also to convey to you Lord Bute's thanks for your kind compliments of congratulation on this occasion.

Thus much as to public news. As to the private negociation between us and France : our ministers are come to a resolution of proposing an Ultimatum, and of obliging the French to speak out, or of ending the negociation. For this end they have sent a paper containing this Ultimatum to Paris, and we have communicated it to-day to all our allies. The terms are exactly the same as before ; denying them, however, any sort of port for their fishery, and proposing that what relates to the East Indies should be settled between the two Companies. I should mention to you that besides the Memorial which Choiseul sent a few days ago, containing the French conditions of peace, Bussy, also, presented two of a very insidious and impertinent nature, trying to engage us in a squabble with Spain. These papers have been returned to that Minister with the indignation they deserve, and have been called offensive[1]. I have, &c., &c.   C. Jenkinson.

MR. JENKINSON TO MR. GRENVILLE.

St. James's, July 28, 1761.

Dear Sir,—I have had the honour of your letter of the 26th instant, and am sorry that my mistake in directing my letter should have been the cause of any delay. Since my last letter of Friday, we have no mail from abroad, so that I can send you no further account of the progress of the different armies ; I can only say that there is good reason to suppose that the enemy has passed the ——— ? so as to be able to secure their communication with Dusseldorff, and by that means procure

[1] See *Parliamentary History*, vol. xv. p. 1018, &c.

themselves subsistence.   I fancy that before this time there has been a battle between the King of Prussia and Loudon.

The Prussian Ministers expected it would happen on the 14th.   We shall now wait with the utmost impatience for the return of the courier that is gone to Stanley, as the issue of the negociation will now depend on the answer he brings.

There is one thing that gives me pleasure in all that passed on this occasion in the Cabinet, which was that all the members of it were unanimous and fell into Lord Bute's sentiments, both in respect to the moderation of the conditions themselves, as to the firmness in proposing them, and the resolution of sending back the insolent memorials that were presented by Bussy.

Mr. Pitt thinks that the Peace is made, but Lord Bute is of a very different opinion.   I agree with you in my own particular that nothing will be concluded 'till November, but I even think further that they will never give us the fishery even in the manner that it is now proposed to them.   I think that they would sooner give up Guadaloupe.   I will take exact care that you shall be informed of everything as it arises.

I am, &c., &c.   C. JENKINSON.

MR. JENKINSON TO MR. GRENVILLE.

St. James's, August 4, 1761.

DEAR SIR,—I had yesterday the honour of your letter, and though I have nothing particular to say by this post, I thought you would excuse the trouble, though my letter contained no more than thanks for your friendship towards me. You will find all the news we have contained in the bulletin which this post will convey to you: you will there see that in Westphalia affairs continue to look better and better. On every other part of the Continent things are at present very critical. Bussy received a courier on Saturday, but whether he brought anything of importance we know not. Yesterday, however, for the first time, Bussy went to Court. He appeared there as a stranger, said nothing in particular to the King, but His Majesty talked to him in general terms a good while.

I agree with you that their manner of negociating the Peace has been more able than their manner of conducting the war.

I wish the reverse of this character may not belong to us.

You say you do not quite understand what our present terms are. They are exactly the same as what we offered before.

Nothing is added on account of our late successes. We have only made all our former conditions at present sine quâ non, and particularly that of refusing them any kind of port for their fishery, declaring that Stanley's and Bussy's commissions shall end if these terms are not complied with.

I am, &c., &c.   C. JENKINSON.

MR. JENKINSON TO MR. GRENVILLE.

St. James's, August 6, 1761.

DEAR SIR,—A courier is just arrived from Paris, and brings a Mémoire containing the Ultimatum of France, in answer to the Ultimatum we sent from hence. This paper carries in my opinion a very hostile appearance with it. It is drawn in very strong terms. A settlement, though unfortified, either on the islands of Cape Breton or St. John, or somewhere else convenient for their fishery, is insisted on; and they will not destroy the fortifications of Dunkirk, nor restore the King of Prussia's territories in Westphalia, nor evacuate at present Nieuport or Ostend, though as to these two last places they pretend to no territorial right, and declare they only garrison them for the Empress Queen, meaning to withdraw their troops when the war is at an end.

They won't accept Belleisle in exchange for Minorca, and desire that we would keep the former, and that they may keep the latter.

These are the general heads of this paper. Stanley has accompanied it with a short letter, and promises a much longer in a day or two; but he says that he thinks that the point where the whole sticks is the fishery. You know my sentiments on this whole affair, both from what I have wrote and said; so that I will not trouble you now with any further ideas upon it. What our Ministers will do I know not as yet. The Duke of Newcastle has already been with Lord Bute to beg that we may not lose sight of peace, and take my word for it that Mr. Pitt is almost as unwilling, though he is too wise to show it. If on this occasion we act firmly and reject these proposals, it will be owing to Lord Bute. I am, &c.   C. JENKINSON.

THE EARL OF EGREMONT TO MR. GRENVILLE.

Petworth, August 6, 1761.

DEAR SIR,—Although I doubt not but you have constant intelligence from Brighthelmstone, yet being returned from London yesterday, and having heard that your son[1] was quite well by a servant just come from thence, I thought the adding my testimony to Mr. Lloyd's was a good pretence for troubling you with a letter to inquire after all at Wotton.

I was in town a week, and Sunday last Lady Egremont[2] was 'listed into the service of one who is at present a foreign Princess: to be sure it was a glorious sight to see his Grace of Manchester[3] mustering his eighteen ladies in the antechamber, and marching into the drawing-room at their head, with a conscious superiority over Grantham[4], Polonius, and all Lord Chamberlains that ever were or ever will be. When we meet I shall tell you how very agreeable this transaction passed with relation to Lady Egremont, who desires her most affectionate compliments to all with you.

Bussy went to Court on Monday, and afforded thereby matter for much speculation and discourse in all the coffee-houses of the metropolis. To be sure you know

[1] George Grenville, afterwards Earl Temple and Marquess of Buckingham.

[2] Lady Egremont was to be one of the Ladies of the Bedchamber to the new Queen.

[3] Robert, third Duke of Manchester, Lord Chamberlain to the Queen. He married Harriett, daughter and co-heir of Edmund Dunch, of Little Wittenham, Berks. He died in the following year, 1762.

[4] Sir Thomas Robinson, recently created Lord Grantham.

of Sir James Lowther's[1] marriage with Lady Mary; perhaps you do not of Lord Willoughby de Broke's[2] with Lady Louisa North, which the London ladies told me was equally fixed.

The great point now in town is whether Thomas of Lincoln, or Hayter of Norwich, should be Bishop of London[3]. I have heard much about it in town, and more in Sussex, the week of Lewes races, and hope very much that firmness may be showed upon this occasion. I know it is of importance. Now I come to the point of negociation, which was the cause of your being troubled with this letter. The future Queen sets out from Strelitz the 17th, and if the winds are fair may arrive at Greenwich the 22nd or 23rd, by which time all the world will be in town. I propose about the 17th or 18th to send for Cockermouth[4], that he may pass three or four days here before we go to town. Now, supposing that my friend George and Mr. Lloyd should come back hither in my coach with Cockermouth and his tutor, and that Mrs. Grenville and you should meet them to see them run about together for three or four days, Lady Egremont and I were thinking how merrily we might all set out together to dance at this wedding. I am, dear Sir, with immutable affection, &c.   EGREMONT.

[1] Afterwards Earl of Lonsdale. He married Lady Mary Stuart, eldest daughter of Lord Bute.

[2] John, sixth Lord Willoughby de Broke, married Lady Louisa North, sister to Lord North, the Minister.

[3] Dr. Hayter was made Bishop of London. He died a year after.

[4] George O'Brien, Lord Cockermouth, succeeded his father as Earl of Egremont, in August, 1763. He died, unmarried, in 1837.

MR. JENKINSON TO MR. GRENVILLE.

St. James's, August 8, 1761.

Dear Sir,—I have just time to acquaint you that Mr. Mackenzie[1], who is arrived from Paris, has brought dispatches from Stanley, the purport of which is, that the French will never consent to any terms of peace in which an *abri* for their fisheries is not included; that they would as soon yield up one of the provinces of their kingdom, as not obtain this necessary security for their fisheries; and until they do obtain it, we shall not hear them speak plain how far they will give up the interests of their allies for the sake of peace. I have, &c., &c.　　　C. Jenkinson.

MR. PITT TO EARL TEMPLE.

Monday, (August) 10, 1761.

My dear Lord,—You will see by the Ultimatum of France that the pleasing prospect of approaching peace is extremely clouded, and I fear at an end. A long dispatch received this morning from Mr. Stanley, gives us to expect that France will be firm: at the same time I find he still thinks that Court has been, and is sincere, in desires of peace.

---

[1] James Stuart, second son of James, second Earl of Bute, and next brother to the Minister, John, Earl of Bute. He assumed the additional surname of Mackenzie, upon succeeding to the estates of his great-grandfather, Sir George Mackenzie. He came into Parliament in 1742, and was made Keeper of the Privy Seal in Scotland in 1763. His removal from that office in May, 1765, was an act forced upon the King by the Grenville Administration, as part of the price stipulated for their return to power. He married his cousin, Lady Elizabeth Campbell, daughter of John, Duke of Argyll, but had no issue. She died in 1799, and he a few months afterwards.

How reconcile with that view her whole conduct? I can find no solution for this political enigma, except that perhaps the French Ministry claim by prescription to perplex by chicane, deceive by perfidy, and impose by insolence, whenever they treat of peace with England.

The Pro-Memoria delivered to Count Viry will, I trust, have your Lordship's approbation.

I am come from Hayes a good deal out of order with a bilious complaint, in which I would hope there is no touch of gout. Writing and business ill suits with such a condition. The Duc de Choiseul does me no small injustice in supposing, as he does, that I wish nothing but to continue war, at any rate. Lady Hester, who has a bilious disorder also, joins in most affectionate wishes for Stowe. I am ever, my dear Lord Temple's most devoted and loving brother,

W. PITT.

(*The following is in the handwriting of Lord Temple*[1], *and dated September* 18, 1761.)

MR. WALL has declared in a paper delivered to the Earl of Bristol the 28th past, that the Memorial which M. de Bussy presented here by order of his Court, concerning the disputes of Spain with Great Britain, was a step taken *with the full consent, approbation, and pleasure of His Catholic Majesty.*

The said French Memorial specifies three points of dissension which subsist between England and Spain.

---

[1] This is the celebrated *advice in writing* given to the King previous to the resignation of Mr. Pitt and Lord Temple. Although it has before appeared in print, its insertion here may be excused, because it illustrates a remarkable incident in the political career of Lord Temple.

1mo, the restitution of prizes taken on the subjects of Spain during the present war. 2do, liberty to the Spanish nation of fishing on the banks of Newfoundland. 3^{tio}, the destruction of the English establishments formed on the Spanish territory in the Bay of Honduras; and farther declares, that if the Catholic King should on account of these disputes determine on war, His most Christian Majesty is engaged to take part therein.

This unjust and unexampled proceeding of the Court of Spain, by inforcing her demands on England through the channel and by the compulsion of a hostile power, denouncing eventually future war in conjunction, while Spain was still professing amity and friendship with Great Britain; and the full declaration and avowal at last made by the Spanish Ministry of a total union of councils and interests between the two monarchies of the House of Bourbon, are matters of so high and urgent a nature as call indispensably on His Majesty to take forthwith such necessary and timely measures as God has put into his hands, for the defence of the honour of his Crown, and of the just and essential interests of His Majesty's people.

It is therefore most humbly submitted to His Majesty's wisdom, that orders be forthwith sent to the Earl of Bristol to deliver a declaration signed by his Excellency to the above effect, and to return immediately to England, without taking leave.

THE EARL OF BUTE TO MR. GRENVILLE.

Friday night, September 25, 1761.

DEAR GEORGE,—Though things look with a very doubtful aspect, and strange events are to be expected every day, there is nothing I can assign for a reason strong enough to desire you to stay in town. You shall know the decision of our present dispatches, and their final issue, the minute it comes to any consistency. I own I think myself very unfortunate, who with the most ardent wishes to serve my King and country, see nothing but rocks and quicksands in my way, and the times, persons, situations, all thwarting every wish of my heart: however, I must go on, while I see the smallest prospect of serving my Prince; but that over, my only care will be to leave Court with the same unblemished character I came into it, and then comfort myself with the testimony of my own conscience, with the approbation of a few friends I highly regard, amongst whom George Grenville stands in the foremost rank. Adieu, my dear George, I am ever, with the greatest regard, most affectionately yours, 　　BUTE.

MR. GRENVILLE TO THE EARL OF BUTE.

Wotton, September 26, 1761.

MY DEAR LORD,—You will see by the date of this letter that I left London this morning, which I should not have done in this unsettled and uncertain state of affairs both at home and abroad, if my longer continuance there could have been of any particular use or service to my friends or the public, to which I always have been, and shall be ready to devote myself. This I desired Mr. Jenkinson to inform you of, and being fully persuaded myself that my stay in the present situation was unnecessary, you will not be surprised, my dear Lord, that I retire from a disagreeable scene, which I have neither light nor discernment sufficient to see through. Your station and judgment must enable you to form a truer judgment in every respect, and I am extremely sorry to find that you entertain so bad an opinion of it, as appears from the melancholy representation you give me in your letter last night; notwithstanding which, I most ardently hope that you will find a happier issue than you seem to promise yourself through all these difficulties, to that most becoming and most honourable object of your wishes, the true service of your King and country in this great and arduous conjuncture. To this object at all times, and at this time more especially from every motive, the views of every honest man ought to be directed with a temper, firmness, and steadiness superior to all private passions, and all public discouragements; the uniform pursuit of it upon these principles, with a resolution adequate to the exigency whatever the event may be, cannot but be attended with universal reputation and honour, and with that unblemished character and peace of mind which you so justly consider as the most desirable end of all public stations. These are my sincere opinions, my dear Lord, and my endeavours have constantly been to make my conduct answerable to these professions; and let me flatter myself that your persuasion of it hath contributed to that very kind and friendly partiality towards me which your letter so warmly expresses, and which I shall ever esteem as the highest honour, and feel with the greatest pleasure. The true and real friendship which I bear to you is the best return I can offer, and will at all times make me happy in proving to you the sincere attachment, with which I am, my dear Lord, your most affectionate and most faithful humble Servant, GEORGE GRENVILLE.

MR. JENKINSON TO MR. GRENVILLE.

(September 29, 1761).

DEAR SIR,—When I saw Lord Bute yesterday he began himself by enquiring what your sentiments were on the situation of affairs and the present conduct of Spain. This gave me an opportunity of explaining to him what you bade me, which I did in the fullest manner. I think he approved of your conduct in going out of town, and appeared in every respect very much pleased. I told him you could be in town at any time in twelve hours if he wanted you.

While I was saying this he opened the letter you wrote to him; he told me it was a letter from you, but did not mention anything of the contents, or give me any orders about it. He seemed to be much less anxious than he had been a day or two before. Pitt had been at Court, and appeared very much out of humour, particularly with those Lords who had been in with the King on a late occasion.

This morning Lord Bute said he had certain intelligence that Mr. Pitt intended to resign, though he was not sure whether he would take the present occasion for it, or whether he would try to shift his ground, and take another pretence for it.

Mr. Pitt had very much pressed for Council in consequence of what had appeared in the intercepted letter you saw on Friday, but this was overruled.

This, with the public news you will receive in the précis, is all the intelligence I know. I would not omit sending it to you, as I thought some parts of it of great importance. I am, &c., &c.

C. JENKINSON.

Stanley is not yet arrived.

MR. JENKINSON TO MR. GRENVILLE.

St. James's, past 5, October 2, 1761.

My DEAR SIR,—The intelligence I have sent you for these last two posts will have prepared you in some degree for the letter of Lord Bute, which I now send you.

In the Council to-day Mr. P. declared his resolution to resign ; he did it in as calm a manner as he was able, and said that he would not continue a Minister of the King's without having the direction of his affairs. He thanked the old Ministers for their civility to him, seeming by that particularly to except Lord B. Lord Temple spoke a little, and declared (as Lord Bute understood) his intention to resign. They tried to bring the Council to a determination about the Spanish war, but the Council said they would not come to a resolution, and did not think affairs ripe for one at present. This is the summary of what passed. My Lord ordered me to acquaint you with this : he wishes that you would come to town as private as you can, by yourself, and that you would lose no time. You may send forward the messenger who brings this to you to order horsesto be ready for you. I should add many things that Lord B. has said to me on this occasion relative to yourself, if he had not expressed himself so warmly in his own letter.

Thank God! he is quite calm on the occasion. Permit me to express my joy for the public's sake, no less than your own, at what is going to happen ; and I flatter myself to see His Majesty's affairs managed the better for this change. I will not tire you with compliments, though whatever I should say you could not doubt of their being sincere, for I have the honour to be, out of gratitude, no less than respect and affection, dear Sir, &c., &c.　　　　　　　　　　　　C. JENKINSON.

THE EARL OF BUTE TO MR. GRENVILLE.

Friday, past 5 (October 2, 1761).

MY DEAR GEORGE,—I write to you in a very painful minute. Mr. P. has taken leave of us, and the King left in a most perilous situation to form a new Ministry. I avoided the desiring you to stay in town, though I thought this event likely, and that out of real tenderness to you, judging it more eligible for my friend to go to the country and remain there 'till the King desired his presence, than by waiting here to seem in a state of expectancy. I hope you will think my opinion no unkind one. I own to you, so impossible have I found it for some time past to go on with any hopes of success that I should have thought it necessary at this juncture for our Sovereign to have taken new Ministers, though untried, inexperienced men; but the high opinion I have of you, the warm friendship I feel for you, and the entire confidence I place in you, makes me see this dereliction with much more indifference than I otherwise should do. I know your love for the King, and I flatter myself, when his service demands your presence, you will not lose a minute in coming here. Jenkinson flatters me I may see you to-morrow at dinner. 'Till then, my dear George, adieu! Yours most entirely,

BUTE.

MR. JENKINSON TO MR. GRENVILLE.

St. James's, October 3, 1761.

DEAR SIR,—You will see by the inclosed note that Lord Bute will be at home from half an hour after one; you may judge of the impatience he has to see you.

When you come I shall take it as a favour if you would just give me notice of it, and whenever you think you shall be at leisure I will attempt to see you. I have, &c., &c. C. JENKINSON.

THE DUKE OF NEWCASTLE TO MR. GRENVILLE.

Newcastle House, Friday morning (October 7, 1761).

DEAR SIR,—I can't possibly come down to the Cockpit this morning, for I must see my Lord Bute before I see the King, as I hope *the great affair* will be settled, and that I shall receive the King's orders to prepare the instruments this morning.

My business is about the Speaker. I find a Tory will not go down well, and that it is thought that if it would, Mr. Prowse[1] would not accept it, and that in all

---

[1] Many years Member for Somersetshire: he died in 1767.

events it would go down better if the offer was first
made to Sir George Savile[1].

I intended to settle this with my Lord Bute and you
at Court.

If you can't come to St. James's I will send Barrington
to you to acquaint you with what shall pass.   Ever yours,

HOLLES NEWCASTLE.

MR. JAMES GRENVILLE TO THE EARL OE BUTE.

October 12, 1761.

MY LORD,—Unhappy differences of opinion with regard to measures of the highest importance having reduced Lord Temple and Mr. Pitt to the necessity of
resigning their employments, it is become unfit and impossible for me to stand separated from them ; I beg
leave therefore to recur to your Lordship's good offices
in laying me at His Majesty's feet in the most respectful
and dutiful manner, and to obtain for me his Royal permission to resign the office of Cofferer, which His Majesty's goodness conferred upon me.

I beg leave at the same time to desire your Lordship
most humbly to offer for me to His Majesty the most
unfeigned sentiments of my inviolable duty and devotion, together with my truly ardent wishes for the pros-
perity and glory of his reign.   I am, with great respect, &c., &c.   JAMES GRENVILLE.

---

[1] Member for Yorkshire: he died in 1784, when the Baronetcy
became extinct. His surviving sister and heir was the wife of Richard,
fourth Earl of Scarborough.

HEADS of LORD BUTE'S LETTER to MR. GRENVILLE, October 13,
1761; delivered by Mr. ELLIOT, and returned to him by LORD BUTE'S
desire, upon account of expressions relative to the DUKE OF NEW-
CASTLE.

[In the handwriting of Mrs. Grenville, with some interlineations by Mr.
Grenville.]

EXPRESSIONS of great concern upon the conversation
with Mr. G. G. upon the preceding day, which, according to Mr. G. G.'s request, he had thought upon very
much : sat down to write to me though very late.   1st
head, regret both from himself and the King, upon the
barbarous usage of my family.   King's consent to the
declining the seals in consequence of my delicacy, which,
if this had been foreseen, he, Lord B., would, instead of
soothing, have exploded : generous offer made by me to
go into the present situation : the King's acceptance :
manner of his reception of it in his Closet : what Lord
Bute said there : my own opening this plan : the delivery of Seals to Earl of Egremont : could not have
been done but upon this plan, otherwise must have been
in the House of Commons : general acquiescence of
everybody to it : difficulty attending the King in depart-
ing from it : imputed by others to wavering, and irreso-
lution or timidity, though not by him : recapitulation of
all my arguments against it (that the King would thereby lose a faithful servant—true, if consequence as I
stated it): will now use his own, not being convinced by
them.   General conduct of the Duke of Newcastle, and
reasons to show the impossibility of him or his friends
acting the part that I suspected : immediate punishment, crazy old man.   Young king, young nobility.   Information from myself of what passed : daily represen-

tation by myself in the Closet of the conduct and proofs
which I should daily receive from experience of the
King's resolution : source from whence the difference of
opinion among us springs : D. of N. does not look upon
him as formidable : detail of N.'s conduct during the
last reign : odious in his, B.'s, opinion : pusillanimity in
the Closet, foreign system, foreign ideas, sole access,
power of calling people rascals and Jacobites : since the
accession, B. has no reason to find fault with his behaviour : great change in his situation in regard to the
King : knew his own power diminished : would insist on
nothing : would press for his friends and acquiesce where
it would not do: had many pledges for the performance
of N.'s promises : to speak more freely, and open himself
more fully than he had done since the accession : his
graces not so desultory ; had bestowed them on men of
worth and character: had certain information that after
the Peace N. would resign when called upon : thought it
therefore better to let this old man tide over a year or
two more of his political life: saw many among his
people who were worthy and fit to be brought forward
in the King's service: opened this plan to remove my
jealousies and any idea I might have formed of being
led into a situation amongst people hostile to me, and to
be dropped in the middle of it: that he loved his King
better than himself, loved his country, his wife, his children, and his friend : that upon this plan he put the
whole, and would abide by it, and risk everything for it;
that he would support it to the utmost; that the King
was upon the same ground, would support me to the utmost, my honour was his honour, my disgrace his disgrace : that these were the genuine and real sentiments
of his heart, of which he wished most earnestly to con-

vince me that they were dictated by the same truth and sincerity with which he was my affectionate and faithful friend.

Wednesday, past three in the morning.

THE DUKE OF NEWCASTLE TO MR. GRENVILLE.

Newcastle House, Tuesday, 4 o'clock (October 13, 1761).

DEAR SIR,—Since I saw you I have received some letters from some of my principal Whig friends (not Courtiers) in the country, and I am very happy to find that Mr. Prowse will go down very well with them, and indeed, better than anybody. This eases me of the only difficulty which I could ever have, and I hope you may make good use of it, as it shows how unanimously and honourably Mr. Prowse will be chose. Though I have scarce the honour to be known to Mr. Prowse, if you think that the making use of my name, as most sincerely concurring with you in wishing he would take this trouble upon him for the sake of the King, and the public, you are at liberty to do as you think most likely to procure the end we wish. I was extremely concerned at what I saw and heard this day : I would scorn to join in engaging you to undertake such a difficult, and in many respects such a disagreeable load, if I was not determined in all events to give you all the little assistance in my power, and to make it as practicable to you as I could, to go through it with honour, ease, and satisfaction ; and of this I beg you will be assured from, Dear Sir, &c., &c.   HOLLES NEWCASTLE.

MR. GRENVILLE TO MR. PROWSE.

Upper Brook Street, October 14, 1761.

DEAR SIR,—The great anxiety which I feel, and which every honest man will feel with me for the success of the business that I now write upon, is the best, and I am persuaded you will think it a sufficient, excuse for the trouble I give you.

The King having been pleased to signify to me his earnest wishes that I should decline going into the Chair of the House of Commons, to which the favourable opinion of many very considerable persons, however unworthy I may be of it, proposed to have called me, it becomes me from every motive both of gratitude and duty to obey, though I will freely own to you, for many reasons, that I do it in this particular and at this time with the greatest reluctancy, as I should have looked upon the Chair as the highest honour that could have befallen me, and as a safe retreat from those storms and that uneasiness to which all other public situations, and more especially at this juncture, are unavoidably exposed.

Upon this occasion it is indispensably necessary that a proper person should be immediately pitched upon for the very honourable and important office of Speaker of the House of Commons.

In this choice every subject of the Kingdom is highly concerned, and I am sure you will agree with me, that if they all concur in calling upon any man from an universal opinion of his ability, candour, and integrity, to undertake this great office, that no private consideration of his own ease and situation should prevail upon him to decline it.

In this circumstance you now stand ; I know your sincere love and reverence to the constitution, and your
constant desire to preserve the credit and authority of
the House of Commons entire : from these motives I
form my strongest hopes that you will not decline the
acceptance of the Speaker's Chair, when you shall know
authentically that all sorts and conditions of men, of
every party and denomination, unite in their earnest
wishes to see you placed in it, and in this public testimony of the approbation of your character.

I have desired Mr. Dyson[1], whom I have apprized of
this proposition, to explain it and enforce it to you, and
I most earnestly beg the favour of you to let me see you
in town, as soon as it is convenient to you, that no time
may be lost, that I may talk to you more at large upon
this subject, and that you will not think of declining it
'till you have heard the reasons I have to urge for your
concurrence with it.

You will I hope be persuaded that I would not make
this proposal to you upon any slight foundations, or if I
had not the strongest reason and best authority to believe
that there can be no other negative voice to it but your
own, and I flatter myself that negative will not be
allowed to be decisive in the present conjuncture. You
have sacrificed your time, your ease, and every other
consideration to a much more laborious and painful service in which you are now engaged ; and can you refuse
to do it in a much less degree, upon a duty of such high
importance to your King and to your country, to which

[1] Jeremiah Dyson, principal Clerk of the House of Commons,
afterwards M.P. for Weymouth, a Lord of Trade, and of the Treasury,
and in 1774 Cofferer of the Household. He died in 1776.

I will venture to say no man was ever more honourably, and more unanimously called?

When you are fully apprized of every circumstance relating to it, I believe I may safely appeal to your own honour and public spirit against every plea of your ease, or even of your health, for the decision of this question. I will, therefore, add no more except the assurances of that real and sincere regard which it is a pleasure to me at all times to express, and with which

I am, dear Sir, &c., &c.　　　GEORGE GRENVILLE.

THE EARL OF HARDWICKE[1] TO MR. GRENVILLE.

Grosvenor Square, Friday morning, October 16, 1761.

DEAR SIR,—I cannot find that any Act of Parliament was passed for naturalizing the late Queen Caroline, either whilst she was Princess of Wales, or after she was Queen. The law of the Crown undoubtedly is that a foreign Princess, being married to the King is ipso facto naturalized, and capable of all the rights and prerogatives belonging to a Queen Consort; and to enjoy dower or a jointure from the King her husband. This was the case of the Consorts of the Kings Charles the First and Second, and of King James the Second, who without being naturalized had all of them large jointures in lands or rents. The only question that can possibly be started, is what you took notice of, upon the restrictive clause in the Act 12 & 13 W. 3, and concerning grants of lands or of tenements, or of offices from the Crown;

---

[1] Philip Yorke, first Earl of Hardwicke, and for many years Lord High Chancellor. He resigned the seals in November, 1756, and died in March, 1764.

and that clause being penned in general words, adapted more especially to other cases, I much doubt whether a Queen Consort is within them.

As to the jointure intended for the Queen, I presume it will be out of the Civil List revenues; and no palace or house of residence can be granted to Her Majesty without a particular Act of Parliament enabling it, for another reason, viz., the restriction in the Civil List Act, primo Annæ.

If the King should upon any occasion be pleased to appoint Her Majesty Regent of the Kingdom, that also will require a particular Act of Parliament for that purpose, as was done 2do Geo. 2^{di}, cap. 27; because otherwise Her Majesty would be obliged to certain qualifications inconsistent with her Royal dignity; which, as I drew that Act, I well remember was the reason of bringing it in. Such particular Acts would fully cure any doubt that might be entertained concerning any grant of lands, tenements, or offices, in the Queen's case.

For these reasons I much wish that this point may be further considered before any expectation or opinion is created by *an Act of Naturalization* being necessary, or intended; for I fear it might be thought to prejudice the general prerogative of the Crown.

The motives from which this trouble proceeds make me rely on your goodness to excuse it, being always with great truth and esteem, dear Sir, &c., &c.

HARDWICKE.

THE EARL OF LINCOLN TO EARL TEMPLE.

Thursday morning (October 9, 1761).

MY DEAREST LORD,—I did not hear 'till yesterday at four o'clock the step you took in the morning[1], and my dear Lord, though I lament from the bottom of a heart (that is totally yours) the thing itself, I can but say I feel great comfort and pleasure, since it was to be done, at the very handsome manner you have chose to do it in; so much dignity to yourself; and I can assure you, my dearest Lord, I have the quickest sensation of gratitude, for that part of it that I *know* myself so infinitely obliged to you for; and what I shall ever remember as long as I live. But my dear friend, things can't remain so; out of disagreeable things happy effects *must* follow. I fully intended, if I had not received your very obliging letter, to have waited upon you this morning, which, if you will give me leave, I will do at a little after eleven; for I long infinitely to express the thankfulness and the warmth of my heart to you. I am ever, with the greatest truth, my dearest, dearest Lord, most unalterably and affectionately yours, LINCOLN.

MR. PROWSE TO MR. GRENVILLE.

Gosport, October 16, 1761

DEAR SIR,—I know not how to express the sense I have of the honour done me by your most obliging letter, nor the distress I feel in declining an offer of one of the highest stations in this country, though attended with every circumstance that can possibly concur to enhance the value of it.

---

[1] His resignation of the Privy Seal.

What I dread, dear Sir, is, that you may think my refusal proceeds either from want of a due sense of the great honour done me, from false notions of popularity, from a love of ease and indolence, from a dread of connections with this or that set of men (where I know there ought to be none), or from any other motive than the true one : not a fear of impairing my health, but being already in such a condition as would make it impossible for me to go through the common and necessary business of the House for one month : for an account of which I must refer you to Mr. Dyson.

There are indeed other objections I cannot but feel, which I will ingenuously confess, great as they are, the vanity of my heart would get the better of. Suffer me only to observe, that as ill health often proves the greatest blessing in a Christian sense, so it may happen on this occasion to be in a political one.

Your authority, and the friendship you have so long honoured me with, give such weight to your commands, that I should immediately set out for London, were my excuse of any other nature, but in this case it is needless to trouble you farther.

Give me leave only to assure you that I shall always retain the most grateful sense of the high honour done me on this occasion, and that I am with the most perfect and unalterable respect,

Dear Sir, your most obliged, &c., &c.

THOMAS PROWSE.

EARL TEMPLE TO MR. WILKES.

Friday night, October 16, 1761.

I AM obliged, my dear Wilkes, to set out early to-morrow morning, and I am sorry I cannot pass half an hour with you to explain a little, and to comment more upon the phenomenon of the times; a public deluded, and the ridiculous instrument of undoing all that for four years together they had so successfully laboured to establish; their idol become the object of their unjust abuse; but virtue and talents are still his in a degree superior to all the rest of the world, his maligners or admirers.

I have only to add to what you know, that when I returned to town, I found the King, upon Mr. Pitt's resignation, had not only acknowledged his great and eminent services in the highest terms and most gracious manner, but insisted likewise on rewarding them, which was finally done in the way the Gazette sets forth, thus confirming by the testimony of the Sovereign all those honours which the public had heaped upon him with such unanimous approbation.

The Duke of Marlborough, Prince Ferdinand, Sir Edward Hawke, &c., &c., did not disdain to receive pecuniary and honorary rewards for their services, perhaps of a very inferior kind to the deserts of Mr. Pitt, and I think he would have been the most insolent, factious, and ungrateful man living to the King, had he waived an offer of this sort, which binds him to nothing, but to love and to honour His Majesty.

The cause of his quitting the Ministry was from a difference of opinion in a capital measure relative to

Spain, as you know; the favourite united with the Minister of numbers[1], bore down the Minister of measures, and by that means in effect removed him from the King's Council, and deprived him of the means of further serving the public. A time will come, I trust, when these matters will be fully explained to both Houses of Parliament.

He is as much a free man as myself. I think that is pretty sufficient, and what fools must they be who cannot read and understand his resignation, attended with the very broad comment of Jemmy's[2] and mine. Good night, and believe me most truly yours, &c.

Temple.

MR. JENKINSON TO MR. GRENVILLE.

St. James's, October 22, 1761.

Dear Sir,—I am sorry it is not in my power to dine with you to day; Lord Harcourt, who has just come to town, has sent me word that he will eat a mutton chop with me, as he is to go very early to the Play with the Queen; but I will wait on you at any time between six and eight this evening, if it is agreeable to you.

I just now read a dispatch from Lord Bristol, which gave me the greatest pleasure: I think I see in it an appearance of good humour and good faith, and an overture made for terminating our disputes with Spain, consistent both with our honour and interest.

I have, &c., &c.   C. Jenkinson.

---

[1] The Duke of Newcastle's great influence over certain members of the House of Commons.

[2] James Grenville, who had resigned the Cofferership, and himself, who had resigned the Privy Seal.

EARL TEMPLE TO MR. WILKES.

Stowe, October 22, 1761.

I SHALL ever be happy my good, though wicked friend, if I can contribute in any way to the giving you the least degree of satisfaction. Your generous and discerning spirit felt as it ought the indignity done to a man who had deserved far other treatment from the public, than to be condemned on bare suspicion, and rolled in the kennel; what amends is it afterwards most graciously to declare him white as the snow on salmon? He was so before, and will, I trust, ever continue so. The burgesses of our ancient and loyal corporation literally refused to drink his health last Wednesday at their club; can your virtuous capital of Aylesbury hundred brag of having shown an equal detestation of corruption?

I am now very happy here at Stowe, and I think if my little woman took as kindly to the country as I do, I could find in my heart to part with my house in town, and bid adieu for ever to all the infamy that flourishes in more parts of our great metropolis than the hundreds of Drury; reserving to myself, however, the hopes of seeing you sometimes here, and assuring you, which I do very sincerely, that I am most truly, my dear Sir, your ever faithfully affectionate and devoted TEMPLE.

EARL TEMPLE TO MR. WILKES.

Stowe, October 29, 1761.

MY DEAR WILKES,—I have but just time to tell you what I forgot to mention to you in my former letters, and likewise at Stowe, namely a matter of no less importance than that I gave your paper concerning Mr. Letheuillier to Mr. Pitt, who with great pleasure promised to obey your commands. Many thanks for your kind though short visit, and be assured of the hearty good will and friendship of your faithfully obedient

TEMPLE.

MR. PITT TO EARL TEMPLE.

Hayes, Sunday, November 1, 1761.

ARDENTLY impatient to embrace my dear Lord Temple, I manfully combat the strong impulse, 'till the great and important day, big with the fate of a Speaker, &c., shall be passed.

On Wednesday noon I hope to see your Lordship, nor do Lady Chatham's[1] hopes yield to mine; and perhaps we shall return back to our village that day; but of these resolves we will, if you please, discourse at large when we meet.

I conclude the first week will be given to forms and swearing, and that the King's Speech will not come 'till the following week; but I forbear these deep mysteries of State : my Horace, with whom I now renew acquaintance, cries,—

> " Quò Musa tendis ? desine, pervicax,
> Sermones referre Deorum."

As to the rest, my dear Lord, Lady Chatham and the little colony are well, except that I have some cold and

----

[1] Lady Hester Pitt had been created Baroness Chatham, with remainder to her heirs male, on the 9th of October.

a small inflammation in my eye. So ends the rural ledger of Hayes. I am ever, my dear Lord Temple's most affectionate and devoted brother,   W. PITT.

Pray tender our loves to Lady Temple.

EARL TEMPLE TO MR. JAMES GRENVILLE.

(November 3, 1761).

I REJOICE, my dear Jemmy, to hear that you have at least rested well last night, or rather this morning.

I must desire your kind acceptance of a bond which I shall forthwith order to be drawn, charging my estate with the sum of 5000*l.*, to be paid at my decease in equal portions to your two amiable sons, and oblige myself in the mean time annually to pay to each of them the sum of one hundred pounds.

Thus far to have done without the power of revocation during my life, will be a sincere pleasure to me ; and I long by this act to show how much I value your noble, disinterested, and affectionate conduct, towards your truly loving brother   TEMPLE.

MR. JAMES GRENVILLE TO EARL TEMPLE.

November 3, 1761.

How can I express, my dearest brother, the content and satisfaction of my mind in finding that the part which I take meets with your most affectionate approbation. I have no need of additional proofs of your friendship to make me love you, or to bind me for ever, as long as life lasts, or longer if possible, to you. I will be bold enough to say that I am attached to your spirit and virtues more than to your fortunes.

My heart is full of gratitude and acknowledgment to you for the noble and generous offer which you make in the instance of my children, of showing your goodness to me. At the same time permit me to decline that part of it which puts it out of your power and mine to recall it, if they or I should not prove to deserve it.

As for myself, if an unalterable esteem and love for your person, and a detestation of a base conduct [1] can merit anything, believe me no time nor conjuncture of things can make me change. I accept therefore with infinite thanks, of what you propose, except in that part which I have mentioned, and which I again entreat you to waive. Give my most sincere love to your good little woman, and believe me to be ever most affectionately yours. J. GRENVILLE.

[THE FOLLOWING NARRATIVE, in Mrs. Grenville's handwriting, ends with the date of November 9th, 1761, and may therefore be placed here, although it appears to have been written at a subsequent time.]

ON Saturday the 3rd of October, 1761, an express arrived at Wotton at two o'clock in the morning, which brought a letter to Mr. Grenville from Mr. Jenkinson (Secretary to Lord Bute), wrote by Lord Bute's order, and sent by the King's command, to acquaint Mr. Grenville that Mr. Pitt had declared his resolution in

---

[1] James Grenville, and his brother, Lord Temple, were now bitter in their resentment against George Grenville, for having adhered to Lord Bute.

Council the preceding day, upon the refusal to commence hostilities against Spain, to resign, and to desire him (Mr. Grenville) to come to London with all possible expedition. He set out at four o'clock in the morning, and between Amersham and Chalfont met Lord Temple, who was coming from London.

Mr. Grenville stopped the chaises, got into Lord Temple's, and told his Lordship he was very sorry for the news he heard, and that he was sent for to town in consequence of it by the King's command. Lord Temple told him what had passed in the Council relating to the War with Spain, and upon which his Lordship and Mr. Pitt had determined to resign. Mr. Grenville said that supposing Mr. Pitt being the hand to execute, thought he had reason to withdraw, and which, as no orders were to be given, Mr. Grenville could not think necessary, said Lord Temple did not stand in the same case, and asked if he had any particular cause of complaint against any of the minority personally to himself, that if he had, he (Mr. Grenville) would adopt it to the utmost; he said no, on the contrary, he believed they would use him well enough, but that he thought he could not, while he held the Privy Seal, withdraw from Council, and he was determined to go there no more; that he came out of town to avoid talking with anybody upon the subject; that the measure singly regarded Mr. Pitt and himself; that he did not see another person in the kingdom who ought to resign for the same cause; that he himself would not have resigned but from the peculiarity of his situation, and that he was going to write to this effect to Mr. James Grenville as soon as he got to Stowe, and desire he would on no account think of leaving the office he then held. Mr. Grenville told him he had been sent for up to town ; he desired he would go and do whatever he thought best for himself, and again repeated that he saw no other person in the kingdom that ought to resign upon that measure except Mr. Pitt and himself.

When Mr. Grenville came to town Lord Bute opened to him the King's intention of giving the seals to him, which Mr. Grenville absolutely declined, though earnestly pressed to it by Lord Bute from the King, by every argument that could be suggested, and afterwards by Lord Egremont, but he remained firm in his determination.

Mr. Pitt was not in town when Mr. Grenville came ; he came on the Monday following. Mr. Grenville went to see him ; the visit passed civilly, though Mr. Grenville differed from him in opinion as to the measure concerning Spain, and his intended resignation. He returned the visit after he had given up the seals, spoke with great decency and gratitude of the King ; and upon Mr. Grenville's saying he was glad to hear His Majesty intended him a mark of his favour, Mr. Pitt assented to it, but said it did not become him to point out what it should be. Mr. Grenville said he saw no impropriety in it if there was anything particular he wished.

The seals were given to Lord Egremont at Mr. Grenville's recommendation, and the King expressed his earnest desire to Mr. Grenville that though he had declined the seals, he should give up the thoughts of being Speaker [1], wishing for the good of his Government that

[1] In the conversation Mr. Grenville had with the King in the spring, 1761, upon the subject of being Speaker, the King repeatedly told him he wished to see him in another situation, and that His

Mr. Grenville should carry on His Majesty's business in the House of Commons. Mr. Grenville made a stand against this proposition, earnestly desiring His Majesty would allow him to go into the Chair, which situation was on many accounts far the most eligible to him; he stated the disjointed situation of the Ministry, his own want of support, the danger His Majesty ran of being obliged to abandon a faithful servant whom he would leave in the midst of his enemies, and by that means deprive of the power of being useful to him.

Lord Bute, to obviate these objections, sent a letter to Mr. Grenville by Mr. Elliot[1], laying down a plan of his future conduct, giving Mr. Grenville the fullest assurances of the King's support of him through all difficulties, saying the King put the whole upon it; "that Mr. Grenville's honour was the King's honour, his disgrace would be the King's disgrace." Mr. Elliot showed him this letter, but said he had orders from Lord Bute to bring it back again to him, which he did; but Mr. Grenville made Mrs. Grenville set down the heads of it immediately, which he repeated to her. Mr. Grenville obeyed the King's commands, and consented to take the lead in the House of Commons, continuing Treasurer of the Navy and Cabinet Councillor, and upon Mr. Prowse declining it, Sir John Cust was determined upon for Speaker.

When Lord Bute told Mr. Grenville of Mr. Pitt's resignation, Mr. Grenville mentioned what he apprehended to be the distressed state of his private affairs,

Majesty only lent him to the public, trusting that whenever the King should think his service required it, Mr. Grenville should leave the Chair. Mr. Grenville assured His Majesty he would, and related these particulars to Lord Temple and Mr. Pitt.—*Note by Mr. Grenville.*

[1] See *ante,* p. 395.

and as much as possible forwarded Lord Bute's disposition to recommend to the King to give him a mark of favour.

Mr. Elliot was the person who transacted it with Mr. Pitt, and he several times pressed him to declare what was the particular thing he wished : the government of Canada, or the Chancellor of the Duchy, were offered and declined.

He then named the peerage, and the fund for the annuity, to avoid its being a pension upon Ireland, and earnestly pressed the peerage for Lady Chatham, notwithstanding what he had before said on that head to Mr. Grenville. The King was with great difficulty brought to consent to this, though Mr. Pitt states it as His Majesty's own *spontaneous* act. When Mr. Pitt went into the Closet to resign the Seals, he was so struck with the King's goodness to him that he burst into tears, wished to remain a private man unrewarded, that his future conduct of duty and loyalty might mark his gratitude to his Sovereign.

Letters passed between Lord Bute and Mr. Pitt upon the subject of the pension and peerage, and were carried by Mr. Elliot[1].

[1] They are printed in the *Chatham Correspondence*, and certainly do not display any " earnest pressing " on the part of Mr. Pitt, or any " great difficulty " on the part of the King. It would rather appear to be, as Mr. Pitt stated, " His Majesty's own *spontaneous* act." The Peerage was scarcely solicited : it is only thus very indistinctly alluded to in one of Mr. Pitt's letters to Lord Bute :—" Too proud to receive any mark of the King's countenance and favour, but, above all, doubly happy could I see those dearer to me than myself comprehended in that monument of Royal approbation and goodness with which His Majesty shall condescend to distinguish me." And Lord Bute replies :— " Having received the King's commands to consider of the most becoming method of carrying his intentions into execution, I have lost no time in my researches. The English Civil List would by no means

It was no secret from any one at that time that Mr. Grenville had, from a delicacy of mind, refused the vacant seals; but notwithstanding *that*, Mr. Pitt never said one word relative to his own situation, nor made the least enquiry whether or no he continued his resolution of going into the Speaker's chair.

Lord Granville informed Mr. Pitt of Mr. Grenville's refusing the seals.

Lord Temple came to town on Thursday the 8th of October, and resigned some days after Mr. Pitt. Mr. Grenville went immediately to call upon him, and repeated his visits frequently for a long time, 'till he was informed Lord Temple had given directions never to let him in; he was therefore never admitted to see him, nor has ever exchanged one word with him since.

Mr. James Grenville resigned his office of Cofferer soon after. Mr. Grenville went to see him and was let in; he found Mr. Elliot there; but Mr. James's behaviour was so very rude and offensive that he went away immediately, and took Mr. Elliot with him.

The arguments chiefly used to Mr. Grenville to induce him to engage in the management of the King's business, was to prevent the seeming danger of the power falling into Mr. Fox's hands, whose party was then very powerful; he was therefore called upon to resist him; but in a conversation with Lord Bute, in which

answer: the Irish had objections: one thing only remained, that could possibly serve the King's generous purpose. This His Majesty approves of, and has directed me accordingly to acquaint you, that as you declined accepting any office, His Majesty will confer the dignity of peerage on Lady Hester Pitt, to descend, through her Ladyship, to your sons, with a grant of three thousand pounds per annum, on the Plantation duties, to yourself and any two other lives you shall name.' It might indeed be imagined that the Peerage was Lord Bute's suggestion, and cheerfully responded to by the King.

Mr. Fox was mentioned, Lord Bute took occasion to desire Mr. Grenville never to name Mr. Fox's name to the King. This conversation happened upon Lord Bute's telling Mr. Grenville that M. Fox had sent to acquaint his Lordship that he was ready to take a part or not in public business, according as Mr. Grenville should wish and think best for the King's service. Mr. Grenville told his Lordship that he had no personal hatred to any man, but that he could have no intercourse of business with Mr. Fox, and did not think it consistent with his opinions to concert any measures with him, and that he meant to say so to His Majesty; upon which Lord Bute desired him not to mention him to the King, who was already so exasperated against him that it would alarm his mind to hear that any such proposition had been made.

The King and Queen went to Guildhall to dine with the Lord Mayor (Sir Samuel Fludyer)[1].

The Privy Councillors met at Whitehall, where Mr. Grenville seeing Lord Temple, asked him how he did ; but Lord Temple turned his back upon him.

Lord Temple and Mr. Pitt went to Guildhall in Mr. Pitt's chariot. Mobs were hired by Alderman Beckford, and posted in different parts, to huzza and clap them as they passed along the streets ; they were clapped as they came into the Hall ; and when they went out, and during the procession, an acclamation was contrived of these hirelings just before the balcony where the King and Queen were sitting (at the Quaker's in Cheapside), as the chariot passed by.

---

[1] On Lord Mayor's-day.

THE EARL OF BUTE TO MR. GRENVILLE.

Wednesday, near 12, November (11), 1761.

DEAR GEORGE,—I have but just received the Duke of Newcastle's answer, the words are these : *Lord Hardwicke is now here, and though he and I see no reason to alter the opinion we gave, we have not any thought of putting a negative upon that which shall be advised by the gentlemen who are to meet to-morrow at Mr. Grenville's*[1].

I have added my brother, believing you would wish him with you, but don't confine yourself to this list; it occurs to me that Mr. Stanley may take it ill if Lord Villiers is sent to and not him, but of that you are the best judge.   I am, dear George, with great affection, yours, &c.   BUTE.

THE EARL OF BUTE TO MR. GRENVILLE.

(November 12, 1761) Thursday night[2].

DEAR GEORGE,—I am extremely concerned that in an affair of such delicacy the whole must be cast upon the King; not but I see through this, and observe very plainly that I shall be presently reported to have taken on me to resist the opinions of the whole Cabinet, and when this comes into the House of Lords (as it certainly must if the paper is given), I shall be feebly sup-

[1] Probably to discuss the terms of the Address proposed to be moved in reply to the King's Speech.

[2] This letter appears to be in anticipation of a demand for papers relative to Spain, to be made on the following day in the House of Commons, on moving the Address. Although much was said about the Spanish question, yet no definite motion was made, and the Address passed without a negative.

ported, perhaps not at all. In this case I wish extremely to gain time, and therefore submit to your better judgment and experience in these matters, whether those who talk of an intention to move for papers may not be answered, that whenever that motion is made, and the reasons given for it, the propriety of an Address for such a paper or papers will be considered.

This will give us the opportunity I wish, to bring us nearer together.

I do own I look on this demand for papers in the light of procuring materials in order to try the cause between the King and his late Secretary, and therefore if the précis of Wall should be granted, I have no conception of not carrying it through, with a spirited Address in justification of the King's measure, though couched in terms neither to give Spain umbrage or to encourage their insolence; this is all I have to trouble you with on this subject, heartily lamenting that in our first consultation the King is to feel the same differences of opinion he has been pestered with so long. I will be early at Court, and I am, my dear George, with the greatest regard, &c., &c. BUTE.

COUNTESS TEMPLE TO EARL TEMPLE.

November 19, 1761.

MY DEAREST LORD,—I am very glad to hear you come back on Monday, for you have had disagreeable weather. I shall go to the Coronation at Covent Garden that night, so if you like to go, I shall keep a place for you. I can send you no news; there has been many things wrote upon that inexhaustible subject the *late resigna-*

tion since you left us; the great man's letter and his friend in the City's answer[1] is put into verse ridiculously enough. I have taken some verses out of *Owen's Weekly Chronicle*, which, I am sure, you can't have seen.

> "No letters more full or expressive can be,
> Than once so respectable W. P.
> The first stands for Wisdom, War, Wonder, and Wit,
> The last points out Peerage, and Pension, and Pitt."

THE EARL OF BUTE TO MR. GRENVILLE.

(December 10, 1761) 45ᵐ past 11.

DEAR GEORGE,—Millions of Congratulations upon your very great, very able, and manly performance[2]: this will do, my dear friend, and shows you to the world in the light I want, and as you deserve. Could you call on me for half an hour? I am a little out of order, and I shall take the air, and I much wish to see you before I go. I am ever, my dear George, most affectionately yours, &c. BUTE.

THE EARL OF BUTE TO MR. GRENVILLE.

Saturday, near 12 (January 9, 1762).

DEAR GEORGE,—I have this minute received your letter, and I can only say that if it depends on me to give the Dean of Exeter[3] effectual assistance, your wishes

---

[1] Mr. Pitt's letter to Beckford. Horace Walpole says that the versification was done by Francis, a clergyman attached to Lord Holland.

[2] His speech the day before in the House of Commons on the German War.

[3] Dr. Charles Lyttelton, Dean of Exeter; upon Mr. Grenville's recommendation he was made Bishop of Carlisle.

will be answered: your recommendation must have great weight with me, and in this case the very respectable character of the Dean, and the regard I have for his family, would plead strongly with me, though you had been silent; but my former disputes with the Duke of Newcastle on Church dignities, and the humour his Grace is in at present, makes it unsafe for me to promise, who am used to look upon my word once given as a serious thing: I had my eye on the Dean of Exeter, very early in this reign, merely from the favourable description I had received of him, and was at that time forced to give way to a person of a different character; following, for the safety of Government, a maxim I abhor, that of doing amiss, that good may come of it. There is no part of my situation arising from the King's partiality to me that I prize more than ecclesiastical patronage, not for the sake of making friends or forming party, but from conviction that a proper choice of the clergy, especially of those in the higher preferments, is rendering to my King and country a most essential service: how far the retrospect of these fifteen months past affords me matter of comfort in this particular, I leave you to judge: I have at this instant a dozen letters before me on Hayter's[1] death, and yet could I decide, few, very few indeed, would demand an answer. Adieu, my dear George. Believe me, with the greatest regard, most affectionately yours, &c. BUTE.

[1] Dr. Osbaldiston, the Bishop of Carlisle, succeeded Hayter in the See of London.

THE EARL OF BUTE TO MR. GRENVILLE.

Past 4 (January 11, 1762).

LORD BUTE'S compliments attend Mr. Grenville; he had not an opportunity of telling him that he mentioned the Dean of Exeter to the Duke of Newcastle, who seemed pretty well satisfied, and owned Lord Hardwicke would be pleased with it, so that he is now at liberty to assure him that he will propose him to-morrow for one of the Sees that shall become vacant.

MR. JENKINSON TO MR. GRENVILLE.

St. James's, April 10, 1762.

DEAR SIR,—When my servant returned yesterday I was surprised to hear that you was getting into your coach to go out of town. It gave me, however, pleasure in this respect, that it was a proof your health was better than it had been for two or three days before. I meant to have called on you that morning, but was prevented by a mail and messenger that arrived. The despatches from Petersburg carry a bad aspect with them in two respects. 1st, It appears that the Emperor[1] is totally Prussian, and is absolutely in the power of the Court of Berlin, so that we shall have no more influence with him than what will arise from our connection with His Prussian Majesty, and in proportion as we are

---

[1] Peter the Third had succeeded to the throne on the death of his aunt, the Empress Elizabeth, who died on the 5th of January. After a reign of about six months, he was dethroned and murdered. His wife became Empress under the name of Catherine the Second.

friends to him.   On the other hand, the Emperor stands alone in this opinion : the Empress and the Chancellor, and not only they, but even the Mistress and the Favourites, are of different opinion, and though not Austrians, they are not so warm friends of His Prussian Majesty as the Emperor.

The Emperor has refused to let Wroughton be presented to him, or to accept his credentials.

Wroughton charges Keith[1] with being the cause of this, who abides by the Emperor's clique, and seems too ready to support the Prussian system.

Keith has asked leave to come home.   The King of Prussia is more angry with us than ever, and he abuses his Ministers here in the grossest terms, saying they have betrayed him, and sold himself to England[2]. There is no Treaty as yet signed between him and the Emperor.   France is very much affected with the news of the loss of Martinique.   This is in general the whole of the news we have received by this mail. The letters from Lisbon of the 29th, which were received yesterday, represent that the Spaniards will soon

[1] Mr. Keith and Mr. Wroughton, British Ministers at the Court of Petersburg.

[2] The following note from the King of Prussia to his Ministers, Messrs. Knyphausen and Michell, is copied by Mr. Grenville from the original in the King's handwriting :—

" Breslau, March 25, 1762.

" Je crois Messieurs que vous êtes les Comis de BUT ; il paroit que vous n'êtes pas Prussiens.

" Vôtre père Knyphausen, avoit pris de l'argent de la France et de l'Angleterre, pourquoi il fut chassé.   Vous auroit il légué cette coutume en héritage ?   F."

It is not stated in what manner this note came to the hands of Mr. Grenville.   It could not have been communicated by the Russian Ministers, and therefore we must suppose either that it was intercepted at the Post Office, or by some other stratagem copied before it arrived at its destination.

begin to act. Tyrawly[1] has as much mauvaise plaisan-terie as ever; he thinks himself there in a very awkward situation.

I saw Lord Egremont this evening, who looks very well. Lord Bute desires me to present his compliments to you. I am, &c., &c. C. JENKINSON.

[THE FOLLOWING NARRATIVE was probably intended to be continued up to the time when Mr. Grenville was appointed Secretary of State, in May, 1762, but the circumstances to which it refers are not of later date than November, 1756, when he was reappointed Treasurer of the Navy. The tone of animosity towards Mr. Pitt and Lord Temple which pervades the whole statement, leaves little doubt that it was written by Mr. Grenville after he had become attached to Lord Bute's Administration.]

Wotton, April 12, 1762.

To recall to mind the circumstances and various causes which have alienated the affection of my brother Lord Temple, and produced a breach between me and that part of my family, is a disagreeable and painful task, but the situation I am in makes it incumbent upon me, however silent I may be upon the subject to the public, to give an account of this transaction through all its stages, that those who may be affected by it may be enabled to judge of the injustice and cruelty I have met with, and how little accountable I am for the con-sequences that may attend it.

The rank and consideration our family has lately risen to was originally owing to the strong affection and unaltered friendship which my uncle Lord Cobham bore to my mother : in consequence of this he procured the honour to be entailed on her and her children,

---

[1] Lord Tyrawly was Commander-in-Chief of the troops sent to succour Portugal. He also acted as British Ambassador at Lisbon.

whom he took care of from their childhood, and almost educated as his own, after my father's death, which happened in February 1726, when Lord Temple and I were at Eton. Lord Temple went abroad to finish his education; by Lord Cobham's advice I went to the Temple, between which place and Stowe I passed all my time.

At Lord Temple's return from abroad in 1733, he found Lord Cobham just beginning to engage in opposition to the Court, and under his directions Lord Lyttelton and Mr. William Pitt, whom Lord Lyttelton had introduced some time before to Lord Cobham, and afterwards to the Prince of Wales. At this period, and in this manner, began the friendship and political intercourse with Mr. Pitt, which has proved so fatal to the peace and happiness of our family.

Soon after this, Lord Cobham and my mother were desirous, from the distressed state of Lord Temple's affairs, that he should marry, and to enable him to do it to the highest advantage, Lord Cobham publicly declared that he would settle his whole estate upon him, which he accordingly did, upon his marriage with Mrs. Anna Chamber, even to the exclusion of Lord Cobham's children by a second marriage.

In the year 1742 I was brought into Parliament for Buckingham by Lord Cobham. In 1743 Mr. William Pitt differed with Lord Cobham and the Opposition about sending the English troops abroad, a measure which the former refused to oppose. In the end of the year 1744 propositions were made to Lord Chesterfield, Lord Cobham, and Lord Gower, who treated for the Opposition with that part of the Court that acted with the Duke of Newcastle and Mr. Pelham.

In consequence of this several alterations were made;

Mr. Pitt was proposed for Secretary-at-War, but rejected by the King; Lord Lyttelton came into the Treasury. Lord Cobham proposed to me, who then lived with Lord Temple, to come into the Admiralty. As Mr. Pitt was not included in this arrangement, and as I knew to what a degree his mind was indisposed to Lord Cobham, I declined this offer, and earnestly begged Lord Cobham to excuse me, the only reasons for which were my friendship to Mr. Pitt, and my apprehension of family uneasinesses. Lord Cobham persisted in pressing, and I in declining it, of which I informed both Lord Temple and Mr. Pitt, who earnestly advised me to comply with it. Lord Cobham having in the meantime complained bitterly to my mother of my refusal, and engaged her to press me likewise upon that subject, I at last accepted it.

The following year, 1745, though in office, I engaged with Mr. Pitt and Lord Temple in opposing the measures of Government; but a new arrangement taking place, by which Mr. Pitt was made Vice-Treasurer of Ireland, and Mr. James Grenville one of the Board of Trade, and Mr. Winnington[1] dying the end of that session, Mr. Pitt wrote strongly to Mr. Pelham to solicit the office of Paymaster General. In this application he succeeded, and from that time took the strongest part with the Administration, and endeavoured by all possible means to gain the confidence of the remains of Sir Robert Walpole's party, for which purpose he publicly disclaimed his former conduct. This gave the last blow to all intercourse between Lord Cobham and him. Having detached Mr. James Grenville from Lord Cobham, he appointed him his Deputy

---

[1] See a curious account of Mr. Winnington's illness and death in a letter to Sir Horace Mann.—*Walpole Correspondence*, vol. ii. p. 118.

Paymaster, which greatly irritated Lord Cobham, and was the occasion of the mark of offence towards him in Lord Cobham's will.

The rupture between Lord Cobham and Mr. Pitt likewise produced great uneasiness and coldness from Lord Cobham to Lord Temple and myself; for though I was determined to preserve every mark of duty and attachment to my uncle, to whom I was so much indebted, I still supported Lord Temple and Mr. Pitt on every occasion which his political conduct gave rise to, Lord Cobham being restored to his regiment at that time, and declining to take any public part whatsoever.

In July, 1746, an alteration was made in the Treasury by the promotion of Mr. Fox and Mr. Arundel, in whose room Mr. Legge and Mr. Campbell were appointed; the former was not in office, and Mr. Legge came into the Admiralty after me, who from the time of my appointment had done the business of that Board in Parliament, in which Mr. Legge had taken little or no share. I therefore considered this preferment over my head as an affront, and determined to resign my office in consequence of it. I applied to Mr. Pelham for that purpose, being unwilling to involve Mr. Pitt, Lord Lyttelton, and my brothers in this dispute, as the former was at that time endeavouring to get upon the best terms with the Administration; nor do I know or believe that any of them took any part in it, except that I have heard Lord Lyttelton, to accommodate this difficulty, offered Mr. Pelham to accept a foreign commission, and by that means to make another vacancy in the Treasury. Mr. Pelham made many excuses to me upon this occasion, and earnestly pressed me to continue, assuring me solemnly that I should be the next to go into the Treasury, and that neither of the gentlemen now preferred should go out of it before me. At the same time that these assurances were made to me, with which Mr. Pitt and my family were acquainted, a proposition was set on foot for providing for my brother Henry Grenville, whose situation required it. The government of Barbadoes was mentioned by Mr. Pelham, and took effect about two months after, by the immediate recommendation of the Duke of Newcastle, in whose department that office was.

These reasons induced me to acquiesce, and in the month of June in the following year, upon the vacancy made by the dismission of Lord Middlesex, I was appointed one of the Lords of the Treasury, without any further difficulty or application.

During all this time I still continued giving my support to Mr. Pitt, notwithstanding the many public proofs I received of his indifference, coldness, and slight of every wish and opinion of mine, in the midst of the nearest intercourse, and of the strongest professions of friendship. Of this I will mention one instance, in which Lord Lyttelton was equally concerned with me. In the year 1748-9, the Bill for punishing Mutiny and Desertion was warmly controverted in the House of Commons, and every clause debated; amongst others, a proviso was offered in the Committee to prevent the revision of a sentence by a Court Martial, after the party was once legally acquitted.

This practice had been used, and the Duke of Cumberland's friends in the House of Commons determined to abide by it and reject the proviso. When the clause was proposed in the Committee it was rejected. Mr. Pitt was absent from illness, and the question never having been agitated till the morning it was proposed, his opinion was not known. Lord Lyttelton, Mr. Campbell, and myself (then all three in the Treasury), voted against Mr. Pelham for the proviso, with many other persons in office, and as the rejection of it made a great deal of noise, the Court thought it necessary to bring in a clause themselves to restrain the revision to once only. When the report was made some time after, Mr. Pitt came down to the House and made a speech on purpose to declare his disapprobation of the proviso that had been offered, and to treat with slight the *conscientious* opinions of those who had voted for it ; to which, however offensive it was, no reply was made, either by Lord Lyttelton or myself.

Soon after this Mr. Dodington resigned the office of Treasurer of the Navy, to which Mr. Legge was appointed, notwithstanding the promise that had been made to me by Mr. Pelham, that he should not go out of the Treasury before me. I was sensible of this breach of promise, but the situation Mr. Pitt was then in must have occasioned a rupture with him, and probably difficulties with my brothers (as none of them expressed any readiness to support my pretensions), had I asserted my claim at that time.

Thus I continued in the same office till Mr. Pelham's death in 1754, giving what support I was able to those who never gave any to me.

Lord Cobham died in 1749, and by his will marked kindness to me, and no indisposition to Lord Temple.

During this whole period, I had cultivated with the utmost care the highest degrees of friendship and affection with Lord Temple, though I had occasionally experienced many transitory coldnesses from him on account of a family uneasiness subsisting between my mother and him, upon occasion of my sister, Lady Hester, who complained of being less kindly treated by him than she thought she deserved. The affection I had borne to her from her childhood made me desirous, if possible, to do her every good office in my power, which some were base enough to represent to Lord Temple as a wish to divide the family, and to put myself at the head of a party in it.

I should not have believed this possible, if my mother had not informed me that Lord Temple himself had told her so, which Lady Chatham very well knows to be true, as well as the earnestness with which I have endeavoured to justify him to my mother, even at the hazard of offending her, of which *both Lord Temple and Lady Chatham know* she has given the most authentic testimony, both to Lord Temple and Lady Chatham. The earnest wish and purpose of her heart was to see her family united in affection; her only ambition to see her family great in the person that should be at the head of it. To these objects she sacrificed her health, her time, and every other passion, and had repeatedly waived and given up every interest of her own, trusting that the power and riches of the head of the family would be the surest means to promote the welfare of every branch of it. With this view the settlements of the Wotton and Stowe estates were made, in which so little consideration was had to the younger part of the family. Lord Temple's marriage, and the settlement made of both estates in consequence of it, furnished an opportunity for securing them both in strict settlement to every branch of her family, according to her own wishes and Lord Cobham's declared intentions;

and nothing prevented this but their firm reliance upon the extraordinary zeal Lord Temple always showed for his family, and their thorough persuasion that the particular affection he had for many years expressed for me would never suffer him to do any act to my prejudice for the defeating of that settlement which he knew she earnestly wished to establish. As a proof of this, Lord Cobham pointed out the same desire in his will, by directing that the money which he left should be laid out in the purchases of lands in the neighbourhood of Stowe or Wotton, and my mother, in a letter delivered to Lord Temple by Lady Chatham after her death, in the most pressing and affectionate terms entreats him never to separate the Wotton from the Stowe estate, (which it had been the labour of her life to unite), a copy of which letter was likewise delivered to me by Lady Chatham, by my mother's directions.

In March, 1754, Mr. Pelham died. Mr. Pitt was at this time at Bath extremely ill, and reported to be in the utmost danger. Notwithstanding the intercourse and intimate union that had been before between the Duke of Newcastle and him, that intercourse and cordiality was diminished before Mr. Pelham's death. A great degree of coldness had arisen between Mr. Pitt and Sir George Lyttelton[1], of whose communication and friendship with the Duke of Newcastle Mr. Pitt had expressed much jealousy. In this situation the Duke of Newcastle and Lord Chancellor Hardwicke applied to Sir George Lyttelton to know the sentiments of Mr. Pitt, Lord Temple, and myself, with regard to the

---

[1] This statement is not consistent with the letters which passed between Mr. Pitt and Sir George Lyttelton at this time.—See *Phillimore's Memoirs and Correspondence of George, Lord Lyttelton.*

arrangements then to be taken; but Mr. Pitt by letter, and Lord Temple and I by frequent declarations to Sir George Lyttelton, desired to speak for ourselves whenever the occasion should require it.

No promotion was destined for Mr. Pitt upon this occasion. The first intention was to make Mr. Fox Secretary of State in the room of the Duke of Newcastle, (made First Lord of the Treasury), and Mr. Legge Chancellor of the Exchequer; but a dispute arising between the Duke of Newcastle and Mr. Fox with regard to the management of the House of Commons, Mr. Fox declined the office, and Sir Thomas Robinson was appointed Secretary of State.

Sir George Lyttelton had pressed Lord Temple, with whom he then lived in friendship, to know what he desired; but Lord Temple declining to give any answer, Sir George Lyttelton informed the Duke of Newcastle that he was satisfied his view was the Garter, and therefore no offer was made to him.

With regard to me, the Duke of Newcastle having determined to have a new Board of Treasury, Mr. Campbell, Sir George Lyttelton, and myself were to be otherwise provided for; the former was satisfied by a place for life, in Scotland, given to his son, and the offices of Cofferer and Treasurer of the Navy, in the room of Lord Lincoln and Mr. Legge, were to be filled by Sir George Lyttelton and me. This was notified to us but a day or two before it was carried into execution, and was not owing to any intervention from Mr. Pitt or Lord Temple, both of whom, and especially the former, were dissatisfied at the turn things took. Mr. Pitt, notwithstanding he was so ill as to have been reported dead, wished to be Secretary of State, and complained that Mr. Fox, Sir Thomas

Robinson, and Mr. Legge, had all been put over his head.

The dispute which Mr. Fox had with the Duke of Newcastle had produced ill blood between them, and Mr. Pitt and Mr. Fox both agreed in resisting the Duke of Newcastle's plan of governing the House of Commons. This brought them nearer together, and in some degree united their interests for the present against the Duke of Newcastle.

At the opening of the new Parliament, in November, 1754, they both attacked Sir Thomas Robinson, and many occasions were taken to mark their discontent. Lord Temple was in the same system, but Sir George Lyttelton declined taking any part in it, which augmented the former coldness and indisposition towards him.

I joined with them, and gave them all the assistance I was able in the House of Commons, though I had personally no complaint, and in private dissuaded Mr. Pitt (who had just married Lady Hester) from pushing things to extremities. I did this from opinion, as there was then no measure on foot to oppose, and from a consideration of Mr. Pitt's circumstances, whose marriage with my sister, out of mere affection to both, I had facilitated to the utmost of my power, the whole transaction having been carried on while my sister lived in the house with us, which she did every summer till her marriage.

There was no consideration of fortune to induce me to consent to this union, neither did I do it with any political view. I had never derived the least advantage to myself from my intercourse with Mr. Pitt, neither did I expect it in this instance; but I own I did not imagine

that my behaviour upon this occasion was to bring an
enemy instead of a friend into our family, and to alien-
ate the affections of a sister, who, I believe, will not
deny that I had every merit of uninterrupted love and
attachment to her.

But to return again to the public situation:—Towards the end of the session of Parliament of the year
1754-5, Mr. Fox, then Secretary at War, was appointed
of the Cabinet Council, notwithstanding which he expressed the most earnest desire to continue his communication with Mr. Pitt and his friends, professing that
his views and ideas were still the same. But this distinction in their situation determined Mr. Pitt to put an
end to the intercourse that had subsisted between them,
which he did by an explanation with Mr. Fox at Lord
Hillsborough's, in which he told him that the road they
travel was so different, it was impossible for them to go
on together, but that he should be very glad to meet him
at their journey's end. Thus we continued at variance
with the Administration, though still in office, and by
this explanation detached from the Duke of Cumberland and Mr. Fox; after which, in a very short time,
a new scene was opened, by a message delivered by Sir
Richard Lyttelton to Mr. Pitt and us, communicated to
Sir Richard through the channel of Lord Bute from
the Princess of Wales, desiring to know the state of our
connection with the Duke of Cumberland and Mr. Fox,
and whether we were at liberty to enter into the closest
engagement with Leicester House.

The answer given to this message, and the immediate
acceptance of the offer contained in it, produced several
interviews with Lord Bute, and in consequence of them,
two at his house between the Princess of Wales and Mr.

Pitt, where the assurances of her protection and support were repeated in the strongest manner.

That Court had been unkindly and harshly treated by the King, and conceived great umbrage at the power and authority of the Duke of Cumberland : these dispositions, which bore so great a resemblance to those we were in, soon formed our union with Lord Bute, under that part of the Royal family.

The marks of favour were given in the most public manner, and our attachment as publicly avowed. A party began to form itself under that standard, and Mr. Pitt's talents and rank in the House of Commons gave him the ascendancy in the measures to be pursued. An occasion for opposition presented itself at the same time, which he immediately resolved to embrace.

The war between Great Britain and France being just begun upon the subject of our American disputes, the Administration determined if possible to strengthen themselves upon the continent of Europe, partly with a view to secure the Electoral dominions, and partly from that principle which had always actuated the late King's councils of carrying on the war against France by land, in Flanders, or in Germany.

For this purpose, attempts were made to bring the House of Austria and the Republic of Holland into the quarrel, and two subsidiary treaties were entered into with the Landgrave of Hesse and the Empress of Russia, upon the former of which a sum of money was issued in the course of the summer.

Mr. Legge, soon after his appointment to the office of Chancellor of the Exchequer, had met with many mortifications, which rendered his situation neither creditable nor agreeable to him. Towards the beginning

of the summer they broke out, and upon this occasion
he refused to sign the warrant for that issue, and connected himself with Mr. Pitt, who introduced him to
Lord Bute, and recommended him in the strongest
terms to Leicester House, as the person the fittest to
put at the head of the revenue, as Chancellor of the
Exchequer, in the future reign.

I had always lived upon good terms with Mr. Legge
long before Mr. Pitt's acquaintance with him, and still
continued to do so; but this destination made by Mr.
Pitt in favour of a new acquaintance, without my knowledge or participation, though he could not forget what
had passed not long before, upon the promotion of that
gentleman over my head, was so contrary to those repeated professions of his wishes to see me at the head
of the House of Commons, that it gave me a proof how
little reason I had to depend upon them.

At the opening of the ensuing session, Mr. Fox was
appointed Secretary of State, in the room of Sir Thomas
Robinson.

Upon the Address in answer to the King's Speech,
the opposition to these treaties, as the beginning of a
continental war, began in a warm debate, which lasted
till five o'clock next morning. We all took our parts in
it, though upon plans a little different.

Mr. Pitt attacked the Ministers personally, as well
as the measure of the German war: I confined myself
to the measure only.

On the 20th of November, we were all turned out
by letters from Lord Holdernesse.

Sir George Lyttelton (who before this time was
entirely broke from Mr. Pitt, and publicly complained
of the usage he had received from him,) accepted the

office of Chancellor of the Exchequer in the room of
Mr. Legge. Upon this principle of resisting the war
in Germany, in which we were supported by Leicester
House and joined by the Tories, our opposition continued during the remainder of the session; in the
course of which Mr. Pitt took occasion to arraign Lady
Yarmouth very strongly (in terms that could not possibly
be mistaken) for the sale of offices, honours, &c. The
loss of Minorca, which happened soon after the rising
of the Parliament, and the unaccountable negligence
to which it was owing, produced a universal discontent.

The Ministry, and particularly the Duke of Newcastle and Mr. Fox, who, from a jealousy of power,
from the time of their coming together, had been
divided amongst themselves, threw the blame alter-
nately on each other, while the public voice blamed
them all. However, though they could agree in nothing else, seeing the danger at last, they agreed in
throwing the whole on Admiral Byng, whose life paid
the forfeit of it. The national clamour and dissatisfaction rose so high on the one hand, and the intestine
dissensions among the principal members of the Administration increased so much on the other, that it
was easy to foresee some change in the Government
would in all probability be the consequence of it.

In the autumn of the year 1756, Mr. Pitt, by the
means of Dr. Wilmot[1], opened a correspondence with
Lady Yarmouth, with whom he had an interview, and a
great deal of conversation upon the state of the kingdom :
the King saw the necessity of making some alteration in

---

[1] Afterwards Sir Edward Wilmot, an eminent physician, much in
the confidence of George the Second. He died in 1786, at the age of
ninety-three.

the Ministry, which Lady Yarmouth expressed very fully,
but Mr. Pitt refusing to come in if the Duke of Newcastle continued in office, or to engage to cover his retreat, this interview ended for the present without any
farther effect than a general explanation of Mr. Pitt's
views and intentions.

On the 16th of October, Mr. Pitt received an invitation to meet Lord Chancellor Hardwicke, which he
consented to.

On the 17th of October he informed Lord Temple
and me by letter of his resolution to go to this conference,
determined to declare that he would not act with the
Duke of Newcastle, nor promise to secure his retreat,
and desired us to come to town to give him the meeting
on the evening of the day appointed for it (Tuesday
the 19th); he likewise mentions in his letter his intention
not to inform Lord Bute of it, 'till after it was over. We
met him at Sir Richard Lyttelton's at the time appointed, when he reported to us the sum of what had
passed both with Lady Yarmouth[1] and Lord Hardwicke,
the negotiation breaking with both upon the same difficulty relative to the Duke of Newcastle.

In the course of this report he informed us that he

---

[1] Lord Hardwicke, in a letter to his son, Lord Royston, giving an
account of the conference with Mr. Pitt, says also, " Mr. Pitt sent this
morning to my Lady Yarmouth, to desire leave to wait upon her. He
had that leave, and was with her a great while. Nobody knows what
he has said to her, except that he has made vast professions to the
King, and proposed to her Ladyship some sort of plan : but whether
he has adhered to, or receded from what he said to me, she has not
said, for she would say nothing 'till she had related it to the King. I
understand he has flattered me black and blue, but if that be all it
passes for nothing. . . . . . What is most remarkable is, that
he had never been with my Lady Yarmouth before in his life."—
Harris's Life of Lord Hardwicke, vol. iii. p. 79.

had stated me for the office of Paymaster, which was then held by Lord Darlington and Lord Dupplin, and that it was consented to without any difficulty.

I thanked him for his attention to me in this instance, which I accepted with pleasure, but said I should have been sorry that any pretensions of mine, however well founded, should have been any obstacle in this transaction.

He answered me that he pretended to no merit, that my rank in the House of Commons entitled me to the step, which was admitted as a thing of course.

This report, and the conversation I have mentioned, passed in the presence of Lord Temple, my brother James Grenville, and Sir Richard Lyttelton.

Thus ended this negotiation for the present, and we all returned into the country, where in a few days we were informed, first of Mr. Fox's resignation, and then of the Duke of Newcastle's.

The Duke of Devonshire was sent by the King to renew the communication with Mr. Pitt and his friends; upon this we were again summoned to town, and Mr. Pitt informed us of what he had settled with the Duke of Devonshire, whom he had with difficulty persuaded to obey the King's commands by accepting the office of First Lord of the Treasury.

By this arrangement Mr. Pitt was to be Secretary of State, Lord Temple First Lord of the Admiralty, with the rest of the Board recommended by himself. Mr. James Grenville was appointed a Lord of the Treasury, and Mr. Legge, Chancellor of the Exchequer. Many other preferments and alterations were made at the same time. With regard to myself, when Mr. Pitt communicated to us what had passed between the Duke of Devonshire and him, he informed me, to my great surprise, that my name and that of Mr. Fox were put down jointly in the paper writ by the Duke of Devonshire, for the two offices of Paymaster and Treasurer of the Navy; that he had insisted on my destination for the Paymaster, but that the Duke of Devonshire had earnestly pressed the putting it down in that manner in the list of preferments made out by him.

From this shuffling account it was easy to foresee what was intended, though it was not ventured to be explained at that meeting.

In a few days after I heard, though not from Mr. Pitt, but from my brothers, that Mr. Fox was to be Paymaster.

Mr. Pitt retired to Hayes, where I saw him but once upon an invitation to us all to meet together in order to consider whether Mr. Pitt should, at the hazard of breaking the whole, not insist upon being appointed Secretary to the Northern Department instead of the Southern, which the King had refused his consent to.

Not one word passed at this meeting relative to myself, nor did Mr. Pitt, however extraordinary it may appear, ever speak to me again upon this subject.

In the mean time Mr. Pitt, being jealous of the consequences of bringing Mr. Fox into that great office, and Mr. Fox being offended at the declaration Mr. Pitt had made to him of his resolution not to act with him any more than with the Duke of Newcastle, the latter refused to take any office whatever, which stopped any farther negotiation upon that head. Thus this office became vacant a second time, but instead of carrying into execution the appointment which had been so repeatedly made of it in my favour, it was now divided and given to Lord Dupplin and Mr. Potter.

This was the more extraordinary as a very agreeable provision might have been made for Mr. Potter, as Treasurer of the Household in the room of Mr. Charles Townshend, to whom the office of Treasurer of the Navy, which was the declared object of his wishes, would by this means have been opened; nor would it have been difficult to have accommodated the Duke of Newcastle's friend Lord Dupplin, if that could be necessary, as was afterwards proved when some time after Mr. Fox was appointed Paymaster.

I have said before that Mr. Pitt never spoke to me again upon this subject, for which his illness at Hayes, where I saw him but twice during this transaction, was the real or pretended excuse.

My two brothers were privy to all that had passed upon this occasion; to them I expressed my surprise and dissatisfaction at a behaviour so contrary not only to the friendship and alliance subsisting between us, but to the engagements of honour and good faith.

I cannot say that either of them interested themselves at all in this complaint, or took any other part than to use their utmost endeavours to persuade me to acquiesce to it.

MR. JENKINSON TO MR. GRENVILLE.

St. James's, April 13, 1762.

DEAR SIR,—Though the news we have received since I wrote last is not of any great importance, I cannot help troubling you with this letter.

We received our Dutch mail on Monday.

The first accounts that were received in France of the loss of Martinique was by the garrison of Fort Royal, which some of our ships landed at Rochelle, the latter end of last month. All their trading towns are in the greatest alarm and consternation upon it: but what is unfortunate, they have accounts that Mons. Blenac's squadron, hearing at sea that Martinique was gone, had changed its course and was gone for St. Domingue.

A great many private accounts from Ireland give the same intelligence of the riots that have happened there, as you will see in the newspapers. It is, however, singular, that Lord Halifax has not as yet mentioned anything about them. The King, however, has ordered Lord Egremont to write to him to-night upon that subject.

I think when you return to town you will find a change of sentiment with respect to continental measures, and I think we begin to turn our thoughts seriously towards putting an end to that burthen. I am, &c., &c. C. JENKINSON.

MR. GRENVILLE TO THE EARL OF BUTE.

Great George Street, April 29, 1762.

MY DEAR LORD,—When I saw you yesterday you expressed your wishes that His Majesty's Message to the House of Commons for the supply of credit might be sent on Monday next, and the last time I saw you before, you desired me to put down in writing the words which I thought necessary for the notice to be taken in

it of the succour to be given to the King of Portugal.
The inclosed paper will show you that I have complied
with your request, which I have done, not from any
eagerness or wish of my own to intermeddle in this or
any other business of this kind, if it is His Majesty's
pleasure that the Messages to be sent to the House of
Commons, and the business to be transacted there, shall
be settled by the Duke of Newcastle, but merely in
compliance with your desire; and however unable I
may be to serve the King as usefully as I wish, yet that
I may not be represented as unwilling to obey His
Majesty's commands, and to perform that service which
I understood it was his pleasure to allot to me, to the
utmost of my power. Your Lordship will see by the
inclosed draft of the Message, that I have thought it
right to particularise the general motives for this measure, and to point out strongly the limitation of the
expense, both which are necessary from the objections
which have been industriously raised, and which I know
to have made a great deal of impression.

In talking to M. de Mello some time ago, I found
that he had no objection to the requisition, and the
motives of it being fully stated to Parliament; however
it seems to me to be advisable to communicate it to
him before it is sent. How far this draft agrees with
that which the Duke of Newcastle said he had settled
with Mr. Dyson, I do not know, as his Grace never
showed it to me, nor spoke to me of it, except when he
mentioned it at the meeting of the Cabinet at Lord
Egremont's. If it is wished to have a day longer for
considering the terms of this Message, I believe you will
lose no time by sending it on Tuesday instead of Mon-

day, as Wednesday will be the first supply day in which it can be taken into consideration.

The strange account which you gave me yesterday, hath furnished matter to me for many reflections, which neither the time, nor my own indisposition, which fitted me much better for a hearer than a Speaker, would then allow me to enter into. My pain returned last night, and my face is much swelled; but as you expressed a strong desire that I should be at the meeting to-morrow, nothing but an increase of my disorder to such a degree as shall make it quite impossible, shall prevent me. I am ever, my dear Lord, &c., &c.

GEORGE GRENVILLE.

(*The following is the inclosure referred to in the foregoing letter.*)

HIS Majesty having received from his good brother and ally, the King of Portugal, an urgent requisition of immediate aid and succour against the most injurious and unprovoked attack, with which the King of Spain, in consequence of his refusal to violate the Treaties, to abandon the alliance, and to put a stop to all the commerce of Portugal with this country, has threatened his Dominions: His Majesty, as well in conformity to his actual engagements by former treaties, as in return for the unshaken firmness and constancy with which his Portuguese Majesty has declared his resolution to risk every hazard, to resist to the utmost every attempt to which he may be exposed on account of his adherence to the ancient alliance and friendship between the two Crowns of Great Britain and Portugal, is desirous to give such aid and succour to the King of Portugal as shall be found consistent with the present situation of his own kingdoms, and with the burthens already imposed upon his people in support of a war of so uncommon an extent and expense; and also considering that, in this critical conjuncture, emergencies may arise which may be of the utmost importance, and be attended with the most pernicious consequences, if proper means should not immediately be applied to prevent or defeat them, relies on the experienced zeal and affection of his faithful Commons that they will enable him to take such measures as His Majesty shall think expedient for the succour and defence of the dominions of the King of Portugal, and to defray any extraordinary expenses of the war, incurred or to be incurred for the service of the year 1762, and to make use of all such means as may be necessary to defeat any enterprises or designs of his enemies, and as the exigency of affairs may require.

THE EARL OF BUTE TO MR. GRENVILLE.

Wednesday, past 9 (May 20, 1762).

MY DEAR GEORGE,—I received an account at four of Gashery's [1] death: how does that borough stand? don't let us be jockeyed in this too, if it can be avoided. What is your opinion concerning Ferrol? I am afraid of the success even alienating the Spaniard, instead of prompting them to peace; besides, a blow struck by them on Portugal, while we are employed there, might

[1] Francis Gashery had been M.P. for the borough of East Looe, through the interest of the Buller family: they were now threatened with a contest by Sir William Trelawney. Lord Palmerston was elected in place of Mr. Gashery.

have a bad effect: however I fling out these thoughts merely to receive satisfactory answers to them from you in case things don't strike you in the same manner ; by no means decided, and very ready to agree in case the enterprise shall be thought expedient. I am ever most entirely yours.　　　　　　　　　　BUTE.

MR. GRENVILLE TO THE EARL OF BUTE.

Great George Street, May 20, 1762, near 12 at night.

MY DEAR LORD,—I entirely agree with you in wishing to secure the vacancy made by Mr. Gashery's death, if it is possible. He was chosen for one of the Looes in Cornwall, and I believe by the interest of Mr. Buller, but Mr. Martin [1] can inform you of that. Mr. Buller, I imagine, will at this time be easily engaged, and there will not be the least difficulty of finding a proper person, if he will accept the recommendation.

The question about Ferrol is a very important one at this conjuncture.

I do not know what degree of likelihood there is of success, and without that knowledge it is not possible to form a positive opinion; if that should be very uncertain the question would be more easily determined, though at all events there is a great deal of weight in your Lordship's observation, which has been of consequence enough to induce you to leave Belleisle at least to a degree undemolished. If you have reason to believe that the Court of Spain has delayed her army entering into Portugal, from the motive of a prospect of peace, the same consideration might then act in the

---

[1] Samuel Martin, Secretary of the Treasury.

same manner upon us; but if that violent step is taken after the proposal is known, Spain has no pretence whatever to entitle her to our forbearance in an instance which, if it succeeds, will be of such great advantage to us, for the carrying on the war, or of such reputation to us at the close of it.

The delay *there* I should suppose cannot be considerable, but if the fleet is to wait for anything upon this occasion before they sail, that would be another objection: a successful impression made there might otherwise be a real advantage and great encouragement to Portugal. I have thrown out my thoughts to you just as they occur to me, without time to review them, because it is so late; if we meet to-morrow at Court, I shall have an opportunity of being more fully informed by you of the several circumstances relating to this subject, which, for many reasons, must be determined immediately, and I dare say will be determined by you in such a manner as upon the whole will be the most desirable.

I will send to Mr. Martin to-morrow morning, and if he can give me any information of consequence about the borough, I will desire him to let you know it immediately, that no time may be lost. I am ever, my dear Lord, GEORGE GRENVILLE.

MR. MARTIN TO MR. GRENVILLE.

Abingdon Street, near 11 o'clock, May 21 (1762).

MR. MARTIN presents his compliments to Mr. Grenville, and acquaints him that Mr. John Buller left London last night, with a design to travel all night, and proceed to East Looe in Cornwall with all possible haste:

alarmed (as Mr. Martin apprehends) with the rumour of an opposition at the ensuing election for that borough, by Sir William Trelawny, who was chosen into Parliament solely by Mr. Buller's interest.

Mr. Martin thinks it may be material to give Mr. Grenville early notice of this affair. He proposes to see Mr. Buller's brother to-morrow morning, and try whether Mr. Martin can learn anything more worth communicating to Mr. Grenville.

THE EARL OF BUTE TO MR. GRENVILLE.

(May 22, 1762).

MY DEAR GEORGE,—After I saw you yesterday, I had directions from the King to write to Lord Egremont.

I do beseech you, leave this whole thing with me, for we cannot go back at present. I have been forced to make an unpleasant arrangement where I am immediately concerned, on your mind revolting against what I had ever looked upon as fixed. The King has suffered me to make all this easy : do not now be overhauling all again. I am ever, most entirely yours.   BUTE.

THE EARL OF BUTE TO MR. GRENVILLE.

Near one (May 22, 1762).

MY DEAR GEORGE,—Elliot surprises me with your ideas on this business, and I take up the pen to write to you the exact state of the case, lest by a message any, the least, mistake, should happen.

The King, in consenting to your having the seals, said two brothers, Secretaries, having the same office, will not be relished, and I am persuaded they themselves will see the impropriety of it; besides I am persuaded Lord Egremont, by what he said to me, would prefer Ireland to his present situation; it was, I have heard, his favourite object; I wish therefore you would sound him upon it, and mention it to Grenville.

I accordingly did so yesterday, and was not surprised at the delicacy you showed; but now, as I have often observed before, a night's meditation, George, has produced millions of fears and difficulties, and above all a refinement that this must proceed from a jealousy infused in me: now mark me, I do most solemnly declare, that not only no such ideas ever entered my head, but that if I was at all susceptible of them, I should be of all men the maddest in the plan I am now following. I myself would not change Lord Egremont for any man you could name: I laugh at the King's notion of impropriety, but I was with him in error, that Lord Egremont would prefer Ireland: I own I thought it so much that I should have mentioned it to him without the least uneasiness; if you think otherwise, the case greatly alters, for it never once was the King's intention to remove him without his own predilection; add to this, I am too much your friend not to combat any measure that gives you so much uneasiness.

I will go to the King to-day, and do everything to put a final end to it, and I am convinced I shall succeed; that over, I must entreat you to let it drop, and to think more favourably of the nobility of my sentiments, and of the affection with which I am ever, my dear George, yours, &c.   BUTE.

THE EARL OF BUTE TO MR. GRENVILLE.

Four. (May 22, 1762.)

DEAR GEORGE,—I just write a line to inform you, that I have kept my word: this affair is quite over, and I entreat you to think no more of it.

I am ever yours, &c.   BUTE.

THE EARL OF BUTE TO MR. GRENVILLE.

Tuesday night (May 25, 1762).

MY DEAR GEORGE,—I spoke to Melcombe, who very readily undertook to sound Tucker; he says that gentleman has a nephew it may be necessary to provide for; that shall not produce any difficulty: he said 48 hours was necessary, but he would lose no time.

The King's conduct to the Duke of Newcastle to-day was great and generous; we shall see to-morrow[1] if he chooses to profit by it. Can you meet me at Court to-morrow before one, having several things to trouble you with? Adieu, my dear George, yours most affectionately.   BUTE.

THE EARL OF BUTE TO MR. GRENVILLE.

Thursday night (May 27, 1762).

DEAR GEORGE,—After I saw you I talked with Dashwood and Melcombe about Tucker, and found that he had had some disputes with Melcombe before, and took the proposition mortally ill, he made to him: upon

---

[1] The Duke of Newcastle resigned on the following day, and the Earl of Bute succeeded him as First Lord of the Treasury.

this I sent Dashwood to him in my own name, to tell him that I would look on this as an obligation done to myself, on which he delivered Dashwood the enclosed message[1], and is to be with me to-morrow, so that I wish you joy of this being secure. I made Sir John Turner[2] very happy to-day, and have signed the warrant to the Attorney-General, so that I hope we may open the Commission to-morrow; at any rate we shall kiss hands, and you will receive the seals[3], of which I beforehand most sincerely wish you joy. I am, dear George, &c.

BUTE.

MR. GRENVILLE'S NARRATIVE.

(Continued from page 439.)

WHEN the vote of credit for two millions was intended to be brought in at the end of the session, Mr. Grenville declared his opinion to the King, and everywhere else, that one was sufficient. The Duke of Newcastle, finding his Treasury Board abandon him in it, thought it expedient to resign.

Lord Bute was made First Lord of the Treasury, and Mr. Grenville was to have the seals Lord Bute had held; but after this was agreed, Lord Bute sent to Mr.

---

[1] " Mr. Tucker desires his best respects to Lord Bute, and consents to give his Lordship this proof of his desire to oblige him, but hopes that when occasion shall offer he may be brought into Parliament at a small expense. Mr. Tucker is obliged to his Lordship for his kind intentions towards Mr. Tucker's nephew."

[2] Sir John Turner was made one of the Commissioners of the Treasury.

[3] Mr. Grenville was made Secretary of State for the Northern Department.

Grenville to tell him that there would be an impropriety, as it would give great umbrage that two brothers should be Secretaries of State at the same time; that therefore it was proposed that Lord Egremont should exchange with Lord Halifax, who was still Lord Lieutenant of Ireland (though at the head of the Admiralty), and that Lord Halifax should be Secretary of State. Mr. Grenville refused to take any part in this proposition, and said it was impossible for him to take the seals, to have a personal affront given at the same moment to Lord Egremont, who he was very confident would not go to Ireland, upon which Lord Bute declined it, and it was never proposed to Lord Egremont[1].

Mr. Grenville was appointed Secretary of State the 28th of May (1762).

During the summer, when the negociation for the Peace was set on foot, Mr. Grenville had many struggles with Lord Bute upon the terms, which he was desirous to keep up higher than Lord Bute (who feared the negociation might break off) could be brought to consent to. Mr. Grenville represented strongly against the giving up Guadaloupe and Santa Lucia, wanted to have an equivalent asked for Guadaloupe, and insisted and prevailed to have a compensation for the Havannah.

Guadaloupe was given up at an Extraordinary Council called when Mr. Grenville was ill in bed, and not able to attend it.

This difference of opinion between Lord Bute and him gave grounds to his enemies to work with greater success than they had hitherto done. In the course of that week Lord Halifax had been employed to sound the Duke of Newcastle, who had declined all treaty.

---

[1] See Lord Bute's letters to Mr. Grenville on the 22nd of May.

Mr. Grenville had seen Lord Bute on the Friday (October 8th), who told him no negociation was then on foot, though it is since known with the utmost certainty that Lord Shelburne went down to Mr. Fox at Margate, on Wednesday the 6th, to know whether he was willing to undertake the King's business[1].

On Saturday, the 9th of October, Mr. Jenkinson came to Lord Egremont's, where Mr. Grenville then was, at an assembly, and desired to speak to him. He went with him into another room, and told him that Lord Bute had ordered him to acquaint him that the King had thought it expedient, to obviate the difficulties likely to arise in Parliament, to call Mr. Fox to take the lead in his Government. Mr. Grenville said he could give no answer to this extraordinary message; that when he saw Lord Bute he should speak to him upon it.

A note came from Lord Bute on Sunday evening, desiring Mr. Grenville to come to him on Monday morning, which when he did, he opened the measure to him : he said some civilities in relation to the King's reluctance in parting with Mr. Grenville, and his own concern at the measure; but that though the King found himself obliged to do this, he hoped it would be but for a time ; that his Majesty hoped Mr. Grenville would still continue in his service; that he intended to make Lord Halifax Secretary of State, and Mr. Grenville First Commissioner of the Admiralty. Mr. Grenville entered his protest very strongly against the step the King was going to take, stated the improbability of facilitating his

---

[1] This statement is corroborated by Mr. Fox's letter to the Duke of Bedford, dated October 13, and printed in the *Bedford Correspondence*, vol. iii. p. 133.

affairs by calling in so unpopular a man as Mr. Fox,
and foretold the ill success which must attend so desperate a measure: that as he himself had been called upon
by His Majesty to resist Mr. Fox's power, that he had
obeyed him by sacrificing to his commands a situation of
ease, profit, and honour; that he did not now shrink
from danger; he saw none to alarm him; but at the same
time if His Majesty thought it expedient to make the
change, he should acquiesce; he never had, nor ever
would, squabble for offices; that in Parliament he should
support the Peace, but, as to everything else, must follow
his own opinions. Mr. Grenville held pretty near the
same language to the King, who seemed pleased with
his acquiescence; he always entered his protest against
the measure, dwelling strongly upon the ill success
which must attend it; the King said "we must call in
bad men to govern bad men;" but often said he hoped
it was but for a time, the expedient of the moment only.

Mr. Fox began his Administration by almost a thorough change in all the offices which were held by the
Duke of Newcastle's friends. The first day of the session of Parliament the mob were so enraged at Lord
Bute that they followed the chariot in which he was,
with gross abuse, and when he came to go away in his
chair, it was almost thrown down, and he was insulted.

In the end of March (1763) Lord Bute sent to Mr.
Grenville to acquaint him that he was determined to
retire from public business; that he had brought the
King to consent to his doing so; that his health and his
ease required it; that in this state there was nobody
whom the King so much wished to see at the head of
the Treasury as Mr. Grenville; that for his own part

he was determined to be a private man for the rest of his days, never to intermeddle in Government, and that he was going out of town with his family to drink the waters at Harrogate.

Mr. Grenville stated many difficulties in regard to his undertaking the situation proposed to him, but desired to be fully apprized of the whole before he could give any answer upon it.

THE EARL OF BUTE TO MR. GRENVILLE.

40 m. past 6, May 28, 1762.

LORD BUTE presents his compliments to Mr. Grenville. The King will consent to suspending the orders given relative to Prince Ferdinand 'till he has made enquiries by another channel.

Lord Bute wishes much to see the outline of the Speech, for a Cabinet must be summoned early next week for deliberating upon it.

MR. GRENVILLE TO THE HIGH BAILIFF OF BUCKINGHAM.

Great George Street, May 28, 1762.

DEAR SIR,—The King having been pleased this day to appoint me to the Office of Secretary of State, my seat in Parliament is thereby become vacant, and Lord Temple having informed me by a message which I received from him this evening, that he leaves me at liberty to offer my service at Buckingham, and that he does not intend to recommend any person upon this vacancy, I apply to you as an old and constant friend to me and to my family, for your vote and interest in order to my re-election at Buckingham[1].

As I certainly should not have made any application to our friends at Buckingham without Lord Temple's consent (which I informed him of), I flatter myself that with his consent I shall meet with no difficulty in prevailing upon my friends to rechoose me for Buckingham, which I have now represented and endeavoured to serve for above twenty years in Parliament, during which time I have wished to show myself a friend to the town in general, and in particular to every individual of my brethren in the Corporation.

The situation the King has called me to, makes it quite impossible for me at this time to go down to Buckingham; I therefore am obliged to take this method of applying to my friends, and have desired Mr. Butler, the clergyman of Wotton, whom I believe you know, to deliver this letter to you upon the subject of it, and to send me your answer, which I hope will be an agreeable and a favourable one to, dear Sir, &c., &c.

GEORGE GRENVILLE.

THE EARL OF BUTE TO MR. GRENVILLE.

Sunday night (May 30, 1762).

MY DEAR GEORGE,—I am extremely pleased with your draught[2]; it touches everything I would wish in the ablest manner. I have read it over and over, weighed every sentence, and have sent you my obser-

---

[1] He was re-elected.

[2] Of the King's Speech at the prorogation of Parliament: it is printed in the *Parliamentary History*, and upon comparison it will be seen that nearly all Lord Bute's suggestions were adopted.

vations with a freedom that I hope you will approve,
or at least excuse. I suppose Lord Egremont has seen
it. When you have settled it with him let me have a
copy, and one must be sent to the Chancellor, and the
King's pleasure taken about a Council, which I could
wish was on Tuesday at two, if there is no objection
to it.

1*st* *Section.* After the word *dispatch* might not
unanimously be inserted?

3*rd* *Section.* Might not this section be shortened
thus: the great and happy change in the situation of
my ally, the King of Prussia, joined to the humane and
generous declaration made by the Emperor of Russia,
to all the Courts in alliance with him, *gives us* (ought
to give us) the most flattering hopes of a speedy pacifi-
cation in those parts of Germany?

4*th* *Section.* Instead of *attack made,* had we not
better put it, *unprovoked attack with which the dominions of my ancient ally, the King of Portugal, is
threatened, &c.?*

In the same section might not the four lines marked
be omitted, and let it run thus: *which have enabled me
to augment considerably my fleets and armies in those
parts where the enemy can be attacked with the greatest
advantage, &c.?*

I insert the last words instead of *vulnerable;* that was
a chosen figure of a late Minister's, and used by him
continually.

5*th* *Section.* I am doubtful about the word *consider*
in the beginning of this section: might it not run thus—
*while I give you my hearty thanks for the ample sub-
sidies, &c.?*

6*th* *Section.* The word *confident,* towards the end,

had better be changed, because confidence follows directly, and instead of it, *will, I am most certain, be found to deserve it.*

8th Section. If it be thought necessary to shorten the Speech, I should imagine this section might be omitted, and the 9th would follow the 7th perfectly well.

THE EARL OF BUTE TO MR. GRENVILLE.

Half-past 3, June (1), 1762.

DEAR GEORGE,—I have been forced to confine myself this morning, and, indeed, to be denied to everybody that called except Lord Mansfield, with whom I had particular business : be so good, therefore, to excuse me to Lord Egremont, and accept of my excuse yourself, as I can't attend you.

I congratulate you on the state of the King's health. His Majesty writes me word that he gave you his orders himself concerning to-morrow [1]. I am directed to send Halifax to the King, who has accepted [2], if His Majesty shall think proper, in the handsomest manner. I am, with the greatest regard,   BUTE.

EARL TEMPLE TO MR. WILKES [3].

(June 14?) 1762.

As to public events, I am sorry to see that the paper hostilities are renewed with so high a degree of acri-

---

[1] The prorogation of Parliament.

[2] To continue First Lord of the Admiralty.

[3] From a corrected and much obliterated draught in Lord Temple's handwriting. The very guarded manner in which this letter is

mony, as now appears on all sides, and though I make
it a rule not to agitate any matter of a political nature
by the *post*, that Argus with at least an hundred eyes,
yet whilst my thoughts agree with Government, I may
venture to hazard them, subject even to that inspection.

I am quite at a loss to guess through what channel
the *North Briton* flows, but I suppose it is meant to be
a Southern stream productive of good to the public; but
I fear the merchandize it bears will be attended with
contrary effects, attacking at once the whole nation of
Scotland, by wholesale and retail in so very invidious a
manner; and Lord B.'s name at full length may be attended with unhappy consequences in many lights, falling afterwards so roughly upon the whole body of country
gentlemen, whose public conduct has been really meritorious; and at the same time attacking a private gentleman
by name, of parts and literary talents, without provocation, are things which cannot meet with the approbation
of the public at large.

But I insensibly grow grave, convinced that the sooner
this scene of indiscriminate and excessive personality is
closed, the better, and that the *Briton* left to himself is
left to his worst enemy.

As the *N. B.* will, I suppose, endeavour by every
means to lie concealed, it will be impossible to ferret

expressed renders it probable that Lord Temple expected it would be
read at the Post Office before it reached its destination, for it cannot
be supposed that he was ignorant of the connection between the *North
Briton* and Wilkes. Almon, mentioning the commencement of that
paper, says, " Lord Temple was not ignorant of his friend's design
before he put it in execution, and certainly approved of it." There is
no date to the above letter, but it appears to have been written after
the publication of the second number of the *North Briton,* and " *the
private gentleman of parts and literary talent*" may mean Horace
Walpole, who is alluded to " *by name.*"

him out, and give him good advice, otherwise I am sure
I could convince him; but of this no more, nor, indeed,
is it a subject that can be treated by letter, but from the
abundance of the conviction the heart speaketh upon
an interesting subject to a friend, who is no otherwise
interested in it than as a well wisher to the public,
which I have ever found you to be, and you will ever
find me, my dear Wilkes, most truly your sincere well-
wisher and devoted Friend and Servant.

THE EARL OF EGREMONT TO MR. GRENVILLE.

Saturday night, 11 o'clock (June 19, 1762).

DEAR SIR,—The Lisbon mail being come in to-day,
I send it to you with some other papers to amuse you
for an hour in your rustication.

The King sent for me this day, and opened his
thoughts to me entirely upon the great business of
Monday.

I think, by what he said, our conversation of
yesterday had its effect with our friend; and I am
desired to open the Council, as I wished to do. Had
he not sent to me I should have taken the opportunity
to day to have talked to him upon a matter I did not
care to open before you, which I have settled to my
satisfaction. Had the Duke of N. been my colleague
I should not have ventured this last sentence. I will
explain my meaning when we meet, which may be very
soon; for if Count La Lippe[1] (who goes on Monday)

---

[1] Sovereign of a petty state, lying on the confines of Hanover and
Westphalia. He was now al out to proceed to Portugal to take the
chief command of the troops. See a good account of this remarkable

does not detain me, I propose coming to dine with Lady Blandford[1] to-morrow. I am, ever, &c.

EGREMONT.

EARL TEMPLE TO MR. WILKES[2].

June 20, 1762.

SIR,—As all the sins of the *Monitor* against the ruling powers are principally charged upon our friend Mr. B.[3], and then by way of rebound upon two other persons, to whom the *Monitor* has been so kindly partial, it is of the more moment to avoid that sort of personality which regards any of the R—— F——. I am, therefore, glad my hint came at least time enough to prevent the publication of what would have filled up the whole measure of offence, and could not but have been much commented upon to the disadvantage of those it might mean to serve: as to other matters, sportsmen I suppose are at liberty to pursue lawful game, I am only solicitous to have them not trespass within the bounds of royal manors, and not start something of a delicate and personal nature, which should be avoided.

I believe there is not the least foundation for the oc-

man in a note by Sir Denis Le Marchant to *Horace Walpole's Memoirs of George the Third*, vol. i. p. 145. His mother is said to have been a daughter of George the First, by the Duchess of Kendal.

[1] Lord Egremont's mother-in-law, the widow of Sir William Wyndham.

[2] From a draught in Lord Temple's hand. It is, no doubt, intended for Wilkes; but was probably copied by another person for transmission by the post, and not signed, as it contains an allusion to Mr. Pitt and Lord Temple, which the latter would not be likely to make in his own handwriting.

[3] Beardmore, an Attorney employed by Lord Temple, was supposed to be a writer in the *Monitor*.

casional reports of Mr. P. and Lord T's return into the King's service. I hope I may be allowed to defray the loss and the expense of laying aside the paper you sent me, and that I shall have the pleasure of seeing you according to your promise.

I am, Sir, your obliged and obedient Servant.

EARL TEMPLE TO MR. WILKES.

Stowe, June 27, 1762.

My dear Colonel,—I lose not a moment's time in certifying the name of Mr. John Hammond to His Majesty, and will send his commission as soon as it is in my power.

You don't mention anything of the commissions I sent you, and of the date you gave to that of Tomkins, but I take it for granted you have received them.

I have no commission of Deputy Lieutenant by me, having left even the form in London; but I must contrive some way to get one, that Tomkins's wish may be gratified. You do not send me the name of the new surgeon (I hope a Scotchman), otherwise I would have certified for him at the same time. In short (wicked as you are), I still find a joy in expediting whatever you wish.

What I writ to you I certainly meant in a most friendly purpose. When I was very very young indeed my father was called in to whip me for   .   .   .
.   .   . ; how dearly did he love me, how much did he grieve at every stroke he gave me? but my mother was peremptory, and all my vivacity could not save me. More wit I never read; but I find the *N. B.*

doth not mend from sage advice. I must, therefore, deliver him over to the tormentors, the *Briton*, the *Auditor*, the *Occasional Writer*[1], and to his own conscience, lulled, though it be for the present, with the sweet music of applauding worlds. We will talk matters over when we meet; in the mean time I am meditating a trip to Beckford's. Believe me, ever, with sincere affection, my dear Colonel's most devoted   TEMPLE.

MR. PITT TO EARL TEMPLE.

(July —, 1762).

MY DEAR LORD,—My boots are greased, and I hold myself in readiness for the welcome summons to Lord Lincoln's, as about the first days of August seemed when we parted at Stowe to be destined provisionally for the pleasing epoque of our meeting at Oatlands. I hope every day to have the pleasure of hearing from your Lordship that the party is finally fixed. I feel the more impatience, lest some *contretems* should happen to prevent a visit which I have at heart to make.

Gout is in the present moment propitious to my purposes, and the thunder showers having spent their rage, give the promise of fair skies and glorious suns, such as the scenes we are going to deserve.

After the late rains, Stowe must be verdure in propriâ personâ, which, added to a few other things, must render it a tolerable place. I trust always that the pregnant clouds may not, among the rest, have dropped any rheumatic sensations upon the Lord of all those beauties, and that I shall have the satisfaction to hear you are

---

[1] Weekly publications :—all of them in favour of the Ministry.

well, as well as the joy to embrace you so very soon.
Lady Chatham and children are all well: the former
joins in all affectionate compliments.

I am ever, &c., &c.   W. PITT.

THE EARL OF EGREMONT TO MR. GRENVILLE.

Saturday afternoon, 3 o'clock, July 3, 1762.

DEAR SIR,—I hope you got safe and well to Wotton,
but you could not be unreasonable enough to expect to
be quiet there for twenty-four hours together.

This morning I received from Viry a large packet
come by express from Versailles, containing a letter from
Comte de Choiseul to me, copy of one from the Duc de
Choiseul to the Comte, enclosing a letter from Grimaldi[1]
with the answer from the Spanish Court to our declaration, signed by Wall: a memorial of the French proposals reduced into articles and signed, and a paper of
observations on the memorial, likewise signed.

The memorial differed little from what came unsigned
before, and my answer must be methodising my former
answer into articles, and my reasonings upon the different
parts into a separate paper.

---

[1] The Spanish Ambassador at Paris. " Grimaldi is more displeasing
than Stahremberg, and much less a gentleman. I am told from the
best authority that his genius goes no further than a mean *ruse*, and
cunning of the Newgate style ; this circumstance, which is well known
here, makes him as little dangerous as his own ill intentions, and the
power of his Court, can give you reason to wish. As his parts may be
very easily surpassed, so even his most distinguishing characteristic,
his pride, will never stand before a man of real spirit, which I have
tried in such little instances not worth mentioning.—*Private Letter
from Mr. Stanley to Mr. Pitt*, June 29, 1761.

Two hours after the first packet, Viry came to me to show me some letters to give light into the Comte Choiseul's packet, some he gave copies of, and others he would not so much as lend me to show the King.

He had wrote you a letter, which on my telling him you were out of town, he desired me to send to your house for, and enclose in my letter to you.

Were I to judge, I think we shall conclude this matter, and think that the managing the Court of Spain, and trusting us with more than they tell at Madrid, is not entirely a farce. I am, &c., &c. EGREMONT.

MR. EDWARD WESTON TO MR. GRENVILLE.

Park Place, July 9 (1762).

SIR,—As it is likely the present proposals of France will be published a little sooner or later, that we may not be reproached by the King of Prussia with having entirely sunk what is therein said about Wesel, Cleves, &c., at the same time that we profess so much regard to his interests, I have thought it necessary to point out in my draught that part of the French plan in such a manner as may be afterwards appealed to as a sufficient communication, though it be not expressly mentioned.

It seems to me that by the way of wording the proposal of France, to give no assistance to our respective allies, they mean to reserve to themselvest he power of succouring theirs with money, which would leave us the same liberty with respect to ours: and, with that tacit reserve, I should think it would be better liked, even by the King of Prussia, that we should stipulate to give him no succour in troops, than a bare reciprocal engagement to withdraw the respective armies; because I apprehend, in case the Peace between him and the Queen should not succeed, if France be not tied up from sending men to her assistance, it will be in her power to do it upon the first pretence, much easier and sooner, who has a standing force always ready upon the frontiers of the Empire; than in ours to give a succour of the same kind to the King of Prussia.

I must own that upon the whole, that a bare stipulation to withdraw the respective armies, appears to me very lame and insufficient, and that it ought to be attended at least with an engagement that they shall not be employed any more in the Empire during the present war, in the quarrel between the Courts of Vienna and Berlin.

As you are pleased to allow of my troubling you with my *idées creuses*, I submit what is above to your consideration and better judgment.　　　　E. W.

THE EARL OF BUTE TO MR. GRENVILLE.

(July 12, 1762) half-past 6.

LORD BUTE presents his compliments to Mr. Grenville: he thinks the dispatch[1] very proper; he would have wished (according to what he took the liberty of hinting to him the other day) that Mitchell had been instructed to insinuate to His Prussian Majesty that our Peace must not be obstructed by any demur on his side: Lord Bute is sensible this may be inferred from the colour of the dispatch, but perhaps this truth dressed in polite expression will not be without its utility.

[1] See *Mitchell Memoirs and Papers*, vol. ii.

MR. GRENVILLE TO THE EARL OF BUTE.

Great George Street, September 1, 1762.

MY DEAR LORD,—I hoped to have had the pleasure of meeting you yesterday at one o'clock at St. James's, agreeably to what I understood you intended when I saw you the day before.

I waited there in order to have shown you the draft of my despatch to Mr. Mitchell[1], and to have talked with you upon the subject of it, which I should have been very glad to have done ; but as I could not see you at Court, I laid it before the King, who was pleased to approve of it, and to direct me to send it without delay, as soon as the other communications which the King ordered me to make to the Landgrave of Hesse, the Duke of Brunswick, &c., can be got ready, which will not be till this evening; I therefore enclose to your Lordship the draft, and beg you will consider it thoroughly, and give me your thoughts upon it in any way that is most convenient and agreeable to you. Your Lordship will see that the whole of it depends upon the repeated declarations made to the King of Prussia, of His Majesty's resolution not to depart from the measure of withdrawing the troops on both sides, as soon as the preliminaries shall be signed ; and consequently, if this letter is sent, no other expedient can be taken.

I think it necessary to observe this to you, as I did yesterday to Lord Egremont, because M. de Choiseul in his two last dispatches takes no notice of this measure, but only says that with regard to Germany both Courts being agreed not to propose to each other anything derogatory to their honour, and to their respective engage-

---

[1] See *Mitchell Memoirs and Papers*, vol. ii.

ments, upon this principle he hopes they will find an *expedient that may satisfy*, and that he agrees that this article *pouvoit être traité et redigé par les Ministres Plenipotentiaires.* I have sent you enclosed with this, and with the draft, the extract from the two last French despatches, that there may be no doubt upon an article of this consequence, and which by this despatch to Mr. Mitchell, and the other communications which the King has ordered me to make, will be circulated all over Europe, and therefore should be thoroughly explained to the Duke of Bedford before he goes, and not considered as a matter subject to future discussion, and to be treated of as such by the Plenipotentiaries.

You will not be surprised at my wishing to know your sentiments upon this before the despatches are sent. I shall be at St. James's a little after one, or I will come to you, if that is more agreeable to you. I am ever, &c., &c.   GEORGE GRENVILLE.

NOTE CONCERNING THE DECLARATION MADE BY MESSRS. KNYPHAUSEN AND MICHELL, SEPTEMBER 8, 1762.

(*In Mr. Grenville's handwriting.*)

THIS day the two Prussian Ministers, Messrs. Knyphausen and Michell came to Mr. Secretary Grenville, and informed him that they had a Declaration to make to him on the part of the King, their master, which M. de Knyphausen repeated verbally.

Mr. Secretary Grenville told them, in answer, that if they had any declaration to make, he desired that, to avoid all mistakes, it might be given in writing, and not by word of mouth, in order that he might lay it before

the King, who would consider what answer should be
proper to be given to it; that this was the more necessary as they had been informed of His Majesty's directions to Mr. Secretary Grenville not to make any communications to them[1], either as to the past or the future,

[1] Mr. Grenville refers to the following, which is copied from his own
Memorandum :—
"Declaration made verbally by me (Mr. Grenville) on the 5th of
August, 1762, by the King's orders, to Messrs. Knyphausen and
Michell, in answer to their repeated demand of communication, or to
know if there was any particular reason for withholding it from them.

"'Que jusqu'à ce que le Roi de Prusse ait des Ministres qui s'ab-
stiennent de se mêler de ce qui concerne l'intérieur de ce royaume,
Sa Majesté jugera convenable de ne pas faire ses communications au
Roi de Prusse que par le canal de son propre Ministre à la Cour de Sa
Majesté Prussienne.'"

The extreme hatred of the King of Prussia towards Lord Bute took
its rise from his determination to withdraw the Annual Subsidy, an
announcement to that effect having been made in a very masterly
despatch from Lord Bute to Mr. Mitchell, on the 26th of May, for
which see *Mitchell Memoirs and Papers*, vol. ii. Lord Bute thus
compares the present state of Prussia with that of Great Britain :—
"We have a very powerful additional enemy to contend with. His
Prussian Majesty has a new and very powerful friend. The weight of
Spain is thrown into our opposite scale : that of Russia and Sweden,
too, is taken out of his. The King of Prussia had Pomerania and
Brandenburg to defend, besides Saxony and Silesia : the two former
are no longer in danger. We had, on our part, a most expensive land
war in Germany : we must now provide for another in Portugal."

It seems, from the following copy of a letter from the King of
Prussia to his Ministers, Knyphausen and Michell, that they had
orders to encourage the opposition to Lord Bute, and to promote the
annoyance and destruction of his Administration, to the extent of
their power, and no doubt that much of the personal abuse which was
so liberally bestowed upon Lord Bute was purchased by Prussian gold.
This letter is in the handwriting of Charles Lloyd, Mr. Grenville's
Secretary, but in what manner it was obtained there is no explanation.

"AU BARON DE KNYPHAUSEN, ET AU SIEUR MICHELL.

"A Dittmansdorff ce 7 d'Août, 1762.

"Votre rapport du 23 de Juillet m'a été fidèlement rendu, au sujet
du quel je ne saurois que vous renvoyer à ce que je vous ai déja écrit
par ma lettre antérieure, par rapport aux communications que Monsr.

and consequently that he could not enter with them into
the subject of the present situation, and that therefore
he must abide by the answer which the King of Prussia
had already given in writing to the late communications
made to that Court, and by the reply which, by His Majesty's orders, had been returned to it from hence
through the channel of Mr. Mitchell.

To this the Prussian Ministers answered that they
had no directions to give it in writing, and therefore did
not dare to do it ; but that they would repeat it, and
that a note of it might be taken in writing to prevent
any mistake.

This was accordingly done, and the note, which is in
the following words, was afterwards read to them :—

" Par un ordre du 21 d'Août, 1762. Que Sa Majesté
le Roi de Prusse espère que le Roi de la Grande Bretagne stipulera la restitution de Clèves, Gueldres, Wesel,
&c., une parité parfaite dans les traitemens de la Grande
Bretagne et de la France envers leurs alliés après la
Paix ; une déclaration que si contre toute attente, on
prenoit des engagemens contraires aux interêts immé-
diats du Roi de Prusse, qu'il ne se tiendroit pas lié, mais
se réserveroit ses droits."

To this they added, that they did not expect that Mr.
Secretary Grenville should give them any answer ; but

Mitchell m'est venu faire de la part de sa Cour, et par rapport aux
mésures que j'ai pris.　Au reste, comme il n'y aura jamais moyen de
parvenir en règle avec le Comte de Bute, vous ne perdrez aucune
occasion qui se présentera pour animer et brouiller sous main la nation
contre lui, et contre l'administration présente, et de rejetter tout ce qui
vient d'arriver de fâcheux à la nation sur lui, comme arrivé par sa
faute.　Enfin vous animérez même autant qu'il se peut les auteurs des
brochûres qu'on met au jour pour décrier la conduite de ce Ministre,
afin de parvenir d'autant plus aisément à le culbuter de son poste.

　　　　　　　　　　　　　　　　　" FEDERIC."

that they made this Declaration, which they hoped they had done in proper terms, in consequence of the orders they had received, and that His Majesty would give such answer, and in such manner, as he should judge proper.

EARL TEMPLE TO MR. WILKES.

Stowe, September 11, 1762.

You will find, my dear Sir, to what an extent of emendation I have dared to proceed ; what, lose so fair an opportunity of doing justice to a great Minister, *in every light the most respectable of his family*[1]? Proh pudor! If any eloquence could persuade Lady T. to appear, even to her own eyes, in print, it would be yours ; but that I must refer to be settled betwixt you.

The Ghost will become every day more formidable, especially if he should take it into his head to haunt our great little man[2], in the horrid shapes of all the conquests which his pusillanimity or fool-hardiness, I know not which, has determined him to butcher in this unmerciful manner.

Pray God the news of the surrender of the Havannah may come time enough to save the fishery ! but I fear a little Havannah more or less will be to make very little difference, unless the cries of the whole City and country, as I hear, united, should disturb the sweet slumbers of that virtuous man.

Lord Gothamstow[3] is charged with haranguing the

---

[1] An ironical allusion to George Grenville.

[2] The Duke of Bedford.

[3] I suspect this to be a *nickname* which had been applied to himself. " I must here observe that there is one merit ascribed to Lord Temple by the *Briton*, to which he has no kind of pretence. I mean

independent Electors, which I am sure is a —— ——, for that worthy personage never so much as set his foot among them. What a number of sins are laid at thy door, Captain Aniseed—they exceed in number all thy natural children at the Foundling Hospital : it is a little hard that I am dragged in to share thy supposed crimes, of which I am totally innocent, thinking, as I do, that I have enough of my own to answer for ; but I care not a fig, and so good night my dear Colonel. Your most faithful and obedient   TEMPLE.

I breakfasted the other day at Gothurst[1] ; it is impossible to express the rage of that whole family ; and he pledges himself in the strongest assurances, that there never was at any period of time so ardent a zeal in the whole body of the country gentlemen, a very few placemen excepted, as at present against the Ministry, which will undoubtedly appear upon the first opportunity.

I tell you my tale, and the tale-bearer. Ask pardon of the dead ! if I write epitaphs it shall be on the living.

I was much vexed to hear that many of my servants were omitted in the Militia list. I took it for granted the parish officers had done the same this time as last, and therefore never enquired ; but to be sure my servants should be in.

the having delivered such fine orations among the independent Electors of Westminster, when he inveighed with such force and energy of argument against the brothers who directed the helm of Government. Now I will venture to say that Lord Temple never once set his foot among the independent Electors of Westminster."— *North Briton*, No. 17.

[1] Gothurst, now more commonly called Gayhurst, an ancient mansion in Buckinghamshire, near Newport Pagnel : at that time the property of a Mr. Wrighte ; it now belongs to Lord Carrington.

EARL TEMPLE TO MR. WILKES.

Tuesday night (September 14, 1762).

I WAITED with infinite impatience, my dear Mr. Wilkes, to hear from Mr. Gascoyne, whom I expected here in the course of the day, the result of the Friday business. I hope and trust, though as he is not come I have not the satisfaction of knowing it, that it has ended there.

It appeared, I think, by your letter, that Saturday had passed peaceably ; I long much for the post of to-morrow.

I am very sorry my old friend and schoolfellow[1] should take the unfortunate North Briton so heinously : in your situation, whether you had any hand in it or not, I think you could act no otherwise than you have done, like a man and a gentleman in every part of it. I am ever, most sincerely, your affectionate and devoted Servant, TEMPLE.

[1] William, second Baron, and first Earl Talbot, at this time Lord Steward of the Household. He died in 1782. The subject of Lord Talbot's complaint against Wilkes was contained in a very silly paragraph in the *North Briton*, published on the 21st of August. His conduct upon the occasion of the duel, and the cause of it, are equally and supremely ridiculous and contemptible. In these days, it is inconceivable how a nobleman, with only an ordinary share of common sense, should have considered it necessary to take such serious notice of a joke so inoffensively stupid. It is impossible not to admire, by contrast, the manner in which Wilkes conducted the correspondence and final issue of this transaction. His letter to Lord Temple, written *on the same evening, two hours after the duel*, and describing all the circumstances of it, is an admirable composition :—it places the whole scene so forcibly before the imagination. It has been already printed in *Almon's Memoirs and Correspondence of Wilkes*, in the *Political Register*, &c., and therefore it is unnecessary to repeat it here.

MR. WILKES TO EARL TEMPLE.

Winchester, September 19, 1762.

My Lord,—I am infinitely obliged by your Lordship's letter of Tuesday, and can never receive any approbation of my conduct, which I shall value equally with Lord Temple's.

I enclosed from hence three letters, which have passed since; five in all.

As I did not hear from Lord T. on the Saturday, I returned here, as I told Mr. Secker I should. I chose the letters should tell the little history, and therefore refer everything which passed between Mr. Secker and me 'till I have the honour of paying my personal respects to your Lordship.

Lord T. had talked much of my not answering his letter, which made the affair very public; a circumstance I avoid, *because* I feel it so much to my honour. Lord Effingham[1], Colonel Harvey, &c., had the whole, and I have their warmest approbation.

I have drawn the whole into a very narrow point, and Lord T. must *at last* stand forth, which he ought to have done on the Saturday, as your Lordship foresaw.

The first letter seemed a mandate from the *Lord Steward*, signed *Talbot*, no *humble servant*. We are more civil in a second letter.

All the new recruits are arrived here, except from Newport. The regiment is far more complete than

---

[1] Thomas Howard, second Earl of Effingham. Deputy Earl Marshal. He died in 1763. At this time he was in command of the troops at Winchester, where Wilkes was on duty as Lieut.-Colonel of the Bucks Militia, his regiment being appointed to guard the French prisoners confined there.

ever, and the front rank beats almost any front rank of the whole Militia.

We already perform the army exercise entire. The utmost harmony prevails among us, and we have healed the unhappy breach between the common men of Lancashire and our own.

I hold the toast constantly at our mess, which I never desert, but have a tolerable number of visitors with us there.

I approve fully all your Lordship's corrections but one. *George* cannot come in there as it were by the bye; because he is to have a separate piece to himself.

My Lord, you have been much abused; but you forgive all, and so do I, excepting only those few words, that *he is in every light the most respectable of his family.* Good God! what a family! In my turn I will call for fine, pillory, and imprisonment, and hope your Lordship will take notice only of this one truth, for the sake of the English Peerage.

I shall suffer no small uneasiness on your Lordship's account 'till I hear that you have recovered the fatiguing ceremonies of Wednesday[1], which I am very apprehensive may, without the utmost care, be followed by the ugly slow fever which so often alarms all your friends. I am, my Lord, your Lordship's most devoted Servant, JOHN WILKES.

---

[1] The Installation at Windsor, upon the occasion of Prince William and the Earl of Bute receiving the Order of the Garter, on Wednesday, the 22nd instant.

EARL TEMPLE TO MR. WILKES.

Wednesday night, September 22, 1762.

MY DEAR SIR,—I have but just time to acknowledge the receipt of both your letters. Very little company here except what the Court itself brings, and the aspect of things not very triumphant. I wish most sincerely I could see any daylight towards terminating the unhappy affair betwixt you and Lord T. in an amicable manner : to such an object I shall lend myself with infinite pleasure, for I need not repeat to you that I am most sincerely, your ever faithfully affectionate TEMPLE.

His Majesty did not condescend to notice me.

The insertion of George before Grenville was only a joke, and to show how time changes compliment into satire.

I wish you would burn those of the latter kind.

THE EARL OF EGREMONT TO MR. GRENVILLE.

(September 24, 1762) Windsor, Friday evening.

DEAR SIR,—No news yet from the Duke of Bedford. M. Nivernois has sent me a *projet de Préliminaires* upon his own ideas, just as if I had not disputed every alteration he had proposed. He seems to insist upon the neutral garrisons being put into Cleves, Wesel, Gueldres, &c. : in sending the packet to the King, I desire him to postpone answering 'till he hears from our Plenipo : I hope he does not defer writing 'till an answer shall come to Nivernois' projet. The latter has received two couriers from Versailles : our minister *tacet*. Pray come to town soon ; I fear you will be much wanted. I hope you got well to your journey's end, and that you found all well at Wotton. Adieu, dear Sir, till Cox comes back from the Castle.

I have been sent for to the King, who took Nivernois' paper as I could have wished him, and agrees we must wait for the Duke of Bedford's letters. I send you the French Ambassador's *projet*, which I beg you will return me by express as soon as you have perused it. Ever your, &c. EGREMONT.

THE EARL OF EGREMONT TO MR. GRENVILLE.

Sunday afternoon (September 26, 1762).

DEAR SIR,—I received yours, by Jackson, this morning; very sorry to draw you from your retreat into so horrid a scene as I fear you will find here. I conclude you lie at Missenden to-night, and therefore send you the Duke of Bedford's despatches, that you may be fully informed before you come to town: you will see that that headstrong silly wretch has already given up two or three points in his conversation with Choiseul, and that his design was to have signed without any communication here. I have been with Lord Bute this morning, and had much talk with him, some I did not like, but I have not given way in anything; nor shall in the attack I expect from the superior, who I am to see after the Drawing-room. I am to meet M. de Nivernois to-morrow morning at Thomond's, at ten, so suppose our conference will be over time enough for me to call upon you before you go to Court. Viry almost gives it up, and says Nivernois is quite ill-intentioned, so we seem to be in a strange condition. Ever yours, &c. EGREMONT.

THE EARL OF ECREMONT TO MR. GRENVILLE.

Brompton, Saturday morning, October —, 1762.

DEAR SIR,—I came to this place last night at ten, little thinking that I should have so disagreeable a salutation on rising this morning, as I found from the Duke of Bedford's voluminous despatch, arrived in the night. I do not suppose that ever there existed such a specimen of falsehood, inconsistency, insolence, &c., &c., &c., as these papers exhibit; and I do not almost see how the negotiation can proceed: the Duke of Bedford is in consternation himself about it. Time does not admit of my telling you many particulars, only imagine that every article almost is altered in a *projet* sent from the Duke de Choiseul to the Duke of Bedford; and all points *tant grands que petits* varied from what was settled and agreed as to France. As to Spain, the *Havannah*, by name proposed to be delivered up, without any compensation to England; and the old treaties to continue in force 'till a new treaty of commerce is to be made, and stipulated to be concluded in the space of one year.

The King comes to town to dinner. Lord Bute is at Kew: for God's sake come up to town; if prudent, steady, and consequential measures, are not soon resolved on, the King will be distressed, the kingdom suffer greatly in its interests, and the Ministers will be undone. I am, &c., &c. EGREMONT.

COLONEL BERKELEY[1] TO EARL TEMPLE.

Camp, near Winchester, October 7, 1762.

MY DEAR LORD,—Lord Talbot having questioned Colonel Wilkes upon the subject of a North Briton in which he was mentioned, and received for answer that his Lordship had no right to question him, and that he would not tell him whether he did or no, Colonel Wilkes was desired by me to meet Lord Talbot, Tuesday evening, and met him accordingly.

Before they walked out, the inclosed was given to me to deliver to your Lordship in case Mr. Wilkes fell. The matter betwixt them was decided by pistols to both their satisfaction, and without hurt to either. When we returned, I offered to give back Colonel Wilkes's letter, but was desired to inclose it to your Lordship as a proof of the regard and affection he bore you at a minute which might have been very near his last. I beg my respects to Lady Temple, and am affectionately yours, N. BERKELEY.

(Inclosure mentioned by Colonel Berkeley.)

MR. WILKES TO EARL TEMPLE.

Bagshot, Tuesday, October 5, seven at night.

MY LORD,—I am here just going to decide a point of honour with Lord Talbot. I have only to thank your Lordship for all your favours to me, and to entreat you to desire Lady Temple to superintend the education of a daughter, whom I love beyond all the world. I am, my Lord, your obliged and affectionate humble Servant, JOHN WILKES.

[1] Norbonne Berkeley, afterwards Lord Botetourt.

EARL TEMPLE TO MR. WILKES.

Wednesday, 1 o'clock (October 6, 1762).

My dear Colonel,—How eagerly do I long to embrace you! What words can express the satisfaction your last letter gave me in every particular? Firmness, coolness, and a manly politeness, makes up the whole of this transaction on your part.

I saw the event was inevitable, and I was sure you would extricate yourself like a man. I fully intended being at Aylesbury at the Quarter Sessions, and how infinitely is every inducement now heightened; but a feverish cold, which has hung upon me near ten days, makes it impossible. As soon as I resign the pen, I must offer my innocent arm to the lancet.

I hope your time will permit you to call here upon one whom you have distinguished by so many marks of cordial friendship at the time of trial. I have received the seven letters[1] you mention: we will talk the whole over at large; the little woman is full of delight, as she interests herself so warmly in your honour and your welfare.

Inclosed, I send you a copy of the Address[2] which I thought of moving, in case of my not being able to attend. I desired Mr. Lowndes, as Knight of the Shire, to take that upon him, which I trust he will do. If there be anything you and he would wish to alter, I submit it to your judgment. The King and Queen have their full share of compliment: the illustrious House of Brunswick can never be too highly extolled.

The consequences that may arise from taking the

---

[1] Correspondence with Lord Talbot, &c., respecting the duel.

[2] To the King, from the Lord-Lieutenant and gentry of Buckinghamshire.

Havannah are only pointed out, according to expressions of Sir G. Pococke[1]; and though the Peace is upheld, yet it is not in my poor opinion at all beyond the just mark.

I suppose much way will not be given on that head. I am ever, with the warmest esteem and cordiality, my dear Wilkes's most truly devoted   TEMPLE.

The Address, when signed, may be sent to me on Saturday by the Buckingham coach, or brought by the most welcome of all conveyances, yourself. I will then sign it and transmit it to Lord Egremont.

EARL TEMPLE TO COLONEL BERKELEY.

(October 7, 1762)

I HAVE many thanks to return to you, my dear Sir, for the obliging trouble you have taken in transmitting to me Colonel Wilkes's letter, which was written with a very steady hand indeed, very laconic, as time pressed, but very expressive of his uniform partiality to me, and warm affection to his daughter. I am the more sensible to this, as I never had it in my power to do him the least favour. I have, indeed, frequently recommended to him as well as to other of my friends, to sail with the new current, which, however, I would not do, and avail themselves of the tide of Court favour before it was spent : how I have prevailed with him you know. I am very sorry for the occasion of this dispute : when Lord T. mentioned it to me at Windsor, if the state of things had admitted of the least hope of reconciliation, I should most gladly have used my best good offices,

---

[1] Admiral, and M.P. for Plymouth.

more especially as two of my friends were concerned; but judging that hopeless, it is no small pleasure to me to see, by your account, that the matter betwixt them was decided by pistols to both their satisfaction, and without hurt to either.

Wilkes called here in his way to Winchester, so I have read all the letters, and am, with many compliments to you from my little woman, ever faithfully yours, TEMPLE.

THE EARL OF EGREMONT TO MR. GRENVILLE.

Piccadilly, October 10 (1762).

DEAR SIR,—The idea I drew my letter upon was a hint given me by Lord Mansfield, which I understood by him he had also communicated to you, which was to write first gently, and then stronger, to the Duke of Bedford, to prepare him by degrees for the alterations he was to expect in his Preliminaries, and make him, if possible, feel the mortification of the total disavowal less sharply: and what I have wrote to him must convey the idea to him, that a compensation will be exacted for the Havannah, although I have not put it so strongly as I have to the Duke of Nivernois, who dispatched another courier, after the conversations he had with you and I, two days ago: and I own I think it would have done mischief to have wrote the first letter stronger to the Duke of Bedford, who for our misfortune is irrevocably our plenipotentiary at Paris[1].

[1] It is evident from these letters, and from others in the *Bedford Correspondence*, that there was much of mutual dislike and distrust between the Duke of Bedford and Lord Egremont; and Rigby's letters to the Duke at this time tended to inflame these feelings, and to include Mr. Grenville and Lord Mansfield in the opposition to the Duke.

I had some fears lest I should not have got leave to have wrote at all, as the King, when I spoke about it yesterday, said nothing : so as soon as Lord Bute told me he thought my idea right, I wrote the letter, and think, by what the Duc de Nivernois must have wrote, if the Duke of Bedford mentions the Havannah at all, it will draw an explanation from them without fail.   I am ever, &c., &c.   EGREMONT.

MR. GRENVILLE TO THE EARL OF EGREMONT.

Sunday, October 10 (1762).

I DO not see any intimation of a compensation for the Havannah in the despatch proposed to be sent to the Duke of Bedford ; but as I am an entire stranger to all that may have been settled within these few days, I must leave the consideration of it to your Lordship, who having seen Lord Bute yesterday, are certainly better informed.

THE EARL OF EGREMONT TO MR. GRENVILLE.

(Sunday, October 10, 1762).

LORD BUTE (who told me yesterday he now was resolved to have a compensation for the Havannah, or continue the war) settled with me according to my proposal that I should write to the Duke of Bedford, to account for our delay, and prepare him for what he was to expect in the answer to his *projet*.

I send you the draft, and if you approve it, and return it, will, after sending it to St. James's, despatch it for France.

THE EARL OF BUTE TO MR. GRENVILLE.

Sunday night (October 10, 1762).

DEAR SIR,—Though I am convinced of the necessity of some new arrangement to carry through the King's measures at this most critical minute, in order to enlarge the too narrow bottom of the Cabinet, and by firmness and unanimity to procure confidence and support; yet my friendship was so extremely sensible to the least uneasiness these ideas might give you, that I determined to open my thoughts at first through the channel of a common friend[1]; this done, I can't too soon have an opportunity of explaining the measures that occur to me as indispensably necessary at present, to resist the most audacious plan that ever was formed, to give the law to the best of Kings, at the risk even of the nation's safety, and at the same time of learning how far these things are agreeable to you, and likely to meet with your concurrence: if, therefore, it will suit your conveniency, I should be glad to see you to-morrow at nine.

I name so early an hour, as I must go out at ten. I am, dear Sir, with the greatest truth and regard, yours most sincerely.   BUTE.

(*The following Narrative is entirely in the handwriting of Mr. Grenville.*)

ON Saturday, October 9, 1762, Mr. Jenkinson, Lord Bute's Secretary, brought me a message from Lord Bute, informing me of an arrangement that was proposed to be made, by which I was to resign the seals of Secretary of State, which were intended

[1] Mr. Jenkinson.

to be given to Lord Halifax, whom I was to succeed as First Lord of the Admiralty, and that it was
proposed that Mr. Fox should take the lead in the
House of Commons, and the next day October 10th,
Lord Bute wrote to me to desire to see me. We accordingly met, October 11th, when the intended plan was
opened fully to me, together with the reasons assigned
for it, which were the necessity of a more extended plan
to resist the design that had been formed to give law to
the King. The opinion I had declared some time ago of
the difficulties to carry on the business of the House of
Commons, without being authorized to talk to the members of that House upon their several claims and pretensions[1], and having them communicated through me
to Lord Bute and to the King, which was a circumstance
that Lord Bute could not consent to ; the frequent differences of opinion in the Cabinet which had transpired,
and were publicly talked of in the City, particularly my
differing with the rest of the King's servants about St².
Lucia being given up, and lately about the Havannah
being restored without a compensation, which, however,
Lord Bute was now determined to insist upon ; and
lastly, with regard to the laying the Preliminaries of the
ensuing Peace before Parliament for their opinion previous to their being signed, which I had earnestly wished
and recommended. These matters were stated with the

---

[1] This seems but a reasonable demand upon the part of Mr. Grenville, and there can be little doubt but that it was stipulated by Fox,
before he accepted the management of the House of Commons, that
the members of that House should be dependant upon himself personally, without the interference of Lord Bute; that he should be enabled
to *talk* to them, or, in other words, to *traffic* with them for the purchase
of their votes : so notoriously corrupt were the Members of the House
of Commons at this period !

utmost civility, but with great marks of uneasiness, and
the warmest expressions of friendship from Lord Bute
to me, desiring and earnestly hoping that neither this
nor any other circumstance might ever diminish it in
the least. To this I answered that I had declined entering into this subject with Mr. Jenkinson, but that I
owned I had received the communication of it with the
greatest surprise; that I desired to know before I gave
any answer whatever, whether the King was in any instance displeased with me, or whether Lord Bute thought
that he had the least reason to complain of me in any
respect; that it was absolutely necessary for me to know
this, and to set it on a right footing in the first place,
before I proceeded to the consideration of anything else.
Lord Bute would scarce suffer me to state this question
before he interrupted me with the strongest assurances
of the high opinion and good-will the King entertained
of me; that this was at no point of time in my life higher
than in the present moment; that the King depended
upon my services to his Government, which he hoped to
avail himself of, even in a more material instance than
what he now destined me to; that he, Lord Bute, knew
my zeal and attachment to the King, and had therefore
always wished to see me at the head of the Treasury;
that he knew my fitness and talents for that great department, and felt thoroughly how unfit he was for it;
that the King had urged him and compelled him first to
take the seals of Secretary of State, and afterwards to
come to the head of the Treasury; that he had been
heartily tired of the first, and was now still more weary
of the second, not knowing the language he was to hold,
and the manner of dealing with the monied people and
the merchants; that from these considerations he had

besought the King for some weeks together to permit him to retire from it, but that his instances had made the King so uneasy, that he frequently sat for hours together leaning his head upon his arm without speaking; that one of the highest rank who was deservedly most dear to the King (by the manner of which expression I was rather led to understand the Queen, although it might be applicable to the Princess Dowager of Wales) having observed it, had earnestly desired him, Lord Bute, to give ease and tranquillity to the King's mind; that accordingly he had told the King that he was ready to do whatever His Majesty liked, being devoted to his service and bound by every tie of duty, gratitude, and inclination, to look upon any sacrifice of himself as nothing when compared to what he owed to His Majesty; that from this motive only he had consented to stay where he was, and to think of some plan to assist the most amiable Prince that ever sat upon the throne, and to prevent his being delivered up to receive the law from a wicked faction who tried to avail themselves of . . .
. . . *(imperfect)*.

MR. WILKES TO EARL TEMPLE.

Winchester, October 12, 1762.

My Lord,—I beg pardon for an omission I was guilty of at Stowe, in not mentioning the unanimous desire of all the gentlemen at the Quarter Sessions that the Address might be presented as soon as possible to His Majesty, and might be inserted in several of the newspapers. I had the earnest command of the whole company to submit both these requests to your Lordship[1].

The affair between Lord T. and me is much talked of, and the camp censure Lord T. for firing only one pistol; the seconds both having declared that before we went out, Lord T. asked me how many rounds we should fire, and my answer was, *Just as many as your Lordship pleases.*

I am caressed more than I will tell; and a most favourite object, whom I have unsuccessfully made tenders to ever since I first saw her here, now whispers me that she will trust her honour at the first Shepherd's minute to a man who takes so much care of his own. I must look into my old friend *Johnson* for what is synonymous to the word *honour*, to guess at the fair one's meaning.

I have been with Dr. Burton, the Master of Winchester College, and desired to see the boy[2] in his presence. This he has absolutely refused from motives of fear to himself, but he gives me to understand that neither himself nor any person there believed the story. Mr. Charles Lowndes accompanied me. I believe the truth is, that the boy, conscious of having grossly abused me often, and fearing a complaint, invented part of this story, which the *Auditor* has finely cooked up. The bookseller is warm in my defence, though his interest

---

[1] The Address from the county of Buckingham was inserted in the *London Gazette* of October 16th.

[2] The boy was a son of Lord Bute's, and a Scholar at Winchester College: he invented some silly story about an imaginary conversation with Wilkes, which had been magnified into a political affair by the *Auditor*, a weekly paper in opposition to the *North Briton*. Some letters on the subject are to be seen in No. 21 of the *North Briton*.

lies so strongly the other way, and your Lordship has seen Dr. Brocklesby's curious narrative.

My last idle song has never been out of my hands, so much do I improve from the kind hints of Stowe. It is, however, much polished, and at last, I hope, not bad. It concludes—

"The King gave but one; but like t'other Scot *Chartres,*
All England to hang him would give him *both* garters:
And, good Lord! how the rabble would laugh and would hoot,
Could they once set a swinging this John Earl of ——."

I forgot to ask if your Lordship had received the cover of the letter opened from Windsor. I beg to subjoin the copy of a note from the College on the complaint of the young gentlemen against one of my men, about a month ago. I am, with the most real regard, your Lordship's most obliged humble Servant,

JOHN WILKES.

(Dr. Burton and the young gentlemen of the College send their compliments to Colonel Wilkes, and are very much obliged to him for doing them justice, but that they desire that the man may be released only for to come to-morrow morning at 10 o'clock to beg the boy's pardon.

Bowyer and Pitt could not stay, and so they wrote it down.

The man begged pardon in form.)

THE EARL OF EGREMONT TO EARL TEMPLE.

Piccadilly, October 12, 1762.

MY LORD,—Yesterday I was honoured with your Lordship's commands, and this day I presented to the

King the Buckinghamshire Address, which was received most graciously by His Majesty.

I feel most sensibly the great honour derived to the arms of this country by the conquest of the Havannah : and your Lordship's obliging expressions to me on the share I may have had in an event so honourable, and I trust so beneficial to my country, deserve my most sincere thanks ; glad at all times of any opportunity of testifying the great respect with which I have the honour to be, my Lord, &c., &c.   EGREMONT.

P.S. This morning I had an express with news of the retaking St. John's Fort at Newfoundland.

EARL TEMPLE TO MR. WILKES.

Stowe, October 17, 1762.

MY DEAR COLONEL,—I transmitted this day se'nnight our Buckinghamshire Address to the Earl of Egremont, and his Lordship informed me by letter, that he presented it to the King on Tuesday last, who was pleased to receive it most graciously : it was not printed in the Gazette of that night, but I take it for granted shows its honest face amongst others in that of yesterday.   I do not recollect seeing others of the same sort in other public papers, and therefore think it is not proper for me to take any step in inserting it : any private individual may if he please.

We are preparing a crown of laurels with myrtles to grace the Hero when next we see him. . . . . Your song is a d——d one : I wish it burnt, as well as I remember it, but I was indeed so ill when I saw you, I did not quite attend to it.

I think it strange that Dr. Burton should decline letting you see the young gentleman: it certainly opens a door to many unfavourable constructions. The *A——r*, I see, is determined to heap falsehood upon falsehood, and then drag me in; this is very infamous, but I despise it all. I received the cover you mention; I am so used to things of this sort at the Post Office, and am so sure that every line I write must be seen, that I never put anything in black and white which might not be read at Charing Cross, for all I care. You say you improve from my kind advice: God knows it is but very slowly; I wish I could brag of it.

Parce puer stimulis et fortiùs utere loris; give yourself up to parliamentary labours, and let applauding senates give testimony to the excellent talents of the gallant gay Lothario. I wish you had been, and were, deprived of pen, ink, and paper for some time, that all your ideas might concentre in the great object of eloquence, even though it were at the expense of my not hearing from you.

George G., first Lord of the Admiralty; Fox the lead in the House of Commons. Adieu! believe me ever most faithfully yours, &c. **T.**

MR. WILKES TO ———[1].

Winchester, Monday, October 18 (1762).

I HAVE at last got the *Auditor*, and I shall send you by next Saturday a letter to the *North Briton*, which is

[1] Probably the publisher of the *North Briton*. There is some mystery attached to this letter: it is ostensibly addressed by Wilkes to

a full justification of myself from the charge of the *boy*. Mr. Churchill undertakes for the next Saturday, but room must be left for a letter of about two pages.

In all events you have a paper with the motto *et cantare pares et respondere parati.*

I am really well pleased with last Saturday's *North Briton.* You remember the public trial of Lord T. and the D. of B. for crim. con. The *Auditor* is getting foolishly civil, I think; but I will soon trim him, and his old master *Fox*, who I hear is now declared a chief Minister, &c. Pray write to me all news, and by every post.

I am impatient for my *Essay on Woman.* Let it be on very good paper: two proofs.

I shall not be in town 'till the second week in November; then no more to quit London. Let everything be sent here. I am, Sir, your most humble Servant, JOHN WILKES.

You may always send to Mr. Churchill, at Mr. Horner's, in Tothill Street, Westminster.

(*No direction.*)

Great George Street.

EARL TEMPLE TO MR. WILKES.

Stowe, October 21, 1762.

MY DEAR COLONEL,—I received both your letters, and have only to recommend you, for your own sake,

a correspondent in London, but *it is entirely in the handwriting of Lord Temple.* Why it should have been copied by Lord T., I am at a loss to conjecture, unless it were for some purpose connected with the subsequent trial of Wilkes for the publication of No. 45, and the *Essay on Woman.* The letter alluded to about the *boy* was inserted in the *North Briton* of the following Saturday.

that of the corps, and of the Militia in general, that the political differences of opinion which will possibly exist betwixt you and your associates, may in no manner whatever clash with the public service; but that you will show by your temper, discretion, reserve, and sobriety of conduct, how much you are an officer, and how well you know the proprieties of situation. Forgive the liberty I take, and be assured it proceeds from the best intentions towards you, the regiment, and the public.

Your own cool reflection will suggest so much to you, stronger and more varied than what I have said, that I quit the subject which you indeed had wisely forestalled.

You have sent me lately several scraps of verses; I would beg of you to send me no more.

It will always be a pleasure to me to hear of the welfare of the corps, but anything of the least delicacy ought never to be conveyed by the post: every day's experience must surely convince you of it.

I am not yet quite recovered, and Lady Temple is fallen ill afresh. I am ever, most truly and affectionately, yours, TEMPLE.

I am glad to hear the *Auditor's* Winchester story is likely to be fully cleared up to your entire disculpation. What I have observed to you cannot be too strongly inculcated amongst your officers.

You say you know all eyes will be upon you; remember, too, all ears will be open in Parliament.

MR. GRENVILLE TO THE EARL OF EGREMONT.

Great George Street, half an hour past 11 at night.
October 24, 1762.

MY DEAR LORD,—The large packet of papers, containing your draft of the observations on the *contre
projet*, and of your very important despatches to the
Duke of Bedford, was brought to me five minutes before
eleven; and although I have scarcely had time to read
them once over in the most cursory manner, yet as you
tell me in the envelope that I am desired to send them
back as soon as may be, His Majesty being very impatient for the despatch of the messenger, I determined
upon no account to detain them, as I dare say they have
been thoroughly considered, which makes any observation of mine still less necessary. I have, however, enclosed a little note, with a short observation upon an expression in the 10th article, in which I am most probably mistaken, as I see by your letter apart to the Duke
of Bedford, that this article has been settled with the
Chairman and Deputy Chairman of the East India
Company, who are chiefly concerned in it.

The 25th article, relative to the captures, is, I take
it for granted, agreeable to former instances, though it
seems to me that the term of twelve days in the Channel
and the Northern Seas, and six months in the East
Indies, is so short a space that it may scarce be possible
for the parties concerned to have notice sent to them.
I cannot close my letter without repeating to you now
upon the subject of the minute of the Cabinet Council
sent to the Duke of Bedford, the same observation that
I made to you upon a former occasion of the same

nature, and which I mentioned at the Cabinet Council the day before yesterday, when this minute was taken.

I have not changed my opinion with regard to the cession of Guadaloupe and St. Lucia, but His Majesty having repeatedly declared to the Court of France his consent to that cession, in consequence of the opinion of the rest of his servants, I do not understand that this article can now be made the subject of deliberation. I am ever, &c., &c.   GEORGE GRENVILLE.

THE EARL OF EGREMONT TO MR. GRENVILLE.

Monday morning (October 25, 1762).

DEAR SIR,—When I ordered the note to be wrote on the back of the case that enclosed the papers, I was in hopes to have despatched this morning, but as I now find it impossible, I send you back the papers for any farther consideration you may please to give them: happy to have your remarks and corrections.

As to your note on the East India Company article, it struck me as you, but it is meant acquisitions made by France.

As to the 25th article, relative to captures, I ordered them to draw it according to former precedents, which, if they have mistaken, it shall be rectified, as I really have not had time to compare it myself.

The article of Santa Lucia having been ceded some months ago, was certainly not a subject of deliberation at the last Council, and the minute was ordered to be sent to the Duke of Bedford, to show his Grace that it was not a private correspondence between him and me, as one might collect from his last two letters. I am &c., &c.   EGREMONT.

EARL TEMPLE TO MR. WILKES.

Stowe, November 2, 1762.

WHAT a *tam Marte quam Mercurio* kind of an insolent triumph! Why am I to be insulted with a narration
of feats worthy of the days of ancient chivalry?—days'
and nights, too, of which I have scarce a faint idea even
in remembrance. Why can you never proceed to single
combat, but I must hear from you? Your last account,
indeed, is of a kind a little more subject to envy than
your former, and I hope you will keep to personal
engagements of that kind only.

You give me hopes of seeing you here before the
Senate meets; always happy in your company, though
the *Auditor's* fertile invention should contrive an
hundred new falsehoods; that egregious one concerning
Master Fred[1]. I think you have fully refuted. I am
ever, my dear Colonel's most devoted   TEMPLE.

[1] See *page* 486—*note.*

END OF VOL. I.